Ethics in Planning

Edited by
Martin Wachs

CENTER
FOR URBAN
POLICY RESEARCH

Published in the United States of America
by The Center for Urban Policy Research
Building 4051 — Kilmer Campus
New Brunswick, New Jersey 08903

Library of Congress Cataloging in Publication Data
Main entry under title:

Ethics in Planning

  Bibliography: p.
  Includes index.
  1. City planning—United States—Moral and ethical
aspects—Addresses, essays, lectures. 2. Urban policy—
United States—Addresses, essays, lectures. 3. Urban
policy—Moral and ethical aspects—Addresses, essays,
lectures. 4. Professional ethics—Addresses, essays,
lectures. I. Wachs, Martin.
HT167.E83   1985   307'.12'0973   84–14992
ISBN 0–88285–103–9

je 4|8|86

Ethics in Planning

Contents

III.   ETHICAL ISSUES IN POLICYMAKING

IV.   THE EMERGENCE OF AN
✳ ENVIRONMENTAL ETHIC

Acknowledgments

I wish to express my appreciation to the authors of the papers included in this volume and to the publishers for permission to reprint those articles published previously. I also wish to thank the staff of the Center for Urban Policy Research for assistance in bringing this volume to fruition. In particular, I am grateful to Carole Baker for guiding this book through the production process in a creative and professional way.

A number of colleagues offered suggestions on the style and contents of this book, and I appreciate their contributions. Among them were George Sternlieb, Peter Marcuse, Peter Marris, Susan Fainstein, Jerome Kaufman, Robert Beauregard, James Hughes and John Friedmann.

About the Contributors

Charles W. Anderson is Professor of Political Science at the University of Wisconsin at Madison. His work deals with liberal democratic theory, political economy, and comparative policy analysis. He has written or edited seven books, including *Statecraft: An Introduction to Political Choice and Judgment*, and *Value Judgment and Income Distribution*.

Edward C. Banfield is Professor of Government at Harvard University. He is the author of *The Unheavenly City; Big City Politics; Politics, Planning and the Public Interest*; and numerous other books and articles dealing with urban planning and politics.

Richard S. Bolan is Professor of Social Planning at the Boston College Graduate School of Social Work. He was formerly Editor of the *Journal of the American Institute of Planners*, and is co-author of *Urban Planning and Politics*.

T. Edwin Boling is Professor of Sociology at Wittenberg University. He is co-author of *Nursing Home Management: A Humanistic Approach*.

John Dempsey is currently President of Belmont-Abbey College in Charlotte, North Carolina.

Frank Fischer is Associate Professor of Political Science and Public Administration at Rutgers University. He is the author of *Politics, Values, and Public Policy: The Problem of Methodology* and co-editor of *Critical Studies in Organization in Bureaucracy*.

Elizabeth Howe is Associate Professor of Urban and Regional Planning at the University of Wisconsin at Madison. She has written many articles about ethics and values in public administration, social work, and urban planning.

Gene G. James is Professor of Philosophy at Memphis State University. He is the co-author of the text *Elementary Logic* and author of several articles on social and political philosophy and applied ethics.

Jerome L. Kaufman is Professor and Chair of the Urban and Regional Planning Department at the University of Wisconsin at Madison. He is the author of many articles on ethics in planning, was a member of the AICP committee which revised the Code of Ethics, and currently is a member of its Standing Committee on Ethics.

Steven Kelman is Associate Professor of Public Policy at the John F. Kennedy School of Public Policy of Harvard University. He has written *What Price Incentives: Economists and the Environment*, and *Regulating America, Regulating Sweden: A Comparative Study of Occupational Safety and Health Policies.*

Richard E. Klosterman is Associate Professor of Urban Studies at the University of Akron. He has published several works on planning theory and is also interested in demographic and economic analysis and land use modeling.

Alasdair MacIntyre is University Professor of Philosophy and Political Science at Boston University. He has written many articles and books, including *After Virtue.*

Peter Marcuse is Professor of Urban Planning at Columbia University. In addition to his works on planning ethics, he has published studies of gentrification and displacement, housing in Vienna in the 1920s, and the history of housing in New York City.

Mark Harrison Moore is Guggenheim Professor of Criminal Justice Policy and Management at Harvard University. He is co-editor of *Alcohol and Public Policy: Beyond the Shadow of Prohibition*, and co-author of *Dangerous Offenders: Elusive Targets of Justice.*

Ernest Partridge is Research Professor at the Center for the Study of Values and Social Policy of the University of Colorado. His specialty is environmental ethics and moral philosophy. He is editor of the anthology *Responsibilities to Future Generations* and author of many articles and two forthcoming books on environmental ethics.

Holmes Rolston, III is Professor of Philosophy at Colorado State University. He is Associate Editor of the journal *Environmental Ethics* and has recently contributed an article on environmental affairs to the book entitled *Just Business*.

Martin Wachs is Professor of Urban Planning at the University of California, Los Angeles. While preparing this book, he was a Visiting Distinguished Professor of Urban and Regional Policy at Rutgers University. He has written many articles on transportation planning and policy and the book *Transportation for the Elderly: Changing Lifestyles, Changing Needs*.

Introduction

Martin Wachs

Some planners would limit discussions of ethics to relatively simple, though important, questions about the propriety of their daily activities. Take, for example, a scenario from a government training program in which government employees are asked if it is proper to use public funds to have their clothing cleaned while on a business trip. After some discussion, participants in the training program agree that it is ethically proper to charge the cleaning bill to the government if the clothing has been soiled in the course of government business, and if prior approval has been obtained from one's supervisor (Rohr, 1978).

This approach to ethics, which John Rohr has called an "office boy mentality," would restrict discussion of professional ethics to the propriety of everyday social and professional relationships. It would ignore the broader ethical content of planning practice, methods, and policies. While narrow definitions of ethical behavior can easily preoccupy public officials and professional associations, they divert attention from more profound moral issues. In the words of a medieval English quatrain:

> The law locks up both man and woman
> Who steals the goose from off the common
> But lets the greater felon loose
> Who steals the common from the goose.

In fact, ethical issues are implicit in nearly all planning decisions, and they confront planners in many guises. For explicatory and pedagogic reasons it is useful, however, to divide ethics in planning into four distinct categories. The first category, illustrated by the example above, includes the moral implications of bureaucratic practices and rules of behavior regarding clients and supervisors. In the second category are ethical judgments which planners make in exercising their "administrative discretion," the authority to make decisions affecting private behavior and property on behalf of the public welfare. More complex, and represented by the third category, are the moral implications of methods and the ethical content of criteria built into planning techniques and models. Benefit-cost analysis and computer simulation models are examples of planning tools containing ethical orientations which should be examined more explicitly than is often the case. The fourth and final type of ethical issues includes those inherent in the consideration of major policy alternatives. These represent the most basic choices which society makes. For planners, they are often the most ambiguous and politically explosive issues. The choice between the preservation of an environmentally sensitive area and its use for the benefit of nearby citizens or between open housing rules and carefully managed racial quotas are two examples of ethical choices which permeate the substance of major policy alternatives.

The relevance of ethics to nearly all planning issues complicates the subject, making it fascinating to some and frustrating to others. Discussions of planning ethics should include all its myriad forms — they are interrelated and they are all important. For purposes of discussion, however, they are here examined independently by category.

The Ethics of Everyday Behavior

May a planner ever accept a gift from a private citizen, disclose information classified as confidential, or use public funds to promote a project which would produce profits for some land owners and losses for others? Why do some planning and zoning organizations have widespread reputations for maintaining the highest of ethical standards while others are routinely described as corrupt? Are there rules, procedures, training programs, and management attitudes which protect the integrity of some planning organizations and others which promote venal behavior by planners?

In many situations, planners face possible conflicts of interest and ambiguities regarding their responsibilities to the public. Codes of professional ethics, because of their generality, can only go so far in promoting ethical conduct in the fulfillment of professional obligations. Venal behavior by planners is the most likely of the topics discussed in this book to gain the attention of the news media and to result in the downfall of insensitive and corrupt public officials. An analysis of the ethical dimensions of everyday professional behavior provides a critical entry point to the study of a wide range of ethical issues in planning.

The Ethics of Administrative Discretion

Planners exercise judgment on behalf of the public. Approval of building plans, determination of the line and grade of a highway, and the choice of location for a sewage treatment plant are examples of planners' decisions which affect the public welfare and deliver gains and losses to individual citizens. Through decisions of this type, planners participate directly in the governance of society. While laws enacted by elected representatives set down basic parameters, they generally leave much unspecified. Thus, planners have wide discretion when making decisions about the nature and location of facilities and the scope of services. They have both responsibility and discretion as "professionals"; yet, in a democratic society, they are rarely directly responsible to the electorate. Planners share with other bureaucrats and professionals a responsibility for shaping the physical and institutional environments within which citizens live. They are, however, removed from the direct accountability which binds elected officials to the citizenry. Planners should examine the special responsibilities and ethical dilemmas posed by their administrative discretion.

The Ethics of Planning Techniques

Planning claims to be a profession partly because of the specialized expertise conveyed through planning education and continually used in practise. Structured data bases, computerized methods of population and economic forecasting, tables of land-use standards and performance criteria, methods of benefit-cost and impact-assessment analysis are a few techniques which constitute the knowledge base of the field. Planners have traditionally presumed that their data, techniques, and criteria were value-neutral. According to this view, newer methods supersede older ones because they constitute advances in understanding rather than a change in tastes. The purpose of planning tools is to provide systematic and neutral information to support decision-making, while the ethical content of planning is assumed to be in the definition of problems and the weighing of information by decisionmakers. Public hearings and citizen comments on proposals supplement "objective" analysis by providing personal and subjective views.

The notion that planning methods and criteria are value-neutral arose from the traditions of positivism which characterized the development of the natural and social sciences from which planning drew its tools. This notion, however, has been under attack for decades by many critics who argue that virtually all methods of analysis and decision-making criteria are value-laden and that the values embodied in planning methods inevitably bias them in favor of certain choices and against others. The position one takes on this issue is in itself a judgment having ethical dimensions and requiring planners to consider the nature of ethical arguments. Furthermore, percep-

tions of the significance and implications of planning flow from views of
the appropriate roles of values in planning technique. The paper in this
volume by Howe and Kaufman indicates that planners differ widely in their
perspectives on this issue. Planners should be aware of this diversity of
views and weigh the value implications of seemingly routine technical evaluations and choices.

The Ethics of Plans and Policies

Plans and programs themselves embody ethical principles. The content of
each and every plan and public policy is a reflection of purposes and priorities which at some level have been considered in ethical terms. Hallett has
said that "planning deals with choices and politics deals with choices, while
ethics, on the other hand, deals with choices" (Hallett, 1967). If a program
houses the poor, enhances individual property values, or limits the freedom
of industries to pollute the air, it is reflective of values regarding what is inherently right or wrong in society. If we agree with many moral philosophers who claim that such principles are ultimately subjective (Zisser,
1983) and best defined by democratic political processes, we find in the
study of ethics the roots of the political nature of planning. Plans and
policies deal with choices among ends and means. Such choices always have
moral implications, and these implications are usually politically charged.
Whether or not planners are explicitly aware of the ethical principles served
by particular choices, the ultimate significance of their plans and policies is
measured in terms of the moral values which they embody.

Purpose of This Anthology

Urban planners have recently focussed attention on professional ethics.
They have been doing so in the public interest and to enhance the status of
planning by promoting professionalism in the field. Several scholars, noting
a dearth of writing on ethics in planning, have addressed this subject from a
variety of critical and analytical perspectives. These studies include a growing number of empirical analyses of planners' attitudes toward ethical
behavior. Watergate, Abscam, and the resultant surge of interest in the
ethical behavior of public officials heightened planners' awareness of the
subject, and in 1981 the American Institute of Certified Planners (AICP)
adopted a revised "Code of Ethics and Professional Conduct." In 1983 the
AICP published a kit of materials entitled "Ethical Awareness in Planning" for use by local chapters in professional development activities. To-

day, many graduate planning programs address ethics in their curricula, although in somewhat disorganized and inconsistent ways (Kaufman, 1981).

Since no single compendium of works on ethics in planning exists, I have assembled a variety of seminal and representative papers in an effort to capture the current state of thinking. This book is intended: 1) to serve as a text for survey classes in professional ethics given by university planning programs; 2) to supplement short courses in planning ethics for practicing professionals; and 3) to provide source materials for discussions of planning ethics sponsored by local chapters of the American Planning Association and similar organizations. Because it gathers together exemplary and critical works, this collection might also interest individual planners. As the AICP Code points out, a "planner owes allegience to a conscientiously attained concept of the public interest." Yet, to most scholars a clear and shared notion of the public interest appears unattainable. If the code is correct when it states that "the definition of the public interest is formulated through continuous debate", then the purpose of this reader is to provide a variety of source materials for such debates.

Overview of Readings

The papers included in this volume span the four categories of ethical concern in planning described above. Most of the authors are planners, though several are policy analysts, political scientists, and philosophers whose work bears directly or indirectly on the concerns of professional planners.

The first five papers explore the ethical dimensions of planning, administration, and public policymaking. Together, they constitute an overview of current thinking on the topic. Peter Marcuse, responding to efforts to revise the AICP Code, in "Professional Ethics and Beyond," rekindled an intellectual interest in planning ethics which had been dormant for more than a decade. Using several case studies he shows how different roles played by planners give rise to distinctly different ethical prescriptions, and that planners are often trapped in situations which provide them with conflicting demands. Marcuse then reviews the planning literature which reveals different prescriptions regarding ethical behavior by professionals. He determines that some prescriptions are "system sustaining" and some "system challenging," but concludes that the mainstream of professional ethics in planning is system sustaining. He challenges planners to go beyond professional ethics which fail to provide opportunities for them to articulate their strongly held moral beliefs.

Elizabeth Howe and Jerome Kaufman, in an empirical investigation of "The Ethics of Contemporary American Planners," report on the results of a survey of professional planners, in which participants were asked to evaluate case studies. The results reveal that planners fall into three distinct categories regarding their attitudes toward ethical behavior. The "technicians" believe that planning is inherently apolitical, that technical methods have a great deal of validity, and that loyalty to their organizations and employers is a primary ethical concern. "Politicians," as the second group is called, see planning as effort to bring about social change and consider manipulation and activism within the realm of ethical behavior. This group values loyalty to principles more than loyalty to organizations and has less confidence in the objectivity of technical analysis. Interestingly, the largest group of planners is the "hybrids," who combine the apparently contradictory characteristics of the first two groups. Since most planners fall into this ambiguous category, they are often drawn in different directions by competing loyalties.

In his article on "Foundations for Normative Planning," Richard Klosterman disputes the view that "value free" planning is possible and argues that planning is inherently normative. Building on the work of contemporary philosophers, he argues that contrary to the logical positivists' position, ethical decisions can be rationally justified despite the fact that their foundation is normative rather than empirical. In "The Structure of Ethical Choice in Planning Practice," Richard Bolan also considers the normative basis of planning, and discusses normative influences on planners under different circumstances. Bolan concludes that ethical choice in planning practice rather than being derived from the fixed norms of the past may be more accurately described as a process of searching for new normative values. Mark Moore, in "Realms of Obligation and Virtue," discusses the attributes of an ideal process of decisionmaking by public policymakers and considers the conflicting obligations which decisionmakers have when they face real choices. He shows that despite conflicting loyalties, the most appropriate decisionmaking procedure is the one which approximates the ideal to the greatest extent possible.

While the first five papers in this volume provide an overview of ethical considerations in planning, the remaining twelve address specific issues spanning all four categories of ethics in planning. The two papers by John Gardiner and Edward Banfield take up the issue of corruption, its meaning and causes, and strategies for avoiding venality. Land use and building regulations are areas in which corruption has been common, and they are central to the field of planning. In "Corruption and Reform in Land-Use and Building Regulation: Incentives and Disincentives," Gardiner examines the conditions, opportunities, rules, and procedures which invite or discourage corrupt behavior in planning and zoning organizations. In "Corruption as a Feature of Governmental Organization," Banfield develops a conceptual model of institutional settings which foster and discourage corruption. He systematically compares private business organizations and government organizations in terms of this model and speculates on the effects recent trends will have on the expectation and toleration of corruption in the future.

"Whistle-blowing," the attempt by a member of an organization to bring information about wrongdoing in that organization to the attention of the public, has in recent years become an issue of discussion in planning. Planners usually profess to be loyal to their own organizations and also to broader concepts of the public interest. They are not infrequently aware of data, situations, and individual actions which could help particular interest groups and potentially damage the planning establishment. A number of planners have been fired for "going public" with objections to the practices of their organizations and releasing potentially embarrassing technical information. In "Whistle Blowing: Its Nature and Justification," philosopher Gene James provides an overview of the issue, its ethical dimensions, and practical considerations. Edwin Boling and John Dempsey consider some of the same issues in their paper "Ethical Dilemmas in Government: Designing an Organizational Response." While recognizing the complex realities of organizational life, they attempt to arrive at a set of principles for structuring governmental organizations which can be effective in carrying out their missions while protecting the rights of employees with respect to individual and organizational ethics.

The next five papers all address the ethical dimensions of the methods, tools, and techniques of planning and policy analysis. In one way or another, each of these papers questions the traditional assumptions of value neutrality in planning methods. Charles Anderson's paper introduces this topic by discussing his conception of "The Place of Principles in Policy Analysis." He rejects the idea that values must be specified externally to policy analysis and shows how moral principles can be understood to be necessary considerations in rationally defensible policy analysis. His views are consistent with those expressed in the papers by Klosterman and Bolan, for example, but they are more sharply focussed on the tools and techniques by which policies are systematically evaluated.

Because cost-benefit analysis is one of the most commonly used methods of policy evaluation, two papers were selected which address the philosophical basis of this technique. Alasdair MacIntyre investigates the relationship between the views of utilitarian philosophy and cost-benefit analysis. Utilitarianism requires recourse to moral principles beyond itself, and he concludes that cost-benefit analysis requires some important assumptions regarding the moral nature of public decisions. In his article, Steven Kellman also looks at cost-benefit analysis. By considering specific definitions of benefits and costs, he concludes that efforts to reduce non-market concepts into commensurables in dollar terms raises serious ethical questions which are not always completely understood by those using cost-benefit models.

Wachs points out, in "Ethical Dilemmas in Forecasting," that similar problems of orientation and valuation arise when forecasting population, economic activity, travel, and other policy variables commonly used by planners. Because forecasts always rely on core assumptions, and assumptions are always more dependent on values than facts, forecasts are always value-laden. Despite this, forecasts, like benefit-cost studies, are presented in political forums as though they were the result of value-neutral technical studies. Frank Fischer, in "Normative Criteria for Organizational Discourse: A Methodological Approach," starts with the conclusion reached by several of the authors of earlier papers that policy analysis is invariably value-laden. He develops the framework of a methodology, based on practical reason, for the evaluation of policy alternatives in such a way as to incorporate both empirical and normative judgments. His paper challenges planners and policy analysts to arrive at evaluation methods which incorporate, rather than exclude, ethical judgments so critical to organizational decisionmaking.

The last three papers in this collection discuss the ethical content of planning policy by focussing specifically on land use and environmental planning. In "Land Planning in an Ethical Perspective," Jerome Kaufman introduces the idea that land use planners should be guided by a commitment to ethical principles regarding the preservation of land as a resource. He notes that conflicting ethical principles lead to dilemmas for land-use planners whose work entails explicit commitments to the preservation *and* exploitation of land as a resource.

In the final two papers, two philosophers address this issue at a more abstract level. In "Is There an Ecological Ethic?" and "Are We Ready for an Ecological Morality?" Ernest Partridge and Holmes Rolston examine the question of environmental preservation. Do we have an ethical responsibility to preserve the environment for future generations or even as an end in itself? Both conclude that it is appropriate for society to regulate and control use of the environment in pursuit of ethical principles which define a better world. They differ, however, in their assessment of the psychological, economic, and political conditions which lead to widespread acceptance of an "environmental ethic."

Taken together, the papers in this volume are representative of a range of ethical concerns which should be considered by students and practitioners of urban planning. They provide an introduction to a subject which underlies every aspect of urban planning and policymaking but which has received surprisingly little attention from planners. While hardly a definitive treatment of the subject, it is hoped that this collection will be provocative, and that it will play a part in elevating ethical discourse to a more prominent place in the contemporary literature of urban planning.

REFERENCES

Hallett, Stanley J. "Planning, Politics, and Ethics," in William R. Ewald, ed., *Environment for Man: The Next Fifty Years.* Bloomington: University of Indiana Press, 1967.

Kaufman, Jerome L. "Teaching Planning Ethics." *Journal of Planning Education and Research*, Vol. 1, No. 1 (Summer 1981), pp. 29–35.

Rohr, John A. *Ethics for Bureaucrats: An Essay on Law and Values.* New York: Marcel Dekker, 1978.

Zisser, Michael H. "Moral Judgments, Ethical Obligations, and the Romantic Planner." Paper presented at the 25th Annual Conference of the Association of Collegiate Schools of Planning, San Francisco, October 1983.

I
Overview of Ethical Issues in Urban Planning and Administration

1

Professional Ethics and Beyond: Values in Planning

Peter Marcuse

Whether planning is a *profession* is a matter of some dispute: a recent outside opinion suggests it isn't yet but may make it very soon (Goode). For planners, such a development would not only mean higher social status and better remuneration but also problems of licensing, registration, educational credentialing, and all the paraphernalia of a *true* profession. The meaning of professional ethics in that context is likely to become of much greater moment for planners than it has been in the past.

At the same time, the apparent end of the social unrest of the '60s, the escalating fiscal crisis of government, and the advent to power of conservative political leadership have resulted in increased soul-searching for many planners. Funded advocacy planning, the solution of the '60s, no longer seems a viable alternative to bureaucratic service in the '70s. New questioning of the role of the profession and its ethical implications is thus understandable.

This article looks at professional ethics in planning from two perspectives. The first is internal. It assumes the social value of the occupation of planning and its professionalization and explores what professional ethics now imply for the conduct of the practicing planner. The second perspective questions the social value of planning and looks at professional ethics in that broader context.

The article begins with several cases suggesting the concrete types of problems with which ethics in planning must deal. It then describes the obligations of existing professional ethics and their application to these issues. It

From the *Journal of the American Institute of Planners*, Vol. 42, No. 3 (July 1976), pp. 264–274. Reprinted by permission.

concludes by looking beyond professional ethics to see how broader decision rules might be framed to guide planners' activities.

Cases in Planning Ethics

Five brief examples will set our stage.[1]

California's Environmental Scorecards

Many professional planners have gone into the business of preparing environmental impact reports (EIR), now required for many private as well as
public projects in California. EIRs are supposed to provide comprehensive
information on the environmental consequences of a project so that public
decision makers may determine whether to approve that project.

Under the headline, "Ecologists Offer Builder A Deal He Can't Refuse,"
one newspaper reported on interviews with a firm of planners active in the
field in which they "claimed a 7–1 scoreboard: seven building permits issued on projects covered by their environmental studies since the court ruling (requiring such reports), and one project turned down because it was
ruled to be inconsistent with official plans for neighborhood land use."

There was no suggestion that this favorable scoreboard arose out of selec-
tivity in the choice of projects, those presenting environmental problems being rejected at the outset. Quite the contrary, the implication was that the
professional preparation of an EIR by professionals was a virtual assurance
of the approval of the project on which it reported.

Most local governments do not have the staff capability to do much independent review of privately prepared EIRs. Two alternatives were seen as
available to local government: to prepare a list of qualified planners from
which a private developer would have to choose or to muddle through with
the situation as it is.[2]

The first alternative was rejected as putting local government in the position of judging the professional competence and integrity of planners.
Developers argued it would be a violation of the client-professional relationship; state licensing, a possible answer, was not on the horizon. The second alternative was thus selected with a real feeling of bitterness on the part
of many government officials as to the uselessness of professional ethical
standards in guaranteeing the integrity of EIRs prepared by professional
planners for private clients.

Oldport: The Hazards of Population Projections

In Oldport the mayor retained a planning firm as consultant to develop a comprehensive twenty-year plan for urban renewal, housing, schools, and social service facilities. The planners' preliminary report projected moderate population growth but a dramatic and continuing shift in racial composition, with minority groups reaching a majority in twelve years. A black majority was predicted within five years in the public schools.

The mayor reacted strongly to the preliminary report. If these findings were released, they would become a self-fulfilling prophecy. All hope of preserving an integrated school system and maintaining stable mixed neighborhoods or developing an ethnically heterogeneous city with a strong residential base would disappear.[3]

The planners were asked to review their figures. They agreed to use the lower range of their projections—minority dominance in the public schools after eight years and a majority in the city in sixteen. The mayor was not satisfied. He told the planners either to change the figures or to cut them out of the report. They refused, feeling they had bent their interpretation of fact as far as they could. Without a discussion of these facts, the balance of the report could not be professionally justified.

The mayor lashed out at them privately for professional arrogance, asked a professional on his own staff to rewrite the report without the projections, and ordered the consultants not to release or disclose their findings on race under any circumstances. The professional on the mayor's staff initially demurred from rewriting the report but ultimately complied. The consultants remained silent, completed the formal requirements of their contract, and left. The mayor never used professional planning consultants again.

Award-Winning Congestion: The Pan Am Building

In 1968 the architect for the Pan Am Building in New York, which added two million square feet of office space to one of the most congested business areas of the world, received an award for structure from the American Institute of Architects. *Architectural Forum* condemned the land speculation which made the Pan Am Building possible at the same time it praised the architect who built it. Robert Goodman (*After the Planners*, pp. 93–6) commented

> The magazine ends with the moral "as professionals, it seems that architects should try to make the best of the world *as it is*—before somebody else fouls it

up even further." With this dreary and negative conclusion, the magazine sums up the profession, unself-consciously and without irony. But is the professional really a tool of whatever system he operates in? Does he have a responsibility for his acts other than to do his job better than someone else? Is the engineer who designed a more painless gas chamber to be lauded as a "realist," or the scientist who designs a cleaner nuclear bomb as a more responsible professional?

Let us assume that a group of Young Turks in the New York AIP chapter, moved by Goodman's eloquence, bring a formal complaint against the planners involved in the project before the executive committee of AIP under AIP's "Code of Professional Responsibility," alleging a violation of its first canon:

> A planner serves the public interest primarily. He shall accept or continue employment only when he can insure accommodation of the client's or employer's interest with the public interest (AIP 1971).

The Young Turks further point to number 4 of the "Guidelines for the Social Responsibility of Planners" adopted by AIP in 1972 (AIP 1973):

> The professional planner should explain clearly to local, state, and national political leaders the seriousness of existing, emerging and anticipated social problems.

The Young Turks argued that the planners should not only have refused to work on the Pan Am project but should also have appeared before the city planning commission to point out its dangers. Expulsion from AIP was asked as the very least penalty for failure to do so.

Evidence presented included a statement from the director of the city planning commission. He himself had recommended approval of the project because he knew that at least four of the five members of the commission favored it. However, citing reasons of congestion, pollution, and inefficiencies of scale, as well as unfair competition to other developments elsewhere in the city, he felt it was against the public interest.

Amid substantial newspaper publicity, the executive committee ruled against the complainants. It found that neither the canons nor the "Guidelines on Social Responsibility" were part of the "Rules of Discipline" of the profession or intended to be enforced by it. For AIP to attempt to arrogate to itself the decision as to whether a given building should be built would be a usurpation of the democratic decision-making process which the committee could not condone.

An editorial in the leading New York newspaper the following day commented on the hypocrisy of the planning profession's claim to serve the public interest and suggested that honesty might dictate repeal by AIP of all references to the public interest anywhere in its canons.

Mass Transit: Planning for Whom?

Central business district revitalization requires the services of a variety of planning professionals. In one large city, a transportation planning firm was engaged by a group of downtown merchants to advise it on the transit aspects of a proposed urban renewal plan for the CBD. The planners recommended a fixed-rail system with lines radiating out from the CBD.

The regional transit agency shortly thereafter (while the planners were still under retainer to the merchants to explain their CBD report on request) also sought a consultant to advise it on the advisability of constructing a fixed-rail system in the region and, if it proved advisable, to suggest routes. The same planning firm was selected; after extensive study it recommended a fixed-rail system with a radial configuration centered on the CBD. A referendum was scheduled on a sales tax to finance construction of the proposed system.

Concern for conflicts of interest on the part of the transportation planners did not surface until the referendum campaign was well under way. Questions were asked about the consultant's recommendations for a radial pattern, which would benefit the CBD, over a grid pattern. How objectively had the arguments for alternatives to fixed-rail been considered? How fairly were they presented? Why was a sales tax recommended as the measure of financing, rather than a special assessment district downtown? How neutral were the technical assumptions used in making the ridership projections on the basis of which the fixed-rail system was recommended in the first place?

The defense contended that the recommendations were strongly supported by the data and the planners' expert professional judgment. Further, the regional transit agency was fully aware of the planners' work for the CBD merchants. It had in fact considered their familiarity with the CBD situation an asset when the firm was selected. Finally, the planners argued that their recommendations to their two different clients were the same because in both cases they were following AIP's exhortation to "serve the public interest primarily."

The sales tax proposition was decisively defeated at the polls. In subsequent interviews, the man in the street told reporters that the only beneficiaries of all the years of studying transit needs in the city seemed to be the planning consultants, who couldn't be trusted further than they could be thrown.

Vietnam: Planners and Foreign Policy

President Nixon resumed the bombing of North Vietnam in the fall of 1971. In the September 1972 *Journal of the American Institute of Planners*, an article appeared entitled "Ecological Effects of the Vietnam War" (Concerned Planners 1972).[4] Its opening paragraph read as follows:

> Planners have no special claim to omniscience or moral virtue. Yet we feel that we must speak out against the escalation of the war in Vietnam, as professionals as well as citizens, for three reasons: because the tools of planning can help to highlight the disastrous consequences of that escalation; because the values which planning should serve in a democracy are violated by that escalation; and because that escalation is being justified by arguments which are a travesty of the approaches of rational long-term planning.

It then continued:

> Our analysis is not value free, nor does it pretend to be. The values that run through it are dictated by the function of the planning profession in our country. Certainly not all individual planners have all the same values, nor ought they to. But the proper role of professional planners on issues of public policy does, we believe, require a commitment to certain basic common values, and we would hope that our profession would be united in its commitment to those values: humaneness, democracy, rationality.

In the following issue of the *Journal* a member of the American Institute of Planners wrote in reply:

> The article also frustrated me because it failed to mention any of the contributions of city planners to South Vietnam . . . Daniel, Mann, Mendenhall, and Johnson, for example, have developed plans for the port of Saigon; a master plan for the growth of Saigon has been prepared by Doxiadis Associates and has been adopted as national policy; Wurster, Bernardi, and Emmons have prepared a set of plans dealing with a land assembly and development process for a sector of Saigon, part of which has already been implemented . . . (Loewenstein 1973, p. 138).

The Concerned Planners responded in the same issue:

> In our article we expressed ourselves as citizens, not merely as planners . . . We . . . wrote to raise questions about the planning mentality that knows how to rebuild cities, but can't think about how to prevent us from knocking them down; that recognizes the moral corruption of the South Vietnam regime, yet is willing to do its street cleaning for it; that says, in effect—well, yes, we do know about the furnaces and concentration camps, but we have our job to get on with (p. 138).

The debate was not pursued thereafter, and the organized profession never expressed itself on the issues.

Obligations of Professional Ethics

Each of the cases posed above is troublesome. Planning does not emerge from them as the highly ethical occupation planners visualize.[5] In most cases, even the rules for telling right from wrong are not clear. Obligations to clients conflict with obligations to the public; following professionally accepted standards of conduct produces results repugnant to most laymen; professional integrity and democratic decision making seem to conflict; the bounds of professional concern are hazy.

While it is accepted that planners should act professionally, how far do the prescriptions of professional ethics bring us in resolving the issues posed by these cases?

Most of the traditionally *professional* obligations of planners have their sources in characteristics of the client-professional relationship.[6] Others arise out of guild characteristics of the occupation. A few are the result of the employer-employee relationships in which many planners find themselves. One arises from planners' frequent role as social scientists. Some may be specifically imposed on planners by statute.

Each of these sources gives rise to ethical prescriptions. Some of these prescriptions are enforced by intraprofessional discipline; others may be publicly enforced; still others are hortatory, enforced only by peer group pressures and judgments about the standing in the profession.

Figure 1 shows these various prescriptive rules, the sources from which they come, and their modes of enforcement; they accept the value of the occupation of planning and are concerned with how that occupation should be carried out. Let us take up each prescription in turn.

Allegiance

Law provides the best-known model for that allegiance which is the heart of the client-professional relationship. The relation imposes certain absolute obligations on the professional: confidentiality within the client-professional relationship, avoidance of representation of conflicting interests, prohibition against personal involvement in affairs undertaken for the client to avoid personal conflict of interest, uniform espousal of the client's interests in dealing with others.

FIGURE 1

Ethical Prescriptions of Planning as an Occupation[7]

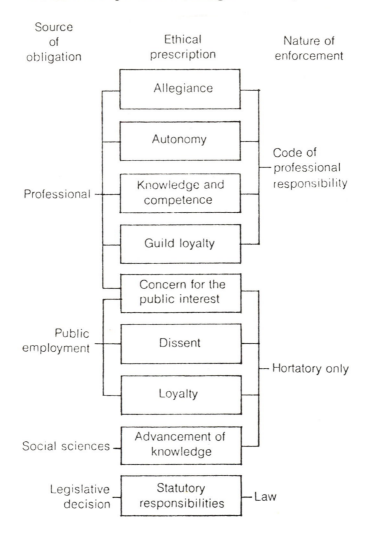

If planners adhered to the rigid standards of allegiance laid out in the canons of ethics for lawyers, the transportation consultants in the mass transit case would be read out of the profession. On the other hand, environmental scorecard keeping would be entirely proper, service to the developer of the Pan Am Building would be all in a day's ethical work, and the decision as to what to do with the consultant's population projections would be entirely up to the mayor of Oldport.

Autonomy

To the extent they are professionals, planners cannot use a common defense that engineers, for instance, have used (Collins) against their assumption of ethical responsibility for the uses of the end product of their labors:

> The typical engineer is an employee of a medium to large company. He usually works with other engineers as part of a hierarchical structure, that also may involve technicians, programmers, draftsmen, etc. His assignments are generally tasks being carried out by other people. He is not usually consulted about the definitions of his task or the criteria to be used in evaluating its successful completion. Nor does he generally have the authority to change these criteria as a result of observations made while carrying out the assignment. He is frequently briefed inadequately or not at all with respect to the overall objectives and strategy for attaining them (Unger).

Planners, to the extent—often limited in fact—that they function as professionals, cannot undertake work on such terms (Hughes). The planner is expected to give a client sound and *independent* advice, whether the client will be offended, whether the advice is likely to be followed, whether it answers directly only the question the client put, or whether it goes beyond it to answer the questions the planner feels the client should have asked.

The professional takes reponsibility for the formulation of the problem as well as of the answer and must be willing to challenge the client's preconceptions and refuse too limited instructions in order to be able to do so. Planners are given problems to solve or objectives to achieve. Everything that may impact on these problems must professionally be considered by them. If congestion renders the Pan Am Building useless, its planners cannot say they were never asked to consider the question.

But this responsibility runs to the client, not to the public. Professional autonomy does not require the same advice be given to New York City.

Knowledge and Competence

New Jersey's pioneering statute for the licensing of planners begins "planning is a profession which requires specialized training" (N.J.). It then sets forth detailed educational and experience requirements for a professional planning license. Even where technical competence is not demanded by law, it is an essential obligation of a professional. Indeed, in the sense of command of a specialized body of knowledge, it is an essential ingredient of every definition of a profession from Flexner to Carr-Saunders to Hughes to Metzger.[8]

The definition of the *specialized knowledge* which is within the unique sphere of planning has provoked seemingly endless discussions about core curricula in planning schools and about qualifications for membership and areas of exclusive jurisdiction in professional organizations. The specialized knowledge of planning probably includes such things as the understanding of the processes required for the making of public decisions; the weighing of cost against benefit; the discounting of long-term against short-term results; the comprehensive handling of physical, social, economic, environmental, and other related aspects of a single proposal; the separation of public from private interests and the differentiation of private interests; the analysis of efficiency; and the understanding of distributional consequences. Exclusive jurisdiction would hardly be claimed by any profession over these broad areas. Yet whatever the boundaries may be of the specialized knowledge of planners, there is agreement that some territory is within it; mastery of its terrain is an essential obligation of the professional planner.

Guild Loyalty

Guild loyalty includes two types of ethical obligations assumed by professionals: one to fellow professionals, the other to the profession as a corporate body. The obligation to fellow professionals produces the bulk of the rules of discipline of AIP: "thou shalt not advertise," "thou shalt not steal thy fellow's client," "thou shalt not cut thy fees," and so on.

To a minor extent these may be justified as contributing to a strong profession better able to fulfill its social role, but primarily they are traditional guild-type rules primarily benefiting members of the profession. Although treated summarily here, historically they stem from that guild membership which lies at the root of what contitutes a profession (Carr-Saunders). They have been the most carefully explicated and vigorously enforced of all the canons of ethics. Only the Department of Justice seems to have occasional qualms about them.

The obligations to the corporate profession include assisting those entering the profession, supporting education and research in the field, and promoting the good name of planning. Obligations to fellow professionals are only tangentially involved in one of our cases. Ironically, they would preclude not the preparation of EIRs so as to achieve a favorable scorecard but the advertising of success in that endeavor.

Loyalty

Like the independent professional's obligation of allegiance to a client, the ethical obligation undertaken by an employee to an employer is loyalty: obedience to instructions within the scope of the employment, service of the employer's interests, and confidentiality. Democracy reinforces the obligation when the employer is a public agency. Matters of policy conflict should be decided by democratically elected governmental bodies. When such a body entrusts decisions to staff in a planning agency, the delegation of power should be respected, even where its substantive wisdom is questioned.

Dissent

From Nader's whistle blowing to Nixon's Watergate, the conflicts between the obligations of loyalty and of moral integrity requiring dissent have recently been much in the news. The conflict becomes an issue in planning when a planner employed by a public agency believes that his agency is not acting in the best interest of the public and yet feels constrained from dissenting by virtue of employment by the city and the obligation of loyalty that arises from it.[9]

The ethical obligation to dissent in such circumstances rests on three grounds: (1) the *public as employer* argument, that the public employee's responsibility runs directly to the public, not to formal superiors; (2) the *whistle-blowing* argument, that any employee has an obligation to report and/or make public disclosure of any facts that come to that employee's attention that may be violations of criminal law or injurious to the public; and (3) the *organizational flexibility* argument, that internal dissent and the right to protest over one's immediate superior's head is an essential ingredient in a responsive and creative organizational structure.

A distinction can be drawn between the impact of these conflicting obligations of loyalty and dissent on a director of planning and on a subordinate employee-planner. At the interface between professional and nonprofessional in the public service, where a director of planning would generally serve, dissent becomes particularly critical, for it is here that the democratic process relies on the integrity of the professional to present a considered independent judgment.

The subordinate professional's advice, on the other hand, is expected to be filtered through his superior to the public. The more responsible the employee's position, the more professional the role; the more egregious the action at issue, the more likely are ethics to demand the expression of dissent. The member of the mayor's staff asked to rewrite the consultant's report in Oldport might thus be justified in doing so, but not the city planning director recommending approval of Pan Am's plans because of the commission's wishes.

Advancement of Knowledge

Of all the client-serving professions, planning is among those which call on the greatest depth and diversity of social science disciplines in much of its day-to-day work.[10] The planner is a social scientist turned practitioner in the arena of public policy.[11]

The social scientist's role creates ethical obligations for the planner—and ethical ambiguities—very much as the economist's role does for the fiscal advisor, or the chemist's for the weapons expert. In each case, the scientific role calls for dedication to the pursuit of knowledge for its own sake, without regard to where it may lead; caution and complete exploration of all facets before arriving at conclusions; full disclosure of methods and results; in other words, the discovery and dissemination of the truth. The planner acting as planner, however, may have quite different, and often conflicting, ethical obligations: to act decisively in accordance with a client's timetable, subject to the client's priorities; to consider the practical impact of disclosures and findings; to economize in the pursuit of alternatives; to be responsible for ultimate products.

It is really as a social scientist that the Oldport consultants object to the suppression of research findings. No secret information, after all, is being withheld from the public; no vested interest is being given a monopoly of key knowledge. Nothing in conventional planning practice requires planners to publicize all the shortcomings as well as all the advantages of their plans after they have been presented to the client. Yet some planners are more social scientists than planners. For them, the answer is an appeal to contract rights, which should be carefully drawn to cover rights to publication, rather than to professional ethics.

Where the role of planner and that of social scientist conflict—and they may—the individual must choose and must tell the client in advance. Planners cannot sell themselves as such and then insist on being treated retroactively as scientists. At the opposite extreme, if local government wants the maximum information with the minimum of bias as to environmental consequences, it must be made clear that planners are relied on in their scientific, rather than their conventional professional client-serving capacity.

Statutory Responsibilities

A profession may be a useful vehicle by which to enforce public policies. If architects are held legally responsible for knowledge of building code provisions, for instance, the enforcement of codes will be simplified. Making attorneys adhere to rigid standards of truthfulness in representations to a court speeds the handling of cases on a docket. Denying the right to practice medicine to doctors who improperly prescribe drugs enforces public policy on drug use. The professional is asked to serve the interests of the public, even where it conflicts with the interest of the client.

The dilemma faced by local governments in the California environmental case suggests two approaches to imposing such responsibilities on planners. One model for planners preparing EIRs is based on the lawyer's role, in which planners see themselves as advocates for their client's projects. The alternate model is that of a certified public accountant, whose balance sheet and profit-and-loss statement, when certified, are intended to be relied upon as accurate and objective by outsiders.[12] The accountant preparing the client's balance sheet has limited discretion to help the client.

In the accounting model, the public looks to the certified statement for objective and fair disclosure of the situation described. The lawyer, on the other hand, prepares a client's case as a partisan advocate. In that model, the public does not expect the lawyer to be evenhanded or objective; that is not the lawyer's role.

Whether planners will be given responsibilities similar to those of the accounting model remains to be seen. Perhaps licensing will bring them. Such responsibilities do not exist now. Until they do, planners cannot be faulted for faithfully acting in their client's interests, unless (and here we come to the last of the professional obligations of planners) there is in fact a duty to the general public that is not subsumed within, and may even run counter to the time-honored professional obligation of allegiance to a client.

Concern for the Public Interest

Some form of concern for the public has been an essential ingredient of every definition of a profession at least since Abraham Flexner first laid down his famous check list (Metzger, p. 3). The first words of the AIP's first canon are "a planner serves the public interest primarily." Some

FIGURE 2

Each Approach Refers to Ultimate Goals

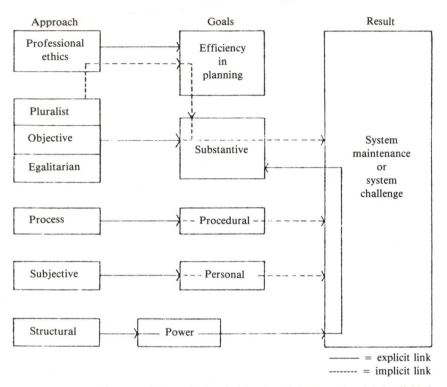

Efficiency is an ultimate goal for professional ethics; for other approaches, it is implicitly instrumental. Systems maintenance/challenge is viewed explicitly as a result, although an instrumental one, by the structural view; other approaches result in systems effects also, but implicitly only.

discussions of planning raise this obligation almost to a religious level (Hoover 1961).

But concern for the public interest may be shown merely by planners acting competently and ethically in performing their everyday professional obligations as planners. They may have a more systematic approach to the "public interest" than the average citizen, but this gives them no right actually to make decisions in public matters, nor any concomitant public responsibility.

The profession formally takes this view. The first canon is specifically intended not to be enforced under the "Rules of Discipline" (Sangster, pp.

5-6), as are the "Guidelines on Social Responsibility." The Young Turks in New York were clearly wrong. No one in California authorized the planning profession there to make public decisions on projects affecting the environment. As individuals, or perhaps even as an organization speaking for the majority of individuals in the profession, a statement might well be made by planners on behalf of strict environmental legislation. As professionals, however, planners could best show their concern for the public interest by representing their clients fairly, honestly, and competently. If, in doing so, they are successful in getting their clients' projects approved, they might well be proud.

These then are the results produced by following the current dictates of professional ethics. They are founded on the theory that, in Charles Frankel's words, "the creation of a planning profession with a reputation for integrity and political/moral independence is (itself) a matter of great social value."[13]

But what is that value?

Professional ethics do not provide that answer. As yet, they do not even provide satisfactory solutions to day-to-day problems of practice. At least in the five cases described earlier, the prescriptions of professional ethics are sometimes contradictory and hardly lead to greater respect for the profession. How then can issues in cases like these be better resolved?

We must look beyond professional ethics for the answer. Indeed, we must look beyond occupationally based ethics. Occupational ethics begin by accepting the social utility of the occupation, and ask how that utility can best be enhanced. The assumption that a reputable planning profession is itself a matter of social value is unquestioned. But perhaps it is precisely in the values the occupation serves that the ethical difficulty lies. What the occupation does, should perhaps not be assumed automatically to be ethically of value. Perhaps it is the effort ethically to fulfill unethical tasks that creates the real dilemmas.

Beyond Professional Ethics

Planning theory has long had much to say of the values inherent in planning and its tasks. Faludi's *Reader in Planning Theory*, Friedmann and Hudson's recent survey of planning theory (1974), and the AIP-sponsored *Planning in America: Learning from Turbulence* each indicate the range of thought that has been devoted to the values of planning. Strictly ethical categories have, however, rarely been explicit in these discussions, and references to professional ethics are even rarer.

Six different approaches to ethics might be deduced from the literature:[14]

1. Subjective approaches, which make ethical action a matter for individual decision
2. Pluralist approaches, which hold that professional services should be made available to *all* potential clients
3. Objective approaches, which attempt to establish formal objective standards for ethical judgment, sometimes using procedural formulations, as in definitions of justice, or quantitative ones, as in concepts relying on welfare economics
4. Egalitarian approaches, which likewise postulate objective standards, such as *expansion of choice*, but are generally framed in broad social terms
5. Process approaches, which see the objective of planning as contributing to a particular process, such as mutual learning
6. Structural approaches, which view ethics in terms of historically defined structural conditions, evaluating actions in terms such as sytem maintaining or system challenging

An important dividing line between the first five and the last formulation is that the structural view is fundamentally historical and the others are not. Professional ethics play a different role in each of the six.

Subjective approaches deal with individual motivation. Self-awareness might be their watchword. Personal integrity, internal consistency, honesty with oneself, clarity of purpose are their guiding values. No attempt is made to define as *right* any particular course of conduct for all individuals; different individuals in the same situation might ethically act very differently, depending on their own values and beliefs.

Each planner may choose among a number of roles he could play. One of those roles is that of the "professional" planner. If chosen, it carries with it the full range of professional ethical obligations. For other roles professional planning ethics would be less important; political leader, private entrepreneur, teacher, advocate—each would have its own set of ethical obligations.

A pluralist approach would place a more uniform emphasis on professional conduct. Since the planner as client-server is modeled on the lawyer, the legal rather than the accounting view of professional obligations would be anticipated. An obligation of the organized profession to serve those otherwise without adequate planning advice would be seen as a part of professional ethics.

The objective approach focuses on results, not the process by which results are achieved. Professional ethics play a secondary role through promoting efficiency in achieving ends defined through nonprofessional objective standards.

Egalitarian approaches often seek to include within professional ethics statements of ultimate values. The extension of choice to those without adequate choices (the new Cleveland plan's formulation), for instance, might be put forward as component of professional ethics. But, given the inclusion of such an objective as a requirement for professional conduct, the expectation as to the behavior of planners can be consistent with conventional professional standards.

Process approaches see planning as much more than a technical process. Certainly it is a process not the exclusive domain of professional planners. Ideas of a learning society and related ideas specifically see the need to broaden the activity of planning into a generalized social activity, to make it an instrument of democratic societal guidance. Professional issues thus are of minor importance. This is not to say that planners are freed from ethical obligations: it is only to say that there are other and higher obligations towards which planning activities should be oriented. And in some cases, as in guild obligations or prescriptions of allegiance, professional ethics may run counter to higher obligations.

The structural view, finally, a view underlying most radical perspectives, sees professional ethics as instrumental in relation to the particular historical system in which they function. Planning in most jobs today is in practice clearly a system-maintaining activity. Professional ethics facilitate that activity.

There are, however, ideological currents within planning, those linked to its utopian aspects, which tend to challenge the limits of the system by posing basic alternatives and *unrealistic* goals, unrealistic because they cannot be achieved within the limits of prevailing structures. There are also social forces challenging structural features of each social system. If structural change in a given system is seen as historically desirable, then service to such system-challenging forces, or pursuit of system-challenging goals, would be the ethical obligation of planners. Such a formulation might put professional ethics at odds with many aspects of professional practice, but it would be a set of professional ethics quite different from those in effect today.

The substantive formulations of such a different set of professional ethics are not necessarily unique to the structural approach. Formulations such as equity or democracy may be common to many approaches. Structural ethics differ in dealing with the question of power.

The distribution of power is historically the determinant of the degree of equity, of democracy, of the distribution of choices among individuals, in any social system. Redistribution of resources requires not only clarifying problems in welfare economics but also overcoming the understandable resistance of those whose resources are being redistributed. A shift in power from those with more to those with less is generally a prerequisite for major changes in the distribution of resources.

Greater democracy by the same token requires not only solving problems of communications, of scale, or of organization, but also broadening decisionmaking power beyond the presently powerful. The powerful may well be expected to resist the weakening of their status through the diffusion of their power.

These are problems of means, but they cannot be separated from a consideration of ends. A more historical formulation of ethics is required than most planning theories afford. A point of view is needed which will in fact look at how, *in practice*, greater equity or democracy can be achieved.

Historical analysis suggests that these problems of means, these issues of power, are inextricably linked to any examination of the ethical aspects of social system structures. Structural system maintenance or system challenge becomes a directly relevant consideration for ethical judgment. The impact of a given action on the power relationships within a system becomes a relevant issue for ethics.

Conclusions

Professional ethics could logically go beyond their present narrow attention to the client-serving, guild-related roles of planners to examine their real effect on the social, economic, and political system in which the planners' activities take place. Professional ethics could logically deal with issues of power and act directly to further values such as equity and democracy. Indeed, professional ethics might even logically support movements towards structural change and new power relationships where planning's own tools and historical analysis show them to be needed. But what can be done in logic will not always be done in practice.

The historical role of professionalization is to seal a social bargain between the members of a profession and the society in which its members work. In return for special prerogatives and privileges, running from social status to restrictions on entry and competition, not to mention direct monetary returns, the profession agrees to a certain measure of self-policing. That is a bargain made entirely within the existing structures of society, supporting those structures and making them operate more effectively. To interpret such self-policing (of which professional ethics are a significant part) to permit or even to require challenge to those same structures could fly in the face of the professional bargain.

The statement on the "Social Responsibility of Planners," adopted by AIP in 1972, and the philosophy of the Cleveland Planning Commission featured in a recent issue of this *Journal,* are the closest statements from the profession challenging the tasks which planners ought to undertake. However, both read as if planners following them may remain entirely within the established limits of professional conduct; the Cleveland plan even suggests that planners might prosper while following its philosophy. Perhaps such formulations are required to achieve at least a minimum level of acceptability for their approaches. But, in the long run, the issue of power will inevitably force itself to the surface and will have to be dealt with. Professional ethics, conventionally interpreted, tend to buttress established power. That certainly seemed to be the result in fact in these five cases. Different results will require different definitions of ethics.

In summary, professional ethics in planning merit a great deal more attention than they have thus far received. They are not as yet well thought through, their prescriptions are often conflicting, their results questionable. The trend towards professionalization of planning makes such attention a matter of high priority for planners.

A clear statement of how planners should conduct themselves requires looking beyond professional ethics to the functions the profession serves, the tasks it is assigned. If a given task is harmful, executing it professionally is not desirable. Planning theories shed some light on the problem, suggesting ethical criteria often differing from the professional criteria but rarely discussing the differences explicitly. The structural view of planning, for instance, requires a serious questioning of the entire movement towards the professionalization of planning. It would call for a historically based view of planning functions focusing on their relationship to the distribution of power in society. It would judge planning's results by whether they contribute to maintaining or to challenging those features of the social system that are judged ethically undesirable.

Professional ethics, in that view, might indeed have the potential to emphasize the utopian, the historically progressive, elements in planning. Realistically, however, professional ethics are likely simply to render more efficient the services provided by planners to those presently with the power to use them. Professional ethics are likely to be system maintaining rather than system challenging. The movement to reshape them in a different direction is likely to be a long and an uphill one.

Author's Note: Those who contributed, very often through strenuous disagreement, to the still incomplete process of working through the ideas outlined in this article are literally too numerous to mention. Their help has been very much appreciated.

NOTES

[1]All are fictional but based on actual situations. Additional aspects of these cases are outlined in Marcuse 1974, pp. 33–71.

[2]Expanding the permanent staff was generally not feasible, especially in smaller communities, because of the expense of very specialized personnel needed and the widely fluctuating work load they would face.

[3]See Paul Davidoff's reading of the new Cleveland plan: "Inequality in Cleveland, as elsewhere in the United States, is both economic and racial, yet the plan is surprisingly silent on the subject of race. The authors may have believed that they could gain wider public support by establishing a concept that could win adherents from many groups. Explicit recognition of racial problems, and the creation of standards for measuring the city's movement toward closing the gap between the whites and the non-whites, may have been judged counterproductive" (1975, p. 318).

[4]The author was a member of Concerned Architects and Planners at the University of California, Los Angeles.

[5]On planners' self-image as professionals, see Alonso, Lee, Miltner, and the collection of materials in Hagman, chs. 2 and 9.

[6]The identifying characteristic used by C. F. Tauesch, among others, for the term *professional* (p. 472).

[7]The chart is not intended to cover general moral rules, such as honesty, presumably equally applicable to all occupations. It does, however, cover the nonprofessional as well as the professional aspects of planning, viewing it broadly as an occupation rather than more narrowly as a profession.

[8]*Esoteric* is the term sometimes used (Freidson, p. 228; Hughes, p. 1).

[9]The controversial nature of the issues it presents can be seen from the fact that the leading discussion of the issue in the planning literature (Finkler 1971), which comes out in favor of the right to dissent, carries with it its own dissent by the executive director of the American Society of Planning Officials, which published it.

[10]The social sciences, for instance, would be the planner's "department of learning" in the Oxford English Dictionary's definition of a professional: "A professional is 'one engaged in a vocation in which a professed knowledge of a department of learning is used in its application to the affairs of others or in the practice of an art founded upon it.' "

[11]More accurately, historically speaking, the practitioner turned social scientist. Planners in the United States originally were overwhelmingly landscape architects, architects, and lawyers; the need for social science knowledge did not become firmly recognized in the profession until the late 1960s. Originally, also, ontogeny recapitulated phylogeny, but now most planners begin their professional studies with a background in the social sciences.

[12]Standards are enforced by the accounting principles board of the American Institute of Certified Public Accountants. For a critical look at some of the consequences of this arrangement, see Britoff 1973.

[13]Letter to the author, September 5, 1973.

[14]Citations are deliberately not given for this or any of the following formulations, because they are not intended to be specific summaries of any individual positions nor any specific body of theory; they often incorporate ideas or phrases from several sources. The formulations are only intended to suggest the implications for ethics that follow from aspects of current planning theories.

REFERENCES

Alonso, W. 1963. Cities and city planners. *Daedalus* 92, no. 4, fall.

American Institute of Planners. 1971. Article 9: code of professional responsibility and rules of procedure. *Roster*. Washington, D.C.: AIP.

_____. 1973. The social responsibility of the planner. Washington, D.C.: AIP.

American Society of Planning Officials. 30 April, 1962. A code of ethics in planning. In *Planning 1962*. Chicago: ASPO.

Britoff, A.J. 1973. *Unaccountable accounting*. New York: Harper and Row.

Carr-Saunders, A. M., and Wilson, P. A. 1934. The professions. *Encyclopedia of the social sciences*. New York: Macmillan Co.

Collins, F. n.d. The social responsibility of engineers. Mimeographed.

Concerned Architects and Planners. 1973. Rejoinder to Mr. Loewenstein's comments. *Journal of the American Institute of Planners* 39, March: 138.

_____. 1972. Ecological effects of the Vietnam war. *Journal of the American Institute of Planners* 38, September: 297–307.

Davidoff, Paul. 1975. Working toward redistributive justice. *Journal of the American Institute of Planners* 41, September: 317–318.

Faludi, A., ed. 1973. *A reader in planning theory*. Urban and regional planning series, vol. 5. New York: Pergamon Press.

Finkler, E. 1971. *Dissent and independent initiative in planning offices*. (With dissent by ASPO's executive director, Israel Stollman). Planning Advisory Service, no. 269. Chicago: ASPO.

Friedson, Eliot. 1971. Professions and the occupational principle. In *The professions and their prospects*, ed. Freidson. Beverly Hills: Sage Publications.

Friedmann, J. 1973. *Retracking America: a theory of transactive planning*. New York: Doubleday.

_____ and Hudson, B. 1974. Knowledge and action: a guide to planning theory. *Journal of the American Institute of Planners* 40, January 2–16.

Godschalk, D. R. ed. 1974. *Planning in America: learning from turbulence*. Washington, D.C.: American Institute of Planners.

Goldstein, H. 1975. Towards a critical theory in planning. In *Symposium on planning theory*, ed. Wilson and Noyelle. University of Pennsylvania, Department of City and Regional Planning, papers on planning no. 1.

Goode, J. November 1975. *The professionalizing occupations*. Seminar report 3, no. 6. New York: Columbia University.

Goodman, R. 1971. *After the planners*. New York: Simon and Schuster.

Hagman, D. G. 1973. *Public planning and control of urban and land development: cases and materials*. St. Paul, Minn.: West.

Hiltner, S. 1957. Planning as a profession. *Journal of the American Institute of Planners* 23, no. 4: 162–167.

Hoover, R. C. 1961. A view of ethics and planning. *Journal of the American Institute of Planners* 27, November: 293.

Hughes, E. 1963. Professions. In *The professions in America*, 2nd ed., eds. K. S. Lynn and editors of *Daedalus*. Cambridge: Riverside Press.

Lee, J. T. 1960. Planning and professionalism. *Journal of American Institute of Planners* 26, February: 25–30.

Loewenstein, L. K. 1973. Letter to the editor. *Journal of American Institute of Planners* 39, March: 138.

Marcuse, P. 1974. *The ethics of the planning profession*. Working paper DP43. Los Angeles: University of California, School of Architecture and Urban Planning.

Metzger, W. P. 1975. *What is a profession?* Seminar report 3, no. 1. New York: Columbia University.

Moore, W. 1970. *The professions: roles and rules*. New York: Basic Books.

New Jersey Chapter, AIP vs. New Jersey Board of Professional Planners. 1967. 48 N.J. 581, 227 A2nd 313.

Sangster, R.P. 1970. Planning: ethics of the profession. Paper delivered at 1970 AIP conference, Minneapolis.

Seeley, J. 1962. What is planning: definition and strategy. *Journal of the American Institute of Planners* 28, May: 91–97.

Tauesch, C. F. 1934. Professional ethics. *Encyclopedia of the social sciences*. New York: Macmillan Co.

Unger, S. H. 1972. Engineering societies and the responsible engineer. Paper delivered at conference on the social responsibility of engineers. New York Academy of Sciences, New York.

Webber, M. 1963. Comprehensive planning and social responsibility. *Journal of the American Institute of Planners* 29, November: 232–241.

Wilson, Robert H. 1975. Has planning theory forgotten its history? In *Symposium on planning theory*, ed. Wilson and Noyelle. University of Pennsylvania, Department of City and Regional Planning, papers on planning no. 1.

2

The Ethics of Contemporary American Planners

Elizabeth Howe and Jerome Kaufman

Suppose a planner who works for a high-income suburb recognizes that the community's land development regulations are exclusionary. This makes it quite difficult for poor people or minority group members to live there, even though job opportunities for them exist in the area. The planner, as part of her regular job activities, decides to organize support from local people she knows are in favor of opening up the community so that they will put pressure on the suburban government's officials to change the community's zoning policy.

In acting this way, does this planner behave ethically or unethically? A study conducted by the authors of a random sample of 616 planners who belong to the American Institute of Planners and work for public planning agencies, indicates that opinions differ sharply.[1] Slightly more than half thought the planner's behavior would be ethical. Slightly more than a third thought it would be unethical; and the rest were not sure, one way or the other. Reactions to this short scenario and fourteen others describing the behavior of planners in situations involving ethical dilemmas are the subject of this study. Figure 1 gives a brief description of each scenario, the tactic the planner used, and the intended beneficiary of the planner's action.

For planners, ethics set the boundaries of acceptable behavior. In theory, a set of commonly held behavioral norms make up the body of professional ethics. Some, but by no means all, of these norms have been codified in the American Institute of Planners' Code of Professional Responsibility. Whether codified or not, these norms ideally represent guidelines for planners to adhere to in conducting themselves as professionals.

From the *Journal of the American Planning Association*, Vol. 45, No. 3 (July 1979), pp. 243–255. Reprinted by permission.

25

FIGURE 1

Description of Ethics Scenarios

Scenario	Tactic	Issue Benefiting
1 City planner gives draft recommendations for pollution control plan to environmental group representative who requests them; no agency policy exists about releasing such information.	Release Draft Recommendation On Request	Environment
2 City planner, who favors low fare to make proposed regional transit system more accessible to the poor, purposely develops estimates showing that system will have high ridership/high revenue yield to counteract low ridership/low revenue yield estimates of regional planners who oppose lower fare.	Distort Information	Mass Transit, Low Income
3 Planning director urges members of important civic group to publicly endorse "park and ride facility" plan, telling them that many neighborhood groups support the plan—director knows, however, that less than half of neighborhood groups consulted so far have agreed to support plan.	Distort Information	Mass Transit
4 City planner assigned to work with particular low income neighborhood, without authorization, gives information to head of the neighborhood organization on study being prepared by another planning agency unit which recommends substantial land clearance in this neighborhood.	Leak Information	Low Income

FIGURE 1 (Continued)

Scenario	Tactic	Issue Benefiting
5 Regional planning director threatens to use agency's A-95 authority to recommend denial of local projects if local officials do not support regional growth management plan.	Threat	Environment
6 Regional planner puts several strong recommendations into fair share housing plan which planner feels are expendable that might be later traded off to get commissioners to support central aspects of plan.	Use Expendables As Trade Offs	Low Income
7 City planner gives draft recommendations for development plan for largely undeveloped part of city to land developer who requests them; no agency policy exists about releasing such information.	Release Draft Recommendations Upon Request	Development
8 Suburban planner decides to organize support from local people to put pressure on suburb's officials to change community's exclusionary zoning policy.	Organize Coalition of Support To Induce Pressure	Low Income
9 Regional planner who worked on a wetlands preservation study, without authorization, gives certain findings to an environmental group, because planner feels the agency's director purposely left out those findings, which were objectively documented, from the study draft because they do not support agency policy.	Leak Information	Environment
10 Planner who favors increased mass transit use and is preparing a study on need for mass transit decides not to include information from a study done several years ago showing that majority of community's residents opposed expanded mass transit system.	Distort Information	Mass Transit

FIGURE 1 (Continued)

Scenario	Tactic	Issue Benefiting
11 Economic planner who initially criticized on technical grounds a proposal by a community development corporation to develop a small industrial park in a ghetto area before the plan commission, later recommends the project to the commission after being told by the director of the director's support for the project.	Change Technical Judgment Due to Pressure	Low Income
12 City planner who is a member of Chamber of Commerce, without authorization, gives information to the head of the Chamber of Commerce on an agency study being prepared that will recommend reducing number of on-street parking meters in CBD to lessen traffic congestion.	Leak Information	Development
13 Planning director undertakes a campaign to create a crisis atmosphere about the pollution and health hazards of the city's waterways by holding press conferences next to the city's most polluted waterways to get media coverage.	Dramatize Problem To Overcome Apathy	Environment
14 City planner gives draft recommendations on scattered site public housing plan to the representative of a white homeowners' group who requests them; no agency policy exists about releasing such information.	Release Draft Recommendations Upon Request	Low Income (anti)
15 County planner, without authorization, gives information and advice on own time to a citizen's group which is trying to overturn in court a county rezoning decision which the county planning staff had opposed; the rezoning allows an oil company to build a refinery on a large, tree-covered waterfront property.	Assist Group to Overturn An Official Planning Action	Environment

Most importantly, they represent the basis for assuring the public who uses planning services that planners will act responsibly in exercising their professional judgment and in applying it.

What makes things difficult for the planner is that some of these norms, or ethical prescriptions, are either so broadly defined that they can be variously interpreted or the norms may conflict when more than one is present in an issue.[2] In the above scenario, for example, two ethical prescriptions are involved—concern for the broader public interest and loyalty to the client community.[3] Partly because of such conflict and ambiguities, all planners may not reach the same conclusion about what is ethical or unethical as the split response to the above scenario indicates.

The primary interest of our study was simply to find out more about how contemporary planners view ethics—what do they agree and disagree about, and what is the nature and extent of their agreement and disagreement. In other words, our intention is to describe what planners think is ethical, not to judge whether or not planners are ethical by some predetermined standard. To our knowledge, no systematic study of this has ever been done. Yet the subject is important since ethical considerations pervade much of what planners do.

Beyond describing what planners think is ethical, we also wanted to examine factors or characteristics of the planners which explain why some view an action as unethical which others see as acceptable.[4] In essence, we wanted to know what motivates planners in practicing their trade. To get at these causal factors, we asked respondents about their professional role orientations, their attitudes toward a variety of substantive issues in the field, their loyalty to their agency, their propensity to express values in their work, and their political preferences, as well as their background and work situation.

The paper is organized into four sections. We start out with a discussion of the study design. We then consider what planners as a whole think is ethical and unethical behavior, looking particularly at areas of consensus and disagreement, and at the fit between planners' attitudes about ethics and what they say they would actually do. Going beyond the descriptive level, we then consider some important reasons why planners make different ethical choices. Here we focus on the variables mentioned above, such as role, political views, and other job related attitudes. Finally we explore some of the implications of our findings for planning theory, practice, and education.

Study Design

We sent a mail survey to 1178 members of the AIP, with an overall response rate of 69 percent, and a useable response from people working in public planning agencies of 616 questionnaires or 53 percent.[5] All responses were completely anonymous. The questionnaire was made up of three parts. The first was made up of a series of 15 short scenarios, each describing how a planner had dealt with a particular ethical dilemma (see Figure 1 for synopses of the scenarios). The respondent was asked if he thought the planner's action was ethical, using a five-point scale; and if he would do the same, using a similar scale.[6]

The issues dealt with in the scenarios were selected to reflect real and difficult ethical dilemmas in the profession. In the interests of keeping the questionnaire to a manageable length, however, we made no attempt to be comprehensive, nor could we provide the respondent with information on the scenario's political and social setting.

The second part of the questionnaire was designed to elicit attitudes about roles in planning, value commitment, orientation toward agency, citizen participation, and about various substantive issues in, or groups affected by, planning: mass transit, the environment, development, and low income and minority groups. The respondent was asked to give his opinion on fifty-three strongly worded statements, using a six-point scale from strongly agree to strongly disagree. The third part of the questionnaire included a variety of demographic questions as well as questions on the respondent's education, political views, and work situation. Of necessity, a mailed questionnaire limited us to information on peoples' *attitudes* about roles, issues, and ethics. We did, however, come closer to actual *behavior* in one respect by asking the respondents not only whether they think the planner's behavior in a given situation is ethical, but whether they would do the same thing if faced with the same situation. Although there have been a number of good in-depth case studies of the behavior of planners on which we could build, none explicitly addressed the question of ethical behavior (Meyerson and Banfield 1955, Altshuler 1965, Rabinovitz 1969, Needleman and Needleman 1974, Jacobs 1978). On the other hand, there has been virtually no research on large numbers of planners—probing into their attitudes on roles, issues, and ethics—so that the tradeoff between behavioral data and larger numbers of respondents seemed well worth making.

What Planners Think is Ethical and Unethical

Today's planners do agree strongly about the ethical propriety or impropriety of some kinds of behaviors. On other kinds of issues, there is considerable disagreement; and on any issue there is always a fairly constant ten percent who are uncertain whether any particular behavior is ethically appropriate or not. Differences in the responses seem mainly to be related to the tactic presented in each scenario rather than to the substantive issue or group that benefits. Initially we will discuss the effect of the tactics, and then we will consider the effect of substantive issues. The order of tactics, ranging from most to least acceptable, is given in Table 1. It should be understood that all the scenarios were designed to include political tactics that we thought would be somewhat questionable. Therefore, the rankings reflect planners' opinions of how unacceptable each tactic is.

For eight of the fifteen scenarios, consensus was high: from 66 to 80 percent of the respondents always answered that the behavior described is either ethical or unethical. In these cases, no more than 25 percent of the respondents ever took the opposite position from the majority. Actions to dramatize a problem to overcome apathy, the use of expendables as a tradeoff, and assistance given on the planner's own time to a group trying to overturn an official action—all of which reflect a fairly activist role in trying to get support for a particular policy—are viewed as the most acceptable tactics. Planners consider threat, distortion of information, and leaking of information as the most unethical tactics, in roughly that order.

It is interesting to note that planners' low toleration for distorting information is consistent with the rule of discipline in AIP's Code of Professional Conduct, which admonishes planners against deceitful conduct. Section (a) of the Rules of Discipline reads: "a planner shall not engage in conduct involving dishonesty, fraud, deceit or misrepresentation." Nevertheless, for the three scenarios in which the planner distorts information (2, 10, and 3), from 13 to 22 percent of the respondents still said that the planner's action was ethical.[7] Strictly interpreted, these planners would be in violation of the AIP rule.

On the other seven scenarios, there was considerably more disagreement. The actions that seemed consistently to provoke such disagreement were releasing the draft recommendations of an unfinished report to a group which requests them, and leaking inside departmental information to an outside group. These issues present particularly clearly the choice between loyalty to one's department and loyalty to some outside group or idea of the public interest.

The scenarios where the planner leaks information to an outside group (4, 8, and 12) actually conflict with Rule of Discipline (d) of the AIP Code, which reads: "Except with the consent of the client or employer . . . a planner shall not reveal . . . information gained in the professional relationship . . . the disclosure of which would likely be detrimental to the client or employer." In each of these scenarios, the planner does in fact reveal infor-

TABLE 1

Rank Order of Tactics by Ethical Acceptability

Rank	Tactic	Scenario	Percent total response ethical[a]	Percent total response unethical	Percent total response not sure	Mean[b]
1	Dramatize problem to overcome apathy	13	82	13	5	1.91
2	Use expendables as tradeoff	6	68	21	11	2.33
3	Assist group to overturn official action	15	67	24	9	2.31
4	Release draft information on request to environmental group	1	64	27	8	2.46
5	Release draft information on request to white homeowners' group	14	54	34	11	2.75
6	Organize coalition of support to induce pressure	8	53	35	11	2.74
7	Release draft information on request to developer	7	47	43	9	2.99
8	Change technical judgment due to pressure	11	42	39	18	3.01
9	Leak information to low income group	4	33	55	12	3.34
10	Leak information to environmental group	9	31	59	10	3.45
11	Distort information	3	22	70	9	3.72
12	Distort information	10	17	74	9	3.87
13	Leak information to Chamber of Commerce	12	16	75	8	3.96
14	Distort information	2	13	81	8	4.05
15	Threaten	5	11	84	5	4.33

[a]Percent for some scenarios is less than 100 percent due to rounding.

[b]The lower the mean score, the higher the number of ethical responses; the higher the mean score, the higher the number of unethical responses. The scale was (1) clearly ethical (2) probably ethical (3) not sure (4) probably unethical (5) clearly unethical.

mation gained in the professional relationship without the employer's consent. Such disclosure might well be interpreted as being "detrimental" to the employer. Although for two of these three scenarios nearly 60 percent thought such an action was unethical, about 33 percent still said the action was ethical. These planners also might be considered to be potential violators of the AIP Code on this point. Clearly, for a minority of planners, the AIP Code of Professional Conduct does not stand up as an irrefutable guide to ethical conduct.

Most planners are generally able to make a choice about the ethical propriety of a particular behavior, even if they do not always agree. But for every one of the scenarios, some always said they were uncertain about the ethical propriety of the behavior described. For all scenarios, the median number of undecideds was 9 percent of the total. The fewest number of undecideds (5 percent) was in the two scenarios where consensus was greatest—scenario 5, where the planner used a threat tactic (the most unacceptable) and scenario 13, where the planner tried to overcome public apathy by dramatizing a problem (the most acceptable). The greatest uncertainty was for scenario 11—where the planner, bowing to pressure from a superior, changed his technical judgment. The split was almost even between those who viewed this behavior as ethical and unethical, but the undecideds accounted for nearly 20 percent of the total response.

Previously, we noted that planners react more to the tactic than to the beneficiary in making their ethical choice. This is clear, for example, in the three scenarios (2, 10, and 3) where the planner distorts information to gain more support for a preferred policy. Respondents overwhelmingly consider such an action to be unethical. In each of these scenarios, the issue benefitting would be mass transit, which planners strongly favor.[8] Therefore, the tactic clearly outweighs the issue in this instance.

Yet the benefitting issue, a possible surrogate for values, apparently has some effect on how planners view ethics. Consider Table 2, which shows the responses to three similarly constructed scenarios (1, 14, and 7) where the planner gives the draft recommendations of a plan to someone who asked for them, when no specific policy exists about releasing such information before a plan is completed. Although the tactic is the same, the beneficiary changes in each scenario. While more respondents view this behavior as ethical than unethical in each of these scenarios, a higher proportion apparently feel that giving such information to the environmental group representative is more acceptable than giving such information to the white homeowners group representative or to the land developer. Since planners are more pro-environment (70 percent) and pro-low income (57 percent) than pro-development (50 percent), as indicated by their averages on the three attitude items in favor of each issue, values apparently have some effect on ethical choice; though the developer may also be less acceptable because he is also an individual who would benefit financially from the information provided.

The three scenarios (12, 9, and 4) dealing with a planner who leaks information to a representative of a group also suggest the possible effect values might have on ethical choice (see Table 3). Although respondents consider

TABLE 2

Effect of Values on Releasing Draft Recommendations

Releasing draft recommendations requested	Percent total responses ethical	Percent total responses unethical
to a representative of an environmental group (scenario 1)	64	27
to a representative of a white homeowners' group (scenario 14)	54	34
to a land developer (scenario 7)	47	43

the planner's behavior in these scenarios as much less ethical than that of the planner described in the releasing information on request scenarios (see Table 2), when the leak is to a representative of a low income group or to an environmental group, the pro-ethical response is almost twice as high as when the leak is to a representative of the Chamber of Commerce. Again, since planners are less favorable to development than to the environment or to low income groups, values also come into play here.[9]

The Relationship Between Attitudes and Behavior

When a respondent says that a planner in one of the scenarios acted ethically, that person is reflecting an attitude about ethics. If, however, that person was faced with the same situation confronting the planner in the scenario, would he behave likewise? To determine whether planners would behave consistently with their ethical perceptions, we not only asked respondents to judge the ethical propriety of the planner's action in each scenario, but we also asked them whether they would behave as that planner did.

We found that there is indeed a strong relation between ethical attitudes and potential behavior. For every scenario, at least 75 percent (in most cases over 80 percent) of the respondents say they would behave consistently.

But this means that for any scenario, from 10 to 25 percent of the respondents would switch—i.e. their attitude does not dovetail with their potential behavior. Two groups of switchers are worth a closer look: those who say the planner's behavior in the scenario is ethical but they would not do it or were not sure they would do it, and those who say the planner's behavior is unethical but they would or might do it anyway. Of the two groups, more judge the behavior as ethical but wouldn't do it than the other way around. Probably the main reason why some say they wouldn't do

TABLE 3

Effect of Values on Leaking Information

Leaking information without authorization	Percent total responses ethical	Percent total responses unethical
to a representative of a low income group (scenario 4)	33	55
to a representative of an environmental group (scenario 9)	31	59
to a representative of the Chamber of Commerce (scenario 12)	16	74

what they see as ethical is because it's risky. Although threatening someone or going around a superior by leaking information to another group, for example, might be viewed by some as ethical, the possibility of being found out and reprimanded or punished in some way is obviously a deterrent. Not surprisingly, the most acceptable tactics are also the least risky ones. For these scenarios, the number of switches in this direction is lowest. The average percentage of switches for the three most acceptable tactics (scenarios 13, 6, and 5) is only 13 percent, while the average percentage of switches for the four least acceptable tactics (scenarios 5, 2, 12, and 10) is nearly three times as high or 35 percent.

Far fewer planners would switch the other way; i.e., judging the behavior to be unethical but still saying they would or might do it. For most scenarios, only 5 to 8 percent of those who say the behavior is unethical would switch. But for three scenarios (13, 11, and 6) about 20 percent of those saying the behavior is unethical would switch. Two of these three scenarios (13 and 6) have the highest ethical responses. So, even some planners who saw the behavior as unethical were likely to behave the same way as the great majority who saw the behavior as ethical.

Why Planners Have Different Ethical Views

What kind of variables seem to explain the differences in ethical choices among planners? Probably the central variable is role. All the scenarios involved situations that were political and actions that were of questionable acceptability. Consistently, the most politically oriented planners found the scenarios more acceptable than did technically oriented ones. In addition to role, there are statistically significant differences on ethics between liberal

and conservative planners, between those more and less committed to their
agencies—if challenging the agency is an aspect of the scenario—and between value committed and value neutral planners.

We had also hoped to be able to examine the effect of these variables on
attitudes about various substantive issues such as the environment, mass
transit, development, and redistribution. However, the substantive attitude
scales did not effectively measure people's attitudes on these subjects,[10] so
that the only way we can get at this effect is by examining the scenarios
where the tactic can be held constant and only the issue varied, as we did in
the last section.

Let us look more closely at the relation between these various independent variables and the dependent variable, acceptable or ethical behavior,
starting with the role/ethics relationship.

Roles and Ethics

Initially, we thought that an important explanation for differences in
ethical perceptions among planners could be traced to a central and continuing conflict in planning: how can planners maintain their technical integrity, yet at the same time, be politically effective? Planning has been strug-
gling over the question of its proper stance as a public profession in a
democratic society for many years. The issue has often been posed as a
choice between the polar models of the planner as technician (Beckman
1964, Walker 1950, Meyerson 1956) and the planner as a political actor
(Rabinovitz 1969, Needleman and Needleman 1974). The former type is
supposed to be technically expert, value neutral, and responsible to the
public through the political decision-makers he serves. But he is also dependent on those same political decision-makers for the implementation of his
"good" advice and plans. The latter, as an ideal type, is more value committed, more responsive to the groups or issues he thinks are particularly
related to the public interest, and more willing to work actively through the
political system to see that plans are implemented. Only in recent years have
there been attempts to think in terms of a role which combines aspects of
both technical and political roles to achieve both integrity and effectiveness
(Meltsner 1976, Benveniste 1972, Catanese 1974).

For the study, a person's role orientation was determined by his score on
two scales, one concerned with technical orientation or attitudes toward
analysis, and one concerned with attitudes toward political behavior in
planning.[11] For ease in interpreting the results, each scale was dichoto-
mized, and three roles were created (see Table 4):[12] technicians, low on the
political scale and high on the technical one; politicians, who had the

TABLE 4

Planners' Roles (n = 577)

		Political scale	
		Low	High
		(not used as a role)	Politicians
Technical scale	Low	n = 26	n = 105
		% = 4.5	% = 18.2
		Technicians	Hybrids
	High	n = 153	n = 293
		% = 26.5	% = 50.8

% is percent of total sample included in table.

reverse pattern; and a third group who are high on both scales, who we called "hybrids."[13]

The large number of hybrids is interesting, since those who have developed models which combine both the technical and political dimensions of role seem to indicate that planners who play the combined role are few and rather special.[14] But if our findings are any indication, these polar role types, even combined, are outnumbered by the people who wish to combine aspects of both roles.

As Table 5 indicates, on all scenarios except 9 and 10, the three roles ranked in the same order, with politicians finding the scenarios most ethical, technicians, the least, and hybrids in between; on the two exceptions, politicians and hybrids were virtually identical. On all the scenarios except 10 and 11, the differences between the two extremes, the politicians and the technicians, were statistically significant at the .05 level or better.

The scores of the hybrids are particularly interesting, since they indicate that there seems to be some tension between the two role dimensions. On all but three of the scenarios, the hybrids were not statistically different from the politicians. However, on scenario 5 (on the punitive use of A-95 review power, one of the most unacceptable tactics to all groups) hybrids were not significantly different from technicians. In the remaining scenarios, on expendables (6) and on organizing opposition to the zoning ordinance (8), where the range of opinions was particularly large, the hybrids were significantly different from both other groups. Thus, although hybrids frequently resemble politicians, they are almost always more moderate than politicians in their judgments, pulled at least somewhat by their similarity to the technicians as well. In some situations, they may shift to an independent middle ground, while in others they may move all the way to the technical

TABLE 5

Means by Role for Each Scenario*

Scenario	Poli-ticians	Hybrids	Tech-nicians
1 release info/env't	2.20	2.37	2.70
2 distort info	3.93	4.02	4.17
3 distort info	3.58	3.64	3.97
4 leak info low income	3.12	3.20	3.64
5 threat	4.03	4.33	4.45
6 "expendables"	2.07	2.28	2.50
7 release info/developer	2.84	2.94	3.13
8 organize coalition	2.20	2.59	3.31
9 leak info/env't	3.30	3.29	3.76
10 distort info	3.80	3.79	4.02
11 technical judgment	2.88	3.01	3.10
12 leak info/C of C	3.74	3.86	4.26
13 media hype	1.70	1.80	2.17
14 release info/whites	2.50	2.68	2.94
15 assist opponents	2.06	2.20	2.55

*The range for the mean score is from 1 (clearly ethical) to 5 (clearly unethical)

side. With more different kinds of scenarios, this pattern might show up more clearly.

In terms of what planners say they would do on each scenario, the three roles ranked the same way as for ethical judgments. It is interesting, also, that respondents generally are somewhat more conservative about what they say they would do, than about what they think is ethical,[15] and that this does not differ by role.

Political Views and Ethics

Political views were measured on a scale from 1 to 7, labeled from radical to conservative. The study indicates that 82 percent of the respondents were in the middle three categories—liberal, liberal-moderate, and moderate. The two extremes contained only 23 people (3.7 percent of the sample), so that each was combined with the next most liberal or conservative group to make five categories, ranging from conservative to radical.

We thought that political groups might rank the same way roles had, with liberals thinking the scenarios were most ethical, and conservatives the least.[16] In fact, two dominant patterns emerged (see Table 6). The

TABLE 6

Means for Ethics Scenarios by Political Views*

Scenarios	Radicals	Liberals	Lib Mod	Moderates	Conservatives
1 release info/env't	1.76	2.31	2.59	2.65	2.80
2 distort info	3.86	4.08	3.97	4.27	3.92
3 distort info	3.56	3.72	3.71	3.86	3.47
4 leak info/low income	2.20	3.25	3.61	3.56	3.47
5 threat	3.88	4.28	4.36	4.50	4.37
6 "expendables"	1.69	2.30	2.31	2.57	2.54
7 release info/developer	2.40	3.01	3.06	3.14	3.00
8 organize coalition	2.02	2.71	2.76	2.87	3.22
9 leak info/env't	2.67	3.39	3.50	3.61	3.83
10 distort info	3.88	3.74	3.89	3.94	4.08
11 technical judgment	3.25	2.98	3.04	2.87	3.33
12 leak info/C of C	3.40	3.98	3.94	4.12	4.06
13 media hype	1.60	1.92	1.84	1.98	2.19
14 release info/whites	2.02	2.75	2.83	2.89	2.83
15 assist opponents	1.58	2.12	2.33	2.67	2.77

*The range for the mean score is from 1 (clearly ethical) to 5 (clearly unethical).

hypothesized pattern did show up for four scenarios (1, 8, 9, and 15) which suggests no obvious logic except that three do deal with environmental issues. Conservatives, however, didn't fit the pattern on five of the scenarios. Surprisingly, on scenarios 3 and 7 they were more like radicals or liberals in their opinions, and on the others they were all to the left of moderate. On 3, 5, and 6, all dealing with tactics, their more liberal stance has a somewhat Machiavellian flavor. On 7 and 14 they were more favorable to the developer and the white homeowners' group, which might have been expected.

In relation to role, we thought that the most political planners might be the most liberal, and technicians the most conservative, with hybrids in between. In actual fact, the single largest group overall is liberals (31 percent of the sample). Politicians were the most liberal, while technicians, though generally more conservative, have a slightly bimodal pattern with high points at both liberal and moderate. Hybrids did have a pattern between the other two, but again it was bimodal like the technicians.

Agency Orientation and Ethics

A classic dilemma found in any public service profession, including planning, is the possible conflict between what the agency, which presumably

serves the public, defines as the public interest, and what the individual professional thinks the public interest is. Whistleblowing (Nader et al. 1972,
Finkler 1971), though risky, is not difficult to justify if the issue involves
dishonesty on the part of the agency, but what if it is purely a difference of
opinion on policy?

In our sample, most planners are quite loyal or committed to their agencies, with 70 percent above the midpoint on the agency orientation scale. On
scenarios which involved a challenge to agency policy—all the leaking
scenarios, helping the environmental group fight the refinery, and organizing support to challenge zoning policy—these agency-oriented planners
thought the action significantly (.05 level) more unethical than the less committed ones. The difference between the two groups was largest on leaking
information about the wetlands study (scenario 9), where the challenge to
the agency director was most open.

Values and Ethics

Overall, 57 percent of the sample had scores above the midpoint scale,
measuring propensity to express values in one's work, indicating that
despite the idea of the value free planner, the majority of planners think it is
acceptable to be open about their values. It is also perhaps not surprising
that the values scale has a high correlation (r_s = .6744) with the political
role scale, indicating that value commitment and a willingness to act on it
possibly go together.

Planners who think that they should act on their values in their work are
different in their ethical judgments from planners who wish to be value
neutral. When the scenarios are grouped together by similar issues, the difference between the value orientations is significant at better than .01 for
giving out recommendations, leaking information, and for the most acceptable tactics (scenarios 6, 8, and 13). There is no significant difference,
however, between the two groups on the scenarios concerned with the
misrepresentation of information.

Moreover, as we saw earlier, many planners do seem to be influenced, at
least to some extent, in what they think is ethical by the intended
beneficiaries of their actions. The same tactic used in behalf of different
groups is judged differently. We expected this effect to be much stronger
for politicians, who approve much more of open value commitment, than
for technicians who generally wish to be value neutral. Actually, the results
are rather mixed. On the scenarios giving out recommendations (1 and 14),
politicians are influenced[17] more by the issue than are technicians; but when
it comes to leaking information, there is no difference between the two
roles. There is, however, an interesting difference on the leaking scenarios

in that the beneficiary is much more important to planners who are not strongly committed to their agencies than for those who are.

Role Types

All the variables discussed so far obviously have an effect on what planners think is ethical. But the key variable seems to be role, with the other variables clustering around it in coherent patterns. We will now look more closely at each role type—the technician, the politician, and the hybrid.

The most traditional image of the planner is as a technician. The two major aspects of the technical role are its faith in the efficacy of analysis and its value neutrality; and on both of these, the comparison between the technicians in the sample and the politicians is dramatic. Fully 81 percent of the technicians indicated that they were value neutral compared with only 15 percent for the politicians. Even more strikingly, 94 percent of the technicians said that a planner's effectiveness is based primarily on his reputation for objective, accurate, and in-depth analysis, while only 51 percent of the politicians agreed. Technicians are also much more likely (63 percent) than politicians (12 percent) to argue that plans should stand or fall for their acceptance on their technical quality and internal logic.

In line also with their value neutrality, technicians were more committed to their agencies, and less likely to challenge agency policy. Grouping together all the scenarios which involved leaking information or challenges to agency policy, the technicians on the average thought that those scenarios were more unethical than all the rest of the scenarios grouped together, while the politicians thought those scenarios were more ethical than all the others combined. Technicians were also more committed to their agencies, with 76 percent over 3.5 on the scale, compared with 64 percent of the politicians. On the scenario involving leaks to outside groups, where the tactic could be held constant, planners who were more oriented to their agencies had a narrower range of scores over the three scenarios, indicating that they were more swayed by the impropriety of the tactic itself, and less by any ties to outside groups.

Given these characteristics and views, it is not surprising that technicians would be the most conservative overall in their view of what is ethical, since the scenarios present situations involving challenging the authority of an agency by leaking information or organizing outsiders to change policy, misrepresenting information in analysis, and generally being politically active in trying to get plans adopted. Thus, there were no scenarios where the mean for all technicians was below 2.00, the point on the scale that indicates a judgment of "probably ethical."

Since the quality and integrity of technical analysis are particularly important to them, it is not surprising to find that misrepresenting information (scenarios 2 and 10) is unacceptable; the mean for all technicians on these two is over 4.00, the score for "probably unethical." Moreover, when faced with a conflict of loyalty between agency and analysis, as in scenario 11, analysis continues to exert a strong pull. Agency oriented technicians were more likely to think that the economic planner's capitulation was ethical, but the difference between them and the non-agency oriented technicians was smaller than for any other agency-oriented scenario except one.[18]

Politicians, of course, are at the opposite extreme from technicians in our typology. Overall, they are more interested in influencing policy than the other groups, and are most willing to use a range of openly political tactics to do it. For example, 51 percent of the politicians ranked influencing policy among the three most important aspects of their job, compared with only 30 percent of the technicians. As Table 7 indicates, politicians clearly are much more prone to lobby, mobilize support, and neutralize opposition than are technicians. They are also more interested than technicians in routinely being involved in policy disputes; and a majority, unlike the technicians, think that the quality and depth of analysis done by planners have little to do with their effectiveness.

In general the politicians are more accepting of the political tactics in the scenarios than the technicians are, although this does not mean they think all tactics are ethical. As Table 5 indicates, the mean for all politicians is less than 2.5—in the probably-to-clearly-ethical range—for six scenarios compared to only two for the technicians. Even though politicians are significantly more accepting than technicians of the use of A-95 power as a threat, and of distorting information, the means for these four scenarios (2, 3, 5, 10) range from 3.58 to 4.03, putting them all in the "probably unethical" range.

Politicians are also somewhat less likely to be committed to their agencies and are more likely to have an independent commitment to issues or client groups. They are as value committed (85 percent) as the technicians are value neutral (81 percent). As indicated previously, they are relatively more willing than technicians to say it is ethical to give recommendations to the environmental group (scenario 1); and although willing to accept the principles as ethical, they are more unwilling actually to give recommendations to the white homeowners' group (scenario 14) or to leak information to the Chamber of Commerce (scenario 13).[19]

Hybrids are the group of planners who are high on both the technical and the political scales. Since they feel the tension between the two role dimensions most, they tend to score between the politicians and the technicians on most variables. Consequently, there are relatively few instances where

TABLE 7

Support for Political Tactics by Role in Percentages (n = 577)

	Poli-ticians	Hybrids	Tech-nicians
lobby actively to defeat harmful pro-posals	94.3	93.8	62.8
develop groups to support plan	89.6	86.4	42.5
neutralize opposition by mobiliz-ing support	73.3	74.4	26.2
may have to work covertly to gain support	70.1	68.2	50.9
planning should be placed in gov't so it can get involved in disputes	66.7	63.0	22.2
quality and depth of analysis have little to do with effectiveness	57.2	36.8	30.7

hybrids are obviously unique by virtue of having scores dramatically higher or lower than the other two groups. Instead, the analysis of this role has to focus on when they seem to be more like politicians, when they are more like technicians, and what kind of overall pattern this produces.

Simply by virtue of the way their role is defined, hybrids are quite close to technicians in their attitudes about analysis, and close to politicians in their attitudes about political tactics. For example, they are similar to technicians in thinking that the effectiveness of planners is based on good analysis, and that plans should stand or fall on their quality and logic. On the political attitudes listed in Table 7, they are virtually identical to the politicians except on the last item on analysis where, again, they are more like the technicians.

In terms of ethics, this means they tend to be more like politicians on tactical scenarios. On the scenarios dealing with leaks and giving out of recommendations, and on the symbolic campaign over pollution, the two groups were statistically indistinguishable. But as the tactics get more varied, and then more questionable, the differences increase. On using expendables as a bargaining device (scenario 6) and on organizing support (scenario 8), they are statistically different from both other groups; while on the use of A-95 review as a punitive tool (scenario 5), they shift to agreement with the technicians.

It is harder to see clearly the effect of their technical values, since the scenarios posing issues of distorting information (2 and 10) or of giving in on a technical judgment (scenario 11) have a much smaller overall range. This means that even if the difference between technicians and politicians is significant, the hybrids in the middle are difficult to sort out from either.

In terms of who they are, they seem generally to be more like politicians than technicians, though they are still always more moderate. They are liberal, though not as much as politicians, with 42 percent left of center and only 34 percent right of center. Sixty-seven percent are value committed, much closer to the politicians' 85 percent than the technicians' 19 percent. A similar pattern holds for orientation to agency, though the overall range is much smaller. As with politicians, these last two characteristics tend to make them more independent, and possibly more active participants in the planning process. This helps to explain the hybrids' greater acceptance of the scenarios on giving out recommendations, leaking information, and challenging agency policy.

There are also a few interesting and unique qualities of hybrids which give a more rounded image of them. They are somewhat more likely to be over 40, and are disproportionately found in the groups with the least (0 to 2) and the most (21 or more) years of planning experience. This might suggest that the attempt to combine the two aspects of role, while a significant characteristic for all kinds of planners, is somewhat more likely to be true of the inexperienced and possibly idealistic young, and the older, more experienced members of the field.

Also the only instance where they hold views stronger than both other role groups was on the belief that planning should be long range. When taken with their combined technical and political approach to planning, this attitude may indicate a more ambitious idea of what planning should be than is held by either other group.

This image of the hybrids gives some support to Meltsner's (1976, pp. 36–47) idea of the entrepreneurial, technically sophisticated politician: a more active, independent, and skilled actor than either of his other kinds of analysts. Because of its base in attitudes, however, our study tends to emphasize the tension and balance aspects of this role. If, on the other hand, the ethical dilemmas posed in our scenarios are seen as a restraint on the political aspects of the planner's role, these hybrids are generally no more limited than their fellow politicians.

Conclusions

Overall, planners' views of ethics fall into two categories. The first are core professional values, shared by virtually all people in the sample. Two core values that clearly emerge from the study are the unacceptability of using threats or distorting information. Then there is a large area where values or ethics seem to be relative, with judgments influenced more by such factors as role, political views, and agency orientation. Tactics or means seem to have a more important effect on ethical choices than do the substantive issues or ends the tactics are used to achieve, though substantive issues do have some impact. Since tactics are important, role, which particularly relates to planning strategy and tactics, is an important determinant of planners' ethics. A variety of other variables closely related to role, such as political views, agency orientation, and value orientation, cluster around it in characteristic patterns, having similar effects on what planners think is ethical. It is also significant that planners say that they would act consistently with their ethical views.

Much of our description of planners simply provides greater insight into the already well developed political and technical role models. Our research can enable us to give an indication of how many are in each group, and what they are like, with more statistical precision than previous studies.

But the role we have called the hybrids provides some new insight into the practice of planning, since these people are trying to bridge the gap, combining the characteristics of both roles. Since there are more hybrids in our sample than politicians and technicians combined, it may perhaps be more difficult to maintain one of the polar roles in practice than in theory. But if hybrids have become, and can be expected to remain the dominant group, this poses a number of issues about the adequacy of the ethical standards now in force in the profession.

Our data indicate that ethical standards in planning are relative. It is certainly true that some kinds of behavior, such as distorting information, are considered unacceptable by the vast majority of all planners. But even for these behaviors, there remain some planners who still consider them ethical. And for many political tactics, planners disagree much more about acceptability, depending on such things as their role orientations, political views, value commitment, or sympathies toward the substantive issues at stake.

This variability in ethical judgments means that it is very difficult to establish any single ethical standard that is meaningful to the whole profession. At the extreme, it is not difficult to think of behavior that most people would agree is unethical. Bribery clearly qualifies, and so, probably, does distortion of information; but what about providing information to outside groups so they can fight your agency, or using threats, tradeoffs, or symbolic appeals to get a plan approved?

One might make the argument that it is better for planning to have a restrictive set of ethical standards. Why? Because in a democratic society planners are not decision makers who can be held responsible by the public. They are experts who "attempt to provide public . . . decision makers with the best possible information, analysis, and recommendations to promote the public welfare" (AIP 1977, p. 2). Such a definition would argue that planners should avoid taking upon themselves the right to define the goals that guide the definition and solution of problems, or trying to openly and actively get their own particular views adopted in the political system. They should have a restrictive view of the scope of planning. Our data indicate that the most effective way to ensure that planners have such a restrictive view of planning and of ethical behavior would be to train people as technicians, since, of our three roles, they have not only the narrowest view of the planners' range of discretion, but are even more restrictive in what they are actually willing to do in practice. This is, in effect, the way the present role of ethics of the AIP is drawn; and historically the dominant role model presented to planners has been the technical one.

But according to our study, hybrids are actually the dominant group in the field. In practice, they have a broader image of the proper role of the planner and a less restrictive view of what is ethical. In this they are quite similar to, though more moderate than, the politicians, and between them the two groups make up 70 percent of our sample.

This raises the question of whether it is useful to have a code of ethics, some provisions of which are more honored by many in the breach than in the observance. As Francine Rabinovitz (1969, pp. 133–134) wrote in 1969:

> The profession . . . still officially discourages political roles, having developed no code of conduct that defines what types of political strategies are ethically acceptable and what types are expedient but unprofessional.

Might it be better to reconsider portions of the code in light of the evolving practice of planning? Planners often make ethical judgments implicitly in making strategy and methodological decisions, but they may not give them the sustained and systematic thought that they give to the more practical issues. Moreover, the more political they are in their planning activities, the more they have to face the kind of dilemmas posed in our scenarios, which are not adequately dealt with in the AIP's code of ethics.

Obviously the possibility of making the code less restrictive raises the problem of the tradeoff between technical integrity and political effectiveness. To be too permissive about tactics might lead, as Rabinovitz suggests (1969, Chapter 6), to a loss of legitimacy. On the other hand, to be too restrictive raises the problem, much discussed since the publication of Altshuler's *The City Planning Process*, of being ineffective and unable to carry plans through to fruition.

But the interesting aspect of our study is that it is the hybrids who dominate, not the politicians; and it is the hybrids who make the greatest effort to combine both the technical and the political aspects of role. This would indicate that they are likely to be sensitive to both the problem of loss of legitimacy and the problem of lack of effectiveness. The two aspects of their role do involve a tension which may at times be difficult to balance. As educators, it may be our role to try to develop ways to either reduce the tension or to enable planners to deal more effectively with it. Simply making clear that it exists and that both the political and the technical aspects of role orientation are legitimate and necessary for a balance, may be a step in that direction. Going further, educators could deal head-on in the classroom with the kinds of ethical dilemmas posed in our scenarios, having students grapple with such problems early instead of waiting until they become practitioners to puzzle through the issues these dilemmas pose. But it may also be the role of the professional organization to provide a more carefully thought out and realistic set of guidelines to behavior in this difficult area of practice.

NOTES

[1] The authors would like to thank all the members of the AIP who participated in the study.

[2] Peter Marcuse (1976) demonstrates quite convincingly the divergent ethical prescriptions that underlie professional planning ethics. These include: allegiance, autonomy, knowledge and competence, guild loyalty, concern for the public interest, dissent, loyalty, advancement of knowledge, and statutory responsibility.

[3] The public interest concern is most directly reflected in Section 1.1(a) of the Canons of AIP's Code of Professional Responsibility—"A planner serves the public interest primarily." The loyalty to the planners' client concern is reflected in Rules of Discipline (d) of the AIP Code.

[4] We also would like to be able to determine what factors are most important in affecting planners' ethical choices. The study was designed with a fairly complex path analysis model in mind. But testing the strength and simultaneous effect of a large number of independent variables (26) on each other and on the dependent variable is a difficult methodological task, especially when, as is the case here, most of the variables are measured only at the ordinal level. This particular paper examines the relationships between six of the twenty-six independent variables and the two dependent variables.

[5] Every sixth person on the AIP mailing list was chosen unless that individual's address clearly indicated that he worked for a planning consulting firm, a university, or a private development, or if the code indicated that the person was a student or an affiliate. (The method of choice was count, discard, recount.) The sampling fraction was increased from 12.3 percent to 18.5 percent to allow for the elimination during the sampling procedure of people who obviously did not belong in the sample, and for an additional estimated 27 percent of the final sample who would also turn out to be in one of the categories listed above. We sampled members of the AIP because their mailing list was the only list of professional planners available. We have no way of knowing, however, whether AIP members were typical of all planners.

[6] The only two other empirical studies of ethics we could find both use the same kind of scenario format (Carlin 1966, Beard & Horn 1975). One, a study of the ethics of congressmen, uses the same five-point scale.

[7] These percentages would increase to 20 to 30 percent if those who were uncertain about the ethical propriety of the action were added to those who said the action was ethical.

[8] Planners come out strongly in favor of mass transit on the transportation scale in Part 2 of the questionnaire. Seventy percent are pro-mass transit while 30 percent are anti-mass transit.

[9] It is interesting to note that, in fact, five of these scenarios form a Guttman scale. A cut-point of 3.0 was used so that the "not sures" were included along with those who thought the

scenarios were unethical. The coefficient of reproducibility for the scale was .9058, and the coefficient of scalability was .7351. The order for the scenarios is the same as in the tables above: scenario 1 is the most acceptable, followed in order by scenarios 14, 7, 4, and 12. This means that the 16 percent of the sample who would leak information to the Chamber of Commerce (scenario 12), would accept providing information to all other kinds of groups; while the 35 percent who would not or were not sure that they would provide information to an environmental group on request, would not provide or leak information to any other kind of group.

[10]The variability on substantive issues was much higher in the final sample than in the pretest group. Items used in the construction of Likert scales, which had explained from 30 to 60 percent of the variance in the pretest, explained only from 4 to 20 percent of the variance for the final sample. This makes them weak tools for analyzing substantive attitudes, and we have not relied on such scales in our analysis.

[11]We were particularly concerned about the construction of the scales measuring role orientation. Originally, following the drift of much of the literature on planners, we thought of role as a single dimension with the technical and political orientations as its two reverse sides. However, a factor analysis of the pretest results indicated that the items should be separated into at least four scales, a political one, a technical one, one concerned with the planner's attitudes toward his agency, and one concerned with attitudes about value commitment. A factor analysis of the final sample showed this pattern even more clearly. The factor analysis used principal factoring with iteration. Both orthogonal (varimax) and oblique rotation were tried, with similar results. For the final construction of the scales, orthogonal (varimax) rotation was used. This grouped the items into six factors. Items with factor loadings of more than .25 were used to create the scales. The political scale included items on political tactics and cynical attitudes toward analysis. The technical scale was made up of two factors, one of which had five items stressing the importance of rationality and technical expertise, and a second with two items on long-range planning and value neutrality.

Generally, Likert scales of this type have about 20 items in them, but scales with as few as 5, 7, and 10 items are acceptable (Likert 1967, Hall 1934). The technical and political scales had six and seven items, respectively. The agency orientation and value commitment scales had five items each. Item analysis of the four role scales came out quite strong. Correlations between each item and its scale were not only significant at the .001 level (due in part to the sample size), but also had in each instance, an r^2 explaining at least 23 percent of the variance.

[12]The fourth possible role, low on both scales, had only 26 respondents in it, so we did not name it or use it. Meltsner (1976, p. 15) calls the comparable category in his typology the "pretenders."

[13]These roles are quite parallel to Meltsner's (1976, Chapter 2) in their underlying dimensions, though not necessarily in their associated characteristics. They were, interestingly enough, developed independently, before either author had read Meltsner's book. They arose logically out of the factor analysis of the pretest results. Meltsner uses the term "entrepreneur" for his high/high category, drawing also on Bardach (1972). The term indicates that these are the most skilled and active analysts of his typology. We wanted a somewhat less value laden term which would indicate that the primary characteristic of our high/high group is that they try to balance the two dimensions of role, and come between the other two roles on a number of our variables. The term "hybrid" denotes "anything of heterogeneous origin or incongruous parts," as animals (especially swine) of mixed parentage.

[14]Of Meltsner's group of 116 analysts at the Federal level, only 23 percent were entrepreneurs. However, he was looking at their political and analytic skills, while we have only been able to look at planners' attitudes about what they "should" do. We cannot infer from our data whether the planners interviewed have the skills, opportunity, or even the personal inclination to play the roles they say are best.

[15]The measure for action was the mean for each scenario. The means for action were lower than for ethics on 11 out of 15 scenarios for each role, though which 11 scenarios had lower means for action differed from one role to another. Only on one scenario for technicians and on two each for politicians and hybrids were the action means higher than the means for ethics.

[16]Overall, the differences between radicals and conservatives were significant for all scenarios except 2, 3, and 10 (among the least acceptable) and scenarios 11 (the most ambivalent). Looking at liberals and moderates reduces the number of scenarios where the difference is significant to seven (1, 2, 4, 5, 6, 9, and 15). Even between the three middle categories, some differences still hold up.

[17]Influence is determined by looking at the difference between the means for each scenario. We would expect that if the tactic is held constant, as it is in scenarios 1 and 14, and also in scenarios 4, 9, and 12, the difference in means would be due to the influence of the issue or beneficiary. The size of the difference can be compared for any other variable such as role or agency orientation; the larger the difference is the more the issue or beneficiary matters. Thus, if the difference between scenarios 1 and 14 is larger for politicians than for technicians, then the issue or beneficiary matters more to the politicians.

[18]The exception was scenario 12, the leak to the Chamber of Commerce. There was no real difference between the two groups. The beneficiary was less acceptable, and all technicians thought the scenario was unethical.

[19]The influence of the environment as an issue was determined in the same way as described in Footnote 17. On unwillingness to act, the mean for action was less than the mean for ethics, and the difference in the means was larger for politicians than for technicians.

REFERENCES

Alinsky, Saul D. 1971. Of means and ends. In *Rules for radicals*. New York: Random House.

Allor, David. 1970–1971. Normative ethics in community planning. *Maxwell Review* 7,1: 113–137.

Altshuler, Alan. 1965. *The city planning process: a political analysis*. Ithaca, N.Y.: Cornell University Press.

American Institute of Planners. 1962. *Code of professional responsibility and rules of procedure*. Washington, D.C.: AIP.

American Institute of Planners. 1973. *The social responsibility of the planner*. Washington, D.C.: AIP.

American Institute of Planners. 1977. *Planning policies, '77*. Washington, D.C.: AIP.

Bardach, Eugene. 1972. *The skill factor in politics*. Berkeley: University of California Press.

Beard, Edmund, and Horn, Stephen. 1975. *Congressional ethics: the view from the House*. Washington, D.C.: Brookings Institution.

Beckman, Norman. 1964. The planner as a bureaucrat. *Journal of the American Institute of Planners* 30, 4: 323–327.

Benveniste, Guy. 1972. *The politics of expertise*. Berkeley, California: The Glendessary Press.

Bok, Sissela. 1978. *Lying: moral choice in public and private life*. New York: Pantheon Books.

Carlin, Jerome. 1966. *Lawyer's ethics*. New York: Russell Sage Foundation.

Catanese, Anthony. 1974. *Planners and local politics: impossible dreams*. Beverly Hills, California: Sage Publications.

Finkler, Earl. 1971. *Dissent and independent initiative in planning offices*. Chicago: American Society of Planning Officials.

Hall, O. Milton. 1934. Attitudes and unemployment. *Archives of Psychology* 165: 5–65.

Howe, Elizabeth. 1978. Ethical issues and the "publicness" of professions. Paper given at the meetings of the American Society for Public Administration. Phoenix, Arizona.

Jacobs, Alan. 1978. *Making city planning work*. Chicago: American Society of Planning Officials Press.

Kelman, Herbert C. 1965. Manipulation of human behavior: an ethical dilemma for the social scientist. *Journal of Social Issues* 21, 2: 31–46.

Klosterman, Richard. 1978. Foundations for normative planning. *Journal of the American Institute of Planners* 44, 1: 37–46.

Likert, Rensis. 1967. The method of constructing an attitude scale. In *Readings in attitude theory and measurement*, ed. Martin Fishbein. New York: John Wiley & Sons.

Marcuse, Peter. 1976. Professional ethics and beyond: values in planning. *Journal of the American Institute of Planners* 42, 3: 264–274.

Meltsner, Arnold. 1976. *Policy analysts in the bureaucracy*. Berkeley: University of California Press.

Meyerson, Martin, and Banfield, Edward. 1955. *Politics, planning and the public interest*. New York: The Free Press.

Meyerson, Martin. 1956. Building the middle range bridge for comprehensive planning. *Journal of the American Institute of Planners* 22, 2: 58–63.

Nader, Ralph; Petkas, Peter; and Blackwell, Kate, eds. 1972. *Whistleblowing: the report of the conference on professional responsibility*. New York: Grossman Publishers.

Needleman, Martin, and Needleman, Carolyn. 1974. *Guerillas in the bureaucracy: the community planning experiment in the United States*. New York: John Wiley & Sons.

Rabinovitz, Francine. 1969. *City politics and planning*. New York: Atherton Press.

Walker, Robert. 1950. *The planning function in urban government*. Chicago: University of Chicago Press.

Zaltman, Gerald, and Duncan, Robert. 1977. Ethics in social change. In *Strategies for planned change*. New York: John Wiley & Sons.

Foundations for Normative Planning

Richard E. Klosterman

The planning profession in the United States and England grew out of and has been in large part shaped by two very important intellectual traditions. Most obvious in this regard is the widespread western faith in rationality and science which has viewed planning as the institutionalized application of the methods and findings of science to social affairs. Equally important, however, has been the great tradition of middle-class reform which has seen planning as a means for improving government and society.[1]

A recurring problem for both planning practice and theory has been the fact that these traditions suggest somewhat conflicting roles for the planning profession and the practicing planner. The rationalist tradition suggests that the planner, as an applied scientist, must be dedicated to objectivity, careful collection and analysis of data, and rigorous adherence to the canons of the scientific method. The reform tradition, on the other hand, suggests that the planner must be committed to change and to ensuring that his proposals promote the best interests of his clients or the population at large. These two roles can conflict not only in planning practice (e.g., when a planner's commitment to impartially analyze all possible courses of action conflicts with a commitment to promote only those alternatives which favor his clients), but also in the definition of the planning profession and planning education (e.g., to emphasize a scientific approach to problem analysis or, perhaps, a commitment to social change).

Evolution of Instrumental Planning

Early planning practice and education were shaped primarily by the profession's roots in the reform tradition. Planning problems—unregulated ur-

Reprinted by permission of the *Journal of the American Institute of Planners*, Vol. 44, No. 1, (January 1978), pp. 37–46.

ban growth, poor sanitation, inadequate transportation and public facilities—were relatively clear-cut. As a result, the profession's early substantive theories were unsophisticated, and its methodologies were straight-forward applications of the "design standards" approach of the more established professions such as engineering, architecture, and public health (Webber 1969). Guided by a rather naive form of environmental determinism, planners assumed a professional responsibility for improving society through changes in the physical environment and saw themselves protecting the public interest from the self-interested and uninformed actions of politicians and private individuals.[2] Planning education reflected this reform emphasis in its neglect of analytic planning methods and social science theory and in its consideration of utopian plans which might define professional ideals.

In the last two decades, however, planning ideology and education have increasingly emphasized the planner's role as an applied scientist. The simplistic assumptions of the early profession have been replaced by an increased reliance on the theories and models of the social sciences. More dramatic has been the replacement of the early design approach by a variety of highly sophisticated, computer-assisted planning tools and techniques from large-scale urban simulation models to linear programming and regression analysis. Contemporary planning education reflects this conception of the planner-as-scientist in its emphasis on statistics, planning methods, and the substantive theories of economics, sociology, regional science, and the other positive social sciences.

With this increased theoretical and methodological sophistication has come a neglect of the profession's reform heritage. That is, implicit in the emphasis on analytic techniques and social science theory is a view of the planner as a "value-free means technician" who collects and analyzes "factual" data concerning the means for achieving public policy objectives but avoids the "value" questions of defining these objectives.

For example, a recurring public policy question at the local level is whether public, low-income (and often minority) housing developments should be located in middle-class residential areas. It seems planners can help communities deal with issues like this in a variety of ways including: estimating the most probable effects of locating a development in a particular area, surveying the experience in other communities, identifying community sentiments on the issue, and determining the least costly way to implement whatever public policy is established. Academic planners, as positive social scientists, may likewise consider the general question of mixed residential neighborhoods by, for example, building predictive models of changes in residential patterns or developing theories of the social and psychological effects of mixed housing.

Under the widely assumed view of planners as technicians, this is all planners can and must do—collect and provide information which will make for more informed policy making. That is, it is assumed planners can help determine the relative costs and benefits of alternative public policies and the most appropriate means for achieving public policy objectives but must leave the determination of these objectives to the public and its elected and appointed representatives.

The Call For Normative Planning

This "instrumental" concept of planning has been increasingly questioned by both planners and non-planners (Fromm 1972, Kreiger 1974, and Long 1975b). Most radical have been the calls by Friedmann (1966), Faludi (1973), and others for "normative" planning in which planners subject both the ends and means of public policy to rational consideration. These proposals are of particular interest because they suggest that the planning profession can combine scientific analysis with reform and change and thus be true to both of its intellectual roots.

However, none of the calls for normative planning has outlined the procedures by which planners are to rationally evaluate public policy ends. More fundamentally, they have not developed the logical foundation for rational consideration of ethical issues in public policy—an activity which runs counter to some of the most fundamental and widely shared assumptions of the positive social sciences.

This article attempts to provide this intellectual foundation for normative planning, the rational consideration of both factual questions of public policy means and ethical questions of public policy ends. First, it argues, planners cannot consider only factual questions of alternative means but also must deal with substantive ethical questions—implicitly if not explicitly. Current attempts to deal with the ethical issues of public policy planning by claims to professionalism and by pragmatic politics are reviewed and judged inadequate. More fundamentally, the "logical-positivist" foundation for the instrumental view is examined and found to be deficient. Further, the "postlogical-positivist" views of contemporary philosophers such as John Rawls are found to suggest that ethical issues can be rationally considered in ways similar to those of the empirical sciences. These views, finally, suggest the foundations for a normative yet rational approach to planning whose implications for planning practice and theory are briefly considered.

The Impossibility of Value-Free Planning

A dominant theme underlying much of the planning literature is the view that planners can and should avoid the consideration of substantive ethical questions. Traditional land use planning was seen by many as a purely technical activity directed by statements of land use goals and objectives which had been approved by the community or were self-evident and needed no approval. Planning on this view was political only in that planners might have to convince public officials to accept and act on their final plans. "Process" approaches to planning utilizing decision theory, linear programming, and operations research have similarly been seen as avoiding substantive ethical questions by limiting the planner's role to identifying the optimal or most efficient means for achieving the objectives of elected and appointed public officials.

While these approaches have been criticized on a variety of grounds, the relevant point here is that neither eliminates the need for planning to deal (implicitly, if not explicitly) with the ethical issues implicit in questions of public policy. Altshuler (1965), Banfield (1959), and others have observed that, for a variety of good reasons, communities and public organizations are reluctant to establish the long-range goals which are presumed to guide planning practice. Goals, when established, are vague and often conflicting; as a result planners and administrators must make substantive decisions in preparing detailed plans and evaluating specific government actions (Appleby 1949).

These traditional approaches have been supplemented by proposals for advocacy planning in which planners promote the interests of community groups (Davidoff 1965) and for limiting planning's role to providing information to existing multicentered policy-making processes (Webber 1965 and Rondinelli 1971). However, neither of these approaches eliminates the need for planners to deal in some way with substantive ethical issues. Advocate planners must select the interests which are (and are not) to be represented in the policy-making process because not all groups can be represented and it is doubtful that any group will be homogeneous in all relevant respects.[3] Even providing additional information to existing market and policy-making processes requires a determination of (among other things) which studies are to be conducted, which data collected, and what findings provided to which community groups (Webber 1965). Because the answers given to each of these questions affect the final policy which is adopted, they necessarily involve substantive ethical issues which must be resolved (either explicitly or implicitly) by planners.[4]

More fundamentally, public policy planning without the explicit or implicit consideration of substantive ethical or political issues seems impossible because planning is itself *essentially* political. As Norton Long pointed out in 1959,

> The question is not whether planning will reflect politics, but whose politics will it reflect . . . Plans are in reality political programs . . . In the broad sense they represent political philosophies, ways of implementing different conceptions of the good life (p. 168).

To the extent that planners are successful in influencing the policies and actions of government, they are acting politically in the most fundamental sense of the word because their actions help determine "who gets what, when, how,"[5] and thus affect the members of society, positively and negatively. As a result, their decisions and actions *necessarily* involve ethical issues of, for example, balancing the conflicting interests of the members of society, and it seems impossible both in practice and in principle to limit planning to only the factual consideration of means.

Attempting to Deal with Normative Issues

It has, of course, been widely recognized by both planning academics and practitioners that value-free planning is impossible.[6] In fact, planners often have strongly felt personal or widely shared professional views on public issues such as the desirability of mixed housing and regularly attempt to get their views enacted at the local, state, or even national level.

Early planners assumed that their views corresponded to an enlightened public interest and saw their attempts to help define public policy objectives as merely the application of their professional judgment to narrow technical issues within their unique competence with issues of land use and related public facilities. Thus, like the professional opinions of doctors and lawyers, planning prescriptions were presumed to be justified by the practitioner's expertise with the relevant issues and their membership in a moral community guided by a well-defined set of professional norms. This emphasis on professionalism is reflected in the repeated attempts to demonstrate that planning is a profession and to develop professional and personal "philosophies" which could guide individual planners (see, for example, Howard 1954 and 1955).

However, planners' claims to professional competence have never been widely accepted by others involved in defining public policy (see, for example, Altshuler 1965, especially pp. 17–83). In addition, the norms which were presumed to guide professional practice have been found to be not only unclear and rarely enforced but often conflicting (see, for example, Marcuse 1976). More importantly, planning issues are now recognized to be important political questions involving the interests of a wide range of actors, and planners' prescriptions have been found to reflect the often unrecognized bias of the profession's middle-class members (see, for example, Davidoff and Reiner 1962 and Davidoff 1965).

Dual Bases for Contemporary Practice

With the recognition of planning's political nature and the questioning of its professional heritage have come a fundamental uncertainty about the way in which planners are to deal with the ethical aspects of their work. For technical or "scientific" issues of understanding the operation of nature and society (the way the world *is*) planners receive relatively clear guidance from the empirical sciences and the loosely defined norms of the scientific method. Thus, it seems, planners should attempt to collect all available data, generalize from particular observations to general theories, laws, and models, and test these by comparing them to reality. However, for political or ethical issues of determining what policies should be enacted (the way the world *ought to be*), no such guidance seems to be available. There may be a variety of opinions about what ought to be done in a particular case; and it is often not clear how these alternative positions can be evaluated or even what information is relevant for comparing them.

Thus, perhaps inevitably, practicing and academic planners are left with a feeling that ethical positions are mere relative matters of individual taste and preference (such as a preference for one color over another) and that planners' views can only compete with my conflicting and equally valid political opinions. Motivated by this belief, contemporary planners have generally adopted two conflicting perspectives on the ethical issues of public policy planning. Some, emphasizing planning's scientific nature and adopting the perspective of the positive social sciences, attempt to avoid all ethical questions by collecting and providing decision makers with factual information on the probable effects of alternative policies. The implicit belief here is simply that better information will lead to better public policy decisions. Others, emphasizing planning's political nature and downgrading policy analysis, just assume their political positions to be "correct" and engage in pragmatic politics in order to, perhaps, promote the interests of underrepresented groups or, more generally, improve their political effectiveness. The implicit belief here is that, by acting politically, planners can improve the political process and its representativeness and, thus, public policy decisions.[7]

However, by emphasizing either the information on which public decisions are made or the decision process and the groups involved, both approaches ignore the inevitable ethical issues of public policy planning, both avoid direct consideration of the *substance* of public policy, particularly the fundamental issue of defining public policy objectives.[8] In addition, by separating scientific analysis from political action, neither approach reflects the profession's traditional concerns with both rationality and reform. To determine whether, in fact, these two concerns can be combined in the rational consideration of substantive questions of public policy it is necessary to examine the intellectual foundation of the instrumental approach.

Foundations of Instrumental Planning

The assumption that planning should be limited to the factual consideration of means reflects, if unconsciously, the long-standing and extremely influential positivist view that the empirically based sciences provide the only means for obtaining systematic and reliable knowledge. In particular, it has been motivated by two important aspects of this tradition: the logical-positivist conception of ethics, developed by the Vienna Circle at the turn of the century, and the means-end conception of rationality.[9]

Logical-Positivist Conception of Ethics

The logical-positivist position is based on an assumed distinction between factual sentences which are "cognitively meaningful" (i.e., can be proven to be correct or incorrect) and nonfactual sentences such as questions, requests, and exclamations which are neither true nor false and thus cannot provide the basis for systematic knowledge. Further, the logical positivists assumed sentences can be cognitively meaningful in only two ways. First, they argued, sentences can be cognitively meaningful if they express statements which are "analytic," i.e., true or false just by virtue of the meaning of the words used. For example, the sentence "A U.S. census standard metropolitan statistical area consists of a county containing at least one city of 50,000 or more inhabitants and any adjacent metropolitan counties" is an analytical truth or tautology true by the meanings of the English terms *U.S. census, standard metropolitan statistical area, county*, etc. Similarly, the sentence "A U.S. census standard metropolitan statistical area consists of only one county containing a city of 50,000 or more inhabitants" is analytically false or self-contradictory on the same grounds, i.e., because of the meanings of the English words *U.S. Census, standard metropolitan statistical area*, etc.

Second, in their famous "verifiability principle," the logical positivists argued that "synthetic" (i.e., non-analytic) sentences can be cognitively meaningful only if they express statements which can be empirically verified, i.e., confirmed or disconfirmed by empirical observations. For example, the sentence "The present population of the New York metropolitan area is thirteen million" is cognitively meaningful under this criterion because it is possible to imagine ways in which it could be empirically confirmed or disconfirmed—using, perhaps, standard census enumeration and sampling techniques.

In the logical-positivist view, sentences which are neither true (or false) by virtue of the meanings of the words they contain nor empirically testable (at least in principle) are cognitively meaningless and, therefore, neither true nor false. In particular, the logical positivists viewed "ethical" sentences (stating that an action is good or bad, right or wrong, etc.) as neither analytic nor empirically verifiable and, thus, cognitively meaningless and neither true nor false. Thus, it was assumed, a clear distinction can be drawn between factual and ethical statements and a "logical gap" separates the two, i.e., that no set of factual statements entails an ethical statement (and the reverse). Disagreements about ethical questions were seen as not resolvable on rational grounds because, in this view, they can reflect differing value systems and the choice between these is itself an ethical decision which cannot be made on rational grounds.[10]

Means-End Conception of Rationality

Closely related to the logical-positivist position is the means-end conception of practical reason revealed in the works of both contemporary writers such as Herbert Simon (1957) and classical writers such as Max Weber (1949) and David Hume (see, for example, the selections in Raphael 1969, pp. 8–14 and 83–90). In this view, actions can be justified only as providing a means for achieving a person's ends and can be rationally evaluated only on this ground (e.g., as providing an adequate means for achieving those ends). An end which guides the selection of one set of means may, of course, provide a means for achieving "higher" or more valued ends and be rationally evaluated with respect to those ends. However, in this view, the chain of means and ends must stop with an "ultimate" end whose selection is a mere matter of individual taste or preference which cannot be justified on rational grounds. For example, it is assumed, planners may justify placing public housing projects in middle-class neighborhoods as a means for reducing racial and class discrimination, but they cannot justify reducing discrimination because they merely dislike or prefer to reduce discrimination.

Implications for Planning

Together the logical-positivist conception of ethics and the means-end conception of rationality imply the instrumental view that public policy planning must be limited to the factual consideration of means toward ends established outside of the planning process. That is, if as is generally assumed, planning is the application of rationality to public policy making, planners must restrict their attention to questions which can be considered rationally. By the means-end view, the rational consideration of courses of action can consist only of the selection of appropriate means for achieving designated ends. While a given end may be justified as a means for achieving a higher end, ultimately the chain of means and ends must stop with an ethical judgment which, under both positions, cannot be justified on rational grounds. Thus, it appears, if planners are to deal only with rational issues, they can only attempt to identify the most appropriate means for achieving ends or goals established by others (e.g., elected officials or client groups). If, however, these two views are mistaken, this widely, if implicitly, assumed argument for limiting planning to the consideration of only public policy means is likewise mistaken.

Examination of the Intellectual Foundation

As was pointed out above, the logical positivists assumed that ethical issues cannot be rationally discussed because, under their verifiability principle, ethical statements were not meaningful. As they recognized (Ayer 1952), however, any statement of their verifiability principle would *itself* satisfy neither of these criteria for identifying meaningful sentences. It could not be a tautology, true by virtue of the meaning of the words, because the crucial word *meaningful* is used in a variety of ways, including several which do not correspond to that implied by the verifiability principle. (For example, the ethical sentence "Stealing is wrong" is *in some sense* meaningful, i.e., different from "Stealing isn't wrong.") It also could not be a synthetic claim or assertion of fact which could be tested empirically because, as a philosophical claim *about meaningfulness*, it is a claim of an entirely different order.

Evading the issue, the logical positivists viewed the verifiability principle as a verbal recommendation which would promote clarity in the discussion of ethical questions. As merely a *recommendation*, however, it can be either rejected or accepted. If it is rejected, the logical-positivist position on which it is based must likewise be rejected. And if it is accepted, even though *by its own criteria* meaningless, there is no reason to believe that ethical

statements should not also be accepted even though they are also meaningless under these criteria. In either case, the logical positivists' assumption
that ethical issues cannot be rationally discussed is severely questioned.[11]

The Basis for Scientific Discourse

More fundamentally, philosophers now recognize that ethical reasoning
is much more like scientific reasoning than the logical positivists recognized.
That is, while the logical positivists were correct in pointing out that empirical evidence alone cannot entail an ethical belief, this is also true for
scientific laws and theories which also cannot be conclusively supported by
observational evidence alone. As philosophers and historians of science
(e.g., Kuhn 1970 and Hempel 1966) have demonstrated repeatedly, there is
always more than one theoretical explanation for any set of observational
data and a degree of choice involved in the selection of one theory or
paradigm over another.

However, the choice between competing theories is not arbitrary; it is
regulated by the loosely defined norms and procedural requirements of the
scientific method, and reliance on these criteria can itself be justified. For
example, while two different explanations (e.g., a sociological one and a
psychological one) may be offered for an observed social phenomenon, the
procedural norms of the scientific method suggest several criteria for choosing between them: which more completely accounts for available empirical
data? which relies on fewer unmeasurable variables? which is more parsimonious? and so on. And, if pressed, one could justify reliance on these
criteria (e.g., argue that it is reasonable to assume that nature is simple
rather than complex and thus that parsimonious explanations are preferred
over less simple ones).[12]

As Gerwirth (1968) has pointed out, the logical positivists and others,
who assumed that science was an entirely cognitive and rational process
while ethics was not, failed to recognize the problem of justifying the norms
and criteria of the scientific method. Their conception of science included
only activities which satisfied these criteria (e.g., neurology, physiology,
and astronomy) and ignored those which did not (e.g., Christian Science,
phrenology, and astrology). Their conception of ethics, however, included
not only the views of Albert Schweitzer, missionaries, and democrats but
also those of Al Capone, cannibals, and Nazis. If their conception of science
had been as broad as their conception of ethics (to include, for example, a
"scientific" dispute between a Christian Scientist and a neurologist) they
would have observed fundamental disagreements in "preference" or "at-

titude" (concerning, perhaps, the type of evidence to be accepted) similar to those in an "ethical" dispute between say, a missionary and a cannibal.

The Basis for Rational Discourse

It is now generally recognized that this pattern of reasoning (i.e., with respect to criteria which must themselves be justified) underlies not only scientific reasoning but all rational discourse.[13] Consider, for example, a purely empirical claim that a healthy individual is mortal. This claim cannot conclusively be proven because, until that person dies, it is at least logically possible that the individual in question will live forever. However, it can be given a great deal of support by an inductive argument pointing out that everyone who has lived to date has been mortal, which makes it *very* likely that the individual in question will also die. A complete justification for the original claim must, however, include a justification for reliance on the rules of inductive logic.

In a similar way the ultimate justification for claims to nonempirical knowledge (e.g., those of mathematics) lies in the rules of inference and substitution of deductive logic. Rational argument, either inductive or deductive, presupposes the reference to one or both sets of principles which are least implicitly agreed upon. While knowledge claims of either type can be supported by demonstrating that their derivation was in accordance with the relevant set of principles, a complete justification for the original claims must include a justification for reliance on those principles.

Reliance on the rules of deductive inference is easily justified on pragmatic grounds because only reasoning which accords with them can insure the transition from true propositions to other true propositions. Similarly, reliance on the rules of inductive logic is pragmatically justified for all attempts to make true inductive inferences because only these rules can be shown (deductively) to provide a self-corrective means for disclosing any underlying order to nature.[14]

The Basis for Means-End Discourse

In addition, contrary to the means-end conception of rationality, a similar two-stage process underlies the rational evaluation not only of means with respect to ends, but of ends themselves. This is best illustrated by graphic, if somewhat unrealistic, examples such as a proposal to collect all the children in a community at their neighborhood schools, load them onto school buses, drive them to a nearby airport, and fly them to a remote mountain region in order to isolate them from the rest of the population. Here is a perfect example of means-end reasoning; and on the means-end conception of rationality the policy is rational because, we can assume, it outlines the most efficient means for achieving the end of isolating the community's children. However, as this example illustrates, a means-end justification is inadequate because the important question is not whether the most appropriate means were selected to achieve the chosen objectives but whether the objective is appropriate. That is, contrary to the means-end view, a complete justification for an action must consider not only the means chosen for achieving selected ends but also the ends themselves.

For example, a community which implemented the public policy outlined above would *seem* to be acting irrationally even if its elected officials preferred to implement it (which, in the instrumental view of planning, is all that is required to justify a policy). The policy would be rational and justified only if there were good reasons for its implementation (e.g., that it provided the only mechanism for protecting the children from an extremely dangerous epidemic). That is, as was true for scientific, inductive, and deductive reasoning, the justification for actions is not dependent on mere irrational preference or taste but, rather, on considerations and criteria. These can, in turn, be rationally justified (in principle) by reference to fundamental empirical characteristics of human beings and the world in which they live (e.g., the fact that, in Hart's words, public policy deals with "social arrangements for continued existence, not with those of a suicide club," 1961, p. 183) which are not mere matters of individual taste but are reflected in the whole structure of our thought and language.[15]

Alternative Foundations

As has been pointed out above, scientific reasoning and indeed all rational discourse is ultimately supported by criteria which, while usually only implicitly assumed, can be rationally justified. Recognizing this, contemporary philosophers (e.g., Rawls 1968 and 1971 and Brandt 1959, pp. 241-70) suggest that the question of the rationality of ethical discourse turns simply on whether similar sets of rationally defensible criteria exist for validating (and invalidating) ethical principles and decisions. That is, as we have seen, scientific reasoning is accepted as rational only because there exist widely accepted and rationally defensible criteria for evaluating scientific observations and theories. Thus, these philosophers argue, if similar sets of criteria for evaluating ethical positions and principles were developed and justified, then ethical discourse can likewise be accepted as a rational activity. From this contemporary perspective, moral philosophy is an attempt to formulate rationally defensible principles and criteria which match our considered moral judgment, just as the philosophy of science attempts to develop systematic principles which agree with accepted scientific practice.

An Example

While the formulation and defense of moral principles have been a continuing concern of philosophers from Plato to the present, these "post-logical-positivist" views have dramatically revived interest in social and political philosophy.[16] The most important example of this contemporary interest and one which best illustrates its implications for planning practice and theory is John Rawls's *A Theory of Justice* (1971).

In *A Theory of Justice* Rawls develops two "principles of justice" to be used to evaluate the major political, economic, and social institutions of society.[17] The first, "the greatest equal liberty principle," holds that each person is to have an equal right to the most extensive basic liberty compatible with an equal liberty for others. The second holds that social and economic inequalities are to be arranged so that they are (1) reasonably expected to be to everyone's advantage, particularly that of the least well off ("the difference principle"); and (2) attached to social positions which are open to all ("the fair equality of opportunity principle").

Rawls defends his principles with two separate, but closely related, arguments. The first, his so-called "contract argument," suggests that his principles are the solution to a hypothetical problem of rational choice under constraints (most importantly, fairness and impartiality) which, he argues, are appropriate for selecting principles of justice. The second, which might be called a "congruence argument," suggests that his principles more nearly match our considered moral judgments than do the alternatives (e.g., unlike classical utilitarianism, his principles would not approve of the institution of slavery even if it benefits the majority).[18]

Implications of the Example

The details of Rawls's arguments are too complex to be considered here and have, in fact, been subject to a great deal of criticism (see, for example, the selections in Daniels 1975). In addition, the importance of Rawls's work for the present discussion lies not in its details but rather in providing an example of the contemporary approach to the consideration of ethical principles (and particular ethical questions). The example is particularly appropriate because it clearly illustrates the parallels with the more traditional consideration of the principles of the scientific method (and particular "scientific" questions) referred to above. In intent, the two approaches are similar in that Rawls's principles are to be used to evaluate the major institutions of society just as the principles of the scientific method are to be used to evaluate the hypotheses and theories of the empirical sciences. In structure, the two are similar in that Rawls's first argument corresponds to placing general restrictions on the selection of the principles which are to guide scientific practice (e.g., requiring that they not be biased toward any particular theory); his second corresponds to requiring that these principles agree with accepted scientific practice.

More importantly, Rawls's work suggests one way in which planners can practice normative planning, rationally evaluating both the means and the ends of public policy. That is, it suggests planners can argue that social institutions with redistributive effects benefiting the least well off are just and can rely on Rawls's principles (and his arguments in their defense) to support their position.[19] In this way the planners' ethical positions would not reflect mere preference or taste but would be supported in a way similar to that of their scientific positions (which are likewise based on principles which must be rationally defended). Other groups could of course pursue other objectives, but under this approach to normative planning, would have to justify *their* perspectives, allowing the bases for the conflicting positions to be rationally evaluated.[20] Thus, while not eliminating the inevitable conflicts over public policy objectives and the groups they favor, this approach would provide a framework within which these conflicts can be rationally considered.

Implications of Normative Planning

Not only would this approach provide a rational basis for planners' ethical positions, it would also unite planners' political and scientific roles, expanding the scope of the latter. Under this approach planners would no longer rely merely on pragmatic politics and claims to professionalism to promote their proposals, but rather, would attempt to defend them on rational grounds. Once they did so it would soon be recognized that their ethical positions (for example, promoting mixed residential neighborhoods) were largely dependent on numerous empirical and thus researchable assumptions. That is, in this case the desirability of mixed housing seems largely dependent on the *empirical* issues of its aggregative and distributive effects under particular circumstances, e.g., whether there is an identifiable tipping point, whether it will reduce property values and increase crime rates or, more positively, will increase racial understanding. While determining these effects may be extremely difficult, they are clearly suitable subjects for empirical research, and information such as this seems essential for adequately supporting recommendations on the advisability of mixed housing.[21] A particularly important new avenue for planning analysis which would seem to follow from a normative, yet rational, approach would be the determination of the *distributive* effects of public policies (i.e., the determination of not merely whether total project benefits exceed total project costs, but also of which groups in society reaped the benefits and which bore the costs).

More generally, Rawls's work points to a need for rationally defensible, normative criteria for evaluating and justifying particular public policies and actions. While Rawls's criteria are applicable only to the evaluation of the major social institutions, it seems that similar criteria could be developed for considering specific government policies and actions. Once developed and (at least provisionally) defended, these criteria would provide a rationally defensible basis for the evaluation of public policies comparable to that which the criteria of the scientific method provide for the evaluation of scientific theories.[22]

These criteria would also provide the basis for the rational evaluation of alternative approaches to planning—which is itself a second order policy decision. Many planning theorists (e.g., Faludi 1973) attempt to avoid all ethical questions by developing predictive hypotheses identifying which of a number of alternative approaches will, in fact, be used in a given situation. However, by merely describing present planning practice, these descriptive hypotheses provide little guidance to practitioners attempting to determine which approach *ought* to be used under particular conditions or to the profession's continuing effort to improve public policy decisions and the processes by which they are made. Given rationally defensible criteria for evaluating these alternative approaches, planning theorists could abandon their present value-neutral approach and evaluate these alternatives as more or less likely to improve existing policy-making processes and, consequently, the community as a whole. Thus, for example, it might be argued that even though a narrowly defined technician role may most effectively get planning proposals implemented in a cohesive political system, a less effective role of advocacy planning may better educate the public and, in the long run, be a more appropriate strategy.

The work of Rawls and the other critics of instrumental planning's positivist foundations is, or course, only suggestive and does not provide detailed guidance for conducting normative planning. However, it seems the most important implications which would follow from a rejection of value-free instrumental planning lie, not in the development of new planning techniques, but rather in fundamentally changing the way individual planners and the profession as a whole view their role in society. The above analysis suggests that planners need not (in fact, cannot) separate planning analysis from planning politics by focusing only on technical questions of public policy means. Rather, it argues, planners can go further and combine their dual commitments to scientific analysis and social reform in the rational consideration of the difficult but important questions of defining public policy objectives. If this does, in fact, happen and the rational evaluation and justification of public policy ends joins the scientific analysis of public policy means as a guiding ideal of the profession, the implications for both theory and practice will certainly be far reaching.

Authors Note: The author gratefully acknowledges the assistance and encouragement of Pierre Clavel of Cornell University's Department of City and Regional Planning and David Lyons of the Sage School of Philosophy at Cornell.

NOTES

[1] The role these traditions played in the development of the American and British planning professions has been well described by Lubove (1967) and Eversley (1973, pp. 43–84).

[2] See, for example, Tugwell (1940).

[3] This has been explicitly recognized in Davidoff's call for "ideological advocacy" in which the advocate planner works with available groups to promote *his own* views (Davidoff, Davidoff, and Gold 1970) and Peattie's (1970) call for planners to choose as clients those groups which seem *to the planner* to be developing issues worthy of support.

[4] In fact, the planner's methods and techniques are not in themselves value free. See, for example, Tribe (1972).

[5] This classic definition of politics is Harold D. Laswell's (1936).

[6] See, for example, Davidoff and Reiner (1962), Altshuler (1965), and Benveniste (1972).

[7] The clearest examples of the second approach are, of course, the calls for advocacy planning by Davidoff (1965), Peattie (1970), and others; it is also reflected in the attempt by Bolan (1967), Rabinovitz (1969), and others to identify roles and strategies which will increase planners' political effectiveness, on the implicit assumption that whatever a planner wants is what ought to be done.

[8] This emphasis on the policy-making process and the groups involved in that process rather than on the *substance* of public policy reflects a similar perspective which dominates both political science and public decision making (see, for example, Cochran 1973 and Lowi 1967).

[9] While revealed only implicitly in the work of practitioners, these intellectual roots are explicitly revealed in arguments for the instrumental approach in Herbert Simon's influential *Administrative Behavior* (1957, especially chapters 1–4) and Davidoff and Reiner's "A Choice Theory of Planning." For brief histories of the positivist tradition and development of logical positivism see Abbagnano (1967) and Passmore (1967).

[10] For an early and influential, if somewhat extreme, version of this position see Ayer (1952, pp. 102–119).

[11] This aspect of the logical-positivist position was pointed out to the author by David Lyons. In fact, the logical positivists never succeeded in stating their verifiability principle in a way that rejected as meaningless the transcendental claims of metaphysics while retaining as meaningful the hypotheses and theories of the empirical sciences (see Ashby 1967).

[12] For an example of this type of argument see Rudner's (1961) discussion of the criterion of simplicity.

[13]The discussion generally follows that in Feigel (1952, pp. 672–80).

[14]Interestingly, as is true for the development of a rationally defensible basis for ethical decision making discussed here, developing a rigorous system of inductive logic which agrees with common sense and accepted scientific practice is exceedingly difficult (see Skyrms 1966).

[15]For more on these points see the suggestive discussion in Hart (1961, pp. 181–95).

[16]See, for example, Germino (1967) and journals such as *American Political Science Review, Political Theory*, and *Philosophy and Public Affairs*.

[17]That is, contrary to the impressions of some (e.g., Berry and Steiker 1974), Rawls does not suggest that these principles be used to evaluate specific governmental actions and policies but, rather, limits their use to more fundamental decisions concerning the nature of major social institutions.

[18]For more complete discussions of Rawls's attempt to defend his principles see Rawls 1971 (pp. 11–22 and 46–53) and Lyons (1974).

[19]An example of this approach in contemporary planning practice is the work of the Cleveland Planning Commission which has pursued an explicit normative position of "promoting a wider range of choices for these Cleveland residents who have few, if any, choices." Unlike other advocacy groups, however, the commission has not merely adopted this position but has attempted to justify it on rational grounds, relying in part on Rawls's arguments (see Krumholz, Cogger, and Linner 1975 and Cleveland City Planning Commission 1975).

[20]For an attempt to defend an alternative to Rawls's principles of justice (in the form of an extreme "libertarian" state, dedicated only to protecting persons against force, fraud, theft, and breach of contract) see Nozick (1974).

[21]A similar point has been made by Norton Long (1975a).

[22]For one such attempt to develop and defend an interpretation of "the public interest" which provides a meaningful, empirically verifiable, and rationally defensible criterion for evaluating public policies and actions see Klosterman (1976, pp. 148–189).

REFERENCES

Abbagnano, Nichola. 1967. Positivism. *The encyclopedia of philosophy*. vol. 6. New York: Macmillan.

Altshuler, Alan A. 1965. *The city planning process: a political analysis*. Ithaca: Cornell University Press.

Appleby, Paul H. 1949. *Policy and administration*. University, Ala.: University of Alabama Press.

Ashby, R. W. 1967. Verifiability principle. *The encyclopedia of philosophy*. vol. 8. New York: Macmillan.

Ayer, Alfred J. 1952. *Language, truth and logic*. New York: Dover.

Banfield, Edward C. 1959. Ends and means in planning. *International Social Science Journal* 11, 4: 361–68.

Benveniste, Guy. 1972. *The politics of expertise*. Berkeley, Calif.: Glendessary Press.

Berry, David, and Steiker, Gene. 1974. The concept of justice in regional planning: justice as fairness. *Journal of the American Institute of Planners* 40, 6: 414–21.

Bolan, Richard S. 1967. Emerging views of planning. *Journal of the American Institute of Planners* 33, 4:234–46.

Brandt, Richard B. 1959. *Ethical theory*. Englewood Cliffs, N.J.: Prentice-Hall.

Cleveland City Planning Commission. 1975. *Cleveland policy planning report: volume 1*. Cleveland: The Commission.

Cochran, Clarke E. 1973. The politics of interest: philosophy and the limitations of the science of politics. *American Journal of Political Science* 17, November: 745–66.

Daniels, Norman, ed. 1975. *Reading Rawls*. New York: Basic Books.

Davidoff, Paul. 1965. Advocacy and pluralism in planning. *Journal of the American Institute of Planners* 31, 6: 331-37.

Davidoff, Paul, and Reiner, Thomas A. 1962. A choice theory of planning. *Journal of the American Institute of Planners* 27, 3: 103-15.

Davidoff, Paul; Davidoff, Linda; and Gold, Neil Newton. 1970. Suburban Action: advocate planning for an open society. *Journal of the American Institute of Planners* 36, 1: 12-21.

Eversley, David. 1973. *The planner in society: the changing role of a profession.* London: Faber and Faber.

Faludi, Andreas. 1973. *Planning theory.* Oxford: Pergamon.

Feigel, Herbert. 1952. Validation and vindication: an analysis of the nature and limits of ethical arguments. In *Readings in ethical theory*, eds. Wilfred Sellars and John Hospers. New York: Appleton-Century-Crofts.

Friedmann, John. 1966. Planning as a vocation. *Plan Canada* 6, April: 99-124; 7, July: 8-26.

Fromm, Erich. 1972. Humanistic planning. *Journal of the American Institute of Planners* 38, 2: 67-71.

Germino, Dante. 1967. *Beyond ideology: the revival of political theory.* New York: Harper and Row.

Gerwirth, Alan. 1968. Positive "ethics" and normative "science." In *Ethics*, eds. Judith J. Thompson and Gerald Dworkin. New York: Harper and Row.

Hart, H. L. A. 1961. *The concept of law.* London: Oxford University Press.

Hempel, Carl G. 1966. *Philosophy of natural science.* Englewood Cliffs, N.J.: Prentice-Hall.

Howard, John T. 1954. Planning as a profession. *Journal of the American Institute of Planners* 20, spring: 58-59.

_____. 1955. The planner in a democratic society—a credo. *Journal of the American Institute of Planners* 21, summer: 62-66.

Klosterman, Richard E. 1976. *Toward a normative theory of planning.* Ph.D. dissertation, Cornell University.

Kreiger, Martin H. 1974. Some new directions for planning theory. *Journal of the American Institute of Planners* 40, 3: 156-63.

Krumholz, Norman; Cogger, Janice M.; and Linner, John H. 1975. The Cleveland policy planning report. *Journal of the American Institute of Planners* 41, 5: 298-304.

Kuhn, Thomas S. 1970. *The structure of scientific revolutions.* 2d ed. Chicago: University of Chicago Press.

Laswell, Harold D. 1936. *Politics: who gets what, when, how.* New York: P. Smith.

Long, Norton E. 1959. Planning and politics in urban development. *Journal of the American Institute of Planners* 25, 6: 167-69.

_____. 1975a. Making urban policy useful and corrigible. *Urban Affairs Quarterly* 10, June: 379-97.

_____. 1975b. Another view of responsible planning. *Journal of the American Institute of Planners* 41, 5: 311-16.

Lowi, Theodore. 1967. The public philosophy: interest-group liberalism. *American Political Science Review* 61, March: 5-24.

Lubove, Roy. 1967. The roots of urban planning. In *The urban community: housing and planning in the progressive era*, ed. Roy Lubove. Englewood Cliffs, N.J.: Prentice-Hall.

Lyons, David. 1974. The nature of the contract argument. *Cornell Law Review* 59, August: 1,064-76.

Marcuse, Peter. 1976. Professional ethics and beyond. *Journal of the American Institute of Planners* 42, 3: 264-74.

Nozick, Robert. 1974. *Anarchy, state and utopia.* New York: Basic Books.

Passmore, John. 1967. Logical positivism. *The encyclopedia of philosophy.* vol. 5. New York: Macmillan.

Peattie, Lisa R. 1970. Drama and advocacy planning. *Journal of the American Institute of Planners* 36, 6: 405–10.

Rabinovitz, Francine F. 1969. *City politics and planning*. Chicago: Aldine.

Raphael, D. D. 1969. *British moralists: 1650–1800, volume 2*. London: Oxford University Press.

Rawls, John. 1971. *A theory of justice*. Cambridge, Mass.: Harvard University Press.

_____. 1968. Outline of a decision procedure for ethics. In *Ethics*, eds. Judith J. Thompson and Gerald Dworkin. New York: Harper and Row.

Rondinelli, Dennis A. 1971. Adjunctive planning and urban development policy. *Urban Affairs Quarterly* 7, September: 13–39.

Rudner, Richard. 1961. An introduction to simplicity. *Philosophy of Science* 28, April: 109–19.

Simon, Herbert A. 1957. *Administrative behavior: a study of decision-making processes in administrative organizations*. 2d ed. New York: Free Press.

Skyrms, Brian. 1966. *Choice and chance: an introduction to inductive logic*. Belmont, Calif: Dickenson.

Tribe, Lawrence H. 1972. Policy science: analysis or ideology? *Philosophy and Public Affairs* 2, fall: 66–110.

Tugwell, R. G. 1940. Implementing the general interest. *Public Administration Review* 1, autumn: 32–49.

Webber, Melvin W. 1965. The roles of intelligence systems in urban-systems planning. *Journal of the American Institute of Planners* 31, 6: 289–96.

_____. 1969. Planning in an environment of change. *Town Planning Review* 39, January: 277–96.

Weber, Max. 1949. "Objectivity" in social science and social policy. In *Methodology of the social sciences*, trans. and eds. Edward G. Shils and Henry A. Finch. New York: Free Press.

4

The Structure of Ethical Choice
In Planning Practice

Richard S. Bolan

Introduction

The recent increase in talk about planning practice has been highlighted
by the declaration that a professional planner is a moral agent (Marcuse
1976; Klosterman 1978; Howe and Kaufman 1979; Bolan 1980; Kaufman
1981). Among the numerous historical ways that planners have seen
themselves—as architects, designers, engineers, social engineers and, most
recently, political actors (bargainers, negotiators; see Schön 1982)—recent
images have stressed that the planner is something more than a bureaucrat
or mere technical functionary. Planners create, influence, speak about, encourage, stimulate, or otherwise take part in the setting of public policy.
They thereby do more than passively carry out the decisions and goals of
others; they are active participants in the articulation of and movement
toward that which is thought to be good, beneficial and valuable for the
planner's client community and its citizens (Kaufman 1978).

Thus, city planners are taking a closer look at the ethical or moral dimensions of their practice. Indeed, even the most mundane, everyday technical
tasks are recognized as having ethical implications. All human action has
meaning, has to be accounted for, and justified. No matter how technical,
specialized, or arcane their work, professionals cannot be exempt from this
fundamental condition.

Having said this, however, one is struck by the poverty of understanding
of the development of a professional ethos. Discussion of professional

Reprinted from Richard S. Bolan. 1983. The Structure of Ethical Choice in Planning Practice. *Journal of Planning Education and Research*. 3: 23–34. Copyright© 1983. Association of
Collegiate Schools of Planning. Reprinted by permission.

ethics usually focuses primarily on the formally promulgated codes of professional conduct. Formal codes, however, typically raise more questions than they answer, often seem more concerned with courtesies professionals should render each other, and rarely exhibit sensitivity for the complex, diverse ethical dilemmas that professionals experience in their practice. They offer a false sense of security and obscure the subtle, tacit and unstated norms that are often instrumental in guiding action.

Turning to philosophy, the discipline traditionally concerned about ethics, one receives only slightly more aid. Philosophers do help us to identify key distinctions and to frame crucial questions; however, they seldom undertake sufficient empirical work that would expose the full complexity of ethical experience. There is only generalized recognition among modern philosophers of the impact of the growing complexity of social order and technology on contemporary ethics.

The goal of this paper, then, is to set forth the structural framework of social influences under which today's professional planner functions in developing ethical decisions and ethical justifications of performance. A "matrix of ethical influences" in professional practice is constructed by reference to traditional views of ethics. The underlying dynamics of this matrix are then analyzed, and this sets the stage for a concluding discussion that equates professional practice with a search for actions that are truly "valuable."

The discussion is not about moral reasoning *per se*. It is neither concerned with the rationality of ethical discourse (Klosterman 1978), nor with the issues of planning for equity or justice (Krumholz, Cogger, and Linner 1975; Berry and Steiker 1974; Lucy 1981; Krumholz 1982). As one author suggests, there is a distinction between a "moral epistemology" and a "moral cartography" (Cua 1978, pp. 7–8). What follows is mostly concerned about the latter. It builds primarily from an earlier, similar work of Marcuse (1976). It is an effort to map the existential framework of professional moral life. Moral reasoning, or the logic of "moral epistemology," generally fails when carried on abstractly in search of a universal principle of conduct. A professional ethics has to be concerned about the processes involved in the "social construction of moral meanings" (Douglas 1970), and it is to this end that the analysis is directed.

A Matrix of Ethical Influences

Grasping the structure of ethical influences on practice begins with examining the range of implications of what one means by the concepts of *responsibility* and *obligation*. Not only professional life, but life in general, is filled with "should" or "ought" statements: "you ought to brush your teeth," "you should do everything possible to prevent murder" and "you ought to do a cost-benefit analysis." Such statements are the foundation of a sense of ethical behavior, an awareness (almost taken for granted) that each of us is a responsible human being.

Any attempt to define what it means to be responsible raises three inter-related questions. The answers to these questions provide the basic framework for developing what I call the "matrix of ethical influences" in planning practice.

First, whom are we responsible to? Who is it that makes a claim on us to be responsible?

Second, what is it that our responsibility obliges us to do? What forms of behavior are considered appropriate responses to a claim of responsibility? Is there a catalog of duties or is our responsibility more profound and less well defined?

Third, under what circumstances are we responsible? Or, to put it another way, do circumstances and situations affect our responsibility?

In the following discussion, the potential range of answers to these questions is presented. In so doing, there is also portrayed the notion that these questions cannot really be taken separately (as they too often are in discussions of ethics)—rather they are a whole, a *gestalt*. Ethical professional behavior simultaneously engages all three questions. A city planner in a practice situation, thereby, continually confronts this primary structure of the ethical milieu. Even the pursuit of technically prescribed behaviors is done within this framework.

Whom Are We Responsible To?

The word "responsibility" in its strictest definition implies the "liability to respond," or the capacity for answering to. Our operating premise starts from the existentialist position where obligation for responding is argued to be a condition of human existence. The self-reflexive and transcendental nature of human life underlies this condition of obligation. Schrader argues:

> Man is responsible, in the first instance, because he is burdened with the *onto-logical necessity* of responding to himself in the sense of having to answer for what he is and does . . . To be is not simply to be liable; it is the original human liability (Schrader 1972, p. 270).

In this sense, our own existence is in our own "care"; people do seek to escape this responsibility (through drugs, suicide, etc.) but such effort to escape would be a conscious choice to opt out of this primary obligation.

Indeed, as Schrader puts it: "To be irresponsible is not to be nonresponsible. One can negate responsibility but one cannot deny it" (ibid., p. 276). One may try to push responsibility aside, but one has not thereby eliminated it.

The responsibility for the self is shaped and influenced through interaction with other selves. We are born into and live in a social world with other human beings and responsibility for the self is integral with the development of a sense of responsibility toward others. Such responsibilities are reciprocal. We cannot unilaterally determine our responsibility to others; by their presence in our social field, others make claims on us just as we make claims on them. Thus, the sense of responsiblity is socially negotiated.

The social field is a structured field. Some within it live more closely to us and with them our sense of responsibility is more intimate and more intense. Kin relations, for example, are the primary frame of reference in our sense of responsibility. They are the relations from which our earliest consciousness and sense of self evolves into a mature ethical consciousness. As our circle of acquaintances extends beyond immediate family, we enter into a wider and wider world of ethical obligations. Each new person we meet extends our ethical world (Levinas 1969, pp. 194–201) and enlarges and diversifies our range of ethical obligation. We enter into and become members of new "moral communities," new alliances of shared intentions (Wren 1974, chapter 5; Cua 1978, pp. 11–15; Golding 1981, pp. 64–68).

Moral communities come into being in diverse and complicated ways. A moral community may be created by the first-hand participation of its members. A planning consultant and a developer entering into a contract, for example, mutually create a new moral community. Even though embedded in a broader and larger culture, the consultant-developer relationship has its unique framework of expectations and obligations. A planner accepting employment with a state planning agency enters into a previously created moral community with an existing web of rules, norms and responsibilities already binding a broad group of people, some of whom the planner may never meet. A student graduating from a city planning school similarly enters a previously established moral community—the city planning profession (Marcuse 1976). Thus, the concept of a moral community embraces the full array of understandings, agreements, expectations, loyalties, norms and obligations of those who comprise its membership. Each moral community, if you will, signifies a particular moral paradigm. As one author puts it, even a den of thieves has a moral order (Wren 1974, p. 113).

The range of different moral communities is depicted on Figure 1. This diagram does not intend to convey that moral communities are hierarchical, however. They are overlapping and, in many respects, interdependent. They form a labyrinth warp-and-woof that makes up the total fabric of each individual's ethical world. Moreover, these many different moral communities can, and frequently do have points of contradiction or inconsistency with one another. What is perceived as good and beneficial in one community may be perceived differently in another, and the individual may frequently feel pulled between them. Codes of professional ethics seldom overtly recognize the multiplicity of moral communities. Even those that do overlook the possiblity of conflict (Howe 1980, pp. 179–191). Moreover, as Wren points out:

> The sorts of communities meant by 'conflicting communities' are not loci of ideals but real force fields of intentions . . . Each . . . is a community of action, a context of absolute obligations (Wren 1974, p. 120).

Moral communities are directly experienced insofar as they extend to the range of personal contacts of the professional during the course of everyday activities. However, obligations go beyond these contacts and extend to responsibilities that transcend both space and time. We possess a sense of obligation to larger moral communities, all of whose members we are not likely to meet or cannot possibly meet. These larger moral communities are the larger society and culture of which we are a part. They embody the general and fundamental moral ideals that inhere in the culture. These ideals have been found to have widespread convergence over many different kinds of societies (Ginsberg 1968, p. 757).[1]

The important point for this discussion, however, is that, whether engaged in professional or other types of activities, we are a part of these broader moral communities. As such, responsibility extends to those who have lived in the past, those who are now alive but not within our general sphere of activity, and those yet unborn. As one author puts it, "To speak of man's shaping his destiny is to talk of human continuity across generations. It is to set forth the obligation of those alive to build for the sake of those to come" (Derr 1981, p. 37). Another writer argues we are obligated to "species-responsible behavior" (Feibleman 1967, p. 284). Indeed, responsibility to successors is one of the primary obligations of the city planning profession. Every plan presupposes a sense of obligation to the future and those who will live in it.

What Does Our Responsibility Oblige Us To Do?

Writings on ethics offer two fundamental views. Weber labelled them the "ethics of ultimate ends" as against the "ethics of responsibility" (Feibleman 1967, p. 277). Philosophers refer to the former as the *teleological* view of ethics in which a moral action is focused on seeking good ends, regardless of the means that might be used to gain such ends. A revolutionary terrorist, for example, is so convinced of the ultimate worth of his cause that killing an opponent is a justifiable means of serving that cause. On the other hand, the "ethics of responsibility," or what is technically termed *deontology*, argues that there is intrinsic rightness and wrongness in individual acts of human conduct. Good ends cannot be justified by wrong actions. In this view, killing is wrong even if the ultimate ends to be served might be judged good. One should forego good ends if they can only be achieved by wrong acts. The wrongness of the acts will, in a sense, contaminate the good ends and make their ultimate attainment less valuable. Fried vigorously gives this argument:

> We must do no wrong—even if by doing wrong, suffering would be reduced and the sum of happiness increased. Indeed, we must not do wrong even in order to prevent more, greater wrongs by others (Fried 1978, p.2).

Consider the debate about urban renewal in the 1960s. Planners with a teleological perspective argued that a good city as an ultimate goal was a worthy objective, and that actions to bring it about were quite ethical even if harm should fall on some people (particularly those who suffer the hardships and trauma of being forced to move from their homes and neighborhoods). In contrast, planners with a deontological perspective argued that the harm done by the forcible relocation of families was wrong regardless of the worthiness of the ultimate goal. Doing harm is a wrong action and cannot be justified by good intentions. In the same manner, Bok argues that lying by a professional in the service of worthy professional goals is wrong, as when a physician lies about the true condition of a patient because, presumably if the patient were told the truth, his illness might worsen (Bok 1978, chapter 15).

While engaged in professional practice, our conscious awareness of activities demanding the foreground of our attention is accompanied by the background awareness of received ideals or norms, which simultaneously reflect both notions of ultimate good and rules of conduct. We are continually pulled and pressured by these two poles. Moreover, these ideals emerge in relation to the multiplicity of moral communities with which we are engaged.

The question of whether a staff planner of a public agency should leak information to, say, an environmental interest group illustrates not only the pull between teleology and deontology, but also simultaneously reflects the pulls of multiple moral communities: e.g. the moral community created by the employment contract, that of the profession, that of the environmental ethos, that of the community, and, indirectly, that of one's self and family (particularly if there is fear that such action might result in loss of employment).

Under What Circumstances Are We Responsible?

In the 1960s, it was argued that ethical judgment was not a case of "either/or" between distant ends and proximate acts. Instead, a number of authors suggested that ethical choice really centered around an integral relationship between the two (Fletcher 1966, pp. 26–31). From this emerged what was popularly known as *situation ethics* which, rather than ascribing to either absolute ends or rules of conduct, attempts to take into account all the complex facts and aspects of a given situation. Fletcher, one of the leading writers on situation ethics, notes: "Situationists are chary about abstractions and generalizations, especially in the absence of concretion and circumstance" (1967, p. 8). Fletcher admits to only one ultimate intrinsic good—love—and all actions should, after taking into account all of the facts of the situation, be focused on increasing or enhancing love.[2] Thus, in situation ethics, all values are relative (save that of love), all prescriptions and codes are qualified "depending on the circumstances." Rigid, legalistic rule-following is eschewed in favor of doing the best one can within the constraints, contingencies, and possibilities of the situation.

The attention to situation ethics reemphasizes a focus on the key aspect of ethical behavior; a concern for ethics is a concern for *action*. As the situationists argue, moral judgments are *decisions*, not conclusions. Decisions are reached in the light of one's estimate of the circumstances, not on the basis of ready-made prescriptions or a prefabricated catalog of duties. In this view, therefore, right and wrong depend upon the situation; rules cannot be created in advance to fit reality—" 'situation ethics' puts its premium on freedom and responsibility" (ibid., p. 25).

This situational dimension of professional practice has seldom been adequately examined. Through this dimension we realize the poverty of professional codes of ethics. They presuppose only the most obvious (and least likely) circumstances of practice situations. In these situations it often appears simple to determine how one's ideals or norms are to be followed and how the moral obligations of various communities are to be met. However, once the complexities of a given situation are given full consideration, one often finds deep conflicts among ideals and norms and the claims of the various moral communities. This was well illustrated by Rittel and Webber's characterization (1973) of planning problems as "wicked problems"—problems arising in situations with no "stopping points," no established decision rules, no correct or incorrect answers, no opportunities to be wrong, and no final solutions.

FIGURE 1

**The Range of Moral Communities of Obligation
In Contemporary Professional Life**

The Professional Has Obligation To:

Self

Family

Friends

Employer

Clients

Colleagues

The Corporate Profession

The Municipal or Local Community

The Nation-state

Past Generations

Future Generations

One approach to examining the influences and demands created by the particular situation is to conceive of a continuum ranging from the simplest of situations at one pole and the most difficult and complex at the other. This is the continuum portrayed on Figure 2. At the simplest pole, we are faced with the choice of either doing good (or right) or doing bad (or wrong). Our choice is obvious; we act so as to do good (right) and reject the bad (wrong).

At the next point on the continuum, we are able to conceive of a range of actions appropriate to the situation, all of which would be good, or right. Planners may immediately recognize this as the usual circumstance from which we draw theoretical discussion of rational problem-solving; we seek methods of calculating the "best" course of action among a number that are already presumed good. A benefit-cost analysis, for example, is one

FIGURE 2

A Continuum of Diversity of Contexts
for Ethical Choice in Planning

Simplest Circumstance
Doing Good Versus
Doing Harm
(Naive Choice)

Doing Good
Versus Doing Best
(Optimality In
Rational Calculation)

Doing Some Good
While Simultaneously
Doing Some Harm
("Wicked Problems")

Most Complex Circumstance
Doing Harm
Versus Doing Worse
(The "Catch-22"
or Hobson's Choice)

technique for choosing the "best" among a number of "good" alternatives.

The next level of complexity, however, introduces the possibility that our choices may concurrently produce some good *and* some harm. Enticing a new chemical plant to the community will create a large number of new jobs and new taxes, but will also increase health hazards due to toxic wastes; building an expressway will ease traffic congestion and provide construction jobs but will displace large number of families and increase air pollution. In the last twenty-five years, planners have become increasingly aware of these conflicting results of their practice. We have even developed methods of analysis that more explicity identify the winners and losers of a given policy or plan (Hill 1968). Of course, even after carrying out such identification, we are still not sure, given the goods and bads, whether we should proceed with the planned action or not.

The most difficult end of the situational continuum is that situation where harm will result no matter what we do, even if we do nothing. These are situations where there are only bad options; the "Catch 22," "Hobson's Choice," a choice "between a rock and a hard place." As one author put it, "there are situations where the best we can do is evil" (Bennett, quoted in Fletcher 1967, p. 15).

We are likely to encounter situations that fit the simplest extreme of the continuum only rarely in our professional lives. I would also estimate that the second situation, where we are only faced with the problem of choosing the best among many good alternatives, is only slightly less rare. The third situation is that most likely to be encountered in practice: in our efforts to do good, we inevitably do both good and harm. The fourth situation, while possibly not frequent, probably occurs more often than the first two.

Summarizing, the concept of responsibility has been examined in the light of three particular questions: Whom are we responsible to?, What does our responsibility oblige us to do?, And how do circumstances influence our responsibility? In any decision process, we always encounter these three questions simultaneously; they are, in effect, a *gestalt* of the structure of responsibility. They cannot be thought of in isolation any more than a single beat of a musical rhythm can be isolated and analyzed. Together they

FIGURE 3

**The Three-Dimensional Matrix
of Ethical Choice in Planning**

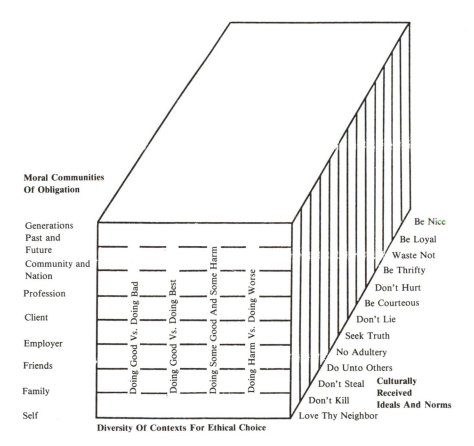

form a single "matrix of ethical influences" in city planning practice. This three-dimensional matrix is portrayed in Figure 3. All perspectives embraced by the matrix are operative in the search for ethical action.

Dynamics Within The Ethical Matrix

The foregoing implies a notion of ethics that is dynamic and ever-changing. This contrasts sharply with views where the propositions of ethics are seen as universal and enduring. Core ethical norms such as prohibitions against murder, lying, stealing, etc. endure; but even with these, nuances and permutations ebb and flow with changing circumstances and shifting social and economic conditions. Concepts such as "justice" and "equity" are similarly elusive as social change constantly pushes us toward their continuing redefinition. The complexities of human interaction require that we consider the sociological and psychological dynamics of ethical choice (Mandelbaum 1955).

Some of this dynamism can be attributed to the same forces that create dynamism in social life in general. Population growth, social and technological innovation, and increasing degrees of specialization, differentiation and complexity create not only social change but also changes in ethical perspectives. The bioethics debate is one shaped and influenced by the present state of medical technology as well as the social and economic conditions in which contemporary medicine is practiced. The ethics of organ transplants have no meaning in a society that does not have the capacity to perform such operations. Similarly, the ethics of transportation planning takes place within a context of the current and immediately foreseeable technologies of ground transportation systems and their role in contemporary social and economic life. The best balance between mass transportation and auto transportation could obviously never have been debated prior to the invention of the automobile. Neither the medical nor the planning debate is purely technical—both are inherently ethical.

In the first instance, then, changes in ethical perspective are driven by changes in situations. Whether or not one subscribes to "situation ethics" as a guiding credo, it is clear that changing circumstances create the conditions for new ethical issues and concerns. The structure suggested in Figure 3 is a dynamic, moving, pulsating structure. The forces for change push us into forming new moral communities and thereby creating new conflicts between values, new perceptions as to what is valuable, and new varieties of possible action. Human creativity and innovation, in a real sense, represent constant challenges to old orders of morality.

These statements may seem obvious and trite. Yet, even with this awareness many of our actions turn out to be perverse. As our plans are implemented, things go awry; people we intended to help are hurt, people we assumed would be innocent bystanders become implicated in harmful ways. Three writings offer different perspectives on this and, in so doing, give insight on deeper aspects of the dynamics of the formation of ethical concepts that lie beneath the surface and entail underlying sociological and psychological forces.

The first of these perspectives is primarily the acknowledgement that we are never fully capable of perceiving all of the relevant circumstances of a decision situation. This has been pointed out by Giddens. He argues that a primary source of unintended consequences in action lies in the unacknowledged conditions in the decision situation (Giddens 1979, pp. 53–59). To put it another way, there are limits to our perceptual capacities. Just as we cannot see all sides of a cube simultaneously, so it is that we cannot "see" all sides of a situation at the instant a decision is called for. We always act in real-time circumstances on the basis of limited information. This may not only inhibit the effectiveness of our action, it may also inhibit the *value* of our action. Thus, limited perception yields limited rationality.

The second perspective is that of Boudon (1982) who offers a socio-economic examination of what he terms "perverse effects." His analysis is an attempt to synthesize the efforts of a number of analysts concerned with the paradoxes experienced through the phenomena of interdependency among active social agents. He begins with Rousseau and goes on to examine the work of Mancur Olsen (1965), Albert Hirschman (1970), Buchanan and Tulloch (1962) and Thomas Schelling (1971).[3]

The beginning paradigm for analysis is basically the familiar "prisoner's dilemma" problem; situations in which individuals attempt to weigh rationally the benefits and costs, in a given circumstance, of cooperating with another individual (or group) as against acting alone. The benefits from cooperation may be greater but so may the risks. "Should I be loyal to my collaborator in the absence of any certainty that he will be loyal to me?"

The prisoner's dilemma shows that cooperative action presupposes loyalty, and if loyalty cannot be guaranteed then independent self-serving action may promise more certain (even though less) payoff. From this it can be seen that each individual's pursuit of what he perceives as his own interest may result in the perverse effect of impeding the good of the society. If loyalty (or other ethical action) can be uniformly coerced, predictable cooperation and social order can take place; if not, unpredictable perversity is possible.

A familiar example is the case of public goods versus private goods, where public goods are those which cannot be divided up for the private use of individual consumers. Thus, their provision cannot rely on the voluntary cooperation of individuals to donate funds for their support. There is no incentive for me to pay, given that others are paying and I can enjoy the services for nothing. Taxation is then introduced as a form of coerced loyalty.

Some social interdependencies can be organized so that loyalty toward cooperative action can be assured, as in the case of taxation. Many others, however, cannot. Consumer protest movements suffer in this regard; if someone else works hard and wins the consumer cause then I, as a bystander consumer, stand to benefit at no cost or effort. Consequently, there is no reason for me to join. Obviously, however, if everyone thinks as I do, there is no consumer movement. There is thus built in a "perversity of composition," akin to the logician's "fallacy of composition." Rational individual behavior can yield irrational social effects. Good social effects may depend on irrational individual behavior. Even though no ethical norms have been overtly violated, different individual perceptions of the virtues and payoffs of loyalty and cooperation yield perverse results.

Some aspects of the interdependency of social agents are such that regulation and enforcement of ethical norms can be carried out, while others cannot. The dynamics of these latter interdependencies exert pressure on the former and create challenges to conceptions of what is right and wrong, good and bad. These anarchic interdependencies, thereby, in subterranean fashion, push toward reformulation of the norms of regulated interdependencies.

A third view, focusing on social-psychological processes, comes from the work of Argyris and Schön (1974, 1978). Their interest in professional effectiveness has evolved a theory which distinguishes between "espoused theory" and "theory-in-use" as two contrasting images of action. After noting the potential for incongruity between the two, they seek to explore the source of the disparity. They claim to find it in a group of what they term "governing variables," principles of action which implicitly guide our behavior. In their "Model I" behavior (their "ineffective" model), these governing variables are: (1) unilaterally define goals and control tasks, (2) maximize winning and minimize losing, (3) minimize generating or expressing negative feelings, and (4) be rational.

The authors also focus on the problems created by assumptions and attributions that are never tested or spoken about. Communication, lacking such testing, is inhibited in effective feedback; norms, values and assumptions get driven underground. What results from the combination of implicit governing variables, inadequate communication, and limited and ambiguous information is a set of *undiscussable* norms that are tacitly accepted even though camouflaged. In short, the Argyris and Schön view suggests the existence of a *covert ethical system*. In our frame of reference, this would mean that there lies within a moral community both explicit and implicit rules of conduct.

Argyris and Schön do not directly examine the ethical origins of the phenomena they describe. However, in a recent publication (Argyris 1982), these norms become more evident. They are variations on traditional ethical strictures that state it is wrong to threaten the autonomy, integrity or dignity of others; it is wrong to confront or challenge others; it is wrong to hurt others not only with physical violence but also with psychological insults. Argyris and Schön's Model I behavior reflects an array of strategies for getting one's way or defending one's *own* autonomy, integrity and dignity without *overtly* violating any of these norms. In some ways, it could be viewed as a hypocritical stance that gives a surface appearance of "loving one's neighbor," even though actually fending for oneself through covert (but accepted) forms of aggression and competition. Moreover, everyone is aware that everyone else is following these same rules (Argyris points out that this too is undiscussable). Thus, the *overt* ethical norms of a given moral community may coincide with those of larger moral communities, but the governing *covert* ethical system is quite another picture. Given the propensity for fallacious assumptions and attributions, any given action by an individual thus might easily have perverse and unforeseen consequences.

One example of this can be found in the recent revelations about the Environmental Protection Agency, referring particularly to those instances where reports from regional staff scientists were ignored, omitted or altered by superiors at policy levels. Such actions are not likely to be a surprise to the professional city planner. Most practitioners in public planning agencies have experienced this happening to their own work. There is widespread acceptance of such practices as part of the "normal" operation of public bureaucracies; thus, such behavior is a well established part of the ethos of public planning. To assert that it is "normal" is to assert that it is the "norm"; that it is embedded in the tacit ethical fabric of the moral community of planning. Such cavalier handling of "the truth" is condemned in the larger political moral community, but it is expected behavior in the smaller, immediate micro-moral community.

In public planning offices, the covert ethos is usually political in nature. In the midst of political games, everyone is guided by a norm designed to camouflage the existence of the games. Following Argyris and Schön, we thus hypothesize the existence of an "espoused" public ethos in a given moral community, underlain by an "ethos-in-use"—a covert, hidden, unspoken ethos that each member of the community tacitly accepts and almost subconsciously employs as a guide to action. In addition, there is the even deeper sublayer norm which prescribes that the covert ethos is not to be talked about.

In summary, we perceive the matrix of ethical influences being impacted by multi-layered forces. On the most visible level, our ethical consciousness is impacted by innovation, complexity and the turbulence of a rapidly changing world. At other levels, more subtle and more deeply rooted dynamic forces are at work as well. The limits of human consciousness, perception and awareness are primary sources of limited rationality, such that good intentions often end up with bad effects. The "perversity of composition" suggests a paradox between individual and social action, so that not only perverse social effects of good actions may occur, but also good actions may be entirely foregone or missed because of unregulated structures of interdependency. Finally, the potential for a two-faced system of ethics, an overt ethics and a covert ethics, results from the limitations of symbolic communication and the reciprocal psychological processes of defense.

Conclusion: The Ethics of Practice

With the foregoing analysis, we begin to grasp why there is no easy or precise method of ethical calculation that might guide and inform practice. We are immersed in a world of multi-layered, countervailing norms. Those likely to be most operative are the most immediate, intimate, personal, and tacit. Professionally, we espouse to act beneficially for macro-level moral communities: the city, the region, the state. But such actions are always taken within the prescribed norms of micro-level moral communities: the planning department, the mayor's office, the city council. We ideally aspire to have our professional practice contribute to broad-scale social improvement, but, on a practical level, we learn the behaviors that will help us to defend, survive and have effect in our immediate organizational settings. We learn the difference between an ideal ethic and a practical ethic quickly.

But what do we mean when we speak of a "practical ethic"? I suspect this means we search for *strategies* and *tactics* for dealing with both the overt and covert dynamics within situations where "good" and "bad" are not really clear and where received ideals are contradictory and inconsistent. As Feibleman suggests (1967, p. 275), we seek to know how to deploy moral force, how to perform moral maneuvers. He argues that such skills are an *art*: more precisely, he suggests the necessity for the "art of *indirection*, and the indirection is made necessary by the fact that the external environment is partly friendly and partly hostile" (ibid., p. 281, emphasis added). I would add as well that the environment is partly obvious and partly camouflaged, partly logical and partly absurd. As a result, ethical professional practice involves traversing treacherous and difficult pathways, and the "art of indirection" suggests that the most direct, or obvious, pathway may not always produce the desired result; circuitous routes may be more ethically effective.

As art, then, we cannot approach the method of ethical judgment in the same manner, as though it were a scientific problem. We face ethical puzzles, it is true, and one might conclude that such puzzles ought to be able to be reduced to some form of precise calculation. However, the premises with which one approaches a scientific problem are not nearly so mischievous and tend to remain fixed. Rules of procedure are similarly stable. Ethical judgement, however, has no such firm anchor points.

In the first instance, the language of ethical judements—the terms and their meanings—immediately puts such judgments on slippery footing. Brennan notes, "moral terms, unlike geometric terms, are 'open-textured'— which means that one cannot state the necessary and sufficient conditions for their correct application" (1977, p. 104). To speak, for example, of the duty of a "father," or of a "professional," or of a "professional city planner," is not to speak of a class of beings whose characteristics are precisely specified. One could not, thereby, *deductively infer* an inexhaustible set of rules that would wholly and unmistakably delineate the actions of a "professional city planner." The label is imprecise—deduced rules of behavior are similarly imprecise.

In ethical judgments, many of the assumptions we make about a problem cannot be tested in any systematic way. Many are only tacit—that is, we are consciously aware of them but we could not easily describe them in words. Many are so taken for granted that they fail to occupy a prominent influence in our consciousness.

Ethical judgments also implicate the person(s) engaged in ways not encountered when solving a scientific problem. As previously noted, an ethical judgment is a decision, not a conclusion. It is a basis for action, not a statement to be filed. This means that the person making the judgment is implicated in the judgment in ways that a scientific problem-solver is not. As Ross points out:

> Science seeks facts and manipulates events to gather information. Action looks to the events themselves . . . We may disconfirm a scientific theory without prejudice to the scientist who proposed it. But our condemnation of a man's deed includes him within it. A person is at stake in action as he is not in science (1973, p. 29).

It is this implied liability that truly differentiates the professional practitioner from the pure scientist.

In overview, then, our linear, cause-and-effect, mechanistic and mathematical forms of reasoning do not help. Similarly, our stock of historically accumulated knowledge is of limited value. In our search to create equity, justice, beauty and value there are simply not the available guideposts that the scientifically oriented mind is accustomed to.

The reason is that ethical practice does not come from a stock of knowledge, or a pre-formed code of conduct, or a previously cataloged list of duties. Ethical professional practice is intrinsically a *process*. It can be seen as a way of being in the world; or, rather, it is *finding* a way of being in the world (Ross 1973, p. 19). We live our lives in search of value as we perceive it. We fundamentally want our actions to be effective not only in the sense that they produce a predicted effect, but that they are *valuable*.

We are born into a matrix of value created by others; and it is a dynamic matrix. Our impulse is not to copy the values or valuable actions of those that preceded us, but to create new values. The artist's search for new forms of expression, new plateaus of beauty, is analogous; we seek to live ethical lives and carry out ethical careers uniquely our own; we seek to give those to whom we are obliged our own individual style of value. As Cua (1978, p. 4) has pointed out: "the agent is concerned with what he will do, not merely in terms of his governing moral principles, but in light of the question 'What will I be?' "

For some, this is expressed in an effort at total negation of past values. For most, however, the striving is to establish one's own unique sense of value and potential for creating new value, within the context of prior expressions of value. Past rules, then do not so much confine us as they *orient* us. It is in this sense that many authors suggest that rules are *both* constraining and *enabling* (Giddens 1979, pp. 67–68; Brittan 1973, p. 118).

In the process of acting, I have an impact on my immediate world and, through the reflexivity of action, I also have an impact on myself in ways that I cannot easily predict. From the transcendental quality of action (i.e., the capacity today to surpass or go beyond what I was yesterday) is derived the ability to create and live with a new sense of value. As Ricoeur points out, "what I shall be is not already given but depends on what I shall do," and this includes how I, and others, sense or "appreciate" my "value" (Ricoeur 1966, p. 64).

In this way, ethics is never complete—neither for the individual nor for the many moral communities to which the individual is obligated. Ethical knowledge is not a "thing," but a continuously unfolding process—constantly opening out to new conceptions of value and new images of what is good. It is an inherent condition of all human action. Thus, we might argue that the Socratic dialogues are more the exemplar of ethics than Plato's *Republic* (Ross 1973, p. 20).

From this, we can infer that we will not be likely to be able to devise a single, general ethical theory of planning practice. A search for universals and stable anchors such as Newton's laws or Planck's constant is likely to prove futile.

Thus, in the same way that the practitioner is the theorist (Bolan 1980), the practitioner is the moralist. It is an inescapable, existential condition of professional practice. It is also the major challenge. As moralist, the practitioner is continually pushed to make ethical judgments and decisions in a social field that is characterized by a thicket of conflicting claims and pulls, some clearly apparent while others are ambiguous, covert, hidden or unspoken. The practitioner's role of moralist, then, is actually the more prominent in terms of professional creativity and imagination as distinct from the scientific, "puzzle-solving" role. The true task of the professional is not to display cleverness and intellectual dexterity but, rather, to create a new sense of value. Thus, the true challenge for every practitioner is to become a creative moralist.

NOTES

[1] Ginsberg reports anthropological research finds a common base of moral concern in every society, primitive and advanced alike. These common elements concern admonitions against murder, violence, stealing, lying, breaking promises (in short life, property and trust). In addition, every society studied has moral codes concerned with reproductive drives; sexual behavior and family relations seem to be universally regulated in some form. (Ginsberg 1968, p. 757).

[2] Fletcher implies a theological conception of love rather than a personal or erotic conception. It is a social attitude rather than a romantic emotion (Fletcher 1967, p. 34); for love, "the essential ingredients are caring and commitment" (1967, p. 39).

[3] The pertinent cases here include: Olson's demonstration that an unstructured group (such as consumers), with its members aware of their common interest and similarly aware of the means to bring about those interests, will still fail to take action as a group (Olson 1965). Hirschman applies his concepts of desertion, protest and loyalty to a variety of examples to suggest different perverse results flowing from each (Hirschman 1970). Buchanan and Tullock's *Calculus of Consent* (1962) explores the zone or threshold where freely given consent breaks down and is replaced by coerced regulation of behavior. Schelling's analysis (1971) shows how, even though no individual advocates segregation, in circumstances where each individual is free to move and each seeks a location where he is not in a minority, the resulting pattern would be highly segregated.

REFERENCES

Argyris, C. 1982. *Reasoning, Learning and Action: Individual and Organizational.* San Francisco: Jossey-Bass.

Argyris, C. and Schön, D.A. 1974. *Theory in Practice: Increasing Professional Effectiveness.* San Francisco: Jossey-Bass.

_____. 1978. *Organizational Learning.* Reading: Addison-Wesley Press.

Berry, D. and Steiker, G. 1974. The Concept of Justice in Regional Planning: Justice as Fairness. *Journal of the American Institute of Planners.* 40:414–421.

Bok, S. 1978. *Lying: Moral Choice in Public and Private Life.* New York: Random House Vintage Books.

Bolan, R.S. 1980. The Practitioner as Theorist: The Phenomenology of the Professional Episode. *Journal of the American Planning Association.* 46:261–274.

Boudon, R. 1982. *The Unintended Consequences of Social Action*. New York: St. Martin's Press.

Brennan, J.M. 1977. *The Open-Texture of Moral Concepts*. London: The Macmillan Press Limited.

Brittan, A. 1973. *Meanings and Situations*. London: Routledge and Kegan Paul.

Buchanan, J.M. and Tullock, G. 1962. *The Calculus of Consent*. Ann Arbor: University of Michigan Press.

Cua, A.S. 1978. *Dimensions of Moral Creativity; Paradigms, Principles and Ideals*. University Park: The Pennsylvania State University Press.

Derr, T.S. 1981. The Obligation to the Future. In *Responsibilities to Future Generations: Environmental Ethics*, ed., E. Partridge. Buffalo: Prometheus Books.

Douglas, J.D. 1970. Deviance and Respectability: The Social Construction of Moral Meanings. In *Deviance and Respectability*, ed., J.D. Douglas. New York: Basic Books.

Drucker, P.F. 1981. What is "Business Ethics"? *The Public Interest*. 63:18–36.

Feibleman, J.K. 1967. *Moral Strategy: An Introduction to the Ethics of Confrontation*. The Hague: Martinus Nijhoff.

Fletcher, J. 1966. *Situation Ethics: The New Morality*. Philadelphia: The Westminster Press.

_____. 1967. *Moral Responsibility: Situation Ethics at Work*. Philadelphia: The Westminster Press.

Fried, C. 1978. *Right and Wrong*. Cambridge: Harvard University Press.

Giddens, A. 1979. *Central Problems in Social Theory: Action, Structure and Contradiction in Social Analysis*. Berkeley: The University of California Press.

Ginsberg, M. 1968. Comparative Ethics. In *Encyclopedia Britannica*. Volume 8. Chicago: William Benton.

Golding, M.P. 1981. Obligations to Future Generations. In *Responsibilities to Future Generations: Environmental Ethics*, ed., E. Partridge. Buffalo: Prometheus Books.

Hill, M. 1968. A Goals-Achievement Matrix for Evaluating Alternative Plans. *Journal of the American Institute of Planners*. 34:19–29.

Hirschman, A.O. 1970. *Exit, Voice and Loyalty*. Cambridge: Harvard University Press.

Howe, E. 1980. Public Professions and the Private Model of Professionalism. *Social Work*. 25:179–191.

Howe, E. and Kaufman, J.L. 1979. The Ethics of Contemporary American Planners. *Journal of the American Planning Association*. 45:243–255.

Kaufman, J.L. 1978. The Planner as Interventionist in Public Policy Issues. In *Planning Theory in the 1980's: A Search for Future Directions*, eds., R.W. Burchell and G. Sternlieb. New Brunswick: The Center for Urban Policy Research.

_____. 1981. Teaching Planning Ethics. *Journal of Planning Education and Research*. 1:29–35.

Klosterman, R.E. 1978. Foundations for Normative Planning. *Journal of the American Institute of Planners*. 44:37–46.

Krumholz, N. 1982. A Retrospective View of Equity Planning: Cleveland 1969–1979. *Journal of the American Planning Association*. 48:163–174.

Krumholz, N.; Cogger, J.M.; and Linner, J.H. 1975. The Cleveland Policy Planning Report. *Journal of the American Institute of Planners*. 41:298–304.

Levinas, E. 1969. *Totality and Infinity*. Pittsburgh: Duquesne University Press.

Lucy, W. 1981. Equity and Planning for Local Services. *Journal of the American Planning Association*. 47:447–457.

Mandelbaum, M. 1955. *The Phenomenology of Moral Experience*. Glencoe: The Free Press.

Marcuse, P. 1976. Professional Ethics and Beyond: Values in Planning. *Journal of the American Institute of Planners*. 42:264–274.

Olson, M. 1965. *The Logic of Collective Action*. Cambridge: Harvard University Press.

Ricoeur, P. 1966. *Freedom and Nature: The Voluntary and the Involuntary*. Evanston: Northwestern University Press.

Rittel, H.W.J. and Webber, M.M. 1973. Dilemmas in a General Theory of Planning. *Policy Sciences*. 4:155–169.

Ross, S.D. 1973. *In Pursuit of Moral Value*.San Francisco: Freeman, Cooper and Company.

Schelling, T. 1971. Dynamic Models of Segregation. *Journal of Mathematical Sociology*. 1:143–185.

Schön, D.A. 1982. Some of What A Planner Knows: A Case Study of Knowing in Practice. *Journal of the American Planning Association*. 48:351–364.

Schrader, G.A. 1972. Responsibility and Existence. In *Existential Phenomenology and Political Theory: A Reader*, ed., H.Y. Yung. Chicago: Henry Regency Company.

Wren, T.E. 1974. *Agency and Urgency: The Origin of Moral Obligation*. New York: Precedent Publishing, Inc.

5

Realms of Obligation and Virtue

Mark H. Moore

The Limitations of Process

Historically, this nation has been reluctant to place much faith in the moral character of its leaders.[1] Instead, we have relied on elaborate procedural and substantive rules to insure good governance by limiting official discretion. We have made officials accountable to us by forcing them to face electoral tests (or to be accountable to people who do). We have made them accountable to one another (and, therefore, to the diverse interests each represents) by dividing power among separate institutions. And we have made them accountable to our most fundamental traditions by subjecting governmental actions to constitutional limitations guarded by a powerful judiciary. Although this system made it difficult for wise and virtuous leaders to bless us with their statecraft, it also gave assurances that no evil men could ever torment us.

The heavy reliance on procedural and substantive rules diminished any sense of urgency about the moral character of public officials. To the extent we thought about it, the virtues of public officials seemed to lie in being respectful toward the rules that circumscribed their action, and in exemplifying upright personal conduct in their daily actions. To many who now consider the question of how public officials should conduct themselves this view still seems the most appropriate. We want nothing more than that officials dutifully satisfy obligations of the decisionmaking process in good faith. The last thing we want is an official who takes liberties with (or even

Reprinted by permission of the publishers from *Public Duties: The Moral Obligations of Government Officials*, edited by Joel L. Fleischman, Lance Liebman and Mark H. Moore, Cambridge, Mass.: Harvard University Press, Copyright © 1981 by the President and Fellows of Harvard College.

operates aggressively within) the mesh of process obligations to pursue an independent view of what the public interest requires.

If one held this view, the questions of what virtues officials might pursue and what duties they are bound to honor would hold little interest. The questions could be answered with a simple list of formal rules guiding official conduct. Several emergent characteristics of our governmental system suggest, however, that we will depend on the moral character of our officials much more in the future than we have in the past.

Corrupted Structures and Processes

For one thing, recent experience with procedural "checks and balances" has, to a degree, jaded our view of their value. Institutional structures and processes originally designed to facilitate widespread participation in public decisions, to focus attention on a limited number of issues, and to occasion choices in which some public values were advanced over others now shelter a horde of narrow and parochial interests attached like barnacles to shards of public power. Within Congress, for example, the specialized committee structure inevitably leads legislators to seek positions on those committees most influential in areas of concern to their constituents. Once ensconced, they use the influence of their office to serve constituency interests.[2] In the executive branch, institutional structures are created to give special attention to specific problems such as drug abuse, environmental protection, energy, and education, and they quickly become the channels through which advocates of particular interests exercise untoward influence over executive branch operations.[3] Similarly, government watchdog agencies (such as the Civil Service Commission, the General Accounting Office, and even the Office of Management and Budget) originally designed to promote accountability now elaborate their rules to such an extent that one suspects they are at least as interested in enlarging their own domains as in promoting effective administration. Since rules, processes, and structures can, therefore, be made to serve narrow purposes as well as broad, bad as well as good, their *general* claim on the allegiance of conscientious public officials may have weakened.

Residual Official Discretion

Even if the moral claim of procedures were not weakening, however, it is apparent that the existing rules and procedures leave substantial discretion to senior public officials. Current case studies of the jobs of senior public officials consistently reveal wide discretion in using the legal authority and resources of the government lodged in their offices (for example, launching major programs to treat heroin addicts with an experimental and potentially dangerous drug, loosening visa restrictions, deciding on aggressive enforcement actions against municipal and industrial polluters, and so forth).[4] Sometimes the discretion is de jure—the system expressly delegates substantial discretion because it was unable (or, in many cases, unwilling) to resolve the difficult issues that would arise as a program began to operate.[5] More often, however, the discretion is de facto. The formal rules are simply silent on an important substantive or procedural issue. Alternatively, the guidance that officials receive from different authorizing positions may be conflicting.[6] Whatever the reasons, it seems clear that the dramatic expansion of the government's undertakings has left many pockets of discretionary authority lodged among individual public officials despite determined efforts to limit discretion with substantive and procedural rules.

The Opportunity to Conceive and Pursue "The Public Interest"

Finally, the governmental expansion has not only left substantial discretionary authority in specific positions, but also created significant competence and expertise. Inevitably, public officials in charge of specific public programs become expert in the substantive problems with which they deal, and the operating characteristics of the programs they direct. They will know whether the authority and resources entrusted to them are being used to greatest effect. And if not, they are well positioned to initiate corrections. This suggests that the nation has an interest in encouraging its officials to accept some responsibility for informing— even shaping—government programs in their areas of expertise. Otherwise a great deal of useful insight and information would be lost. One possible implication is that the duties of public officials are not simply to be passive instruments in policymaking but to work actively in establishing goals for public policy in their area, and in advocating those goals among the people who share their responsibility. In short, they have the opportunity and duty to conceive of and pursue the public interest.

Despite our best efforts, then, we have not succeeded in constructing a governmental system that is independent of the moral qualities of its leaders. This makes questions about the duties, obligations, and virtues of public officials more urgent than we suppose, and particularly so for those who teach in professional schools establishing professional standards for public officials. My purposes in this essay are two: first, to sketch three realms within which virtues may be pursued and obligations arise; second, to begin the analysis of where the paths of duty and virtue lie within each realm. Since the discussion risks becoming excessively abstract without specific examples, it is useful to begin with some actual cases.

Three Realms of Official Obligation and Virtue

Consider a few vignettes of official action:

Gordon Chase, the administrator of the Health Service Administration of New York City, launches a large-scale methadone maintenance program to combat an epidemic growth of the heroin problem in New York City. The program is a controversial one that holds substantial risks for patients and produces uncertain but apparently significant improvements in their lives. Chase is not directly responsible for addiction treatment programs in New York. Instead, the responsibility is lodged in the Addiction Service Agency, which is adamantly opposed to methadone maintenance programs. Chase seizes the initiative by assembling the program, assuming the necessary authority and resources will be available. Furthermore, to build momentum, Chase claims that he will be able to treat 15,000 addicts within a year—a claim that is demonstrably exaggerated.[7]

Orville Freeman, the Secretary of Agriculture, hears testimony that people are severly malnourished, even starving, in the rural South. He has the resources within his department to act to alleviate the hunger, but fears the wrath of congressional overseers who oppose such efforts. He is responsive to their views not only because they can affect the entire range of his department's programs, but also because President Johnson expressly cautioned him to avoid antagonizing the congressmen who head his authorizing and appropriating subcommittees. Although the demand for action comes from a congressional committee, it is *not* the committee that has jurisdiction over his agency's programs or funds. Consequently, Freeman takes no action except to send a few aides to the South who report that no emergency exists there.[8]

Dave Goldman, an official with "California Legal Services, Inc.," reports to the press and the officials who finance his program in Washington that he has *not* been representing a local farmworkers union or giving them legal advice. In fact, he has repeatedly met with the union leader to discuss both legal and political tactics. The terms of Goldman's contract with the federal agency prohibit California Legal Services from assisting the union.[9]

Caspar Weinberger, the newly appointed chairman of the Federal Trade Commission, encounters Representative Evins, the chairman of the FTC's appropriations subcommittee outside the hearing room just before his first appearance before the subcommittee. The congressman hands him a note with three names on it and asks Weinberger to "take care of these people." Weinberger, who has assumd responsibility for reforming the FTC and who believes that the core of the FTC's problems is its reliance on patronage appointments, returns to his office and suggests that his personnel officer begin the process of terminating the employees whom Evins named.[10]

These examples of official action are useful for our purposes because in each instance the official acts in a way that violates widely shared notions of officials' obligations. Chase cavalierly ignores a formal policymaking process and launches a risky treatment program for heroin addicts. Freeman fails to meet a basic human need despite the availability of resources to deal with the problem. Goldman lies to his superiors about his activities. Weinberger acts precipitately and perhaps unfairly towards his subordinates.

Interestingly, however, in each instance the official can present an excuse for his actions. Chase would argue that, on balance, methadone maintenance programs were likely to produce more good than harm, and since the mayor could have halted his activities at any time, his silence constituted approval. Freeman would point out that, of course, he would have liked to respond to hungry people in Mississippi, but he received no instructions to do so from either the Congress or the president. In fact, he received contrary messages. Besides, it was not clear that the problem was as bad as alleged. Goldman would defend his actions by arguing that lying was necessary to protect a fragile effort to redistribute political power. Otherwise, the program would be crushed into irrelevance by those who were then powerful. Besides, he suspected that his overseers in Washington really wanted him to behave as he did. Weinberger would explain that his actions were ordinary managerial tactics to rejuvenate and redirect a failing agency, and that the benefits of the energized agency far outweighed any apparent unfairness to the employees.

The sins and excuses offered in these cases suggest the richness, ambiguities, and dilemmas of the moral life of public officials. Conscientious officials ask themselves questions like the following: What substantive objectives should they pursue? What programmatic uses of governmental authority and resources are appropriate to consider in reaching those goals? What process of consultation is required to legitimate a given policy decision? Can they take shortcuts in the process of consultation leading to authorization? Can they manipulate procedures? Does it matter if their opponents are manipulating procedures and expect them to do so as well? What do officials owe to colleagues whose positions and personal relationships entitle them to frequent, familiar access to the officials? What do they owe to subordinates whose careers depend on their stewardship? To what extent should officials' personal interests play a role in the decisions they make?

To lend order to these questions, it is useful to think of obligations arising in three different realms. Officials are bound, first, by obligations to respect the processes that legitimate their actions. Typically, these processes require them to share their authority with others, and to subject proposed uses of government authority to the scrutiny of the public and their representatives. Second, they are obligated both by a general duty to beneficence and by their oath of office to serve the public interest—to use the powers of their offices to accomplish public purposes as effectively, efficiently, and decently as they can. Third, like all of us, on a more intimate and personal basis, they are obliged to treat their colleagues and subordinates—the individuals with whom they deal on a daily basis and who depend on them in important ways—with respect, honesty, and fairness.

While these realms of obligation usefully order the questions that officials might ask themselves, they also highlight two central difficulties. First, the nature of the obligations within each realm are often ambiguous. It is hard for an official like Chase or Freeman to know what the public interest requires of them in confronting heroin addiction or hunger. It is hard for Goldman to understand what programmatic activities are being authorized. And it is hard for Weinberger to know the extent of his responsibilities to the employees of FTC. Second, the obligations, once discerned, often conflict. Chase's, Freeman's and Goldman's perceived duties to pursue the public interest conflict with the obligation to protect authorizing procedures. Similarly, Weinberger's duty to serve the public interest and pursue a reform mandate for the FTC conflicts with his duties to his employees.

Given ambiguity and conflicts, virtue in public officials lies in the skill and judgment they reveal in discerning the obligations and resolving conflicts among them. The rest of this essay seeks to help conscientious public officials (and those who train them) pursue virtue by exploring the realms of obligation. I do not assume that the realms can be fully charted, nor that a complete chart could guarantee reliable navigation. In fact, my view is the opposite: that character and motivation to behave virtuously are much more important than concepts or technique. But given character and motivation, officials might still be aided by some discussion of the nature of their obligations. In any event, we will examine the nature of the obligations and virtues of public officials in pursuing the public interest, in protecting and authorizing processes, in preserving relationships with colleagues and friends, and, finally, in confronting their own conscience.

Obligations to Pursue the Public Interest

Public officials are obliged to pursue the public interest—to use the powers and resources of their offices to accomplish public purposes efficiently and effectively. In part, this duty derives from normal obligations that attach to administrative offices in which an agent works with the authority and resources of others to accomplish their purposes. But the duty also partakes of a general duty of beneficence—to do what one can to help others.

For private individuals, the duty of beneficence is a modest one, largely because the scope of plausibly effective private action (and hence the scope of moral responsibility) is comparatively small.[11] When, however, an individual assumes responsibility for broad public purposes, and has been granted discretionary command over the substantial powers and resources of the government, the duty of beneficence takes on a markedly different aspect. The difference is partly one of scale. Since the capacity to do things for people is so much greater for public officials than for private individuals, the relative importance of this general duty of beneficence must increase. But the difference seems to be based on the *public* character of the responsibility and the routine use of coercive power in pursuing the good as well. The hope of realizing broad public goals in which many take satisfaction and the concern about inflicting harm through clumsiness or a deliberate choice to sacrifice some interests to advance others make the duty of beneficence both more important and more difficult than in the private realm. The problem for a public official is to discern what the simple duty to "do good" requires in the complex undertakings of the public sector.

To argue that officials have an obligation to the public interest does not necessarily imply that they have either the duty or the right to develop their own conceptions of what the public interest requires in particular situations. One can argue, for example, that their purposes have already been established when they arrive. They can be discovered in explicit legislative mandates, inferred from prior policies, or guided by tacit understandings with the people who hire them. Moreover, if officials are in doubt about their mandate or want to change it, they can always seek explicit new authority by consulting with others who have authority or interests in their area. They need not, indeed *should* not, feel that they have to make all the decisions about purposes and programs themselves.

On the other hand, to argue that officials should take guidance from others in formulating and deciding matters of public policy does not relieve the officials of responsibility for taking some initiative in conceiving and proposing alternative uses of the powers vested in their office. After all, mandates are often quite ambiguous. Moreover, even when they are not, senior public officials are in an unusually good position to see new opportunities, or to discern the changing character of a given problem. Because they possess information and expertise, they are expected to play a special, but not necessarily dominant, role in making policy. Finally, on some occasions, when there is a compelling need that they can satisfy, and when there is reason to be distrustful of the process that would authorize action, officials may even be under some obligation to risk violating process obligations on behalf of an overriding obligation to serve the public interest. The point is that regardless of whether we consider the officials' role as discreet, neutral administrators giving operational content to well-established mandates, or as respectful advocates proposing changes in policy with full attention to authorizing procedures, or even as officials pursuing a public need at the moral risk of violating existing authorizing procedures, senior public officials must inevitably think about the purposes their current policies are serving.

In conceiving of the public interest in particular situations, conscientious officials must be careful to avoid some common pitfalls. Some concern the nature of their responsibilities for foreseeing the consequences of the policies they recommend. Others have to do with the way they size up or appraise the diverse effects they foresee.

Foreseeing Consequences of Policies

Intuitively, awareness of the consequences of one's actions seems a necessary if not sufficient condition for moral conduct. While this point is debated among philosophers with respect to private conduct, the principle seems beyond dispute for public officials deciding important policy issues. Officials have a duty to anticipate the important consequences of policies they advocate or implement.[12] This, in turn, requires them to conceive of categories of effect that would influence their judgment about the wisdom of pursuing given policies. Since these categories of effect become the terms in which old policies are evaluated and new policies advocated, they define the officials' moral vision of the social values at stake in their domain. The discerning sensibility officials reveal in developing these categories is, then, an important mark of their virtue. In actual practice, characteristic shortcomings occur.

Perhaps the most common pitfall is to miss entirely the importance of the activity. In a system that encourages public officials to avoid taking responsibility for advancing policies, it is all too easy for officials to shrink from the intellectually and politically demanding task of describing the important values that are at stake in their domain. Instead, they refer to terms established in legislative or policy mandates no matter how inadequate for describing actual effects, or to a few very broad goals which are commonly shared but are difficult to relate to the particular decisions at hand. They also commonly seek refuge by describing operational objectives that describe their activities well but do not connect easily with important social values. Worst of all, perhaps, they sometimes act as though the problem of developing a suitable accounting system was a technical matter best left to experts. Of course, it is not easy for officials to be aware of even the immediate effects of their actions. It is also difficult to connect the proximate effects of their programs with the ultimate effects envisioned somewhere further along elaborate chains of causation. And it is still more difficult to connect a wide variety of ultimate effects with a few overarching social values. But of such skills is discerning judgment made, and it is precisely these skills that are the virtues of responsible public officials.

A second common pitfall is to develop conceptions that are too narrow—that capture too few of the important effects of a given policy. Somewhat ironically, the narrowing can result from two radically different notions about the "proper" way to develop views of social values at stake in policy choices. Sometimes it occurs because officials become preoccupied with "quantifying" effects. They look primarily at those effects whose magnitudes can be reliably measured. Even worse, in a vain attempt to establish an "objective" measure of social value, they focus exclusively on effects that can be valued in terms of market prices. Alternatively, however, their vision may become improperly narrowed if they decide in advance that all policies will be ruled out if they produce harmful effects (however small) in areas that the officials regard as inviolable. In the end, of course, a principled stand basing a policy on one important effect may be seen as the proper choice since it was the only one that suitably honored an important social principle. But still, to refuse from the outset even to explore other consequences of the choice seems a moral luxury that cannot be afforded to public officials.[13] Public officials should have the discipline and detachment to see *all* the things at stake in their choices—even consequences that are "unthinkable."

It is not too difficult to resist these temptations to narrow one's vision, and expose one's sensibilities to a suitably far-ranging array of consequences. But even if officials free their minds to roam widely over the terrain of important effects, they are still likely to overlook or fail to accommodate an important class of consequences—namely, the long-run effects of given policies on institutions and institutional relationships in the society.[14] Such effects occur through several different mechanisms. Sometimes policies will create important precedents that give rise to new expectations or shape policy debates in other policy areas. Other times policies create new institutions whose future operations will importantly shape governmental actions in ways that are difficult to foresee. Perhaps the most common and important institutional effect, however, is the effect of each policy initiative on the authority, credibility, and prestige of government itself. Every policy claims for itself some of the government's prestige and some of the polity's attention. As our recent history makes clear, these are hardly inexhaustible resources. In fact, the recent sprawl of policy initiatives has shown just how quickly government credibility can be dissipated among a confused and increasingly disenchanted citizenry. It is not always true, of course, that a policy initiative saps the legitimacy of the government. When a policy initiative solves a salient public problem (such as polio or air pollution), or reaffirms an important public value (such as equal voting rights or equality of educational opportunity), the prestige of the government is enhanced, not reduced. The point, rather, is that it is insufficient for a public official to explore each policy exclusively in its own substantive terms—even when the terms have been expanded to accommodate many diverse effects, extended forward in causal systems to capture ultimate as well as proximate effects, and connected to broad social values. Beyond this, an official must assume the statesmanlike burdens of foreseeing the effects of policies on institutions, including, in particular, effects on the legitimacy of the government itself.

A third pitfall for public officials in foreseeing consequences is to mishandle the inevitable uncertainty in the choices they make. Perhaps the most common errors in this domain are to pretend that uncertainty does not exist or to try to exorcise it with the tools of science. Such temptations are an inevitable feature of a system in which officials take their responsibility to foresee consequences seriously. It is only natural for conscientious public officials to want to appear knowledgeable. And it is natural for them to reach out to experts and to science to bolster both the image and the reality of confident knowledge. On the whole, reaching out to science to provide certainty in the judgments they make is admirable. The problems arise only when the drive for certainty stands in the way of using current knowledge effectively.

This paradoxical result can occur in two different situations. First, when officials claim greater certainty than is warranted by current knowledge, major distortions can occur. By acting as though some consequences were certain, officials are, in effect, obscuring the possibility (perhaps even the probability) that some effects quite different from those they imagine could occur. In shrinking their conception of what might happen, some useful knowledge is lost. Second, officials can err by refusing to decide a question until science reduces all the major uncertainties to very low levels. For officials caught between an obligation to foresee consequences precisely and an apparent obligation to be conservative in using scientific information, it often seems desirable to delay choices until science reduces major uncertainties to very low levels. The problem with this, of course, is that delaying a decision is the same as deciding to live with the consequence of not deciding. Since some information about the consequences of failing to decide is often available, as well as some information about the possible consequences of different decisions, it is possible for officials to compare delay with some alternative choice. To the extent that officials fail to use this information and make the comparison, they leave us less well positioned against possible events than current knowledge would allow. Thus, the determined pursuit of confident knowledge can often drive out useful information.[15]

The alternative to the unrealistic drive for certain knowledge is simply to acknowledge the uncertainty in the choices that officials make. This has the enormous virtue of corresponding to the actual state of affairs. But it has the great liability of emphasizing the painful fact that, ordinarily, we do not know precisely what will happen as a consequence of policy choices. To say that we are uncertain is not the same as saying we know nothing, of course. We can imagine possible effects. We can usually even say that some effects are more probable than others. What we cannot say with a high degree of confidence is exactly what will happen. In this sense, then, officials are often "gambling" with the lives and fortunes of citizens. What standards should guide officials as they face these gambles?

Some activists hold the view that any uncertainty about the effects of a given policy should prevent the government from acting. The government simply should not gamble with the welfare of its citizens. The certain benefits of inexpensive electric power that could be guaranteed by the construction of nuclear power plants cannot offset the remote chance of a nuclear accident. Nor, presumably, can the uncertain benefits of prison reform or forced school integration justify the certain, immediate costs of these policies respectively to victims of crime and parents who want their children in neighborhood schools. It is simply wrong to expose people to risks of bad outcomes, or to try to justify certain losses in one area with uncertain gains in others. Unless the government can be sure of the consequences of a policy it should not act.

Other times we adopt a slightly less conservative stance: the government should not act if there is a chance (however small) of a very bad consequence. It is all right if there is uncertainty about potential benefits. It is even all right if there is a chance that there will be some small bad effects. The problem arises when there is a chance of a real catastrophe. Thus, the uncertain benefits of school integration could conceivably justify the imposition of certain costs if we think the likely benefits of school integration are sufficiently large, but subsidies to nuclear power plants could never be justified because some chance of a real disaster undeniably exists.

A third stance is less conservative still. It says that society should look at the relative likelihood of conceivable effects in all the relevant areas of potential impact and calculate the "expected magnitude" of a policy's effects in given areas. Of course, it could choose to weigh the possibility of very large bad effects disproportionately to other kinds of effects. But the mere possibility of very bad effects would not be an absolute bar to a policy. It would all depend on the probability of the very bad effect, and the other offsetting (or not quite offsetting) advantages of the policy.

My own view is that public officials should strike the third stance described above: they should look at the expected magnitude of the effects in given areas, and should count prospects of large losses much more heavily than other kinds of effects. I think the first stance, that the government should take no action if there is any uncertainty, is absurd. Since virtually all government actions, including the establishment of government itself, involve uncertain consequences, no government at all would be possible if we adhere to this rule. The second stance is more respectable, but still inappropriate since it rules out policy actions even where the chance of a bad effect is small, to the point of vanishing, and the potential benefits very large and quite certain. There seems to me no choice but to face up to the fact of uncertainty, explicitly assess the relative probabilities of different results in all areas of concern, and decide on the basis of some expected result appropriately weighted.

Discerning the Public Interest

It is one thing to have the discipline, competence, and vision to foresee the diverse consequences of policies. It is quite another to discern the thread of the public interest in the tangle. Two broadly different concepts of the public interest or public welfare have been developed to help officials make the judgments with confidence and precision. One conception is the analysis of benefits and costs based on the logic of welfare economics. The second is the analysis of rights and responsibilities drawn from specific conceptions of justice. While specialists offer these conceptions as complete in themselves and antagonistic toward one another, I think it is more useful for public officials to know the strengths and limitations of each and to use both in searching for policies that move most surely in the direction of the commonweal.

The "benefit-cost" approach to discerning the public interest begins with the notion that the appropriate way to value the diverse effects of a given policy is to let their values be assigned by those who are affected.[16] Intuitively, this notion is extremely attractive. It reserves an important right—the right to say what is valuable and what costly, what dignified and what un-dignified, what virtuous and what contemptible—to individuals. In doing so, welfare economics honors the capacity to assign value as something fundamental to human existence. A practical problem soon appears however: how to discover the value that affected individuals actually do assign to the imagined effects. For this problem, welfare economics proposes several solutions. Economic theory demonstrates, on the basis of a rigorous deductive logic, that in a world where consumers with stable, well-ordered preferences purchase goods in perfectly competitive markets populated by firms whose managers maximize profits by choosing efficient solutions to well-defined production problems, the set of prices one observes in the market will be pareto-efficient. At that set of prices, at the margins, individuals will be trading things of exactly equivalent value. If we go farther and assume that the initial distribution of rights and responsibilities in the society is fair, or that the current distribution of wealth and income is in some sense appropriate, then we can also say that the observed set of prices gives a fairly precise estimate of the *social* value attached to production and consumption of things traded on the market. Consequently, for things traded in markets, the observed prices provide a rough approximation of their social value. For things *not* traded in markets, welfare economics proposes a less elegant (and much more expensive) but still eminently practical solution: simply ask the individuals what they would be "willing to pay" to add additional units (or avoid losses) or whatever it is that is being affected by a policy. To the extent that we can observe market prices related to effects of policies or collect data on citizens' "willingness to pay" for given kinds of effects, we will have a convenient way of assigning social value to the diverse effects of a given policy.

The merits of this approach are formidable. It delegates to the affected individuals the right to assign value to the effects. In addition, it exploits some relatively inexpensive information (market prices) to suggest the value of alternative actions. Finally, and most important, the methods lead to results in which the value of diverse effects are all expressed in the same units. Thus, one can "add up" different effects, not only across different kinds of effects, but also across groups that are differentially affected. The sum of these values will represent the "net social value" of a given policy.

While these features commend the benefit-cost approach to our attention and make it prudent to gather information about the values that individuals attach to policy effects when convenient, several important limitations of the approach make it unwise to use this conception exclusively to fix a conception of the public interest in a particular situation. For one thing, information about prices and willingness to pay is likely to be distorted for technical reasons. Since actual market conditions rarely correspond to those required by the theory, observed market prices can be taken only as rough approximations of social value. Similarly, simple introspection suggests that it would be difficult to give meaningful responses to a survey of "willingness to pay." It is difficult to think of how much one would pay for a park, cleaner air, and national defense, to say nothing of more complicated effects such as integrated schools or a society in which satisfactory nutrition was guaranteed to everyone. Finally, both market prices and expressions of willingness to pay are dependent on the current distribution of wealth and income. If the current distribution is unfair, then these prices cannot be interpreted as appropriate expressions of social welfare. Since welfare economists have no theory that justifies a particular distribution of income, however, and since in any case their ability to gather information conveniently and inexpensively depends on accepting the current distribution of wealth and income, they are inclined to ignore the theoretical problem in order to get on with the practical task.

Second, although welfare economics accepts the relevance of distributional concerns in evaluating the outcomes of given policies, the theory handles these concerns quite cavalierly. The fundamental moral issue is whether losses to one group of citizens can be justified by "larger" gains for others. The welfare economist's answer to this question is that as long as the overall contribution to social welfare is positive, that is the gains to the gainers are "larger" than the losses to the losers, the policy should be adopted. The justification for this position is simply that the existence of a net social gain means that, in principle, the gainers from a policy decision could compensate the losers and both would be better off, in their own view, than if the policy were not adopted.[17] The curious part of this solution, however, is that there is no requirement that the losers actually be compensated. That is treated as a different problem to be addressed at a different time. The crucial thing is that the compensation could, in principle, occur. Thus, although distributional issues arise both in estimating the values of specific effects and in determining whether a policy should be adopted, they are often ignored when actually evaluating a policy or deciding exactly how to execute it.

The standard of rights and responsibilities based on conceptions of justice starts from a much different premise. The idea is that with respect to some goods, activities, and conditions individual preferences should *not* be the basis for assigning social value. Instead, society as a whole should establish the value without reference to individual preferences. Far from being disinterested in the distribution of the socially valued goods, activities, and conditions, society takes responsibility for guaranteeing that the rights and responsibilities are distributed equally in the society. Thus, even in liberal societies we require everyone to attend school, to be immunized against some diseases, to accept the right to vote, to remain free from slavery, and to repress desires to attack their friends and neighbors, despite the fact that individuals would often be "better off" in their own eyes if they could exchange the rights for something they valued more, or escape an obligation by contributing something else. In effect, by requiring individuals to accept rights and duties, and by preventing exchanges in these areas, society forces individuals to act as though the rights and duties had infinite value.

Socially established rights and duties, then, are special things. They are established by collective decisions rather than individual preferences. They are distributed equally throughout the society. And citizens are not allowed to exchange them. Insofar as their creation overwhelms individual preferences and frustrates exchanges, the conception presents a stark challenge to the idea that social values should be nothing more than the sum of individual preferences. Insofar as we conceive of the exclusive purposes of the state as doing justice by guaranteeing these rights, an alternative conception of where the public interest lies is established.[18]

This conception of the public interest also has some enormously appealing features. While the conception of welfare economics celebrates our diversity, the conception of equal rights and responsibilities celebrates the idea that in some important areas we are (or should be) equal. If there are some areas in which we are the same, these must be the defining characteristics of being human. If they are the defining characteristics of being human, then they must be invested with a special significance: they represent minimal conceptions of human dignity which cannot be trespassed without making someone less than human. To establish such conceptions of human equality and dignity collectively, and to honor them reliably in public policy decisions is clearly consistent with an attractive notion of how officials might pursue the public interest.

Note that while part of the appeal of establishing conceptions of socially established rights is the sheer satisfaction of celebrating shared conceptions of human dignity and citizenship in a just society, the creation and maintenance of rights produce important individually consumed satisfactions as well. By allowing people to develop legitimate expectations that their rights will not be violated, they create a kind of wealth for individuals in the society. Some fears that might impoverish their lives can more or less safely be put aside. Similarly, the existence of rights creates a degree of equality in bargaining relationships because they give individuals enough security to withstand substantial economic or physical power. In fact, rights prevent individuals from yielding to temptations to abandon some virtues. So, the establishment of generally shared rights and duties meets individual and social needs to define the place of individuals in a collective enterprise—a need that has both expressive and instrumental value. Moreover, rights define the areas in which individuals will be powerful and autonomous, not only with respect to one another, but also with respect to the government.

But just as there are problematic aspects of the utilitarian standard of the welfare economists, difficulties also exist with this notion of rights and justice. One problem is that the strength of the obligation to protect a given right is often uncertain. Rights often conflict, and it is not usually obvious in advance which rights should take precedence in given situations. For example, do the rights of some citizens to equality of educational opportunity outweigh the rights of other citizens to attend schools in their own neighborhoods? Or, do the rights of citizens to accumulate wealth and pass it on to their children outweigh the rights of less advantaged people to have an "equal opportunity" to pursue their conception of virtue and satisfaction in their individual lives? Similarly, there are often good reasons to override specific rights in given situations as long as the rights are well defended by procedural safeguards and as long as some reasonable compensation is paid. So, like all contracts, establishing rights is not entirely free from uncertainty: apparently clear duties may not be honored. When this could or should occur will not always be clear to a public official who is seeking to protect the most important rights of citizens.

A second problem, related to the first, is that it is rarely clear which rights have been established within a society at a given moment. Academic justifications for different conceptions of justice always exist. They range from a notion that individual rights to life, liberty, and property are so far-reaching that almost any state action infringes on them significantly,[19] to a notion that rights leading to significant economic equality could be justified.[20] In the most commonly accepted formulations, rights are established primarily in civil and political areas. Rights to property in these schemes are only licenses to accumulate as much economic value as one can by using one's labor and enterprise in production and exchange. No guarantees are offered in the struggle with nature. More recently, however, as we have accumulated wealth, entitlements have been created that to some extent *do* provide guarantees in the struggle with nature. We now provide some levels of income, food, housing, jobs and health care *almost* as a matter of right. Whether programs providing benefits in these areas represent extensions of rights to cover economic struggles that were previously left to chance, or whether these are simply charitable gifts that may be withdrawn by the rest of the society if economic conditions deteriorate or if the behavior of people accepting the entitlements departs from social expectations, is a major unresolved issue in our current politics.

While public officials weighing the consequences of policies should recognize effects on the current distribution of socially established rights, entitlements, and duties, which of these demand overriding allegiance is unclear. In many areas, recognition of relevant rights and entitlements may prove insufficient to guide the officials' judgment about whether and how to proceed with a given program. They may meet the objective of protecting all relevant rights, and still have some latitude about how to distribute additional costs and benefits of the proposed policy. So, as a practical matter in many areas the concept of justice turns out to be as ambiguous as the conception of maximizing individual satisfaction.

In my view, then, officials searching for the public interest must accommodate two fundamental problems. The first, discussed above, is the insufficiency of either the welfare standard or the justice standard when each is taken alone. The simple summation of individual preferences attached to effects fails to guide policy because it ignores legitimate *social*, as opposed to individual, values, and the distribution of gains and losses among individuals in different social positions. The assertion of a more or less limited number of absolute rights and inescapable duties is either inadequate in guiding policy (because it leaves many important effects of policies unvalued) or distorting (because it forces us to reject policies where rights are abridged even in situations where the rights are defended by elaborate procedures and suitable compensation can be arranged). The second problem for officials is that the specific content of both conceptions changes over time as a result of changing social conditions. Values that individuals assign to certain kinds of effects change with social conditions. So do the kinds of things that are called rights and duties.

To accommodate these difficulties, conscientious officials should make two broad commitments. The first is that in valuing the consequences of given policies they should adopt elements of both the welfare economics and the justice criteria. From the welfare economics criterion they should accept the responsibility to foresee the consequences of policies for individuals, and, when it is convenient, gather information about the values that individuals place on the diverse effects. But they should also go beyond the welfare economics criterion to see that the social interest in guaranteeing rights in some areas and promoting equality in others is reflected in the policy choice.

From the justice criterion, they should accept the notion that society as a whole has a legitimate interest in guaranteeing rights, even when individuals would abandon them and other individuals in the society would benefit from the abandonment. But, they should also understand that individual rights may be abridged when compelling reasons for doing so exist, and when the rights have been protected by procedures that force the state to establish compelling reasons, and, sometimes, arrange suitable compensation. Moreover, since rights and duties can change over time, and since governmental action in a just society inevitably creates precedents (since it always carries an expectation of equal treatment across individuals and over time), officials should consider how current policies affect the *future* structure of rights, entitlements, and duties. Moreover, they must realize that their actions are not only *reflecting* but also *shaping* these future rights and duties.

The second broad commitment of conscientious public officials is to accept responsibility for deciding issues and explaining their decisions in ways that strengthen the *process* of defining social and individual values. This commitment is important precisely because the domain and content of social values change, and because the officials' actions affect these things. While the structure of the government frees officials to choose for all of us, and while they must do this as conscientiously as possible, they must ultimately acknowledge their subordination to social processes and their general obligation to make broad social processes work as well as possible. At the very least this means that in deciding on specific policies, they must give their reasons. They must explain which values are taking precedence, which are being subordinated, and why. At the most basic level these are obligations of the officials to themselves—otherwise how could they justify their own actions to themselves? But they are also their obligations to the rest of us. We need them to explain their actions partly so that they become accountable to us, and partly so that they can help our political choices become what they ought to be—a deliberate social weighing of relevant values in particular decisions against the backdrop of a changing context of individual preferences, rights, entitlements, and duties. Their justifications are part of the process of discovering what individual and social lives are possible at a given moment.

Obligations to Authorizing Processes and Procedures

Beyond, and, as we have seen, part of, the obligation to explain and justify policy choices in terms of anticipated results, public officials have obligations to expose their views and judgments to elaborate mechanisms of consultation that legitimate their choices. This obligation can be derived both from a prima facie duty to respect and accommodate the interests of others whenever possible, buttressed by a long political tradition of solicitousness toward the interests of minorities,[21] and from a variety of utilitarian arguments that emphasize the instrumental values of consultation in making complex and controversial choices.[22]

At the heart of the prima facie duty is the notion that people should be asked to consent to actions that affect their interests. This presumption is very strong in situations where contemplated actions will produce adverse effects. It is also present, however, even when the expected results will be beneficial. No other posture is consistent with the notion that individuals or their representatives have independent capabilities to assign value and choose, and that in deciding on actions that affect us all, we confront one another as approximate equals. Of course, in the political realm, where the interests of many often stand in opposition to the interests of a few, we do not always insist on the strong condition that the consent of the few be secured (which would, in effect, grant veto power to the few). But we do often assume that a good-faith effort will be made to understand those interests, accommodate them as much as possible in the design of policies, and provide explanations, as well as occasional compensation, when those interests cannot be accommodated. Such actions are necessary to show respect for the equal status and legitimate interests of others in the society.

Three different utilitarian justifications for consultation can also be offered. One justification is based on technical considerations. Consultation is good because it develops better information on the likely consequences of policy choices and the preferences of affected parties than would be available without the elaborate machinery. Forced to confront interested parties, officials will see more clearly and vividly what is at stake in their policies and will make more informed decisions.[23] A second justification emphasizes the fact that the use of procedures granting "due process" will facilitate the execution of the ultimate choice. Parties whose interests are adversely affected will nonetheless accept the decision because they have been dealt with "fairly": they have been granted the expressive satisfaction of making their case as convincingly as they can, and they have been implicitly assured that their right to be heard in future decisions is intact. In fact, if they are gracious losers, they may legitimately think that their interests will attract greater solicitousness on the next decision.[24] A third justification is even more far-reaching. Processes of consultation, discussion, and negotiation are valuable because they teach people to be good democratic citizens. By confronting one another on an equal basis in situations where interests conflict, the parties learn skills in reaching compromises as well as an attitude of respect toward their opponents. These are extremely valuable for citizens in democratic societies.

Whichever justification appeals more strongly, good reasons for officials to feel generally obligated to consult extensively with affected parties clearly exist. In fact, the obligation cuts even more deeply because we all carry in the back of our minds a model of an "ideal" decision process. In this ideal, all parties interested in a choice are invited to participate. Their opportunities to participate are arranged to be more or less equal. Their aggressiveness in exploiting their opportunities reflects their degree of interest in the issues under consideration. They participate in the choice by emphasizing some values at the expense of others, by proposing alternative actions that seem well designed to achieve important values, and by presenting arguments and evidence that their proposals will produce attractive results that are consistent with common values or represent a fair distribution of costs and benefits. Because the participants expect to encounter others in the process who are more or less equally influential in the final choice, but have different interests and equal capabilities to make arguments, they are motivated to express their position in ways that show sympathy for the interests of the others, and to make truthful statements. Otherwise, their good faith can be questioned and, if it is, some increment of their influence in the final choice will be lost. Moreover, there is enough agreement within the group concerning appropriate values, institutional relationships, and concepts of justice and fairness that nothing offered as a reasonable proposal by one group sounds outrageous or beyond the pale to others. Finally, all parties feel motivated to confront the decision because no parties gain by the continuation of the status quo. (Or if they do, there is enough power among the others to force the other parties to negotiate.) In this situation, satisfactory decisions agreed to by people with different interests and knowledge can ordinarily be made.

To a very great degree, we have designed our governmental institutions to create such processes throughout our political system. The system of representation is designed to give citizens more or less equal, as well as ready, access to political power. The Administrative Procedure Act created highly structured proceedings to prevent agency administrators from ignoring major interests in wielding their substantial discretionary authority.[25] And we continue to tinker with our process of governmental decisionmaking through such things as the Freedom of Information Act, Government in the Sunshine Act, legislation designed to control ex parte communications between regulatory agencies and affected parties, and so on. Not only do we have a commonly shared ideal of an attractive decisionmaking process, then, we have also created laws and institutions which require officials to approach this ideal.

The problem, of course, is that despite our ideals, institutions, and laws, the actual process of decisionmaking rarely comes close to the ideal. The representation of interested parties in a decision is usually far from complete or fair. Similarly, simple busyness, as well as limitations on human cognitive capabilities, routinely frustrate intellectual ambitions for creative and thorough joint analyses of given issues.[26] Finally, and perhaps most important, it is always tempting to behave strategically in the process of discussion and negotiation rather than to enter the process in "good faith." The process can be deliberately biased by ignoring relevant interests or by granting formal rights of participation that are substantively meaningless. Similarly, in discussions, information about important consequences can be withheld or distorted, and preferences can be disguised so that a "fair division" of losses and benefits turns out to be much more favorable to one party's actual interests. Since such ploys are always possible and often occur, it is difficult for any party to enter the process of deliberation and negotiation in good faith. One's sense of competence and worldliness is at stake as well as the actual substantive and procedural stakes that will be affected in the process of choosing. In most actual circumstances, then, the problem for officials is how they should cope with a process that is likely to fall far short of an ideal process. What obligations do they have in confronting this common situation?

Three different standards for officials could be advocated. One standard is that officials should behave as though they were in fact operating within an ideal process. The justification for this standard is the categorical imperative: if officials are unwilling to discipline their own behavior to create a fair process they can hardly expect others to do so, and as a result, all hopes for a fair process will disappear. A second standard of conduct is that officials must manage their own actions in the process to compensate for the apparent weaknesses and injustices of the existing process governing their area of responsibility by deciding issues in ways that would be the result if the process were, in fact, fair and rational. The justification for this standard is that the officials' responsibility to do justice or serve the public interest takes precedence over the obligation to meet *apparent* process obligations where they depart from the basic requirements of an ideal process. A third standard is that officials must work to make the process "fairer." In the short run they must conform to the existing process, but because the current process is deficient, they must try to correct the process by drawing in additional interests, or shaping the process of deliberation in different ways.

In practice, each of these standards presents difficulties. The first standard—to behave as though one were involved in an ideal process regardless of its actual status—seems to me to run the risk of continuing both an unfair process and an unfair result. It is a noble position, but it seems to me to sacrifice too much of the officials' continuing responsibilities to create both fair processes and attractive results. The officials miss an opportunity to restructure the process, to represent unrepresented interests, and to insist on the value of their expertise.

The second standard—operating within the process to insure a result that officials think is just without regard to the rules that would govern their conduct in a fair process—runs the opposite risk. Justice may be done or the public interest served in a particular instance, but only at the price of further weakening the process. Moreover, there is always the chance that the officials' perception of the appropriate outcome is faulty because they do not have the ideal process to instruct them. Thus, they may weaken the process by championing nonexistent interests or by utilizing distorted information without doing any greater justice, or serving the public interest more effectively.

The third standard—making adjustments in the process to bring it closer to the ideal—seems the most attractive of the three. The only problem is that the officials' capacity to affect the process will usually be quite limited. Typically they face procedures built on law, well-defined institutional relationships, and custom. Many other officials and citizens will have important stakes in this process. Often no convenient forum to discuss a change in process will exist, nor will any authority to change the process be available. While this situation does not preclude officials from cumulatively making changes in the process, their term in office is often too short to produce much effect. To be sure, officials may, for some specific choices, be able to improve the typical process. And, of course, the force of this third standard is to oblige them to do so when they can. But still, there will be many situations in which they are more or less powerless to change the process in any significant way, and they will then face a choice between the first two standards.

In making up one's mind about what one owes to the process in a given situation, I would suggest the following principles. First, I think that public officials must accept the notion that the legitimacy of their actions depends crucially (I am tempted to say exclusively) on the extent to which the authorizing process for their actions approximated the ideal decision process. The closer the approximation, the greater the legitimacy. This means that officials have strong obligations to improve the decisionmaking process in their areas of responsibility, and to give great respect to the laws, institutional relationships, and customs that currently structure the process. It also implies that in ignoring or frustrating the process to achieve a specific aim, officials must accept a particularly heavy burden, since in this case the legitimation of their actions will be even weaker than it would have been if they had continued with the unfair but well-established process. Finally, this principle implies that most officials most of the time operate with surprisingly slender degrees of legitimacy. This does not necessarily mean that their actions are unjustified, but one of the conditions that could justify their action is often absent.

Second, as a corollary to the first principle, the officials' obligation to seek legitimacy through a process that approximates the ideal process increases as the action they contemplate becomes more important. An action may be important because it affects many people, produces effects in very sensitive areas, establishes new precedents, or involves some risk, however small, of very large adverse consequences. In effect, some actions require less elaborate procedures because the consent that is required covers a smaller, less important domain.

Third, I think it can be argued that the amount of legitimacy officials must secure through an elaborate process of consultation *diminishes* with the officials' own degree of accountability. If officials can be easily removed from office, they may be able to take greater risks with the legitimating process than they could if they were solidly entrenched. The reason is that removal from office is so thorough a repudiation of the officials' actions that the process cannot only be repaired but strengthened. No permanent damage can be caused by someone who can easily be removed from office. So a civil servant with civil service protection should take fewer risks with the process than a political appointee who serves at the pleasure of an elected chief executive.

Obligations to Friends and Colleagues

The ambiguities of an official's obligation to pursue the public interest and to conform to authorizing processes lead many conscientious officials to seek help and advice about where their duty lies. For such advice, officials are apt to turn to a relatively intimate circle of colleagues and friends. They turn to them partly because they trust their judgment and partly because they need their support. They need the good opinion of friends to comfort them when they are being criticized. And they particularly need the good opinions of colleagues to give them instrumental assistance and assure their future on the job. Moreover, when they turn to this circle of friends and colleagues, officials will find that not only do the intimates give advice, they also impose obligations of their own. The officials find that they owe them something that derives from personal loyalty and shared conceptions of ultimate purposes.[27] Thus, the advice and claims of colleagues and friends will figure quite prominently in the moral environment of a public official.

It is important to recognize that advice and claims from intimates are apt to be very powerful. The obligations are concrete and personal—not abstract. Moreover, they are familiar because they are similar to bonds that spring up in other realms of the official's life and are routinely honored, such as obligations to family and personal friends. Finally, the sanctions that these intimates can impose if they are disappointed, or, in their view, betrayed, are swift, vivid and devastating to a person's conception of himself. Because duties to colleagues and friends are personal, familiar, and effectively guarded by social sanctions, these duties may often be given great prominence by officials.

These observations raise the question of exactly how much prominence should be given to these claims. We can see that they will be psychologically powerful. My view is that while one does owe friends and colleagues personal loyalty, these claims are much less important than the other claims we have discussed, and much less important that most officials make them. My guess is that more officials have been tempted into bad actions by responding to strongly felt obligations to friends and colleagues than by a badly distorted idea of what the public interest requires or a contemptuous attitude toward process.

Public officials owe colleagues and friends two things. First, they owe them notice that in their professional lives they serve their conception of what the public interest and authorizing processes require. They are obliged to do the *public's* business, not that of their friends or their own personal business. The interests and access of friends and colleagues with respect to public decisions must conform to these obligations. Of course, it will be difficult to maintain this distance. It requires an emotional attachment to conceptions of the public interest and authorizing processes that is as strong as an obligation felt to a friend. But I think this is the direction in which moral responsibility runs.

Second, officials owe friends and colleagues consistency in the independent stance they take toward the public interest and authorizing processes. I think this predictability and consistency are often what officials mean when they talk about another official's "integrity." They know where a person stands, understand the individual's reasons, and can trust that person not to change a position capriciously. It is capricious changes rather than disagreements that create a sense of betrayal. And the sense of betrayal is the sin that must be avoided in these intimate relationships. Given the "distance principle" cited above, friends or colleagues cannot reasonably feel betrayed if their interests are not accommodated or their advice not taken. They can feel betrayed only if they could not have guessed at the outset what stance their friend or colleague would take.

So officials owe their colleagues and friends clear signals of how they view obligations to the public interest and authorizing processes in particular circumstances.

Obligations to Oneself

Notice that we have finally returned to the beginning of our inquiry. If obligations to the public interest and to authorizing processes are ambiguous in specific situations; and if friends and colleagues must be held at arm's length by a confidently held view of the duties of office; then, in the end, much depends on the individual official's conscience. Ultimately that individual must develop and remain loyal to a conception of the duties of a particular office, in a particular form of government, at a particular time, for the range of issues that occur. If much depends upon personal conceptions of duty, it is worth noting two troubling elements that insinuate themselves as one privately reflects on where duty and virtue lie. One element is personal ambition. The other is an astonishing capacity for rationalization. The two together are particularly poisonous.

Personal ambition is likely to be a major problem for public officials. After all, one must be more than a little arrogant to presume to govern others. With arrogance often comes ambition. Moreover, since continuing success seems to vindicate past actions, and since officials operating in their morally ambiguous environments often feel an acute need for vindication, officials may have a more than ordinary interest in continuing to be successful. Finally, we often think we see officials acting as though they were primarily interested in keeping their office or aggrandizing themselves rather than doing the right thing. It seems all too frequent that officials will explain inaction in an area where the public interest seems clearly to demand action but a suspect process of authorization prevents it by arguing that they are protecting their capacity to act effectively in other areas. Cynically we suspect the official is merely trying to survive in office. Similarly, active officials may claim that their unwillingness to rely on an elaborate process of consultation was necessary to achieve their purposes. Again, we cynically suspect the officials ignored the process to insure that they might claim credit for the action.

Clearly, selfish motives of public officials create moral difficulties when they guide actions.[28] That is particularly true in cases where simple stealing or deliberate deceptions of the public are involved. But I would argue that the desire to retain an office or to seek personal glory are hardly the worst sins of a public official. In fact, in our system of government, personal ambition is a key ingredient. We harness personal ambition to public purposes by forcing officials to be accountable. The best way for officials to stay in office and be praised is to meet their obligations to the public as they understand them. Note that because the system is designed in this way, the issue of whether public officials are acting out of self-serving or public-serving motives will always be obscure. When officials act on a policy, neither they nor we can be sure exactly what their motives are. If the action is well conceived and consistent with our aspirations, it will always be possible to see a self-serving as well as a public-serving motive. Perhaps the fact that we have designed the system in this way is part of the reason it is easy to become cynical about the motives of public officials: both self-serving and public-serving motives can always be inferred. Perhaps we err, then, and overestimate the importance of personal ambition as a threat to the moral stature of public officials.

Still, conscientious officials should determine how significant personal ambition is in guiding their actions. Fortunately, there are two rather simple tests they can apply. The first is to ask themselves whether they would be willing to be replaced in office by someone who shares the same values with respect to both outcomes and processes. Of course, it will always be easy to exaggerate the importance of modest differences in the stance of the proposed replacement in comparison with one's own stance. But if officials find themselves reluctant to leave office, or exaggerating small differences as they contemplate the imagined change, they should begin to be suspicious that personal ambitions and interests might be carrying too much weight in their actions.

The second test is particularly appropriate where officials seem to be sacrificing important values in one area because they believe they can make contributions in others. This situation often arises when officials feel particularly constrained by ties of personal loyalty to colleagues, and feel those with whom they serve are honorable despite their actions in given areas, but worry that their desire to stay in office is what is really influencing their willingness to continue in a job when important values are being sacrificed. The simple test here is simply to establish an arbitrary deadline in the future for reappraisal. If by that time the official has not been able to take actions that *advanced* important values, the apparent justification for "going along" can be readily seen as a rationalization and the official should leave office.[29]

In my view, the capacity for rationalization is a far greater enemy than personal ambition. It is a greater problem because the errors one can make if one allows this capacity full sway are much greater, and because it is much harder to see when it is operating on one's conception of duty. The only device that can protect one against rationalizations is a rather thoroughgoing, relentless skepticism about one's own conceptions, and enough time to become settled on a view that withstands this skepticism. Of course, one cannot take this time and effort with every action, but one should do it with *some*.

To the extent that the observations made in this essay will assist officials in rooting out rationalization and leaving only real justification for their actions, I will feel that I have accomplished a useful purpose. But I worry that I may only facilitate rationalization. And that is how skepticism works.

NOTES

[1]See *The Federalist* (New York: Heritage Press, 1945), in particular, no 51. "If men were angels, no government would be necessary. If angels were to govern men, neither external nor internal controls would be necessary. In forming a government which is to be administered by men over men, the great difficulty lies in this: you must first enable the government to control the governed; and in the next place oblige it to control itself."

[2]For an example of this kind of activity see Philip B. Heymann and others, *The Federal Trade Commission: A Failing Agency*, Kennedy School of Government Case *C14-76-119*, Harvard University.

[3]The establishment of a separate cabinet level Department of Education is probably the most dramatic recent example of a shift in organizational structure that left the executive branch more vulnerable to influence by a narrowly interested professional group. For a general discussion of how structure affects the distribution of power, see Harold Seidman, *Politics, Position and Power* (New York: Oxford University Press, 1970).

[4]See the following cases: Mark H. Moore and others, *Methadone Maintenance (A) and (B)*, Kennedy School of Government Case *C94-77-065*; Philip B. Heymann and others, *The Bureau of Security and Consular Affairs*, Kennedy School of Government Case *C14-75-003*; and Joseph Bower and others, *William D. Ruckleshaus and the Environmental Protection Agency*, Kennedy School of Government Case *C16-74-028*.

[5]A standard current complaint of public officials is that goals of legislation are left hopelessly vague, even contradictory, to allow passage in the legislature, and then turned over to officials to administer. The ambiguity and conflicts in the statutes then provide ample cause for interested parties to sue the government no matter what action an official takes, and the management of the program ends up in court. The court, in turn, tries to discern Congress's real intent by examining the legislative history. It also checks on the adequacy of the procedures an official used to reach a particular decision. It is a very clumsy process that puts officials in a difficult and ultimately hopeless position: they can work very hard in setting up a process and making a choice, but they have little reason to believe that their decision will be accepted as legitimate, final, and binding.

[6]There are notorious cases of these in the literature on federal program implementation. See in particular Jeffrey Pressman and Aaron Wildavsky, *Implementation* (Berkeley: University of California Press, 1973).

[7]Moore, *Methadone Maintenance (A) and (B)* (Case C94-77-065).

[8]Nicholas Kotz, *Let Them Eat Promises: The Politics of Hunger in America* (Englewood, N.J.: Prentice-Hall, 1969).

[9]Private correspondence with an official whose pseudonym is David Goldman.

[10]Heymann, *The Federal Trade Commission* (Case C14-76-119).

[11]For a discussion of the relationship between the extent of one's responsibilities and one's capacity to act see Charles Fried's concept of the "realm of efficacious action," in Charles Fried, *Right and Wrong* (Cambridge, Mass.: Harvard University Press, 1978), pp. 24–28.

[12]This statement reveals a commitment to utilitarianism, since it suggests that a necessary if not sufficient condition for moral action is that one be aware of the consequences of one's action. A nonutilitarian, of course, could argue that the rightness of an action depended not at all on the consequences of the act, but only on the character of the action.

[13]Again, throughout this discussion I am aware that I am revealing a strong utilitarian bias.

[14]For a more complete argument on this point see Mark H. Moore, "Statesmanship in a World of Particular Substantive Choice," in Robert A. Goldwin, ed., *Bureaucrats, Policy Analysts, Statesmen: Who Leads?* (Washington, D.C.: American Enterprise Institute, 1980).

[15]For an admirably clear discussion of the role of uncertainty in choices see Howard Raiffa, *Decision Analysis* (Reading, Mass.: Addison-Wesley, 1968). The fact of uncertainty in choices has important but as yet unstated implications for exactly how social science findings should be used in policy deliberations.

[16]For a useful introductory discussion of these principles see Edith Stokey and Richard Zeckhauser, *A Primer for Policy Analysis* (New York: Norton, 1978), chap. 13.

[17]Ibid., p. 279.

[18]John Rawls, *A Theory of Justice* (Cambridge, Mass.: Harvard University Press, 1971).

[19]Robert Nozick, *Anarchy, State and Utopia* (New York: Basic Books, 1974).

[20]Rawls, *A Theory of Justice.*

[21]On the concept of prima facie duties see R.M. Hare, *The Right and the Good* (Oxford, Eng.: Oxford University Press, 1973).

[22]For an extended utilitarian justification for consultative processes see Charles E. Lindblom, *The Intelligence of Democracy* (New York: Free Press, 1965).

[23]Ibid.

[24]For a discussion of the important role that "due process" plays in facilitating implementation of choices see Roger B. Porter, *Presidential Decision Making: The Economic Policy Board*, chaps. 7, 8 (New York: Cambridge University Press, 1980).

[25]For an excellent discussion of this important statute see Richard B. Stewart, "The Reformation of American Administrative Law," *Harvard Law Review*, vol. 88, no. 8 (June 1975).

[26]For a stimulating discussion of the limits of individual cognitive capacities and the implications for policy deliberations see John D. Steinbruner, *The Cybernetic Theory of Decision* (Princeton: Princeton University Press, 1974).

[27]For an illuminating discussion of this subject in a different context see Michael Walzer, *Obligations: Essays on Disobedience, War, and Citizenship* (Cambridge, Mass.: Harvard University Press, 1970), chap. 9.

[28]For a discussion of this problem see Joel Fleishman's essay in this volume.

[29]I am indebted to Jonathan Moore for this idea.

II

Corruption and Whistle-Blowing in Planning Organizations

6

Corruption and Reform in Land-Use and Building Regulation: Incentives and Disincentives

John A. Gardiner

A survey of American newspapers over the period 1970–1976 identified at least 372 incidents of corruption involving local government officials.[1] The largest number of incidents, 112, concerned government contracting—the purchasing of supplies or professional services, or the construction of highways and public buildings. The second largest group, 83 cases, concerned land use—the approval of subdivision plans, zoning variances, building permits, and so forth. Reported incidents ranged from giving a clerk $10 or $20 to expedite the processing of an application, to giving building inspectors $50 to overlook code violations, to $50,000 and up for approval of zoning changes and subdivision plans (Gardiner and Lyman, 1978: 6–8).

A variety of opportunities for corruption are built into land-use and building regulatory systems. Planning and zoning commissioners must decide which of many possible land uses are in the best interest of the community; specific building and site plans must be reviewed; building inspectors must decide whether code violations require redesign or reconstruction, and so forth.

The fact that our land-use and building systems involve many discretionary decisions does not, however, necessarily mean that these decisions will be made corruptly. Journalistic accounts tend to provide localized or ad hominem explanations for the occurrence of corruption in specific cases—"Smith got in with a bad crowd," "The agency was understaffed," or "There was just too much money riding on this decision." While such factors may help to explain why *these* individuals became involved in corruption in *these* cities at *these* points in time, they do little to help us develop a general understanding of the nature of corruption or to provide a theoretical basis for changes which might reduce the frequency or impact of corruption. The basic assumption of this article is that participation in corruption by officials and the persons and businesses they regulate can be understood in terms of the *opportunities* which are available for corruption and *incentives* to take advantage of those opportunities.

Opportunities for Corruption

Corruption can *only* occur when an official has an opportunity to use his or her authority in a way which would lead someone to want to pay for favorable treatment. However, some decisions made in land-use and building regulation are more attractive than others as opportunities for corruption. Recognizing that attractiveness is both objective and subjective in nature (some officials may perceive opportunities which others never thought existed), we might expect that attractiveness would be affected by (1) the visibility of the decision, (2) the decision's congruence with other community policies, (3) the number of officials involved in the decision, (4) who takes the initiative in corruption negotiations, (5) the impact of the decision on the applicant's activities, and (6) relationships between this decision and past and future activities (see Rose-Ackerman, 1978).

Visibility of the Decision

Regulatory decisions are made in varying settings, are accompanied by varying levels of documentation, and are varyingly preceded or followed by reviews by other officials. In the simplest case, an inspector visits a construction site or apartment building. In the presence of the contractor or landlord, the inspector decides whether or not to cite code violations. Like the policeman who decides not to ticket the speeding motorist or arrest the streetcorner numbers runner, the inspector who takes no action has left no trace of his inaction. Some agencies may not even keep records of which inspectors were instructed to visit a site. In some situations, however, evidence of a citable violation remains; while no one except an eyewitness could prove that the inspector observed a traffic or safety violation, the use of substandard materials or deviations from approved blueprints could be checked for years afterward.

In contrast with the on-site, low-visibility decision making of the inspectors, land-use regulation (for example, master plans, subdivision proposals, or applications for variances) usually involves group decisions in public settings on the basis of written applications. The applicant's plans will be reviewed by city employees, discussed by the zoning commission, and then voted upon by the city council. While this procedure usually makes it possible to determine *who* has decided *what*, visibility may still be limited. Applications may be sketchy regarding the materials and procedures to be used in construction. Commission and council proceedings may not be transcribed, and individual votes may not be recorded. Even where advertised, hearings may be poorly attended by the public. Standard operating procedures may not require written evaluation of an application by the planning staff or the zoning commission. Finally, even where proceedings are open and records are kept, there may be no official standards against which an inquisitive public might evaluate decisions made; if a zoning ordinance simply states that a parcel of land should be developed for "residential" purposes, a pro-developer decision by the city council will be less suspicious than in situations where ordinances spell out limits on housing densities, acceptable levels of impact on surrounding area or public facilities, the contributions which must be made by the developers, and so on.

While not part of the regulatory decision itself, we should also note that the form of payoff used can influence its after-the-fact visibility. Corruption is easier to prove when payments are made by check rather than cash; it is also easier to link to the decision direct payments to the officials on the day the decision is made than campaign contributions, legal retainers, or commissions to brokers months later. Even less attributable to specific decisions are the Christmas presents and gratuities which are common in many cities.

As these illustrations indicate, the visibility of regulatory decision and the subsequent possibility that corruption can be proven will vary according to the setting in which the decision is made (for example, on-site vs. formal meetings), the "paper trail" which is left concerning both the proposed activity and its assessment by the regulator(s), and the likelihood that others will review the decision (see below). Presumably, an opportunity for corruption which has maximum visibility would be less attractive than one where no one can or is likely to detect misfeasance. This proposition can be summarized as follows: *The attractiveness of an opportunity for corruption declines as its visibility increases.*

Congruence with Community Policies

Transactions involving corruption range from violations of clear legal requirements, to "judgment calls" where officials are authorized to exercise their discretion, to totally legal decisions where applicants were simply seeking to guarantee speedy decisions or a minimum of "nitpicking." Why might congruence with city policies make some decisions more attractive opportunities for corruption? In part this may be just another aspect of the visibility factor: deviations from clear policies are more likely to raise questions than judgment calls or expedited decisions on legitimate applications. It may also relate to officials' identification with the policies which they are charged with implementing; taking money for approval of a legitimate or discretionary decision will be less likely to test their loyalties than participating in an activity clearly disapproved by the community. (This issue will be considered more fully in later discussions of official incentives to participate in corruption.) Finally, Susan Rose-Ackerman (1978: Chapter Six) notes that where community goals are vague, mutually inconsistent, or nonexistent, a bribe offer may constitute the only basis which a regulator can find for his decision. In any event, we can summarize this proposition as follows: *The attractiveness of an opportunity for corruption increases with its congruence with city policies.*

The Number of Officials Involved

Land-use and building regulation decisions involve varying numbers of officials. In the simplest case, a single inspector visits a construction site or home and cites or does not cite a code violation. In a second set of cases, the decision involves a sequence of reviews; a subdivision proposal, for example, will be reviewed by the planning staff, then the zoning commission, then the city council. In a third set of cases, several officials or agencies share jurisdiction; construction might be stopped by building, electrical, plumbing, or fire inspectors, by the police, and so on; a home or apartment might be declared uninhabitable by the housing or fire or health inspectors. These three basic situations can be further subdivided in several ways: is there a single official who must concur in an action, or can the applicant "shop around" among a group of officials (for example, inspectors or plans examiners), any one of whom can provide the necessary approval? Is an appeal mechanism available to challenge the first decision (can the applicant go to the head of the buildings department, to the courts, to the prosecutor or other city officials)? Where an appeal mechanism exists, are its policies and procedures so hostile or costly as to be prohibitive?

This classification scheme has thus far been confined to official organization charts and allocations of authority. In some cities, however, control over decisions may be informally dispersed even further (Smith won't act until Jones and Brown agree) or centralized. In Chicago, for example, it is frequently alleged that all city bureaucracies will defer to an alderman's decision on a project affecting his ward. In Long Beach, California, architects came to the conclusion that no project would gain the approval of the Planning Commission without the approval of its director. "If you wished to have a project developed in Long Beach, you had to have his approval or you got no further . . . The planning director had assumed over the years a posture where his recommendations were couched virtually as a fiat to the commission," one architect told a grand jury (Morris, 1976).

How do these variations in the number of officials involved in regulatory decision making affect opportunities for corruption? At a minimum, they determine which officials are important enough to be worth corrupting if the city council regularly ignores zoning recommendations of the planning staff, there would be no reason to deal with the subordinates. If the building official can't (or won't) overrule the inspectors in his department, however, then the lowest level official is the one with whom the applicant must come to terms. Where authority is in fact shared (either sequentially or among agencies with overlapping jurisdictions), applicants must satisfy all of them or run the risk that one will jeopardize an accommodation reached with another agency or official. From the point of view of an official, the fact that other officials can or will become involved in a decision will raise the possibility that an honest official will question his decision or that a corrupt official will insist on a share of the bribe. As result, we might conclude that: *Increasing the number of officials actually or potentially involved in decision making both increases the number who may wish to share in corruption and increases the danger that any one may "blow the whistle."*

Who Initiates Negotiations?

In some cities, it appears that applicants initiate the discussion of payoffs; in other cities, however, officials spell out the rules of the game: "You know how the buildings department works, don't you," a New York clerk asked an architect who sought to bypass professional expediters; elsewhere, officials came to the applicants, indicating "what it would take to avoid problems." In a third set of cities, the process has become so routinized that—if you can believe those who were willing to talk—neither party even mentions the $20 included with the application or the case of scotch which "appeared" in the inspector's car.

We need not attempt to make judgments—indeed the evidence in these cases is usually so sketchy and self-serving that it would be foolish to attempt them—about which participants were telling the truth about the initiation of corruption negotiations. We might guess, however, that the locus of initiation might affect the attractiveness of a corruption opportunity: assuming that a participant has an incentive to engage in corruption, the opportunity will be more attractive if the other party suggests it. (If he has no incentive to participate, or feels that he can attain his goal without participating, he would still not participate no matter how attractive the opportunity qua opportunity.) This seems paradoxical: why would you want someone else to get you involved in criminal activity? If this speculation is correct, there may be several explanations. First, you would then be able to claim, if an investigation ensued, that you were the victim of official extortion or, if you are the official, that the applicant "forced" the bribe on you. Second, because the other party took the lead, he will be precluded from backing out, blowing the whistle, or otherwise endangering the transaction; a willing collaborator is a less dangerous partner than someone you have coerced. Third, particularly if the other party is experienced in consummating corrupt transactions, you can transfer to him much of the labor and risk involved in covering your tracks. Finally, as was indicated in discussing the importance of congruence with community policies, the fact that the other party suggested the deal may be psychologically reassuring, allowing you to retain the belief that you are a "good guy" even if you are momentarily doing business with a "bad buy."

While no data is available to test this proposition, we might venture the guess that: *Opportunities for corruption are more attractive when the other party initiates negotiations.*

Impact on Applicants' Activities

Regulatory decisions affect development and property management in different ways. Some decisions are essential preconditions to private sector activity while others pose only a threat of interruption of ongoing activities. Construction requires the approval of plans and building permits; building utilization requires a certificate of occupancy. While construction or building occupancy is underway, by comparison, regulatory decisions are reactive; unless regulators learn of a problem and choose to take action, the applicants may proceed about their business. (If an inspector orders construction or occupancy to cease, however, activity will once again require an affirmative regulatory decision.)

Why would this factor of proactive vs. reactive regulation affect opportunities for corruption? Below, I will discuss the obvious point that applicants will have a strong incentive to bribe where official endorsement is a precondition to their activities; at this point, I might simply note that every administrative requirement which has this effect will create an opportunity for corruption to occur. Thus, we might conclude: *Opportunities for corruption will be increased by any legal or administrative requirement which is a precondition to private sector activity.*

Impact of Past and Future Activities

Some encounters between applicants and regulators can be treated as single events: Once a decision has been made, either honestly or corruptly, the parties will never see each other again. Other encounters, however, are only part of a chain of events which began in the past or will continue in the future. The applicant for rezoning must return for building permits and certificates of occupancy; the contractor or landlord has seen before or will see the inspector at a later date, on other sites, for example. In these latter situations, participants may have to consider the impact of behavior in this transaction on other transactions. If a developer offers a bribe today, will he (a) be guaranteed smooth sailing throughout the development process, (b) have to pay off every regulator encountered during development, or (c) be forever barred from working in the city because it proved highly sensitive to integrity issues? If he refuses to pay off, will he be closely scrutinized and stalled by other officials? Conversely, if he has paid off in the past, will he be bound to pay every time he returns, precluded by his past actions from "blowing the whistle" when the price gets too high? We might expect that anticipated continuing relationships will generate more frequent opportunities for corruption. Beyond the simple numerical increase in transactions, ongoing relationships may involve increased perceptions of mutual dependence ("we're in this together") and increased understanding of the other's dependability ("I know that I can count on Smith, but I've never met Jones before"). In any event, we might say: *Opportunities for corruption will be increased where applicants and regulators participate in an ongoing relationship.*

Conclusion

The local systems which have been established to regulate land use, construction, and building quality involve thousands of applicants and officials, and hundreds of thousands of regulatory decisions each year. While each of these decisions could serve as an opportunity for corruption, they vary in ways which influence their attractiveness to participants. Opportunities for corruption will be more attractive when they are less visible to outsiders, when they involve actions congruent with community policies, when few officials are involved, when the other participant initiates discussion of payoffs, when the decision is essential to the applicant's activities, and when past or future activities are related to the present opportunity. We turn now to an analysis of the incentives which might cause applicants and officials to act honestly or corruptly vis-à-vis specific opportunities.

Incentives for Corruption

Assuming that an opportunity for corruption has arisen, how would it be perceived by officials and applicants (the developers, builders, and landlords affected by regulation)? When would they decide to act corruptly rather than to comply with official rules and procedures? Before analyzing these issues, I must note that I do not assume that officials and applicants are either more or less virtuous than others in American society; as Pogo observed in the 1950s, "I have met the enemy and he is us." Furthermore, I am not assuming that each opportunity for corruption will undergo a detailed assessment—in many if not most situations, individual yes/no decisions reflect the results of years of confronting similar issues.

Applicants' Perspectives

An opportunity to buy one's way out of regulatory requirements will mean different things to different applicants. In some cases, the regulator's decision is essential[2] to the applicant's business (a negative decision can put the applicant out of business or prevent him/her from ever entering the business), while in other cases the decision "only" affects profit margins. If the applicant has already invested in land or equipment, a payoff may be the only way to retrieve sunk costs. More broadly, we must note that the profitability of a new development or an existing building is affected by a number of factors including tax laws, interest rates, market conditions (demand for new housing or commercial space, vacancy rates in existing structures), alternative uses available for capital or other resources, land prices, and construction and/or maintenance costs. Depending on time and place, some of these profit factors are stable while others are fluctuating, some are predictable while others can only be guessed. Finally, some decisions regarding development can be made at leisure while others must be made rapidly (as when a desirable site comes on the market, or costly capital or other resources must be financed whether utilized or not).

Regulatory decisions and the possibility of having to participate in corruption to secure them thus vary in their significance to applicants. Some decisions will determine whether an applicant can engage in his business; some will make a great difference in the profitability of a transaction; some will mean only a minor increase or decrease in profits. My first prediction about incentives for corruption, therefore, is: *Applicants' incentives to comply with official requirements, either corrupt or honest, will increase with the importance of regulatory decisions to their activities.*

Other issues affecting an applicant's calculation of incentives and disincentives might be summarized as follows:

1. Will differences between compliance costs (the costs of complying with official policies and procedures) and bribe costs put the applicant at a *competitive disadvantage*? If all competitors in the same market are treated equally (honestly or corruptly), the applicant will be ambivalent about corruption, but he will prefer corruption if it will put him at an equal or superior marketing position (e.g., if it allows him to construct buildings at a lower cost than can his competitors, and buyers are unaware of or uninterested in the code violations).

2. Is this contact with the regulator part of a *continuing relationship* or is this likely to be the only contact? If you are likely to maintain continuous contact, you will want to satisfy the regulator's demands (whether for compliance or for bribes); if this will be the sole contact, you will simply seek the least cost resolution of the interaction. Extended contact can also convert an official relationship into a personal one ("Bill has helped me out in the past, so I'll cut him in on this deal").

3. Do the *community and the industry* (the planning society, engineers in the county, the trade unions) have norms about corruption? Does the applicant consider himself to be part of the community or industry or an outsider? If the applicant violates those norms, will the violation be punished? (N.B., these norms may encourage or condemn corruption, but we must first ask whether they exist and are enforced by any significant sanctions.)

4. Does the applicant have any *personal or organizational norms* regarding corruption? Some people and some organizations have clearly defined ethical definitions of what behaviors are and are not morally acceptable, while others are vague on these questions. Even if the individual's preferred behavior is clear, he may separate his personal code from his business code: "I know this is wrong, but that's how you do business here— you pay off or get out." While I cannot say precisely how people would weigh moral losses against financial gains, we must at least note that many people do not perceive payoffs (or at least gifts and expediting fees) to involve moral issues.[3]

Out of these complex calculations, applicants can form, with varying degrees of accuracy (i.e., reliable information about present and future events) and clarity (resolution of relevant ambiguities), perceptions of his or her incentives and disincentives to engage in a specific act of corruption. As indicated, the calculations may intermingle normative and economic factors; personal, group, and community value systems; and short-, mid-, and long-term perspectives. But however their calculations are made, we might conclude that *an applicant will have an incentive to engage in corruption when the perceived benefits of corruption, less its costs, exceed the perceived benefits of legitimate (noncorrupt) activities, less their costs.* Developers can estimate the profitability of land uses which planning commissions would accept with and without bribes, builders can estimate the construction costs of complying and not complying with codes, and so forth.[4] Ultimately, I would argue that the frequency of corruption in a regulatory system is a function of the ratio between the costs and benefits of corruption and the costs and benefits of legitimate behavior: when corruption promises large benefits and few costs, and there are few legitimate alternatives, there will be substantial corruption; where legitimate activities are rewarding and corruption hazardous, corruption will be infrequent.

Officials' Perspectives

Like the applicants, we might expect that officials involved in land-use and building regulation will have an incentive to engage in corruption when its net benefits exceed those which might be expected from legitimate activities. Like the applicants, the officials will have received "messages" from their peers, fellow residents, superiors, and so forth as to the behaviors which are labeled corruption and as to whether rewards will follow from compliance with these messages. We can not be certain, however, that officials have received *consistent* messages, or that messages regarding corruption are the only factors which will influence their actions.

Instead of a simple model which assumes that officials' behavior will be influenced only by organizational and community norms concerning corruption and integrity, we must envision multiple norm systems which may generate consistent or inconsistent pressures upon officials. To illustrate the cross-pressures which might be felt by regulatory officials, let us focus on relationships with the development and housing industry, with the political process, and with other members of the regulatory system.

Land development and building management are multibillion dollar industries, the profitability of which may be affected by the standards imposed by the regulatory system. While there are numerous instances of conflict between officials and applicants, they are in many ways partners in the real estate industry. Officials become familiar with the economics and technological capabilities of the industry and know the impact of regulations on developers' and landlords' operations. They are also sensitive to community land-use goals, for example, to build as rapidly as possible or to accept only a certain type of growth, to close down substandard housing or to keep as much housing as possible open to low-income residents. While they know that they *can* enforce the rules, they also know that some enforcement decisions will have the effect of putting applicants out of business or of leaving the intended beneficiaries of the system, for example, home buyers and tenants, in worse shape than they were before. These personal relationships may pull regulators in divergent directions: to the extent that inspectors empathize with tenants, they may well want to improve their living conditions by forcing landlords to make repairs, yet will hesitate to "push them over the brink" to abandon the building, leaving the tenants out on the street. To the extent that they empathize with landlords (recognizing their narrow profit margins or regarding the tenants as "animals"), they will want to give them as long as possible to remedy code violations. In some cities tenants or landlords may be well-organized and have the political "clout" necessary to influence enforcement policies. Finally, the mere fact that regulators will encounter tenants, landlords, or developers at a later date will make them less willing to stimulate their hostility. As a result, it is not surprising that many will feel that "bending the rules" is a worthwhile tradeoff in order to "get the job done" under impossible circumstances and may be necessary simply to survive on the job.

There is also a substantial overlap between the interests of regulators and the interests of local political officials. In some cities, the content of regulatory policies is matter of open community conflict, e.g., in battles between "no-growth" and "slow-growth" advocates. The overlap also carries over into staffing and decision making; positions on planning and zoning commissions frequently are given to campaign backers of mayors and councilmen. Campaign contributors expect a favorable hearing when they seek approval for variances or new developments. For officials, then, the regulatory system may provide opportunities for patronage, in the form of either jobs or decisions, which will help to keep contributions of both labor and funds flowing into their organizations.

Finally, "official" norms concerning both regulatory policies and integrity policies can be tempered by repeated interactions among regulators. Some officials have been neighbors, social acquaintances, or political allies for years before they became fellow regulators; others become close friends in the course of official collaboration. These contacts generate both organizational norms—this is the way we do things here—and mutual obligation—we're in this together. The content of organizational norms can vary from intensive reinforcement of official policies ("The community has given us an important responsibility and we've got to show that we can do the job") to legitimation of self-serving activities ("Nobody gives a damn about our work, so let's look out for ourselves"). To the extent that these norms and interactions develop, however, they tend to constrain individuals' actions: the incipient rotten apple will be less likely to capitalize on an opportunity for corruption if he senses that his colleagues will condemn him, while the individually honest official will hesitate to blow the whistle on widespread corruption in his organization. Where corruption is widely encouraged or condoned, individuals may even find it difficult to avoid becoming involved, as nonparticipation becomes ridiculed or punished by peers.

Without attitudinal data on members of communities, industries, and organizations, it is difficult to determine whether the individual officials who participate in corruption are acting in accordance with or contrary to the prevailing norms concerning corruption, or the relative intensity of integrity and other community policies; we might predict that intense support for integrity would predominate over moderate emphasis on alternative, conflicting goals ("keep development moving," "don't put poor tenants out on the streets," "don't rat on another inspector"), but that intense support for these other goals would outweigh casually articulated integrity norms. Therefore: *Officials' incentives to participate in corruption will be increased by community or organizational norms which emphasize policies which conflict with "official" policies or which do not emphasize integrity.*

In addition to the role of personal, organizational, and community norms, two characteristics of land-use and building regulation systems appear to be particularly relevant to the creation of opportunities and incentives for corruption. The first concerns the policies that officials are authorized to enforce: some regulations are very explicit—this land will be used only for single-family homes; all foundations must have six inches of concrete over eight inches of gravel—while others leave officials a great deal of discretion—land should be developed in ways which serve the public interest, apartments must be safe and clean, and so forth. Where the policies to be implemented are unambiguous, as noted above, deviations will be more visible and thus less attractive as opportunities for corruption.

The second characteristic of regulatory systems concerns agency structures and decision-making processes (see Rose-Ackerman, 1978: Chapters Seven and Eight). Is the official acting alone or as part of a group? Is his decision final or must it be ratified by superiors? Does the official have a monopoly on authority to grant or withhold approval, or can the applicant turn elsewhere? Earlier, it was predicted that an official who could act on his own would have more opportunities for corruption than one who worked in a group or needed a superior's approval. The following two factors may also work to increase officials' incentives to take advantage of opportunities. First, if the applicant is seeking *legal* ends and bribes are being sought to expedite action, corruption would be reduced if other officials are available to issue the necessary approvals. If the applicant is seeking *illegal* ends, however, corruption might be reduced by increasing requirements for approval of officials' decisions by supervisors or by other agencies. (If they also were corrupt, however, the review mechanisms would only serve to increase the extent and costs of bribes.)

I hypothesized at the outset of this analysis that officials might estimate the attractiveness of corruption by comparing the benefits of corruption, less its costs, with the benefits to be gained from noncorrupt performance of official duties, less its costs. It must be noted that there are great variations in the job security and pay scales of regulatory officials in different cities. There are also variations among officials: while city councilmen and zoning commissioners act in more visible settings, they do not have supervisors reviewing their decisions and can only be removed by local voters; inspectors and plan examiners, on the other hand, frequently have civil service job security but are more routinely supervised. Finally, the two types of officials vary in their exposure to the threat of prosecution: corruption laws tend to be more explicit about bureaucrats' violations of existing laws than about corruption in the legislative process. (However, prosecutors *may* be more interested in catching a "big fish" city official than "small fry" bureaucrats.)

In the analysis of applicants' incentives to participate in corruption, I noted the combined importance of probabilities of detection and the scale of likely punishment in determining the risks or costs of corruption. Officials would similarly need to assess local detection mechanisms—are supervisor, prosecutors, or watchdog groups regularly reviewing official decisions to identify questionable acts—and the sanctions which are imposed upon exposed officials. Will they lose their jobs? Will they be barred from future professional activities? Will fines or jail sentences exceed expected bribes? Summarizing these factors, we might predict that: *Officials' incentives to engage in corruption will be increased by structures which increase their independent authority, which provide vague decision rules, or which pose minimal risks through limited detection capabilities or light sanction policies.*

Implications for Corruption Control

This analysis of patterns of corruption in land-use regulation suggests that while individual wrongdoers can be found in many settings, the probability of corruption will be increased where there are incentives for applicants to evade regulations, where officials have incentives and opportunities to make decisions favoring interests, and, where, for both applicants and officials, the benefits of corruption less its costs exceed the benefits of noncorrupt behavior less its costs. Accordingly, strategies to prevent or reduce corruption must reduce incentives and opportunities for corrupt behavior and the costs of noncorrupt behavior, and increase incentives and opportunities for noncorrupt behavior and the costs of corrupt behavior. Because of the complexity of the corruption problem, a variety of control strategies must be considered, each of which addresses opportunities and incentives in different ways.

Before describing these control strategies, however, I must note that several factors will affect the design and implementation of programs to alter incentives and opportunities for corruption.

First, for both regulators and regulated industries, "corruption" and "integrity" rarely surface as discrete policy choices, but more frequently are minor parts of more complex decisions. For developers tax and interest rates, alternate investment opportunites, and so forth, create an economic framework within which payoffs may be only minor offsets to large profits. Similarly, peer pressures within regulatory agencies create social relationships and work patterns which may encourage or condone payoffs. Under these conditions, even greatly increased prointegrity influences or costs of corruption may fail to change individuals' orientations.

Second, in many communities and organizations, corruption and integrity are *not* issues of high visibility and salience. Except in those situations where revelations have produced "scandals," citizens, officials, and regulators, are usually thinking about other issues. (Where scandals *have* surfaced, however, public officials usually find that high investments in fighting corruption—or at least in appearing to do so—are essential for political survival.) In the absence of scandal, proposals to prevent corruption are viewed in terms of their impact on other policy goals and priorities: Will stricter enforcement practices attract or repel potential developers (who might bring higher land values or lower tax rates to the community), upgrade existing properties or just put slum dwellers out on the street? Will conflict-of-interest regulations keep otherwise valuable job applicants from accepting regulatory positions? Will time and material investments in monitoring integrity jeopardize "getting the job done"? To the extent that officials who wish to implement anticorruption programs must also consider these other issues, they will be less free to expend resources on integrity goals. In general, officials should be willing to "invest" in controlling corruption amounts equal to the damage which corruption can do to the organization, although in practice it is difficult to estimate either the costs of control strategies or the organizational costs of corruption.

Third, many factors which create opportunities or incentives for corruption are beyond the control of individuals or groups seeking to control corruption. Changes in local or national economies will affect building markets, tax and interest rates, and the structure of competition in the development, construction, and building management industries. The local tax base and tax rates affect city land-use policies and the pay scales which might attract city employees. Personnel practices, whether stressing patronage appointment of political supporters or "merit" appointment through civil service examinations, influence the types of individuals assigned to regulatory positions and how closely supervisors can control them. A reform-minded head of the building department may have to work with policies set by the personnel and finance departments. Zoning decisions may be made by officials answerable only to the electorate. Civil service laws and the statutes governing both corruption and land-use regulation are often set at the state level, and prosecutors and judges are rarely under the control of local officials. These factors will affect opportunities and incentives for corruption, yet are unlikely to respond to the types of programs which can be implemented at the local level.

Fourth, the corruption I have discussed involves many different types of acts and actors, including $10 payoffs to building inspectors on code violations, and $50,000 payoffs to city councilmen on zoning changes. Some participants may participate in only one transaction while others may engage in corruption routinely over a period of years. It is likely that policies to prevent a single large payoff ($50,000 on a rezoning case) would differ from those aimed at recurring small payoffs ($10 to the building department clerk or inspector). And perhaps nothing can be done to wipe out all small single transactions; to the extent that the participants in these transactions are amateurs in corruption, however, they may respond best to the deterrence policies described below.

Within the limits set by these factors, several strategies can be used to reduce opportunities and incentives for corruption. Some strategies confront corruption directly by increasing supervision over decision making and penalties imposed on wrongdoers; others operate indirectly, providing incentives to perform tasks properly by withdrawing the anticipated benefits of corruption or simply by increasing the visibility of government activities. The direct strategies may be most appropriate for dealing with specific and known targets, while the indirect strategies will affect broad audiences, only some of whom may be likely participants in corruption. Somewhat arbitrarily, since their effects will overlap, these strategies are discussed under the headings of reducing opportunities for corruption, increasing the costs of corruption, and reinforcing expectations of integrity.

Reducing Opportunities for Corruption

In most forms of crime, it is easier to take small sums of money than large sums; possessors of large sums of money usually have the foresight and resources to guard their assets closely. In land-use and building regulation, the opposite situation exists: the building code decisions which generate small-scale payoffs are tightly structured while the planning and zoning decisions which are worth thousands or millions of dollars rest on discretionary judgments about the "public interest." Building inspectors and office clerks are likely to be recruited and supervised through civil service systems, but planning and zoning commissioners are usually appointed on a part-time basis by the city council, and the councillors who react to their recommendations are directly chosen by the electorate.

Where regulatory systems are used to achieve land-use and building goals, opportunities for corruption can be reduced through procedures which make the process and content of decisionmaking more visible. Policymakers can rarely spell out all of the factors to be considered in development, construction, and housing decisions. Yet, clear policy goals will tell implementing officials what they should be doing and will identify deviant actions which might involve corruption. On the other hand, policies that are too complex (or even self-contradictory) will force officials to negotiate compromises, providing opportunities for corruption. Official discretion, in other words, is a two-edged sword; it provides both working space for officials to adapt policy goals to specific situations and room for officials and applicants to negotiate corrupt compromises. The best arrangement, of course, would balance clarity of policies with freedom to develop consistent applications of those policies in specific cases.

Similarly, regulatory procedures can be modified to raise the visibility of decision making. Some conflicts over planning goals are aired through extensive and well-attended public meetings. When applications for land-use changes must include data related to specified decision criteria (housing density, access to transportation, public facilities, and so on), a decision inconsistent with those criteria (for example, allowing high-rise apartments in a single-family neighborhood) would more quickly raise a suspicion of corruption. Where decision procedures require the regulator to record his decision (for example, formal votes on zoning applications or written statements by an inspector that a structure meets code requirements or that requirements have been waived for specified reasons) or set time deadlines (a building permit application will be approved within X days, a zoning application within Y months), deviations will be both more identifiable and more attributable to specific persons.

In addition to strategies which increase the visibility of specific decisions, communities can adopt policies which provide greater information about the individuals assigned to regulatory positions. Some communities require officials to file financial disclosure statements listing sources of income and outside employment, identifying real or potential conflicts of interest. These communities have also required applicants to specify the owners of the land proposed for development. As they reduce perceived opportunities for corruption, these strategies also raise the costs of potential corruption (by raising the probability of detection) and encourage noncorrupt behavior (by showing that the organization condemns corruption).

Several other forms of reorganization might be mentioned briefly. First, agency reviews can be organized in "parallel" rather than in sequence: if an applicant can turn to more than one permit clerk or plan examiner, he may be less subject to extortion for approval of a legitimate request. Second, managers might consider systems to rotate assignments among officials: if plan examiners and building inspectors are periodically reassigned to different geographic areas, or at least to different projects, the chance that a single official will form close contacts with an individual developer, contractor, or landlord will be reduced (although it may also reduce the information which he utilizes to make decisions).

Raising the Costs of Corruption

I have noted that many of the positive incentives to corruption, the profits applicants derive from evading regulatory requirements, are beyond the control of local governments. The costs imposed by regulatory procedures (forms, supporting data, time delays, and so on) and the standards set by regulations (permitted land uses, construction quality, and so forth) influence the profitability of development and building ownership and set up trade-offs between regulatory goals and inducements to corruption. Incentives can either be reduced, by setting lower construction standards and permitting the most profitable land uses, or increased, with high standards and limited uses. When communities pursue their land-use goals with regulatory systems consonant with probable growth patterns, up-to-date construction codes, competent management, and efficient paper processing arrangements, incentives will be reduced; when communities use land-use policies and procedures which create incentives to corruption (for example, by banning high-density housing or setting high construction standards), however, they can reduce *net* incentives by raising the costs of corruption.

The risk posed by engaging in any criminal act combines both the probability of detection and the penalties of being caught. A prevention program must insure that the net costs of corruption exceed the gains it promises, and corruption must be less attractive than legitimate alternatives. The first factor implies that higher risks must be posed where corruption promises high payoffs; even a small penalty (a fine, reprimand, or brief suspension) might outweigh the small bribes paid to inspectors, but more serious sanctions are needed against the zoning commissioners and city officials involved in land-use decisions where payoffs can exceed several years' salary. Designing sanction systems involves a delicate balance; sanctions must be tough enough to deter corruption but not so harsh that enforcers will overlook the offense rather than subject violators to "excessive" punishment.

While these steps make it more *possible* to detect corruption, there may be a greater need to establish organizations which are trying to detect it. In New York City, for example, the Department of Investigations is actively seeking to identify corruption problems. In some areas, state and federal prosecutors both respond to complaints about corruption and conduct extensive investigations. Where city officials and prosecutors are inactive, investigative journalists and citizen watchdog organizations can provide an alternative mechanism to search out corruption. Research on other forms of illegal behavior suggests that steps which raise the likelihood that corruption will be detected are likely to have a greater deterrent impact than policies which simply increase the severity of the sentences meted out to those who are detected.

Defining and Reinforcing Integrity Expectations

Applicants and officials bring to their current roles a lifetime of experiences which shape, with varying degrees of clarity, definitions of corruption and expectations about the consequences of corrupt and noncorrupt behavior. The influence of these past experiences will persist. Yet, they can be counteracted by current experiences which illustrate the agency's definitions of prescribed and proscribed behaviors and the rewards and punishments which will follow from conformity and nonconformity. Definitions and expectations are likely to be learned through contacts with both organizational superiors and peers, from official policy directives and training sessions, and from the word-of-mouth folk wisdom of "those who have been around." To the extent that goal consensus can be built through group participation—through discussion among those who will be affected by the goal statements and implementing policies—it is likely to have a greater influence on behavior than goals announced by the unilateral fiat of supervisors. In Cincinnati, for example, a city manager asked his Middle

Management Board to develop a new code of ethics, concluding that a staff-generated code would be more readily accepted by city employees than a code issued from his office. In Arlington Heights, Illinois, officials established committees representing both regulatory agencies and the construction industry to develop regulatory policies.

Whether evolving unilaterally as an edict from the agency leader or collectively as a peer norm, a crucial part of an anticorruption program is a clear *definition* of what is meant by corruption. Unless the agency spells out the kinds of things that employees should and should not do, it cannot assume that they will know that a specific activity is improper, or that it will be punished. Three steps are involved: the organization must issue clear statements of permissible and impermissible behavior, the consequences of violations must be announced, and these definitions should be consistently reinforced.

Inevitably, definitions of corruption become fuzzy in many "gray areas." All would agree that a regulator should reject a cash payment from someone he regulates, but what about a free meal (for example, a contractor taking the inspector to a cafeteria, or a developer taking the city council to a supper club "so we can get to know each other")? What about a low-interest loan from the developer's bank? Tickets to the Super Bowl? A bottle of liquor at Christmas? A contribution to the mayor's reelection campaign?

It is hard to draw a line that will distinguish expressions of friendship from compromising obligations. Officials and applicants alike will always say "[the gift, the bank loan, the campaign contribution] never entered our minds—of course we were dealing with each other at arm's length when [the subdivision application, building permit, fire inspection] came around." It may well be that no single point divides the harmless from the harmful; one official may bend the rules for the person who gives him a bottle of Scotch at Christmas while another will go by the book even with the banker/developer who holds his mortgage. The relevant guideline may not be defined by objective characteristics of the gratuity but rather by community perceptions: if local residents feel that the inspector who has a hamburger with the builder has "sold out," the political costs to officials may be as great as if cash had changed hands. As a result, many city officials take the safe way out—they forbid anything that either is improper or gives the appearance of impropriety, even knowing that this strict a guideline may prove unenforceable.

Having decided where to draw the line, the next task is to inform both officials and the applicants they deal with about these policies. Some cities issue formal ethics codes to every new employee, and cover ethical issues in training sessions. Such formal strategies are likely to be viewed as either irrelevant or hypocritical unless indications are frequently and clearly given that "official" policies will be "real" policies. In Arlington Heights, Illinois, the fact that the village prohibited the acceptance of gratuities from firms doing business with city probably mattered less than the fact that the village manager enforced the policy. He regularly reminded insiders and outsiders of the policy, and anticipated the Christmas present problem by sending to all businesses dealing with the city a letter stating, "We would be embarrassed if you thought of us with more than a card." Gifts sent by businessmen who didn't get the message were returned by city policemen, employees' outside jobs were terminated when they conflicted with city duties, and so forth. Fairfax County, Virginia had officially discouraged fraternization between inspectors and contractors for years; the policy was routinely ignored until an assistant county executive threatened to fire anyone caught attending the contractors' Christmas parties. He sent each inspector a copy of the official personnel rules, with the message "This means, in simple terms, that no employee may accept any gift from any person or firm that he is involved with in the line of duty. Any violation of these rules is considered unacceptable conduct and requires that it be dealt with severely."

While setting definitions is an important first step, subsequent enforcement may be more important in affecting regulators' behavior; indeed, official policies which later go unenforced may suggest to subordinates that not even supervisors take the matter seriously. Reinforcement systems can utilize both positive and negative sanctions, and can focus on both corruption/integrity and the substantive policies regulators are to implement.

Designing reinforcement systems appropriate to specific situations depends heavily on the leader's familiarity with the work and staff involved—knowledge of their character, the temptations they will encounter on the job, cross-pressures they will face, and idiosyncratic matters such as their family situations, debts, gambling habits, and so forth. Obvious positive sanctions include salaries, pay raises, bonuses, promotions, work assignments, and public awards; negative sanctions can range from a private "chewing out" to reprimands, suspension without pay, dismissal, and prosecution. The availability of these sanctions may vary with budgets, local civil service laws, administrative requirements for promotion and demotion, and so on. More importantly, the effectiveness of these sanctions varies greatly; if the supply of positive sanctions is limited, employees may learn when no further rewards are available, and the targets of negative sanctioning may learn the techniques of evading detection or "wearing the boss down." Depending on the ingenuity of regulators and the requirements of courts or civil service hearing examiners, the costs of a negative sanction strategy may finally exceed benefits in terms of deterrence. Finally, supervisors should be conscious of the virtues (and lower costs) of informal sanctioning strategies, including the simple word of praise for proper performance that will reinforce training session homilies. When employees are being conditioned to handle new activities, reinforcements should be continuous; therefore, supervisors should intervene intermittently to maintain desired responses. Since the effectiveness of specific reinforcers may decline over time, supervisors should also be alert to the necessity of changing their approaches.

Transforming these positive and negative sanctions into reinforcements for integrity is a complex art greatly dependent on an understanding of the current predispositions of the personnel involved and probable corruption opportunities. A supervisor creating a new department has the luxury of recruiting subordinates who share his values or are at least amenable to beginning with his ground rules; a supervisor working with a group generally supportive of integrity can capitalize upon those feelings to ostracize the occasional deviant. Where such sentiments are not present or where many of the regulators condone or participate in corruption, the task is harder. A necessary first step may be to make compliance possible, protecting those who wish to comply from retribution or further contamination by peers. The compliant group can then be expanded through allocations of formal and informal rewards, showing that integrity is both accepted and rewarded. To the extent that the supervisor can implement positive sanction strategies first (which may be impossible under scandal conditions with public officials and the press demanding immediate action), he will be able to focus his negative sanctions on that segment of his work force which will not respond to positive approaches. Applying negative reinforcements can be as delicate as using positive reinforcements; negative reinforcements and/or punishments may change the behavior of most problem cases. Totally rotten apples should, if possible, be dismissed; where that is precluded by civil service protections, they can only be isolated from other personnel to minimize contamination. In all of these steps, it is essential that the supervisor build upon whatever latent or manifest support for integrity exists within the group, selling integrity as a collective goal rather than as an ultimatum delivered from on high.

NOTES

[1]This article is based on research conducted under a grant from the National Institute of Justice and reported in greater detail in Gardiner and Lyman (1978).

[2]Earlier, I noted one issue which complicates the labeling of a specific decision as "essential." While applicants will need approval from *some* representative of the regulatory system, an unfavorable reaction from the first regulator encountered may not be decisive;

supervisors or other agencies may be willing and able to produce the necessary clearances, or simple stalling tactics may lead the regulators to give in. One real estate lawyer offered this example. "We represented a developer seeking a variance which was consistent with the community's land-use policies. When our client was told that a bribe would be necessary, we went to court to force the city to issue the variance. The judge sensed the extortion issue and quietly told the city to quit fooling around. In my opinion, no one ever *has* to pay." This *caveat* is legitimate in those situations where an alternative forum is available (that is, where a supervisor or court and the costs of appeal or delay do not exceed the costs of acquiescing in the original official's demands).

[3]For survey data on legislators' perceptions of when behavior should be defined as "corrupt," see Peters and Welch (1978).

[4]For detailed illustrations of this calculation process, see Gardiner and Lyman (1978), Chapter Twelve.

REFERENCES

Gardiner, J., and T. Lyman. 1978. *Decisions for Sale: Corruption and Reform in Land-Use and Building Regulation*. New York: Praeger.

Morris, J. 1976. "Transcript Reveals Mayer Fear" *Long Beach Independent Press-Telegram*, July 3.

Peters, J., and S. Welch. 1978. "Political Corruption in America: A Search for Definitions and a Theory." *American Political Science Review* 72 (September) pp. 974–984.

Rose-Ackerman, S. 1978. *Corruption: A Study in Political Economy*. New York: Academic Press.

7

Corruption as a Feature of Governmental Organization*

Edward C. Banfield

This is an exploratory paper the purposes of which are to identify the principal variables having to do with corruption in governmental organizations in the United States and to point out some significant relationships among them. The paper begins by setting forth a conceptual scheme for the description and analysis of corruption in all sorts of organizational settings. This is applied first to the "typical" business and then to the "typical" governmental organization. (The reason for introducing the business organization into the discussion is to create a contrast that will highlight the characteristic features of governmental organization.) In the concluding section some dynamic factors are noted.

The Conceptual Scheme

The frame of reference is one in which an *agent* serves (or fails to serve) the *interest* of a *principal*. The agent is a person who has accepted an obligation (as in an employment contract) to act on behalf of his principal in some range of matters and, in doing so, to serve the principal's interest as if it were his own. The principal may be a person or an entity such as an organization or public. In acting on behalf of his principal an agent must

From *Journal of Law and Economics*, Vol. 18 (December 1975), pp. 587–605. © 1975. Reprinted by permission of The University of Chicago Press.

*The writer is grateful for the encouragement and suggestions given by his colleague, Julius Margolis, and for criticisms by Susan Rose-Ackerman and Barry M. Mitnick. He has also benefited greatly from reading Mitnick's The Theory of Agency: The Concept of Fiduciary Rationality and Some Consequences (unpublished Ph.D. dissertation, Univ. of Pa., Dep't Pol. Sci., 1974).

exercise some *discretion*; the wider the range (measured in terms of effects on the principal's interest) among which he may choose, the broader is his discretion. The situation includes *third parties* (persons or abstract entities) who stand to gain or lose by the action of the agent. There are *rules* (both laws and generally accepted standards of right conduct) violation of which entails some probability of a penalty (cost) being imposed upon the violator. A rule may be more or less indefinite (vague, ambiguous or both), and there is more or less uncertainty as to whether it will be enforced.

An agent is *personally corrupt* if he knowingly sacrifices his principal's interest to his own, that is, if he betrays his trust. He is *officially corrupt* if, in serving his principal's interest, he knowingly violates a rule, that is, acts illegally or unethically albeit in his principal's interest.

Agents are in varying degrees *dependable*. The more dependable an agent, the larger the psychic costs to him of a corrupt act and accordingly the higher his reservation price for the performance of the act.

Minimizing Corruption: Constraints

As a means of showing the relationships among these and other variables it will be useful to imagine a situation every feature of which tends to minimize corruption. In such a situation agents are selected after an elaborate search on the basis of their exceptional dependability and law-abidingness, all of their other qualities being deemed of no importance as compared to these. The agents are given whatever kinds and amounts of in-centives will motivate them to loyal service and whatever disincentives (for example, high risk of discovery followed by dismissal with loss of pension rights) will deter them from disloyalty. The principal's interest (ends, objec-tives, goals, purposes, etc.) is fully explicated, and agents are given discre-tion no broader than is judged necessary to fully serve that interest. Rules are definite (that is, neither vague nor ambiguous) and it is known whether or not they will be enforced. If an agent's duty requires him to try to attain mutually exclusive or competing ends, his dilemma is resolved by his prin-cipal. An agent's performance is carefully monitored; if there is any doubt about his loyalty, he is dismissed forthwith. Monitors are themselves carefully monitored.

Obviously all of this implies centralized control: there must be an authori-ty (that of a chief executive or "top management") capable of selecting dependable agents, establishing an effective incentive system, explicating the principal's interest, monitoring monitors, and so on.

It will be seen that the situation just described—one in which everything possible is done to minimize corruption—is in many respects highly unrealistic. The principal may be an abstract entity such as a corporation, labor union, or public, in which case some surrogate—a board of directors or chief executive—must explicate its interest and be a monitor-in-chief who cannot himself (or themselves) be monitored.[1] There may be no central authority capable of doing the things necessary to minimize corruption—for example, to dismiss agents whose loyalty is questionable. The rules may be indefinite,[2] and there may be much uncertainty as to whether they will be enforced.[3]

Perhaps the least realistic feature of the "ideal" situation is the implicit assumption that there exists only one objective—viz. to minimize corruption. In the real world there are always competing objectives, a condition that makes it necessary to give up something in terms of one in order to get more in terms of another. Each of the measures that might be taken to reduce corruption entails costs. Getting the information upon which an estimate of the dependability of a prospective agent can be based is costly, and to secure the services of one who has this scarce, and hence valuable, quality is also costly—costly not only in money and other resources that are paid out, but also, and perhaps chiefly, in terms of opportunities foregone, it being highly unlikely that the candidates standing highest in dependability will also stand highest in all other qualities (for example, intelligence, energy, willingness to take risks, etc.) which may be of value to the organization.[4] Similarly supplying the incentives and the disincentives necessary to secure loyalty is costly in resources and in opportunities foregone.[5] So is the explication of the principal's objective and the negotiation of an agreement between a principal and an agent.[6] So also is monitoring: it entails not only direct costs, such as the salaries of monitors,[7] but also indirect ones such as the lowering of morale that may occur when agents feel "spied upon." The same may be said of narrowing agents' discretion: it is costly to form an estimate of the amount of the corruption that would be prevented by setting this or that limit; moreover, narrowing discretion may injure morale (the exercise of discretion being for many an important non-monetary reward) and, while preventing the agent from doing (corrupt) things that are slightly injurious to the principal, it may at the same time prevent him from doing (non-corrupt) ones that would be very beneficial to him. If simply to prevent corruption an agent is given a narrower discretion than would be optimal if there were no possibility of corruption, whatever losses are occasioned by his having a sub-optimal breadth of discretion must be counted as costs of preventing corruption.[8]

It is evident that the costs of eliminating, or controlling, corruption may on occasion be greater than the gains from doing so. One can imagine a firm's spending itself into bankruptcy in an effort to end corruption or a labor union's sacrificing the advantage of its monopoly position by employing an honest but incompetent business agent.[9]

This being so, one might expect the management of an organization to try to discover: a) what level of corruption is optimal for it—that is, the level at which the marginal cost of anti-corruption measures equals the gain from them, and b) what trade-offs among the variously "priced" anti-corruption measures will yield an optimal set, that is, one in which the marginal return from each measure is the same.

Because of technological factors the substitution possibilities may be severely limited. For example, in certain circumstances it may be impossible to substitute monitoring for dependability (the agent's work may have to be done in absolute secrecy); similarly, in certain circumstances it may be impossible to substitute a narrowing of discretion for dependability (the work may require the exercise of a very broad discretion).[10]

It should be noted also that the nature of corruption puts special difficulties in the way of getting information on the basis of which to make a rational allocation of resources. Thus, for example, a principal cannot know how much a third party may bid to secure a corrupt action from an agent and therefore he cannot know how much it will pay him (the principal) to invest in agent loyalty.

Institutional Forms: Business

The concepts and relationships that have been set forth in the abstract will be useful in describing some of the main structural features of a concrete form of organization: the "typical" business (more precisely, the competitive corporation). The reason for discussing the business organization here is to provide a contrasting background, so to say, against which the characteristic features of governmental organization can be more readily seen.

1. In a business organization the principal's interest consists of one—or of a very few—objectives the parameters of which—for example, a satisfactory level or profit and beyond that the maximization of emoluments (including staff and expenses) to managers—are easily ascertained. The goods and services produced by the organization can generally be brought under the measuring rod of money and can be distributed via market competition, thus reducing, and to some extent eliminating, the need to exercise discretion. If over time the revenues of the firm do not cover its costs it must go out of business.

2. The incentive system of a business organization is based very largely upon personal, material incentives, especially money. Although the employee may find his work intrinsically interesting and may get satisfaction from

"associational benefits," money rewards, or the expectation of them, are in the usual case by far the most significant of the inducements which motivate him. Business executives whose attachment to the organization they serve is almost purely pecuniary are probably not at all uncommon.

3. There exists a highly integrated system of control through which a chief executive (sometimes a team: "top management") can: a) reduce the objectives of the organization to lower levels of generality by defining "targets," b) select agents, c) fix limits on their discretion, d) give or withhold rewards and punishments, e) arrange for monitoring the performance of agents (and also of monitors). The chief executive may himself be chosen and monitored by a board of directors.[11] So long as profits are satisfactory he is not likely to be disciplined or removed by his board. Frequently its monitoring of him is *pro forma* since it must depend largely upon him for information (although some boards have independent auditing committees) and he is likely to have selected most of its membership.

4. Since there exists in a business organization an ultimate authority (the chief executive or, in some matters, the board of directors), it is possible, in principle at least, for agents to get authoritative rulings as to the terms on which conflicts among ends should be settled. Questions which lie outside an agent's discretion—for example, which of two mutually exclusive criteria of choice should be invoked in a concrete situation—are passed up the hierarchy to one who *has* discretion in the matter.

5. The chief executive of a business organization normally continues in office if profits are "satisfactory" until he reaches retirement age. That is, the one condition he must normally meet in order to maintain his control of the organization is business success.[12] Apart from a poor showing on the balance sheet, the principal danger to his tenure is from a hostile takeover or a merger; this danger exists only as outsiders believe they could operate the corporation enough more profitably to yield them a net gain over the costs of acquiring control—costs which the incumbent chief executive is usually in a position to make discouragingly high.[13]

6. The business organization may do whatever is not prohibited by law or government regulation. (Technically a corporation may do only what its charter allows, but as a practical matter it is usually possible to obtain a charter that allows almost anything lawful.) Within the limits set by law and regulation, the business organization may withdraw from one line of activity and enter upon another; it may hire and fire, reward and punish as it sees fit, and it may purchase what it pleases (including the services of consultants of all sorts) at whatever price it is able and willing to pay. Except as it must make disclosures in accordance with government regulations, its affairs are secret.

Some Implications

These features of business organization have several implications relevant to a discussion of corruption:

a) Its principal—perhaps its only—object being profit, the business organiz-
    ation will incur costs to prevent corruption insofar—but *only* insofar—as
    it expects them to yield marginal returns equal to those that could be had
    from other investments. Similarly, it will incur costs in order to corrupt
    (that is, to induce the agents of others to betray their trust) insofar—but
    again *only* insofar—as it expects them to contribute to profit.

b) The business organization will invest heavily in search costs and in incen-
    tives to assure that its chief executive: 1) will not be personally corrupt,
    and 2) will be officially corrupt insofar as may be necessary to secure the
    success, or at least avoid the failure, of the business. These qualities, al-
    though obviously not sufficient conditions of a good chief executive (abil-
    ity is probably much more important), are surely necessary ones and in
    the effort to secure them the board of directors may choose someone who
    has close family or friendship ties with a principal (large stockholder) or
    who has "come up through the organization"—that is, whose "loyalty"
    has been tested over a long period in positions of successively greater re-
    sponsibility. In order to identify the interest of the chief executive even
    more closely with that of his principal the board may give him not only a
    high salary and generous pension rights but also bonuses in the form of
    stock or stock options.

c) The task of the business executive being to optimize rather than to mini-
    mize corruption, he may follow a policy of "leniency" in dealing with
    certain types of personal corruption (for example, petty pilfering of sup-
    plies) because to do otherwise might create disaffection among employees
    who object to being "checked up on." What Dalton calls "unofficial re-
    ward"—in plain language, petty graft—is sometimes a significant ele-
    ment in an incentive system.[14]

d) In dealing with personal corruption at a high level of hierarchy the chief
    executive is likely to shun publicity; rather than prosecute an offender he
    may transfer him, force him to resign, or if there is no other way, arrange
    for his early retirement. To acknowledge that there was personal corrup-
    tion in a high place would be "bad for the organization": it might pro-
    duce unfavorable publicity and, worse, encourage a take-over bid, that
    sort of corruption being widely regarded as indicative of poor manage-
    ment. (Insofar as the chief executive chooses to ignore or "cover up"
    such corruption because the revelation of it would reflect on his own
    work he is of course personally corrupt.) On the other hand, personal cor-
    ruption at the bottom of the hierarchy in excess of the permitted limit
    may be dealt with harshly, for the exposure of such corruption is general-
    ly taken as a sign of good management.

e) Obviously to be effective a monitoring system in a business organization
    must operate selectively; its mission is: a) to keep corruption at the lower
    levels within permitted levels and, b) to inform the chief executive about
    corruption at the higher levels but in a manner that does not oblige him to
    let its existence become generally known.

f) Although the structure of the business organization makes possible the
    resolution of the dilemma faced by an agent who is required to attain mu-
    tually exclusive objectives, in practice it may fail to do so. When "top
    management" insists—presumably unwittingly—that agents do what they
    cannot possibly do without violating rules (that is, without being official-

ly corrupt) the monitoring system is likely to be bypassed, or if it is not, to adapt itself to the situation by "turning a blind eye" on all except the most flagrant rule violations. There will be a tendency also for colleague-groups and perhaps monitors as well to define the situation so as to reduce the psychic costs of rule violations (for example, it was "against the rules" but "not really wrong or unethical").[15]

g)   Arrangements which allow for the by-passing of monitors or for selective monitoring may easily become dysfunctional by withholding, sometimes for a monitor's own corrupt purposes, information that a chief executive wants and expects to have. A situation which produces rule-violation in the line of duty (that is, official corruption) in effect taxes dependable agents (that is, those for whom rule-violation entails psychic costs) and subsidizes the undependable. One would expect that under these circumstances the undependable would eventually replace the dependable.

h)   If its sole purpose is the maximization of profit, the business organization may have an incentive to corrupt the agents of other organizations—competitors, labor unions, government agencies, etc.[16] Its only disincentives are in the nature of business risks—for example loss of reputation within the trade, unfavorable publicity, and fines and other legal penalties (until recently criminal sanctions have rarely been imposed upon officers of corporations which violated the law). The expected disutility of these will presumably be weighed against the expected gain of successful corruption.

i)   One would expect the tendency to corrupt other organizations to be the strongest among those profit-maximizing businesses which must depend upon a small number of customers or suppliers (whether of capital, labor, or materials) and whose profit margin in the absence of corruption would be non-existent or nearly so. These might fail if they indulged in any form of "social responsibility."[17] Oligopolistic businesses, having ample "slack," although avoiding the vulgar *quid-pro-quo* forms of corruption, probably tend to be lavish in entertainment, consultants' fees, and other expenditures intended to "create goodwill," "maintain good working relations," and "make friends." Insofar as such expenditures cause corruption, it is likely to be of a kind difficult or impossible to identify clearly as such.

Institutional Forms: Government

The structural features of "typical" American governmental organization differ strikingly from those of business.

1.   Fragmentation of authority both within and among federal, state and local jurisdictions, a conspicuous and distinctive feature of the American political system, gives incentive to the formation and energetic activity of a multitude of pressure groups. Accordingly American governmental organizations characteristically have objectives that are numerous, unordered, vague and ambiguous, and mutually antagonistic if not downright contradictory.[18] The product (services generally) of a governmental orga-

nization is frequently of such a nature as not to be susceptible to being priced in a market or perhaps to quantitative measurement of any kind. Almost all government regulation is of this character.[19] Governmental products that might be priced usually are not, and if they are, the price is usually set so low as to subsidize the consumer and (if the supply is short) to create a rationing problem which necessitates exercises of discretion on the part of governmental agents.[20] As Robert C. Brooks wrote early in the present century, " . . . as soon as regulation is undertaken by the state a motive is supplied . . . to break the law or bribe its executors."[21] When, as is often the case, the governmental organization has a monopoly a strong incentive exists for third parties to seek to influence the agent's exercise of discretion by offering a bribe—that is, to pay a monopoly price, the money going not to the government but to the agent.

The governmental organization's existence is not jeopardized by selling its products at prices that are below the cost of production since typically it gets some or all of its revenue by taxation. If there is any threat to its existence, it is likely to arise from its having failed to distribute enough in subsidies to get the support it needs in the legislature or at the polls.

2. Although the incentive system of the governmental organization is based mainly on money and other personal material incentives, other types of incentives usually bulk larger in it than in the incentive system of business organization. At the lower levels of government hierarchy job security is an important incentive. At the middle levels the satisfactions of participating in large affairs, "serving in a good cause," and of sharing (albeit perhaps vicariously) in the charisma that attaches to an elite corps (for example, the F.B.I.) or to a leader (for example, J. Edgar Hoover or Robert Moses) are also of importance. At the top level power and glory are among the principal incentives (for example, Hoover and Moses). It would probably be hard to find in government a very high level official whose attachment to his job is purely pecuniary.[22]

3. From a legal-formal standpoint and often in fact, control of a governmental agency is in many more hands than is control of a business. Normally a chief executive or a small team ("top management") has authority over all of the operations of a business. A governmental agency, by contrast, is usually run by a loose and unstable coalition of individuals each of whom has independent legal-formal authority over some of its operations. Not only is there separation among legislative, judicial and executive functions, but the executive function is itself divided. In the Federal government, for example, there are numerous independent bodies (for example, the Federal Reserve System) which exercise an authority independent of the President's. In state and local government, executive authority is much more widely distributed.[23] The mayor of a moderate-sized city, for example, has no control whatever over at least a dozen bodies whose collaboration is indispensable. The comptroller and district attorney, for example, are usually independently elected, and there are numerous bodies, notably the civil service commission, in which the mayor has little or no voice. The governmental chief executive appoints his principal subordinates (subject usually however to their confirmation by a separate authority), but the incentive system is fixed by law and regulation and is as a rule of such a nature as to preclude competition with business organiza-

tions for executive talent. Moreover the governmental chief executive and his principal subordinates, having no control over the tenure or pay of lesser ("career") executives, have not much more than nominal authority over the lower levels of bureaucracy. For example, the mayor of New York, according to Sayre, has few levers to move the several hundred bureau chiefs; he works "at the margins of bureau autonomy" by creating and staffing new bureaus and by praising or attacking those who are or are not responsive to him but "his victories are temporary and touch only a few bureaus."[24]

4. Whereas the business organization may hire, promote or demote, and dismiss salaried employees at will (subject to civil rights and other such laws), the governmental one is severely restricted by civil service regulations. The governmental executive cannot dismiss a career civil servant whom he considers untrustworthy; instead he may prefer formal charges supported by evidence before a trial board from the decision of which the employee may usually appeal. The procedure is so time-consuming and dismissals so hard to get that it is invoked only in cases so flagrant as to make it unavoidable.[25]

5. The fragmentation of formal authority in government is overcome to a greater or lesser degree by informal arrangements: officials exchange favors (for example, voting support, jobs, opportunities to make money by legal or other means) with other officials and with interest groups and voters in order to assemble the authority they require to maintain and if possible increase their power.[26] In the extreme case the result is a stable structure in which control is as highly integrated as in the business organization; this is the "machine," the chief executive of which (who may or may not be the chief executive of a governmental organization) is the "boss."[27] One difference between the machine and the business organization requires particular notice: the business executive's control, resting as it does on a solid legal-formal base, is stable as compared to that of the boss, which arises from extra-legal, if not illegal, arrangements, is *ad hoc*, and must be continually renewed by "deals" in order to prevent it from collapsing.

6. The agent of a governmental organization is both likely to be required to serve objectives that compete or are mutually exclusive (this is because, as noted, the objective function of a government organization is characteristically vague, ambiguous, and unordered) and unlikely to get the dilemma that he faces resolved by passing it up the hierarchy: there is hardly ever a chief executive with authority over all the matters involved in the conflict and, if there is and if the conflict is passed up the hierarchy to him, the answer that will come back to the agent will probably be: "Maximize *all* objectives."[28] The fundamental fact of the situation is that the electorate or some set of interest groups (that is the principal) *demands* states of affairs that are mutually exclusive.

7. The chief executive of a governmental organization normally serves a two- or a four-year term after which he must face "take-over" bids first in a primary and then in a general election; in many jurisdictions he may not succeed himself more than once or twice. As compared to his opposite number in business his tenure is uncertain and brief.[29] Although as an incumbent he has a decided advantage, much of what he does or fails to do in office is with a view to increasing the probability of his reelection.

8. Unlike the shareholder, the citizen cannot easily disassociate himself from a corrupt organization: to escape it he must incur the costs of moving to another city, state, or country. Nevertheless, in the usual case he will have no incentive to invest in its reduction because it, or rather the absence of it, is a "public good" the benefits of which will accrue as much to "free riders" as to others.[30] There are, however, institutions, notably the media and the ambitious district attorney, that stand to gain by searching out and making much of corruption, whether real or seeming.

9. From a formal standpoint, a governmental organization may do *only* what the law expressly authorizes and it *must* do what the law expressly requires. In fact, when public opinion permits, it sometimes withdraws from tasks assigned by law which expose it to corruption.[31] Its freedom to avoid exposure to corrupting influences is small as compared to that of the business organization however.

10. A governmental organization may have few secrets. To a large and increasing extent, its affairs (for example, the salaries of employees, the number of widgets bought and the price paid, etc.) are matters of public record. Generally public hearings must be held and public participation secured before a governmental undertaking may get under way. Sometimes there must be a referendum. Meetings at which decisions are to be made must often be open to the public. In many instances officials are required to disclose their property holdings and business connections. As "public figures" they are for all practical purposes unprotected by laws against slander and libel.

Consequences of These Differences

Obviously the structural differences between business and governmental organizations have consequences affecting corruption:

a) In governmental organization the costs of preventing or reducing corruption are not balanced against gains with a view to finding an optimal investment. Instead corruption is thought of (when it comes under notice) as something that must be eliminated "no matter what the cost." Even when no deterrent effect could be expected, a governmental organization—the IRS, for example—would not act uncharacteristically in spending, say, $50,000 to uncover and punish a misdeed which could not possibly have cost the government more than, say, $500.

b) In the absence of central control there is no real (as opposed to nominal) chief executive or "top management" which can make substitutions among anti-corruption measures (for example, more investment in dependability and less in monitoring) in an effort to "balance the margins."

c) In the absence of central control, an agent whose duties are mutually incompatible cannot get a resolution of his dilemma by administrative action; therefore—unless he resigns—he must act corruptly. As Rubinstein remarks in *City Police*, "a policeman cannot escape the contradictions imposed on him by his obligations."[32]

d) Where authority is highly fragmented there is no centralized system of monitoring or, more generally, of control. Under these circumstances corruption is likely to occur "because the potential corrupter needs to influence only a segment of the government, and because in a fragmented system there are fewer centralized forces and agencies to enforce honesty."[33] Although there may be officials in roles specialized to perform monitoring or other anti-corruption functions—typically an independently elected district attorney—these frequently fail to perform vigorously when doing so would be contrary to their political or other interests; in any case no chief executive can *require* them to—that is, there is no effective provision for monitoring the monitors.

e) Because of the inflexibility of government pay scales and promotion rules a government executive is often unable to offer an agent incentives (monetary and nonmonetary) equal to those he could earn elsewhere. One consequence is that the government agent is likely to be less dependable and less able than his business organization counterpart. Of more importance, perhaps, the government agent has less to lose from dismissal.[34]

f) The nature of governmental activity often precludes precisely stating or narrowly limiting the breadth of an agent's discretion.[35] If the objective is no more definite than to "improve the quality of life," the agent's decisions must necessarily be on grounds that are highly subjective. The monitoring of such decisions presents obvious difficulties: almost any can be given a plausible rationale.

g) When output standards cannot be made definite, the organization may try to compensate by making input specifications very detailed. The effect of this, however, is to reduce the number of competitive suppliers, thereby making collusion easier between sellers and corrupt purchasing agents. Sometimes an agent establishes specifications that only one supplier can meet.

h) Both because of the relatively open (not secret) nature of most government activities and because of the fragmentation of control, monitoring agents from *outside* the organization is probably more common in government than in business. "Unplanned feedback" (that is, information and clues that come to the organization from clients, competitive agencies, the mass media, public prosecutors, civic groups, etc.) may be of special importance in governmental organizations because of the lack (due to fragmentation) of *planned* feedback.[36] Selective monitoring (that is, the filtering out of information damaging to certain "higher ups" or posing a threat to the successful functioning of the organization) is difficult to manage when there is much "unplanned feedback."

i) Governmental organizations are much less likely than business ones to be permissive about petty corruption ("unofficial rewards"). For one thing, the governmental organization, which is not seeking to maximize profit, is willing to accept whatever loss of productivity may result from employees' disaffection at being closely watched. For another, no one in the organization has authority to permit "stealing from the government." Such petty corruption as exists within a governmental organization reflects a failure of management, not, as it might in a business organization, a cost deliberately incurred to avoid a still larger one.

j) Insofar as government executives are motivated more by non-pecuniary values (for example, power, participation in large affairs, "serving in a good cause," etc.) than are business executives, they are probably less susceptible to pecuniary inducements to corruption. By the same token, they are probably *more* susceptible to non-pecuniary inducements such as "the good of the organization."[37]

k)   Because the opportunity to exercise wide discretion in important matters (that is, to wield power) normally comprises a larger part of the "package" of incentives offered to government executives than of that offered to business executives, close monitoring is probably more disruptive of management in government than in business.

l)   The existence of governmental organizations in which authority is highly fragmented presents an opportunity for a political entrepreneur to "purchase" pieces of authority (that is, to bribe or otherwise influence the possessors of authority to use it as the "purchaser" requires) and thus to create a highly integrated system of control (machine).

m)   Where the formal decentralization is not overcome by an informal centralization (that is, a machine) corruption is likely to be widespread, there being no mechanism capable of regulating it. "Prudential considerations restraining corruption," Brooks wrote early in the present century, "are apt to be much more keenly felt by a thoroughly organized machine than in cases where corruption is practiced by disorganized groups and individuals each seeking its own or his own advantage regardless of any common interest.[38]

n)   To the extent that there is a machine, that is, to the extent that the formal fragmentation of authority has been replaced by an informal centralization, the governmental organization will resemble the typical business organization. Its chief executive ("boss") will have reasonably secure tenure, a well-defined objective function (to maintain and enhance the organization), and the ability to exercise control.[39] He will invest heavily in the dependability of his principal subordinates (one "comes up through" a machine by demonstrating loyalty over time),[40] regulate the breadth of their discretion, maintain an incentive system that motivates machine workers (especially job patronage, legal fees, the purchase of insurance, construction contracts, etc.), and monitor them to check unauthorized corruption.

Some Dynamic Factors

In the nature of the case it is impossible to know how much corruption there is at any given time. On theoretical grounds, however, it seems safe to say that for several decades corruption has been increasing in the United States and that it will continue to do so.

Adam Smith remarked that those who trade often with each other find that honesty is the best policy.[41] For traders, mutual adherence to rules constitutes a public good. If the traders are fewer than some critical number, each will find it to his advantage to abide by the rule and even to contribute to its enforcement upon others. But if they exceed the critical number, each may find it to his advantage to violate the rule and none will voluntarily contribute to its enforcement because each will know that the situation will be essentially the same no matter what he does and that therefore it will pay him to be a "free rider."[42]

It is easy to point out instances in which honesty is still the best policy (the Chicago grain pit is one example and the Chicago political "machine" another). Nevertheless, it seems likely that for several decades the proportion of situations of the large-number type, in which dishonesty is likely to be the best (that is, most profitable) policy, has been increasing. Certainly there are relatively few executives who think of their organization as an entity (for example, a "house") that will exist in essentially the same environment for generations to come. This being so, there is now relatively little incentive to invest in acquiring reputation ("character," to use Smith's word), something which, unlike an "image," can only be had by consistent adherence to the rules over a long period of time.

A second factor tending to increase corruption in the United States has been the dramatic enlargement of the scope and scale of government, local, state and national. Doubtless this enlargement has been to some extent a response to problems that have arisen because of the inability of traders who interact in large numbers and over short periods to maintain the rules that could be taken for granted when most traders interacted frequently and over long periods of time. As honesty gradually ceased to be the best policy, there were more demands that government offer incentives and disincentives to make it so once again. Moreover, the American passion for equality has always encouraged the replacement of the invisible hand of competition by the visible—and supposedly fairer—one of bureaucracy. (As Tocqueville remarked, "equality singularly facilitates, extends, and secures the influence of a central power" and every central power "worships uniformity [because] it relieves it from inquiry into an infinity of details . . . ").[43] But uniformity was bound to leave many individuals dissatisfied—the infinity of details could not be ignored without cost—, and thus to create pressures for special treatment.

Whatever their causes, every extension of government authority has created new opportunities and incentives for corruption. Over the long run this has helped to make it appear normal, tolerable, and even laudable.[44]

Had the growth of government been accompanied by the centralization of control and certain other structural changes, the increase in corruption would doubtless have been less. But the structural changes that occurred were mainly in the "wrong" direction: executive control has been reduced by merit system practices, recognition of public employee unions, civil rights legislation, laws requiring "citizen participation," "sunshine" laws, and the like. At the same time, the extra-legal arrangements through which control was informally centralized in a "machine" which, sometimes at least, found it advantageous to moderate and limit corruption have in most instances been wiped out or rendered less effectual by "good government" reforms.

A third factor, closely related to the second, has been the imposition upon business organizations of constraints much like those under which government operates. Public opinion (including often that of businessmen!) more or less obliges the business organization to subordinate the profit criterion to other objectives—ones which, as in government, are vague and conflicting. Like government organizations, businesses are more and more expected to tolerate, even to encourage, participation in their affairs by out-siders ("public interest groups") and to give the public details of dealings the success of which requires secrecy. Frequently courts and regulatory agencies play leading roles in making business decisions.[45]

If these are indeed the trends, one may well ponder what their outcomes will be. Presumably the culture that is being formed today contains a much smaller stock of dependability than did that formed a generation, or two, or three ago. Substitutes (for example, monitoring) can take the place of much dependability, but they will surely be relatively costly and there is doubtless some "technological" limit to the amount of substitution that is feasible: it is hard to believe that complex social organizations can exist in the complete absence of dependability.[46] In any case there are more important questions. In a society in which *dishonesty* is the best policy, will not the individual feel contempt for himself and for his fellows and will he not conclude—rightly perhaps—that he and they are "not worth saving"?

NOTES

[1] "[U]nfortunately," writes Frederick Andrews, "no one has devised a way to impose effec-tive [internal] controls on the very top officers, those whose rank enables them to over-ride controls." Wall Street Journal, June 12, 1975, at 1, col.5.

[2] The recently enacted Federal pension law "requires that fiduciaries follow the 'prudent man rule' which requires them to act 'with the care, skill, prudence and diligence' that a prudent man 'acting in a like capacity and familiar with such matters would use in the conduct of an enterprise of a like character and with like aims'." Wall Street Journal, Feb. 14, 1975, at 28, col. 1.

The bribery conviction of former Senator Daniel B. Brewster was overturned by a U.S. Court of Appeals because the "trial court's instructions did not set forth a clear and com-prehensive standard for the jury to make the distinction between receiving bribery payment in return for being influenced in the performance of an official act, receiving illegal gratuities and receiving legal, normal campaign contributions." Philadelphia Evening Bulletin, Aug. 2, 1974, at p. 1.

[3] The uncertainties regarding enforcement of some rules may be seen from the following: "If the Public Officers Law [of New York state] were enforced, and those who accepted or promised a reward in return for a vote were actually incarcerated, few of the state's legislators would re-main outside prison bars."

" . . . the act of paying for a judgeship is, after all, an indictable offense, though never enforced."

"To survive politically, most congressmen must overlook the Corrupt Practices Act, which places a ceiling on campaign expenditures, and pretend ignorance on the subject of where their money originates." Martin & Susan Tolchin, To the Victor—Political Patronage from the Clubhouse to the White House, 94, 146, 246 (1971.)

⁴Ancient Athens provides an interesting exception. There magistrates, whether chosen by lot or elected, were subjected to an examination not to prove capacity or talent but "concerning the probity of the man." Fustel de Coulanges, The Ancient City 330 (1956). For a close analysis of the costs of policing the agent see Barry Mitnick, The Theory of Agency: The Concept of Fiduciary Rationality and Some Consequences (unpublished Ph.D. dissertation, Univ. of Pa., Dep't Pol. Sci., 1974). With regard to "indirect" costs of such policing, see his The Theory of Agency: The Policing "Paradox" and Regulatory Behavior, Public Choice (forthcoming, Spring 1976).

⁵Gary S. Becker & George J. Stigler, Law Enforcement, Malfeasance,and Compensation of Enforcers, in Capitalism and Freedom, Problems and Prospects 242 (Richard T. Selden ed. 1975). This article first appeared in 3 J. Leg. Studies 1 (1974). One of the methods proposed by Becker and Stigler to deter malfeasance or nonfeasance is "to raise the salaries of enforcers [agents] above what they could get elsewhere, by an amount that is inversely related to the probability of detection and directly related to the size of bribes and other benefits from malfeasance." However, malfeasance, Becker and Stigler say, can be eliminated without paying the enforcers lifetime salaries exceeding what they could get elsewhere by requiring them to post a bond which they would forfeit if fired for malfeasance. *Id.* at 237.

In some jurisdictions an official who resigns before charges are brought may retain his pension rights. The Knapp Commission remarked on this and another practical difficulty in the way of making the threat of pension rights effective. "The result of the present [New York] forfeiture rule," it said, "has been that the courts on appeal have directed the reinstatement of patently unfit officers because they could not tolerate the injustice involved in the forfeiture of vested pension rights." New York City, The Knapp Commission Report on Police Corruption, 228–29, 26 (1972) [hereinafter cited as Knapp Commission].

⁶"With some recent exceptions, police agencies have tended to keep the policies under which they act ambiguous and unwritten. The reasons may include the fear of articulating clear guidelines because of possible controversy and the difficulties in formulating rules for the varied situations police encounter" Police Foundation, Toward a New Potential (1974).

For a homely example see William A. Niskanen's account of his difficulties in including a selling agent to maximize his (N's) returns from the sale of a house, in Capitalism and Freedom, Problems and Prospects 26 (Richard T. Selden ed. 1975).

⁷" 'If we examined every item over $100,000—which really isn't much for a huge corporation—that would drive our fees sky-high. There's a real cost-benefit problem here,' says . . . a top partner at . . . the largest audit firm." Wall Street Journal, June 12, 1975.

⁸For example, the cost to New York City of prohibiting a uniformed patrolman from making a gambling arrest unless a superior officer is present. Knapp Commission 90.

⁹Cf. Simon Rottenberg, A Theory of Corruption in Labor Unions, in Am. Ass'n for the Advancement of Sci., Symposia Studies Series No. 3, at 4 (Nat'l Inst. of Soc. & Behav. Sci., June 1960) reprinted in Univ. of Chicago, Industrial Relations Center, Reprint Series, No. 96.

¹⁰Gary S. Becker & George J. Stigler, *supra* note 5, at 243, remark that the role of trust in an employment contract is larger: the less easily and quickly the quality of performance can be ascertained, the more diverse the activities of the enterprise, the more rapidly it is growing or declining, and the more unstable the industries in which it is operating in each case.

[11]On the changing role of the corporate director see the article by John V. Conti, Wall Street Journal, Sept. 17, 1974, at 1, col.6.

[12]Union members not uncommonly tolerate corruption on the part of agents who win them advantageous contracts. Philip Taft, Corruption and Racketeering in the Labor Movement 6, 28 (N.Y. St. Sch. Ind. & Labor Rel. Bull. 38, 1958). Similarly, voters sometimes prefer candidates whom they have reason to believe corrupt. Of a sample of 1,059 Boston homeowners (taken in 1966), 41% agreed that "a mayor who gets things done but takes a little graft is better than a mayor who doesn't get much done but doesn't take any graft." Unpublished data gathered by James Q. Wilson and the writer.

[13]See Henry G. Manne, Mergers and the Market for Corporate Control, 73 J. Pol. Econ. 110 (1965). Also, Company Executives Shore Up Defenses Against Take-Overs, Wall Street Journal, Oct. 21, 1974, at 1, col.6.

[14]Melville Dalton, Men Who Manage, ch. 6 (1959). See also Alvin W. Gouldner, Patterns of Industrial Bureaucracy 87, 159-62, 176 (1954).

[15]For an account of a business organization (GE) in which "disjointed authority" led to men being required to do what was illegal see Richard Austin Smith, Corporations in Crisis ch. 5-6 (1963). Striking parallels are to be found in Joseph S. Berliner, Factory and Manager in the USSR, chs. 11 & 12 (1957).

[16]Taft found that racketeering in labor unions tends to appear in industries that are highly competitive and have a highly mobile labor force, and that when these conditions coexist some corruption is "almost inevitable." Philip Taft, *supra* note 12, at 33. The Knapp Commission found the second largest source of police corruption in New York City (the first was organized crime) to be "legitimate business seeking to ease its way through the maze of City ordinances and regulations. Major offenders are construction contractors and subcontractors, liquor licensees, and managers of businesses like trucking firms and parking lots, which are likely to park large number of vehicles illegally. If the police were completely honest, it is likely that members of these groups would seek to corrupt them, since most seem to feel that *paying off the police is easier and cheaper than obeying the laws or paying fines and answering summonses . . . .* " (Italics added.) Knapp Commission 68.

[17]Arrow has remarked that an ethical code "may be of value to the running of the system as a whole, it may be of advantage to all firms if all firms maintain it, and yet it will be to the advantage of any one firm to cheat—in fact the more so, the more other firms are sticking to it." But he concludes that the value of maintaining the system "may well" be apparent to all and that "no doubt" ways will be found to make ethical codes a positive asset in attracting consumers and workers. Kenneth J. Arrow, Social Responsibility and Economic Efficiency, 21 Public Policy, 330, 315-16 (1973).

[18]These points are elaborated in Edward C. Banfield, Political Influence (1961), esp. pt. 2.

[19]These features of governmental organization are illustrated and analyzed by James Q. Wilson, Varieties of Police Behavior (1968).

[20]See Arnold J. Meltsner, The Politics of City Revenue 33-35 (1971).

[21]Robert C. Brooks, Corruption in American Politics and Life 166 (1910). The construction industry provides a case in point. New York City has a 843-page building code; a builder is required to get at least 40-50 permits and licenses (for a very large project as many as 130) from a maze of city departments. "Each stage," John Darnton writes in the New York Times, July 13, 1975, sec. 4, at 5, col. 3, " . . . is an invitation to a payoff. By withholding approval, or concentrating on a minor infraction, or simply not showing up at all, an inspector can cost a builder dearly or delay his recouping a multi-million-dollar investment." In practice, the Knapp Commission found, "most builders don't bother to get all the permits required by law. Instead, they apply for a handful of the more important ones (often making a payoff to personnel at the appropriate agency to insure prompt issuance of the permit). Payments to the

police and inspectors from other departments insure that builders won't be hounded for not having other permits.'' Knapp Commission 125. Recently two-thirds of the construction inspectors in Manhattan were suspended without pay on bribery charges. None of the charges seems to have resulted from a builder's effort to get around the requirements of the building code. What was being bought and sold, an official said, was time. Robert E. Tomasson in the New York Times, July 18, 1975, at 5.

[22]Moses, Caro writes, found ''a hundred ways around'' civil service pay and promotion rules. But his men were mainly attached to him because they were ''caught up in his sense of purpose'' and because they ''admired and respected'' him. Moses himself, Caro asserts, came to be motivated solely by an insatiable lust for power and glory. Robert A. Caro, The Power Broker, Robert Moses and the Fall of New York 273 (1974).

[23]See Edward C. Banfield & James Q. Wilson, City Politics, ch. 6 (1963).

[24]Wallace S. Sayre, in Agenda for a City 576 (Lyle C. Fitch & Annmarie Hauek eds. 1970).

[25]General Motors' procedure in dismissing salaried employees is in sharp contrast to that of the New York Police Department. When there was reason to believe that some of them were accepting favors and ''kickbacks,'' GM marched salaried employees, some of whom had been with the company for more than 25 years, through an ''assembly line'' for questioning by two company investigators. Forty-three who admitted taking gifts of more than nominal value were fired on the spot. Wall Street Journal, April 24, 1975, at 1, col. 6 and New York Times, June 15, 1975, at 1, col. 6.

In the New York Police Department, on the other hand, an officer under indictment for a felony may not be suspended; instead he is placed on ''modified assignment,'' retaining his salary, fringe benefits, and gun until final disposition of his case, which may take three or four years. New York Times, July 19, 1974, at 39, col. 1.

[26]For an account of the patronage, favors, and ''honest graft'' distributed in a relatively ''clean'' medium-sized city (New Haven) see Raymond E. Wolfinger, The Politics of Progress, ch. 4 (1974).

[27]On the machine, see Edward C. Banfield & James Q. Wilson, *supra* note 23, at ch. 9.

[28]In the Federal bureaucracy, Kaufman writes, subordinates may have to pick and choose among many directives for justification. ''This obligation may be thrust upon them by the inescapable ambiguities as well as inconsistencies of the instructions to them.'' Herbert Kaufman [with the collaboration of Michael Couzens], Administrative Feedback: Monitoring Subordinates' Behavior 2 (Brookings Inst. 1973).

In Oakland, California, the city manager sends a guidance letter to officials involved in the budget process. ''The important thing to understand about the manager's letter is that it contains nonoperational guidance, or decision rules that are not decision rules.'' Arnold J. Meltsner, *supra* note 20, at 165 & 271.

[29]On turn-over of mayors, see Raymond E. Wolfinger, *supra* note 26, at 394–95.

[30]See Mancur Olson, The Logic of Collective Action (1965).

[31]The New York Police Department announced that as an anti-corruption measure it would not arrest low-level figures in gambling combines or enforce the Sabbath laws (except upon complaint) or the laws pertaining to construction sites (unless pedestrians are endangered or traffic impeded). New York Times, Aug. 19, 1972, at 1.

[32]Jonathan Rubinstein, City Police (1973).

[33]Raymond E. Wolfinger, *supra* note 26, at 114.

[34]As Becker and Stigler remark, *supra* note 5, at 242, 'Trust calls for a salary premium not necessarily because better-quality persons are thereby attracted, but because higher salaries impose a cost on violations of trust.'' The principle was applied by New York Police Commissioner Murphy who limited the ''exposure [to temptations offered by gambling and narcotics interests] to officers of higher rank who presumably have a greater stake in maintaining their reputations.'' Knapp Commission 238.

[35]Recently the General Services administrator took steps to monitor some of his own necessarily subjective decisions by delegating the choice of architects to a panel of career civil servants which will rate candidates in writing on the basis of published criteria. Final decisions remain the administrator's reponsibility. Wall Street Journal, June 11, 1974, at 7, col. 1. For an account of the difficulties police administrators have in managing the discretion of policemen see James Q. Wilson, *supra* note 19, at 64–65 and *passim.*

[36]Herbert Kaufman, *supra* note 28, at 10, writing about the Federal bureaucracy, describes the sources of "unplanned feedback" as follows: "Clientele or customer objections, the normal interactions of organizations with each other, for example, staff agencies such as budget, personnel, administrative management, audit, legal counsel, and public relations can be expected to turn up some information for line executives about the behavior of line subordinates. Competitive agencies may reveal a good deal about each other's field activities. Some individuals and organizations thrive on exposing shortcomings in public agencies employing sensational publicity, reporters from the mass media, public prosecutors, grand juries, civic groups, public investigatory commissions. Subordinates themselves give clues about their own activities when they seek clarification of policy announcements, overlapping circles of acquaintances, membership in clubs and community groups, gossip and humor." See also, *id.* at 35, 41 & 74.

[37]Barnard believed corrupt acts such as falsifying books "for the good of the organization" to be rare in industrial organizations "but undoubtedly have occurred not infrequently in political, governmental, and religious organizations." Chester I. Barnard, The Functions of the Executive 277 (1938).

[38]Robert C. Brooks, *supra* note 21, at 107. See also Raymond E. Wolfinger, who writes, *supra* note 26, at 114: "John A. Gardiner's study of the notoriously corrupt city of Wincanton provides evidence for the proposition that decentralized political systems are *more* corruptible, because the potential corrupter needs to influence only a segment of the government, and because in a fragmented system there are fewer centralized forces and agencies to enforce honesty. The Wincanton political system is formally and informally fragmented; neither parties nor interest groups (including the criminal syndicate) exercise overall coordination. The ample patronage and outright graft in Wincanton are not used as a means of centralization. Indeed, governmental coordination clearly would not be in the interests of the private citizens there who benefit from corruption, nor of the officials who take bribes. Attempts by reformers to stop graft or patronage founder on the city's commission form of government, which is both the apotheosis of local governmental fragmentation and a hospitable environment for machine politics."

[39]Early in the present century an observer found New York state's formal administration "a drifting, amorphous mass, as helpless as a field of seaweed in the ocean" with power dispersed among nearly 170 units and "no head, no manager, no directing will *legally committed* to preside." At the same time the extra-legal side—that is, the political parties—had "no loose ends, no irresponsible agents—that is, "authority is clearly defined, obedience is punctiliously exacted; the hierarchy is closely interlinked, complete, effective." Quoted in Clifton K. Yearley, The Money Machines 254 (1970).

[40]Writing of James Marcus, a high official of the Lindsay administration who was convicted of bribery, Moscow remarks: "Marcus could not have happened in a Tammany administration, in which a man of loose morals might have been appointed, but not without full knowledge of his weaknesses." Warren Moscow, The Last of the Big-Time Bosses 202–03 (1971).

[41]Quoted from Adam Smith's Lectures by Edwin Cannan in his introduction to The Wealth of Nations, at xxxii (Mod. Libr. ed. 1937).

⁴²For a general discussion see James M. Buchanan, Ethical Rules, Expected Values, and Large Numbers, 76 Ethics, Oct. 1965, at 1–13 and his further remarks on The Samaritan's Dilemma, in Altruism, Morality and Economic Theory 71 (Edmund S. Phelps ed. 1975).

⁴³2 Alexis de Tocqueville, Democracy in America 295 (Knopf ed. 1945).

⁴⁴Indeed, as has been frequently noted, corruption frequently serves socially desirable functions—for example, it may make a grossly unfair tax more nearly equitable, it may keep the government going in a time of hyperinflation, it may deter a policeman from beating an innocent person, etc.

⁴⁵Consider, for example, the ruling by an administrative law judge of the National Labor Relations Board that a newspaper may not prohibit its reporters and editors from accepting gifts ("freebies") from news sources. New York Times, Jan. 17, 1975, at 43, col. 4. Weidenbaum has written recently of a "second managerial revolution" involving a shift " . . . from the professional management selected by the corporation's board of directors to the vast cadre of government regulators that influences and often controls the key decisions of the typical business firm." Murray L. Weidenbaum, Government-Mandated Price Increases 98 (Am. Enterprise Inst. for Public Policy Res., 1975).

⁴⁶Cf. J. S. Mill: "There are countries in Europe, of first-rate industrial capabilities, where the most serious impediment to conducting business concerns on a large scale, is the rarity of persons who are supposed fit to be trusted with the receipt and expenditure of large sums of money." 1 Principles of Political Economy 151 (5th ed.). See also Edward C. Banfield, The Moral Basis of a Backward Society (1958).

8

Whistle Blowing:
Its Nature and Justification

Gene G. James

Whistle blowing has increased significantly in American during the last two decades. Like blowing a whistle to call attention to a thief, whistle blowing is an attempt by a member or former member of an organization to bring illegal or socially harmful activities of the organization to the attention of the public. This may be done openly or anonymously and may involve any kind of organization, although business corporations and government agencies are most frequently involved. It may also require the whistle blower to violate laws or rules such as national security regulations which prohibit the release of certain information. However, because whistle blowing involving national security raises a number of issues not raised by other types, the present discussion is restricted to situations involving business corporations and government agencies concerned with domestic matters.

I

It is no accident that whistle blowing gained prominence during the last two decades which have been a period of great government and corporate wrongdoing. The Viet Nam war, Watergate, illicit activities by intelligence agencies both at home and abroad, the manufacture and sale of defective and unsafe products, misleading and fraudulent advertising, pollution of the environment, depletion of scarce natural resources, illegal bribes and campaign contributions, and attempts by corporations to influence political

Gene G. James, "Whistle Blowing: Its Nature and Justification," *Philosophy in Context*, Vol. 10, Copyright© 1980, pp. 99–117. Reprinted by permission of the Department of Philosophy, Cleveland State University, Cleveland, Ohio 44115.

activities in third world nations are only some of the events occurring during this period. Viewed in this perspective it is surprising that more whistle blowing has not occurred. Yet few employees of organizations involved in wrongdoing have spoken out in protest. Why are such people the first to know but usually the last to speak out?

The reason most often given for the relative infrequency of whistle blowing is loyalty to the organization. I do not doubt that this is sometimes a deterrent to whistle blowing. Daniel Ellsberg, e.g., mentions it as the main obstacle he had to overcome in deciding to make the Pentagon Papers public.[1] But by far the greatest deterrent, in my opinion, is self-interest. People are afraid that they will lose their job, be demoted, suspended, transferred, given less interesting or more demanding work, fail to obtain a bonus, salary increase, promotion, etc. This deterrent alone is sufficient to keep most people from speaking out even when they see great wrongdoing going on around them.

Fear of personal retaliation is another deterrent. Since whistle blowers seem to renounce loyalty to the organization, and threaten the self-interest of fellow employees, they are almost certain to be attacked in a variety of ways. In addition to such charges as they are unqualified to judge, are misinformed, and do not have all the facts, they are likely to be said to be traitors, squealers, rat finks, etc. They may be said to be disgruntled, known troublemakers, people who make an issue out of nothing, self-seeking and doing it for the publicity. Their veracity, life style, sex life and mental stability may also be questioned. Most of these accusations, of course, have nothing to do with the issues raised by whistle blowers. As Dr. John Goffman, who blew the whistle on the AEC for inadequate radiation standards, said of his critics, they "attack my style, my emotion, my sanity, my loyalty, my public forums, my motives. Everything except the issue."[2] Abuse of their families, physical assaults, and even murder, are not unknown as retaliation to whistle blowers.

The charge that they are self-seeking or acting for the publicity is one that bothers many whistle blowers. Although whistle blowing may be anonymous, if it is to be effective it frequently requires not only that the whistle blower reveal his or her identity, but also that he or she seek ways of publicizing the wrongdoing. Because this may make the whistle blower appear a self-appointed messiah, it prevents some people from speaking out. Whistle blowing may also appear, or be claimed to be, politically motivated when it is not.

Since whistle blowing may require one to do something illegal such as copy confidential records, threat of prosecution and prison may be additional deterrents.

II

Not only laws which forbid the release of information but agency law which governs the obligations of employees to employers seems to prohibit whistle blowing.[3] Agency law imposes three primary duties on employees: obedience, loyalty and confidentiality. These may be summed up by saying that in general employees are expected to obey all reasonable directives of their employers, to not engage in any economic activities detrimental to their employers, and to not communicate any information learned through their employment which either might harm their employer or which he might not want revealed. This last duty holds even after the employee no longer works for the employer. However, all three duties are qualified in certain respects. For example, although the employee is under an obligation to not start a competing business, he or she does have the right to advocate passage of laws and regulations which adversely affect the employer's business. And while the employee has a general obligation of confidentiality, this obligation does not hold if he has knowledge that his employer has committed, or is about to commit, a crime. Finally, in carrying out the duty of obeying all reasonable directives, the employee is given the discretion to consult codes of business and professional ethics in deciding what is and is not reasonable.

One problem with the law of agency is that there are no provisions in it to penalize an employer who harasses or fires employees for doing any of the things the law permits them to do. Thus, employees who advocate passage of laws which adversely affect their employers, who report or testify regarding a crime, or who refuse to obey a directive they consider illegal or immoral, are likely to be fired. Employees have even been fired on the last day before their pensions would become effective after thirty years of work and for testifying under subpoena against their employers without the courts doing anything to aid them. Agency law in effect presupposes an absolute right of employers to dismiss employees at will. That is, unless there are statutes or contractual agreements to the contrary, an employer may dismiss an employee at any time for any reason, or even for no reason, without being accountable at law. This doctrine which is an integral part of contract law goes all the way back to the code of Hammurabi in 632 B.C., which stated that an organizer could staff his workforce with whomever he wished. It was also influenced by Roman law which referred to employers and employees as "masters" and "servants," and by Adam Smith's notion of freedom of contract according to which employers and employees freely enter into the employment contract so either has the right to terminate it at will. Philip Blumberg, Dean of the School of Law at the University of Connecticut, sums up the current status of the right of employers to discharge as follows: "Over the years, this right of discharge has been increasingly restricted by statute and by collective bargaining agreements, but the basic principle of the employer's legal right to discharge, although challenged on the theoretical level, is still unimpaired."[4] The full significance of this remark is not apparent until one examines the extent to which existing statutes and collective bargaining agreements protect whistle blowers. As we shall see below, they provide very little protection. Furthermore, since in the absence of statutes or agreements to the contrary, employers can dismiss employees at will, it is obvious that they can also demote, transfer, suspend or otherwise retaliate against employees who speak out against, or refuse to participate in, illegal or socially harmful activities.

A second problem with the law of agency is that it seems to put one under an absolute obligation to not disclose any information about one's employer unless one can document that a crime has been, or is about to be, committed. This means that disclosing activities which are harmful to the public, but not presently prohibited by law, can result in one's being prosecuted or sued for damages. As Arthur S. Miller puts it: "The law at present provides very little protection to the person who would blow the whistle; in fact, it is more likely to assess him with criminal or civil penalties."[5] All that the whistle blower has to protect himself is the hope that the judge will be lenient, or that there will be a public outcry against his employer so great that he will not proceed against him.

III

There are some laws which encourage or protect whistle blowing. The Refuse Act of 1899 gives anyone who reports pollution one half of any fine that is assessed. Federal tax laws provide for the Secretary of the Treasury to pay a reward for information about violations of the Internal Revenue Code. The Commissioner of Narcotics is similarly authorized to pay a reward for information about contraband narcotics. The Federal Fair Labor Standards Act prohibits discharge of employees who complain or testify about violations of federal wage and hours laws. The Coal Mine Safety Act and the Water Pollution Control Act have similar clauses. And the Occupational Safety and Health Act prohibits discrimination against, or discharge of, employees who report violations of the act.

The main problem with all these laws, however, is that they must be enforced to be effective. The Refuse Act of 1899, for example, was not enforced prior to 1969 and fines imposed since then have been minimal. A study of the enforcement of the Occupational Safety and Health Act in 1976 by Morton Corn,[6] then an Assistant Secretary of Labor, showed that there were

700 complaints in FY 1975 and 1600 in FY 1976 by employees who claimed they were discharged or discriminated against because they had reported a violation of the act. Only about 20 percent of these complaints were judged valid by OSHA investigators. More than half of these, that is to say, less than three hundred, were settled out of court. The remaining complaints were either dropped or taken to court. Of the 60 cases taken to court at the time of Corn's report in November 1976, one had been won, eight lost and the others were still pending. Hardly a record to encourage further complaints.

What help can whistle blowers who belong to a union expect from it? In some cases unions have intervened to keep whistle blowers from being fired or to help them gain reinstatement. But for the most part they have restricted themselves to economic issues, not speaking out on behalf of free speech for their members. Also, some unions are as bad offenders as any corporation. David Ewing has well stated this problem: "While many unions are run by energetic, capable, and high-minded officials, other unions seem to be as despotic and corrupt as the worst corporate management teams. Run by mossbacks who couldn't care less about ideals like due process, these unions are not likely to feed a hawk that may come to prey in their own barnyard."[7]

The record of professional societies is not much better. Despite the fact that the code of ethics of nearly every profession requires the professional to place his duty to the public above his duty to his employer, very few professional societies have come to the aid of members who have blown the whistle. However, there are some indications that this is changing. The American Association for the Advancement of Science recently created a standing committee on Scientific Freedom and Responsibility which sponsored a symposium on whistle blowing at the 1978 meeting and is encouraging scientific societies and journals to take a more active role in whistle blowing situations. A sub-committee to review individual cases has also been formed.[8]

Many employees of the federal government are in theory protected from arbitrary treatment by civil service regulations. However, these have provided little protection for whistle blowers in the past. Indeed, the failure of civil service regulations to protect whistle blowers was one of the factors which helped bring about the Civil Service Reform Act of 1978. This act explicitly prohibits reprisal against employees who release information they believe is evidence of: (a) violation of law, rules, or regulations, (b) abuse of authority, mismanagement, or gross waste of funds, (c) specific and substantial danger to public health or safety. The act also sets up mechanisms to enforce its provisions. Unfortunately, it excludes all employees of intelligence agencies, even when the issue involved is not one of national security, except employees of the FBI who are empowered to go to the Attorney General with information about wrongdoing. Although it is too early to determine how vigorously the act will be enforced, it seems on paper to offer a great deal of protection for whistle blowers.

Although state and local laws usually do not offer much protection, thanks to a series of federal court decisions, people who work for state and municipal governments are also better off than people who work for private corporations. In the first of these in 1968 the Supreme Court ordered the reinstatement of a high school teacher named Pickering who had publicly criticized his school board. This was followed by a 1970 district court decision reinstating a Chicago policeman who had accused his superiors of covering up thefts by policemen. In 1971 another teacher who criticized unsafe playground conditions was reinstated. And in 1973 a fireman and a psychiatric nurse who criticized their agencies were reinstated. In all of these decisions, however, a key factor seems to have been that the action of the employee did not disrupt the morale of fellow employees. Also no documents of the organizations were made public. Had either of these factors been different the decisions would have probably gone the other way.[9]

Given the lack of support whistle blowers have received in the past from the law, unions, professional societies, and government agencies, the fear that one will be harassed or lose one's job for blowing the whistle is well founded, especially if one works for private industry. Moreover, since whistle blowers are unlikely to be given favorable letters of recommendation, finding another job is not easy. Thus despite some changes for the better, unless there are major changes in agency law, the operation and goals of unions and professional societies, and more effective enforcement of laws protecting government employees, we should not expect whistle blowing to increase significantly in the near future. This means that much organization wrongdoing will go unchecked.

IV

Whistle blowing is not lacking in critics. When Ralph Nader issued a call for more whistle blowing in an article in the *New York Times* in 1971, James M. Roche, Chairman of the Board of General Motors Corporation responded:

> Some of the enemies of business now encourage an employee to be disloyal to the enterprise. They want to create suspicion and disharmony and pry into the proprietary interests of the business. However this is labelled—industrial espionage, whistle blowing or professional responsibility—it is another tactic for spreading disunity and creating conflict.[10]

The premise upon which Roche's remarks seems to be based is that an employee's only obligation is to the company for which he works. Thus he sees no difference between industrial espionage—stealing information from one company to benefit another economically—and the disclosure of activities harmful to the public. Both injure the company involved, so both are equally wrong. This position is similar to another held by many businessmen, viz., that the sole obligation of corporate executives is to make a profit for stockholders for whom they serve as agents. This is tantamount to saying that employees of corporations have no obligations to the public. However, this is not true because corporations are chartered by governments with the expectation that they will function in ways that are compatible with the public interest. Whenever they cease to do this, they violate the understanding under which they were chartered and allowed to exist, and may be legitimately penalized or even have their charters revoked. Furthermore, part of the expectation with which corporations are chartered in democratic societies is that not only will they obey the law, but in addition they will not do anything which undermines basic democratic processes. Corporations, that is, are expected to be not only legal persons but good citizens as well. This does not mean that corporations must donate money to charity or undertake other philanthropic endeavors, although it is admirable if they do. It means rather that the minimum conduct expected of them is that they will make money only in ways that are consistent with the public good. As officers of corporations it is the obligation of corporate executives to see that this is done. It is only within this framework of expectations that the executive can be said to have an obligation to stockholders to return maximum profit on their investments. It is only within this framework, also, that employees of a corporation have an obligation to obey its directives. This is the reason the law of agency exempts employees from obeying illegal or unethical commands. It is also the reason that there is a significant moral difference between industrial espionage and whistle blowing. The failure of Roche and other corporate officials to realize this, believing instead that their sole obligation is to operate their companies profitably, and that the sole obligation of employees is to obey their directives without question, is one of the central reasons corporate wrongdoing exists and whistle blowing is needed.

Another objection to whistle blowing advanced by some businessmen is that it increases costs, thereby reducing profits and raising prices for consumers. There is no doubt that it has cost companies considerable money to correct situations disclosed by whistle blowers. However, this must be balanced against costs incurred when the public eventually comes to learn, without the aid of whistle blowers, that corporate wrongdoing has taken place. Would Ford Motor Company or Firestone Rubber Company have made less money in the long run had they listened to their engineers who warned that the gas tank of the Pinto and Firestone radial tires were unsafe? I think a good case could be made that they would not. Indeed, if corporate executives were to listen to employees troubled by their companies' practices and products, in many cases they would improve their earnings. So strong, however, is the feeling that employees should obey orders without questioning, that when an oil pipeline salesman for U.S. Steel went over the head of unresponsive supervisors to report defective pipelines to top company officials, he was fired even though the disclosure saved the company thousands of dollars.

I am not arguing that corporate crime never pays, for often it pays quite handsomely. But the fact that there are situations in which corporate crime is more profitable than responsible action, is hardly an argument against whistle blowing. It would be an argument against it only if one were to accept the premise that the sole obligation of corporations is to make as much money as possible by any means whatever. But as we saw above this premise cannot be defended and its acceptance by corporate executives in fact provides a justification for whistle blowing.

The argument that employees owe total allegiance to the organizations for which they work has also been put forth by people in government. For example, Frederick Malek, former Deputy Secretary of HEW states:

> The employee, whether he is civil service or a political appointee, has not only the right but the obligation to make his views known in the most strenuous way possible to his superiors, and through them, to their superiors. He should try like hell to get his views across and adopted within the organization—but not publicly, and only until a decision is reached by those superiors. Once the decision is made, he must do the best he can to live with it and put it into practice. If he finds that he cannot do it, then he ought not to stay with the organization.[11]

And William Rehnquist, Justice of the Supreme Court, says "I think one may fairly generalize that a government employee . . . is seriously restricted in his freedom of speech with respect to any matter for which he has been assigned responsibility."[12]

Malek's argument presupposes that disclosure of wrongdoing to one's superior will be relayed to higher officials. But often it is one's immediate superiors who are responsible for the wrongdoing. Furthermore, even if they are not, there is no guarantee that they will relay one's protest. Malek also assumes that there are always means of protest within organizations and that these function effectively. This, too, is frequently not the case. For example, Peter Gail who resigned his position as an attorney for the Office of Civil Rights Division of HEW because the Nixon administration was fail-

ing to enforce desegregation laws, and who along with a number of colleagues sent a public letter of protest to President Nixon, says in response to
Malek that:

> as far as I am concerned, his recommended line of action would have been a
> waste of everyone's time. To begin with, the OCR staff members probably
> would have made their protest to Secretary Finch if they had felt that Finch's
> views were being listened to, or acted upon, at the White House . . .[13]

And in defense of sending the public letter to Nixon he states that:

> A chief reason we decided to flout protocol and make the text of the letter
> public was that we felt that the only way the President would even become
> aware of . . . the letter was through publicity. We had answered too many let-
> ters—including those bitterly attacking the retreat on segregation—referred
> unread by the White House . . . to have any illusion about what the fate of
> our letter would be. In fact, our standing joke . . . was that we would prob-
> ably be asked to answer it ourselves.[14]

Even when there are effective channels of protest within an organization,
there may be situations in which it is justifiable to by-pass them, for example, if there is imminent danger to public health or safety, if one is criticiz-
ing the overall operation of an agency, or if using standard channels of protest would jeopardize the interests one is trying to protect.

If Justice Rehnquist's remark is meant as a recommendation that people
whose responsibility is to protect the health, safety and rights of the
American people should not speak out when they see continued wrongdoing, then it must be said to be grossly immoral. The viewpoint it represents
is one that Americans repudiated at Nuremberg. Daniel Ellsberg's comments on why he finally decided to release the Pentagon Papers put this
point well.

> I think the principle of "company loyalty," as emphasized in the indoctrina-
> tion within any bureaucratic structure, governmental or private, has come to
> sum up the notion of loyalty for many people. That is not a healthy situation,
> because the loyalty that a democracy requires to function is a . . . varied set of
> loyalties which includes loyalty to one's fellow citizens, and certainly loyalty to
> the Constitution and to the broader institutions of the country. Obviously,
> these loyalties can come into conflict, and merely mentioning the word "loyal-
> ty" doesn't dissolve those dilemmas . . . The Code of Ethics of Government
> Service, passed by both the House and Senate, starts with the principle that
> every employee of the government should put loyalty to the highest moral
> principles and to country above loyalty to persons, parties, or government
> department . . . To believe that the government cannot run unless one puts
> loyalty to the President above everything else is a formula for a dictatorship,
> and not for a republic.[15]

V

Even some people who are favorable to whistle blowing are afraid that it might become too widespread. For example, Arthur S. Miller writes: "One should be very careful about extending the principle of whistle blowing unduly. Surely it can be carried too far. Surely, too, an employee owes his employer enough loyalty to try to work, first of all, within the organization to attempt to effect change."[16] And Philip Blumberg expresses the fear that "once the duty of loyalty yields to the primacy of what the individual . . . regards as the 'public interest,' the door is open to widespread abuse."[17]

It would be unfortunate if employees were to make public pronouncements every time they thought they saw something wrong within an organization without making sure they have the facts. And employees ought to exhaust all channels of protest within an organization before blowing the whistle, *provided* it is feasible to do so. Indeed, as Ralph Nader and his associates point out, in many cases "going to management first minimizes the risk of retaliatory dismissal, as you may not have to go public with your demands if the corporation or government agency takes action to correct the situation. It may also strengthen your case if you ultimately go outside . . . since the managers are likely to point out any weaknesses in your arguments and any factual deficiencies in your evidence in order to persuade you that there is really no problem."[18] But this is subject to the qualifications mentioned in connection with Malek's argument.

If it is true, as I argued above, that self-interest and narrow loyalties will always keep the majority of people from speaking out even when they see great wrongdoing going on around them, then the fear that whistle blowing could become so prevalent as to threaten the everyday working of organizations seems groundless. However, Miller's and Blumberg's remarks do call to our attention the fact that whistle blowers have certain obligations. All whistle blowers should ask themselves the following kinds of questions before acting: What exactly is the objectionable practice? What laws are being broken or specific harm done? Do I have adequate and accurate information about the wrongdoing? How could I get additional information? Is it feasible to report the wrongdoing to someone within the organization? Is there a procedure for doing this? What are the results likely to be? Will doing this make it easier or more difficult if I decide to go outside? Will I be violating the law or shirking my duty if I do not report the matter to people outside the organization? If I go outside to whom should I go? Should I do this openly or anonymously? Should I resign and look for another job before doing it? What will be the likely response of those whom I inform? What can I hope to achieve in going outside? What will be the consequences for me, my family and friends? What will the consequences of *not* speaking out be for me, my family and friends? What will the consequences be for the public? Could I live with my conscience if I do not speak out?

There is one respect in which whistle blowing might be taken too far. However, this requires explanation. Proponents of whistle blowing often write as though it were by definition a morally praiseworthy activity. For example, whistle blowing is defined in the preface of Nader's book as

> the act of a man or woman who, believing that the public interest overrides the interest of the organization he serves, publicly "blows the whistle" if the organization is involved in corrupt, illegal, fraudulent, or harmful activity . . .[19]

And Charles Peters and Taylor Branch, defending whistle blowers against the charge that they are traitors, say:

> The traitor was always hated, because he was the enemy, but there was a special edge on the scorn that historically made traitors hated everywhere . . . For the traitor was excoriated as a person without honor of any kind, who, among people willing to die for cause or principle . . . could shuffle back and forth between opposing camps, sniffing for the highest bidder, unmoved by higher loyalty or human bond . . . Benedict Arnold was hated for defecting . . ., but he was despised as a real traitor because people found out that he had bargained at length over the pension he would receive—and even the number of calico dresses his wife would obtain—for switching sides.
>
> The whistle-blowers have actually reversed the operation of the classical traitor, as they have usually been the *only* people in their organizations taking a stand on some kind of ideal.[20]

They go on to argue that whistle blowers have been so successful in winning public admiration that "looking at the problem through the eyes of future whistle-blowers, the dilemmas are likely to center not on the morality of proposed actions but on their utility."[21]

The problem with both this definition and defense of whistle blowing is that they fuse motives with goals. That is, they seem to take for granted that because the whistle blower discloses wrongdoing, his or her motives must be praiseworthy. In fact, people may blow the whistle for a variety of reasons: to seek revenge, gain prosecutorial immunity, attract publicity, etc. Furthermore, from the standpoint of immediate public good, the motives of whistle blowers are unimportant. All that matters is whether the situation is as the whistle blower describes it. That is, does a situation exist which is harmful to the public?

However, consideration of the motives of whistle blowers does raise an interesting problem. To what extent should there be laws which encourage whistle blowing for self-interested reasons? Should there, e.g., be more laws like the federal tax law which furthers disclosure of tax violations by paying informers part of any money that is collected? Do not laws such as these bring about a situation which encourages suspicion, revenge, and profit seeking among citizens? And would not a society which relied heavily on this type of law be "taking whistle blowing too far?" I think that the answer to the last two questions must be affirmative. This does not mean, however, that society should never adopt laws which encourage whistle blowing for base motives. The extent to which a given law furthers spiteful behavior among citizens must be balanced against the amount of good it produces. In some cases, although I do not think in very many, the good clearly outweighs the harm of furthering vengeful behavior.

It would seem that anyone who was in favor of whistle blowing would also be in favor of laws protecting whistle blowers from arbitrary discharge from their jobs. However, Peters and Branch argue that with one exception

> freedom to hire and fire without red tape is essential to good government and . . . potential whistle-blowers should not be promised a world free of risks. Of course, our society should offer everyone a cushion against catastrophic job loss in the form of a decent guaranteed annual income and free health care. Beyond that we resist depriving life of adventure.[22]

The one exception they allow is that of people in situations like that of Dr. Jacqueline Verrett, the FDA employee who informed the press that her superiors were distorting the results of experiments she had performed which showed that cyclamates cause growth deformities in chicken embryos. All other whistle blowers, they say, even those such as Daniel Ellsberg whom they admire greatly, should be subject to being fired. But, exactly why people in situations such as Dr. Verrett's should be treated as exceptions is not made clear. Perhaps they consider threats to people's health more important than other threats to their well-being. Nor do they give any argument to justify why not depriving life of adventure is more important than preventing the discharge of people they claim are usually the most conscientious employees of organizations. Their position also seems to be inconsistent since they say elsewhere that whistle blowing "should be encouraged, even by . . . employers themselves."[23]

The reason they arrive at such a contradictory position, in my opinion, is that they too fear that whistle blowing might get out of hand. Shortly after making the foregoing remark they say:

> There should be more protection for the whistle-blowers who prove right . . . without making whistle-blowing an automatic free ride. The risk must be preserved, for otherwise whistle-blowing would become banal, the

country would be inundated with exposures, and the good cases would become uselessly lost in a sea of bad ones.[24]

This is to abandon the view that all whistle blowers should be fired, in favor of the one that people whose claims turn out to be false should be fired. But should all whistle blowers be fired whose claims turn out to be false? If so, what about those whose claims are partially true and partially false? Their position is a variation of the view that speech should be protected only when what is said is true. I doubt that they would accept this view if applied to the press. As working journalists they are more likely to believe that the press should be penalized only when it can be shown that false statements were made with malicious intent. Why should it be different in the case of whistle blowers? To believe that it should is not only to deprive life of adventure, it is to actively discourage whistle blowing and to allow corporate and governmental wrongdoing to flourish.

Rosemary Chalk, Staff Officer for the American Association for the Advancement of Science, arguing for greater involvement of scientific societies in whistle blowing, is correct, in my opinion, when she says that: "It should not be necessary for the whistle-blower to be 100 percent correct in order to gain support from his or her professional colleagues. The basis for scientific society involvement should not rest exclusively on whether the whistle-blower is right or wrong, but rather on whether the issue . . . is important in terms of its effect on the public interest."[25] Philip Blumberg is also correct when he says: "The public interest in the free discussion of ideas does not rest on the validity of the point of view expressed. Where dissent involves *no unauthorized disclosure*, the cost of sanctioning such conduct is low and of prohibiting it, high."[26] But unlike Blumberg, I believe that the area of authorized disclosure should be as wide as possible. This means that the law of agency should be superseded by federal legislation which would prevent employers from discharging or otherwise penalizing whistle blowers unless it can be proven both that their claims are false and were made with malicious intent. However, the situation must be one in which the public interest is at stake. Disclosure of trade secrets, customer lists, plans for marketing, personnel records, etc., should not be protected unless releasing them was necessary for the whistle blowing and the damage resulting is clearly outweighed by benefits to the public.

Many people are opposed to legislation protecting whistle blowers because they believe it unwarranted interference with freedom of contract. However, the traditional doctrine of freedom of contract rested on an assumption of equality between employers and employees which no longer exists. It is far easier today for employers to find another employee than for employees to find a new job. Furthermore, as Lawrence E. Blades has pointed out, the freedom of the individual to terminate his employment is more important than the freedom of employers to hire and fire at will.[27] The rights of the individual to dispose of his labor as he wishes and to be protected from retaliation in exercising his civil rights are fundamental to the existence of democratic societies. The courts have recognized this to some extent by limiting the right of employers to dismiss employees for union activities. The current practice of allowing employers to dismiss employees who are performing their jobs competently and whose sole "offense" is disclosure of situations harmful to the public is, therefore, one that ought to be abolished.

If legislation to protect whistle blowers is effective, it should provide for punitive damages against employers when it can be proven that they dismissed or penalized employees for justified whistle blowing. But how is the employee to show this? Both Blades and Ewing believe that the burden of proof should be on the employee. Blades writes:

> Ordinarily, when both sides present equally credible versions of the facts, the plaintiff will have failed to carry his burden. However, there is the danger that the average jury will identify with . . . the employee. This . . . could give rise to vexatious lawsuits . . .
>
> Certainly, the employee should not be allowed to shift to the employer the burden of showing that the discharge was motivated by good cause by proving only that he capably performed the duties required by his job and was discharged for no apparent reason . . . The employee should be required . . . to prove by affirmative and substantial evidence that his discharge was actuated by reasons violative of his personal freedom or integrity.[28]

Both Blades and Ewing qualify their position by suggesting that longevity of service be taken as evidence that an employee was doing his job effectively. Blades says "in cases like mine, where the discharged employee had served the employer for 17 years as a branch manager and 32 years in all, a jury would probably be quite justified in finding little merit in an explanation that the plaintiff was fired for 'chronic' inefficiency and incompetence."[29] And Ewing states: "The longer the employee was on the job, the better his or her case . . . If management was doing its job, such employees (who have served eight or more years) must have been working competently or they would not have stayed on the payroll all that time."[30]

The problem with these remarks is that if the burden of proof is on the employee to show by "affirmative and substantial" evidence that his discharge was for reasons which violate his personal freedom or integrity, and at the same time, the employer is under no obligation to show that the discharge was for good cause, establishing that an employee has competently performed his job for a number of years would be irrelevant to the issue at dispute. Showing this would be relevant only if the employer were under an obligation to show that he or she had not performed competently. And in cases involving discrimination against, or the firing of, whistle blowers, this is exactly what employers should be required to do. To require that employees show by affirmative and substantial evidence that they were not fired for good reasons, when employers are under no obligation to demonstrate why they were fired, is to require a degree of evidence impossible to fulfill. Such a law would offer no protection to whistle blowers and is in fact a reversion to the doctrine of the absolute right of employers to discharge at will which laws protecting whistle blowers should be designed to overcome.

The fear that unless the burden of proof is placed on the whistle blower, vexatious lawsuits will result is unrealistic for two reasons. First, as I argued above, self-interest will always keep the majority of people from engaging in whistle blowing. Second, only employees who could show that an act of whistle blowing preceded their being dismissed or penalized would be able to seek redress under the law.

VI

Laws preventing whistle blowers from being dismissed or penalized are, of course, only one way of dealing with corporate and government wrongdoing. Laws and other measures aimed at changing the nature of organizations to prevent wrongdoing and encourage whistle blowing are equally important. Changing the role of corporate directors, appointing ombudspersons and high level executives to review charges of wrongdoing, requiring that certain types of information be compiled and retained, and reforming regulatory agencies are some of the proposals which have been advanced for doing this. Unions and professional societies also need to act to further the rights of their members and protect the public good. Professional societies, e.g., should reformulate their codes of ethics to make obligations to the public more central, investigate violations of member's rights, provide advice and legal aid if needed, censure organizations found guilty, attempt to secure legislation protecting members' rights, and in some cases set up central pension funds to free members from undue dependence on the organization for which they work.

Since my primary purposes were to clarify the nature of whistle blowing, defend it against criticisms and show its importance for democratic societies, detailed discussion of the topics mentioned in this section is beyond the scope of this paper. Whistle blowing is not a means of eliminating all organizational wrongdoing. But in conjunction with other measures to insure that organizations act responsibly, it can be an important factor in maintaining democratic freedom.

NOTES

[1]See Charles Peters and Taylor Branch, *Blowing the Whistle: Dissent in the Public Interest*, New York, 1972, Praeger Publishers, Chapter Sixteen.

[2]Quoted in Ralph Nader, Peter J. Petkas and Kate Blackwell, *Whistle Blowing*, New York, 1972, Grossman Publishers, p. 72.

[3]For a discussion of agency law and its relation to whistle blowers see Lawrence E. Blades, "Employment at Will vs. Individual Freedom: On Limiting the Abusive Exercise of Employer Power," *Columbia Law Review* 67 (1967), and Philip Blumberg, "Corporate Responsibility and the Employee's Duty of Loyalty and Obedience: A Preliminary Inquiry," *Oklahoma Law Review* 24 (1971), reprinted in part in Tom L. Beauchamp and Norman E. Bowie, *Ethical Theory and Business*, New York, 1979, Prentice Hall; and Clyde W. Summers, "Individual Protection Against Unjust Dismissal: Time for a Statute," *Virginia Law Review* 62 (1976). See also Nader, *Op. Cit.*, and David W. Ewing, *Freedom Inside the Organization*, New York, 1977, E. P. Dutton.

[4]Blumberg, *Op. Cit.*, in Beauchamp and Bowie, p. 311.

[5]Arthur S. Miller, "Whistle Blowing and the Law" in Nader, *Op. Cit.*, p. 25.

[6]Corn's report is discussed by Frank von Hipple in "Professional Freedom and Responsibility: The Role of the Professional Society," in the *Newsletter on Science, Technology and Human Values*, Number 22, January 1978, pp. 37–42.

[7]Ewing, *Op. Cit.*, pp. 165–166.

[8]Discussion of the role professional societies have played in whistle blowing can be found in Nader, *Op. Cit.*, von Hipple, *Op. Cit.*, and in Rosemary Chalk, "Scientific Involvement in Whistle Blowing" in the *Newsletter on Science, Technology and Human Values, Op. Cit.*, pp. 47–51.

[9]These decisions are discussed by Ewing, *Op. Cit.*, Chapter Six.

[10]Quoted in Blumberg, *Opt. Cit.*, p. 305.

[11]Quoted in Peters and Branch, *Op. Cit.*, pp. 178–179.

[12]*Ibid.*, pp. x-xi.

[13]*Ibid.*, p. 179.

[14]*Ibid.*, p. 178.

[15]*Ibid.*, p. 269.

[16]Miller, *Op. Cit.*, p. 30.

[17]Blumberg, *Op. Cit.*, p. 313.

[18]Nader, *Op. Cit.*, pp. 230–231.

[19]*Ibid.*, p. vii.

[20]Peters and Branch, *Op. Cit.*, p. 288.

[21]*Ibid.*, p. 290.

[22]*Ibid.*, p. xi.

[23]*Ibid.*, p. 298.

[24]*Ibid.*

[25]Chalk, *Op. Cit.*, p. 50.

[26]Philip Blumberg, "Commentary on 'Professional Freedom and Responsibility: The Role of the Professional Society'," in the *Newsletter on Science, Technology and Human Values, Op. Cit.*, p. 45.

[27]Blades, *Op. Cit.*

[28]*Ibid.*, pp. 1425–1426.
[29]*Ibid.*, pp. 1428–1429.
[30]Ewing, *Op. Cit.*, p. 202.

9

Ethical Dilemmas in Government: Designing an Organizational Response

T. Edwin Boling
and
John Dempsey

The subject of ethics is currently an extensive concern in the field of public management. Ethics, and ethics-related subjects, have begun to occupy a prominent place in the literature of the field, on the agendas of professional meetings, and in the educational programs which train future managers.[1] Many hope that the effects of this renewed focus on ethical questions will be salutary. If it has no other consequence than to raise the ethical consciousness of public managers—to make them more sensitive to the important normative dimensions of their work—its purpose will have been at least partly achieved. Still, one is left with the disquieting feeling that ethical "awareness" alone is not the total solution.

A review of the recent emphasis on ethics in public administration shows several important limitations. First, it tends to focus on personal ethical standards and on how administrators can make ethical choices concerning public policies. These are certainly important concerns, but they represent only a small range of ethical problems common to public life. Second, most of the current literature points to individuals as bearing exclusive responsibility for ethical behavior in organizations. While this emphasis may be laudable, its implied reliance on individual administrators both underestimates the complexity of the problem and fails to contribute to a systemic solution. The analysis presented in this article, by contrast, focuses

From *Public Personnel Management Journal*, Vol. 10 (1981) pp. 11–19. Reprinted by permission.

on conceptual clarification and organizational reform as the building blocks which must underlie efforts to improve the ethical tenor of organizational life.

Dimensions of the Problem

The kinds of ethical problems that are likely to confront public administrators can be categorized into three distinct, but related, types: (a) the ethics of public policy, (b) personal ethical standards, and (c) organizational role demands.

The Ethics of Public Policy. In view of the widely held belief that administrators share policy-making power with elected officials, it is only fair that their policy decisions be made to stand the same ethical tests as those to which legislative decisions are subjected. In short, administrators must ask—from an ethical point of view—what is the 'right' decision in a given situation. They must ask themselves " . . . which (policy) choice is the fairest in this case?", and "which choice is the most just?" These questions are never easy ones to answer, particularly since they involve concepts that elude precise definition.

Public administrators admit that the subject of ethics is a difficult one. Ethics seem to be identified as both rules (law) and expectations (ideals). Consequently, some acclaim high ethical attainment when the law is met, feeling no sense of need for stretching toward an ideal. However, practitioners do not have a corner on the confusion about ethics. Among academicians very diverse definitions have been generated.[2]

Personal Ethical Standards. All serious persons must grapple from time to time with questions of right and wrong action. In public life, the development of personal ethical standards is crucial because of the "public trust" involved, and because of the large number of people affected by the "personal" decisions of public officials. Government service often exposes one to the kinds of temptations which sharply test an individual's ethical mettle. The very nature of public employment—both because of the money administered by public officials and because of the power which those managers possess—exposes administrators to the temptations. Further, because officials are also private citizens with their own economic concerns, public employment can also create severe conflicts of interest. While laws and the simple norms of decency may prohibit the grossest forms of these activities, there are some situations where laws are either hazy or inapplicable.

Moral and ethical action is often assumed under the idea that everyone knows what a moral judgment is.[3] Thus, by intuition, individuals are expected to "draw distinctions between right and wrong, good and bad, all of them without being cognizant of the criteria we are employing."[4] Intuition, an ethical approach of behavioral simplicity, centers in an individual philosophy of human action. Golembiewski presents this theme in the form of Judaeo-Christian religion. Even in public life, it is possible to be guided by a limited set of personal values effectively derived from this religious tradition.[5] Pressing the individualistic theme toward the public sector, Presthus concludes that "we are in truth forced to rely upon officials themselves for responsible public administration."[6] In this same pattern, Appleby admonishes individual officials to have "moral purpose and strength" while guarding "social life (and) carefully avoiding involvements of a questionable nature."[7]

The intuitive orientation continues to receive high marks in public administration. In an award winning manuscript (honored by the American Society for Public Administration), Wakefield assesses "where we are in terms of ethics and the public service."[8] She defines a system of values which reaches back into Judaeo-Christian tradition; the system sets *individual responsibility* as the primary and ultimate source of ethics in the public service.

Although rather infrequently, the intuitive approach to ethical behavior has been criticized. In a cross-cultural study of personal value systems among managers, England found that there were large individual differences. Personal value systems were rigid and tended not to change over time.[9] In another example, Walton made the following critical assessment of the intuitive approach:

> . . . a personal ethic devised from traditional religious or moral codes is, of itself, too simplistic an approach to the problem of professional behavior in a large organization. Loftiness of purpose and purity of motive are insufficient bases on which to rest an ethical system totally adequate to mid-twentieth century organizational realities.[10]

Organizational Role Demands. Knowing which policy choices are ethical, and knowing right from wrong in personal behavior are essential elements of responsible, effective public administration. However, since almost all public administrators work in organizational settings, there is another dimension to personal behavior which must be explored. This is the dilemma which occurs when personal ethics standards, or policy choices, are at variance with established organizational policy.

Whether these situations involve organizational coercion on an individual to perform an action he or she believes to be unethical or the simple demands of obedience to the dictates of "organizational gospel," an environment is created where an employee must choose a course of action from among options which Albert O. Hirschman has labeled, "exit, voice, and loyalty."[11] According to Hirschman "exit" means "resignation," "leaving under your own steam, quitting, switching, resigning, deserting, escaping from."[12] Comparatively neat and impersonal, exit is the end of loyalty. "Loyalty," on the other hand, means keeping silent in the hope that one can "win the next battle," or believing that one's departure will result in further deterioration of the organization's ethical standards.

In between exit and loyalty is Hirschman's third option, "voice":

> . . . an attempt to change things through articulation whether by your dissatisfaction to those in a position to make changes, or by grousing to anyone who will listen . . . Voice is essentially an art, constantly evolving in creative new directions. In contrast to exit, voice implies a continuing (if strained) loyalty to the entity that is causing stress.[13]

It is the instance of "voice"—particularly when it involves "grousing to anyone who will listen"—which creates the much-publicized phenomenon of "whistle-blowing."[14] "Whistle-blowing" is a significant form of ethical behavior, particularly if one agrees with the first article of the Code of Ethics for Government Service, which instructs public employees to "Put loyalty to the highest moral principles and country above loyalty to persons, party, or Government department."[15]

A Model for Reform

In arriving at solutions to the above problems, there are two possible avenues along which action might proceed. One could try to instill in individual public administrators the courage necessary to make the tough moral choices which the Code of Ethics seems to require. Perhaps we should redouble our efforts to inculcate the values of that Code, and to persuade public administrators to develop ethical consciousness. However, a different approach—one with more realistic prospects for long-term success—is to focus not on individual public administrators, but on the organizational settings in which they work. It is an approach which asserts that if we wish to improve the ethical tenor of organizational life we must devote our attention to a restructuring of the organization itself.

Boulding speaks of an "organizational revolution"[16] in modern society, stating that in political, economic and ethical thinking there is as much as a one hundred year lag. Specifically, he writes:

> We are still . . . thinking in terms of a society in which organizations are rather small and weak, and in which the family is the dominant institution.[17]

In his analysis, Boulding establishes ethics as a major organizational component. In the following pages this paper identifies three areas for the "ethical" reform of organizations—conceptual clarification, protection for dissenters, and a program of normative enrichment.

Conceptual Clarification

The problem of ethics in organizations is at least in part one of definition; it is not new and it remains unresolved. Resolution of the problem demands that ethics be extended to the realm of group properties, that normative structure be separated into various parts, and that each part be examined in detail. A procedure not unlike this was suggested by Leys more than 35 years ago. Concerned with the ethics of public policy, Leys noted the contention of many that one should go "beyond conscience" for establishing political morality. He continued by stating that conscience urges respect for "two sorts of values": (a) to respect and conserve good things that already exist, and (b) to seek and honor ideals not yet realized.[18] The implications here are that morality is the upholding of values which already exist while ethics, imaginatively, create new values.

More recently, Barnsley demonstrated a similar concern for conceptual clarification. He alludes to the separation of much of the terminology which has been used interchangeably.[19] Others, without giving an obvious nod to conceptual clarification, have suggested that ethics are really beyond rules of conduct; ethics are creative ideals from which values, norms and moral behavior receive stimulus for change.[20]

To secure individual behavior of a collective nature, societies specify rules through a normative system—the *normative ethos* or the guiding rules plus acceptable action and ideals that characterize social systems. Organizations, as systems within the larger social structure, are expected to develop normative patterns in league with those of society. Therefore, a program of normative enrichment should clarify an organization's normative system as it relates to and supports the ethos of the larger society. To generate this clarification, the normative ethos must be defined in terms of its basic elements—*values* supported by *norms, morals* and *ethics*. Although often used interchangeably, each of these concepts has its own distinct place in a normative constellation.

Basic to the normative ethos are *values*, abstract standards that persist over time and that identify what is right and proper for people in a society or group.[21] These standards provide a framework that influences individual behavior and affects social expectations, principally determining what is regarded as right, good, worthy, beautiful, and so on.[22] Supporting the values are regulations which guide conduct or *norms*. Norms define what is acceptable or required. These are rules which are mediated to the individual through his/her particular group memberships. Norms are sometimes internalized and taken for granted, thereby ordering the activities of persons in social groups, often as if by habit.

Whereas norms are group rules which specify what behavior ought to be, *morals* are personal judgments—relative to behavior—and morality is the behavior carried out under those judgments. Both judgments and behavior are based upon values and norms.[23],[24] One senses a "rightness" in compliance with norms and a "wrongness" in violation or non-compliance. In the struggle to set rationally acceptable justification for regulation of behavior through moral judgment, persons often develop different views about what is moral or immoral.[25]

The concept *ethics* represents the idealistic dimension of the normative ethos, and as such it extends beyond practice (as shown by moral conformity to norms). Berkson writes:

> The ethical . . . derives from man's imaginative power, from his tendency to idealize, to envision perfection, to extend his selfhood in identification with humanity as a whole. Ethics is concerned with the quality of life . . . it sees the good as a form of beauty to be prized for its own sake.[26]

Ethics direct a rigorous examination of "what is" in terms of expected behavior in the norms as well as that reflected in morality. Out of this examination a "what ought to be" ideal is generated, leading to change in norms and morals. This interpretation is reflected in a recent statement by Hill which contends that ethics "generate new patterns of behavior that are ahead of and above the law."[27]

This clarification identifies values as societal standards which organizations are committed to support. Norms are specific rules designed for that support. However, group members must know these rules before behavior (morality) can be in conformity with expectations and before an idealistic stretch (ethics) beyond conformity is possible. Consequently, normative behavior in organizational decision making should not be left totally to individual intuition. Toward a correction of this practice, organizations have a responsibility in establishing and extending normative behavior.

In applying a *social* interpretation of morality and ethics to policy decisions, administrators are not without other conceptual models to guide their choices. One such model is provided by John Rohr, who suggests that administrators can look to "regime norms" to provide guidance.[28] Rohr notes that important regime norms, such as justice, equality, and liberty, are useful in helping aministrators to decide among various policy options. He suggests further that these norms can be made operational through the study of Supreme Court decisions. By studying and observing how the court views and defines "justice" when dealing with concrete situations, the administrator can gain insight into how "justice" might be applied to specific cases with which he or she has to deal.[29]

Protection for Dissenters

Whistle-blowing and other forms of ethical behavior which run counter to organizational policy can be dangerous, especially for the unfortunate persons who do not manage to capture significant media attention. In some instances, whistle-blowing can turn "voice" into (involuntary) "exit." In other cases it can lead to undesirable reassignment or transfer, ostracism by peers, or a reputation as an organizational trouble-maker. It may even limit the whistle-blower's ability to change jobs should other pressures make the present job unbearable. In short, the cost of whistle-blowing can be high—so high, in fact, that instances of whistle-blowing probably occur in but a small fraction of the cases where it is merited. This is a troublesome thought, especially if one believes that government employees should obey their pledge to give first loyalty to the "highest moral principles."

Under the assumption that whistle-blowing, and the conditions which make it necessary, are not going to disappear, a priority in organization design is to reduce the immediate and specific costs of legitimate whistle-blowing. One element of such a strategy is the development of an appeal mechanism for those individuals who feel themselves aggrieved for their whistle-blowing activities. The Civil Service Reform Act of 1978 has taken a step in this direction with the creation of the Special Counsel's Office, linked organizationally with the Merit System Protection Board.

The Special Counsel's Office has major responsibilities in whistle-blowing cases. It is empowered to receive and investigate allegations of agency or personal employee misconduct. The creation of the Special Counsel's Office may be a breakthrough, since it provides an "in house" opportunity for government employees to report misconduct without having to blow the whistle to an outside (the government) party. Further, since these allegations can be made anonymously, the arrangement provides an amount of protection.

One of the most puzzling aspects of legitimate whistle-blowing is why it is necessary in the first place. If the cause is just, why is dissent often limited to one or a very few individuals? Why is it that organizational supervisors—presumably rational men and women—refuse to see the error of their ways, and the ways of their agencies? Why must the truth (and here we are presuming that whistle-blowers possess the truth) seek outside agents to guide it to the light of day?

One possible answer is that the merits of a given argument may not be obvious to those who are unable to view it with the detachment which objectivity requires. Looked at in this light, whistle-blowing is not a phenomenon to be viewed in good versus evil terms, but as a seemingly intractable problem in which fair and honest individuals have a legitimate difference of opinion about an issue. If this is so, and if it is conceded that the merits of the case are on the side of the whistle-blower, we must seek to determine what forces have clouded the views of other agency officials. Part of the answer may lie in what Albert Hirschman and Stanley Hauerwas call self-deception—the unconscious internalization of organization norms to the extent that one's individual judgment becomes clouded.[30] It is wise to try to minimize self-deception if we want the arguments of whistle-blowers (as well as other arguments) to be decided on their merits.

One useful vehicle to help minimize self-deception is active participation in professional associations, especially those associations which cross agency lines. Particularly useful for government officials are those associations like the American Society for Public Administration, the American Management Association, and other groups which include government officials at all levels, academics from a variety of disciplines, and private sector managers. These associations, their conferences and publications, raise issues in ways which make it difficult for their members to remain myopic about the specific problems of their particular organizational settings.

An even more useful vehicle, one which enables the public administrator to "step back" from the press of daily duties to regain a detached perspective on agency problems, is a program of periodic sabbatical leaves. While one may not expect taxpayers to fund a program of sabbaticals on the scale to which college professors have become accustomed, there still exists a wide range of programs which make it possible for government officials to experience a "change of pace" at frequent intervals in their careers. Opportunities exist through the Intergovernmental Personnel Act for public administrators in the federal government to exchange positions with officials at the state and local levels. That program could be expanded and opportunities provided for federal officials to arrange temporary exchanges with other federal employees. The program of the Federal Executive Institute might also be expanded, and more federal managers could be given the opportunity to participate at the Charlottesville center and at other "regional" campuses. Finally, the civilian agencies might take a page from the books of their military counterparts and send rising managers to enroll in graduate programs at both private and state-supported universities.

Another element of organizational redesign which can have a positive effect on the ethical tenor of government is an improved system of personnel evaluation. Such a system must work in two directions. In the first direction, it must be a system in which supervisors are required to discuss the relevant character traits of the individuals in their charge. "Integrity" (or some synonymous virtue) must be counted in developing employees' evaluation files, and, more importantly, employees must know that it is to be counted. In the second direction, employees must have the opportunity to speak to the relative merits of their supervisors. Evalution must be a two way street, and employee evaluations of supervisors must be scrutinized (along with other appropriate data) by the agency's highest levels. An important component of this phase of the evaluation is the inclusion of a statement which judges the supervisor's openmindedness and willingness to tolerate opinions different from his/her own. If supervisors are aware that open-mindedness and tolerance for legitimate dissent are laudable attributes, and that their performance will be judged by subordinates and reviewed by superiors, they are less likely to foreclose dissent in ways that may eventually result in the necessity for whistle-blowing.

One of the messages contained in the Civil Service Reform Act of 1978 is that employees do differ with regard to performance and that a sound personnel system recognizes those differences and rewards people accordingly. If the existing system can be revised to include the evaluation of normatively relevant criteria, and if an opportunity can be provided for employees to judge the qualities of their supervisors, progress will have been made toward preventing both whistle-blowing and the conditions which seem to cause it.

Normative Enrichment. Organizations are cooperative social systems. Most have certain moral and ethical expectations which are prescribed for members, and management has been largely dependent on individual integrity for achieving these expectations. In a changing world, organizations are part of an environment which demands corporate integrity. Individual and collective integrity are not always synonymous and integrated. Therefore, organizations ought to give more attention to that part of their "premises of decision making" which contains the rules, regulations and standards for behavior. Since members of organizations may hold conflicting standards, each may need instruction in organization expectations; hence, the necessity for each organization to put its members into psychological environments that lead to cognitive change and adaptation to the proper value, moral or ethical objectives. To be sure, no organization can survive if it neglects productivity and sound management practices. In a similar sense, it seems reasonable to assume that attention to moral and ethical goals is also necessary for survival. At any rate, each organization sets its values, norms, and ethics; and each should motivate members toward moral behavior.[31]

This motivation treats the normative ethos with the same respect and seriousness given other elements of the organization—goals, positions and roles. Because of systemic qualities, normative dimensions are as important as productivity. Correcting the normative dilemmas of organizational behavior needs more than a new or a revised "Code of Ethics." Priority might be given to the development of a program of *normative enrichment*, i.e., an evaluation of overall organizational conduct, clarification of rules, and normative training for organization members. Toward this end, a series of steps for such a program is proposed.

First, the organization should adopt a definite normative stance toward its environment. This would include a policy of creative, corporate citizenship where "social responsibility" and the advancement of "quality of life" are accepted goals. Second, through an evaluative process, a normative profile of the organization should be established and kept up-to-date. Along with a measure of adherence to environmental norms, this profile would depict the value orientation of members; knowledge of agency rules; most consistent patterns of rule violation; and the presence or absence of an idealistic, creative spirit of moral concern. Third, organizational rules for conduct should be made specific and very public. Along with a general acknowledgement of social responsibility, individual members should be informed of moral expectations toward fundamental rules. Penalties for violation ought to be written, distributed, and applied. If there are no written rules already, then standards for conduct would be democratically codified with the assumption that persons who help to make rules are more likely to respect the rules. Fourth, members of the organization should be given special training toward normative enrichment. Primary purposes for this value training would be to determine higher principles for improving the quality of life, to generate new values, and to promote constant reformation of existing standards.

Conclusion

This article has looked at the kinds of ethical problems which public administrators have to face. We have discussed the difficulties inherent in trying to make ethical policy choices, in developing personal standards of ethical conduct, and in making difficult moral decisions in the face of likely organizational reprisals.

The ethics problem is essentially a problem with the normative ethos; it is futile to talk about ethics with a projection toward the drafting of codes of ethics where organizational rules are easily abused. Today's popular call for ethical reform demands that we first adhere to basic values and norms. Then, perhaps through laborious normative practice and training, a desire for the higher principles will be born and nurtured.

In the final analysis, the most realistic solutions to the problems of morality and ethics may lie in redesigning the organizational structures that constitute our public agencies. Organizations must use rules for their intended purposes; but, beyond the use of rules there should be a demonstration of concern for imaginative idealism. It is this imaginative process, this idealistic turn, this creative and innovative spirit that in reality comprises "organizational ethics."

Perhaps a restructuring of the appeals mechanisms available to whistle-blowers will help solve the problem; or perhaps some much-needed revisions to our personnel evaluation system or a realistic sabbatical leave policy interrupting continuous service will help avoid the problems of self-deception. Whatever the ultimate solution, it is most likely to be found in the structures and policies of the agencies where public officials work. To look elsewhere is to search in vain for a formula that will continue to elude most public servants.

NOTES

[1] See T. Edwin Boling, "The Management Ethics 'Crisis': An Organizational Perspective," *The Academy of Management Review*, 3 (April, 1978), pp. 360–365, for citations relative to the empirical nature of the ethics crisis and a discussion of the relationship of this behavior to organizations. Derek Bok, "Can Ethics Be Taught?", *Change*, 8 (October, 1976), argues that ethically relevant courses should be included in the curricula of pre-professional education programs—if only for the purpose of raising the "ethical consciousness of future professionals."

[2] T. Edwin Boling, "Organizational Ethics: Rules, Creativity and Idealism," in John W. Sutherland, ed., *Management Handbook for Public Administrators* (New York: Van Nostrand Reinhold Co., 1978), pp. 221–253.

[3] John H. Barnsley, *The Social Reality of Ethics: The Comparative Analysis of Moral Codes* (London: Routledge and Kegan Paul, 1972).

[4] *Ibid.*, p. 9.

[5] Robert Golembiewski, *Men, Management and Morality* (New York: McGraw Hill Book Company, 1965).

[6] Robert V. Presthus, *Public Administration* (New York: Ronald Press Company, 1975), p. 410.

[7] Paul Henson Appleby, *Morality and Administration in Democratic Government* (New York: Greenwood Press, 1969), p. 220.

[8] Susan Wakefield, "Ethics and the Public Service: A Case for Individual Responsibility," *Public Administration Review*, 36 (November/December, 1976), pp. 661–666.

[9]George W. England, "Personal Value Systems of Managers—So What?" *The Personnel Administrator*, 20 (April, 1975), pp. 20–23.

[10]Clarence C. Walton, *Ethos and the Executives: Value in Managerial Decision Making* (Englewood Cliffs, N.J.: Prentice-Hall, Inc., 1969), p. 125.

[11]Albert O. Hirschman, "Exit, Voice, and Loyalty," in Charles Peters and Michael Nelson, eds., *The Culture of Bureaucracy* (New York: Holt, Rinehart, and Winston, 1979), pp. 209–217.

[12]*Ibid.*, p. 209.

[13]*Ibid.*

[14]An interesting collection of articles on whistle-blowing, including several case studies of prominent whistle-blowers, is available in the Winter, 1977 issue of *The Bureaucrat*. Also see James S. Bowman, *Managerial Ethics: Whistle-Blowing in Organizations: An Annotated Bibliography and Resource Guide* (New York: Garland Publishing, Inc., 1982).

[15]*Code of Ethics for Government Service*, approved as House Concurrent Resolution 175 in the Second Session of the 85th Congress.

[16]Kenneth Boulding, *The Organizational Revolution* (New York: Harper and Row, 1953).

[17]*Ibid.*, p. 4.

[18]Wayne Albert R. Leys, *Ethics and Social Policy* (New York: Prentice-Hall, 1941), p. 278.

[19]J. Barnsley, *op. cit.*

[20]Isaac Baer Berkson, *Ethics, Politics and Education* (Eugene, Oregon: University of Oregon, 1968).

[21]Clyde Kluckhohn, *Culture and Behavior* (New York: The Free Press, 1962).

[22]Robert N. McMurray, "Conflicts in Human Values," in Robert T. Golembiewski, Frank Gibson and Geoffrey Y. Cornog, eds., *Public Administration*, Chicago: Rand McNally and Company, 1966), pp. 314–327.

[23]Thomas E. Davitt, *The Ethics in the Situation* (New York: Appleton-Century-Crofts, 1970).

[24]Berkson, *op. cit.*

[25]Barnsley, *op. cit.*

[26]Berkson, *op. cit.*, p. 238.

[27]Hill, *op. cit.*, p. 4.

[28]John Rohr, *Ethics for Bureaucrats* (New York: Marcel Decker, 1978).

[29]Other possibilities are available as well, e.g., John Rawls' theory of "justice as fairness." An interesting look at Rawls' theory is available in Nicholas Henry, "Public Administration and the Public Interest: Notes on Some Philosophic Abstractions," presented to the 1974 meeting of the Southern Political Science Association. In his paper, Henry uses Rawls' "justice as fairness" theory as a yardstick to measure the propriety of affirmative action in federal government hiring.

[30]Hirschman, *op. cit.*, and Stanley Hauerwas (with David B. Burrell), "Self-Deception and Autobiography: Reflections on Speer's *Inside The Third Reich*," in Stanley Hauerwas, *Truthfulness and Tragedy* (Notre Dame, Indiana: University of Notre Dame Press, 1977), pp. 83–98.

[31]Herbert A. Simon, *Administrative Behavior* (New York: The Free Press, 1976).

III
Ethical Issues in Policymaking

10
The Place of Principles in Policy Analysis*

Charles W. Anderson

In order to make a policy decision, one must invoke some criteria of evaluation. We cannot decide whether a proposal for public action is desirable or undesirable, whether the results of a public program are to be adjudged a success or a failure, except in the light of a standard. We have to make a decision on some basis, for some reason. We can favor a specific program for the reason that the benefits seem to outweigh the costs. We can base our decision on the grounds of legality, or on the grounds that one option appears more politically feasible than the rest. We can decide on the basis of majority will or fundamental fairness or because of self-interest, organizational interest or the interest of some group whose cause we are trying to advance. We can decide on instrumental grounds, that this policy would rectify a balance of payments disequilibrium or provide a consistent, low-cost energy supply. Failing all else, we can make a decision because heads came up rather than tails.

All of these are potential criteria for choice, and all identify standards for public judgment. One could incorporate any or all of them into a model of the decision-making process, and each, except perhaps for the last, has been highlighted somewhere in the policy-making literature as constituting the essence of decision. Nonetheless, the essential question is not how we can decide, or how we in fact do decide, but how we ought to decide. What counts as a good reason for a policy decision and what is an inappropriate basis for political judgment?

*I gratefully acknowledge the helpful comments of Murray Edelman, Booth Fowler, Leon Lindberg, Ben Page, Gina Sapiro, and John Witte on earlier drafts of this manuscript.

From *American Political Science Review*, Vol. 73, No. 3 (September 1979), pp. 711–723. Reprinted by permission.

Any theory of policy evaluation[1] has to address the problem of the choice of criteria for decision making. This is as true for those who would propose models to explain the behavior of policy makers as it is for those whose interest is in trying to clarify what "policy rationality" or "good judgment" entails. However, it is probably fair to say that even purely "empirical" theories of policy process cannot escape the normative implications of policy evaluation. The move from the empirical to the prescriptive is easy and natural for the consumers of policy theory, and in the eyes of students and practitioners, current models of policy making readily become standards for the craft of policy analysis. Such has been the fate both of pluralist interest-group theory and incrementalist models of the budgetary process. (It is very easy for those who look upon political science as a repository of practical wisdom to conclude that it is "good practice" to inflate a budget request by approximately the amount of the anticipated legislative cut.) In any event, the "fact-value distinction" is not a profound stumbling block in policy theory. There are few enough students of policy analysis who are not concerned with the implications of different modes of policy choice and many significant works in the field—those of Dror, Lindblom and Simon, for example—are overt arguments for preferred strategies of decision.

Logically, the choice of criteria is the first element in any theory of policy evaluation. How we perceive a problem depends on how we propose to evaluate it. Problems are not just "out there" waiting to be resolved. The first act of evaluation is to make a distinction between "problems" and "the way things are." Poverty is not a problem for a society that believes that "the poor are always with us"—or that they get precisely what they deserve. Inflation can be regarded as a "condition" rather than a "problem," for it means no more than a rise in the price structure. Inflation has to be regarded as a problem for a reason, as, for example, that it affects business confidence, or represents an illegitimate confiscation of some forms of property, or redistributes income in socially undesirable ways. A policy problem, in short, is a political condition that does not meet some standard.

It is not merely in the phase of problem identification that the choice of standards is important. Each step in the process of decision making depends on the initial stipulation of values to be served. We cannot just "weigh" or "compare" policy alternatives. We must weigh and compare them against something. At the end of analysis, we cannot merely make decisions. We also have to justify them. However whimsically or equivocally we *came* to our conclusions, good reasons have to be given for our policy preferences if they are to be taken seriously in the forums of policy deliberation. Ultimately, policy analysis has less to do with problem solving than with the process of argument. The better metaphor for policy analysis may not be the mathematical equation but the legal brief—it is a reasoned case for a preferred course of public action.

The Stipulation and Ranking of Values

Like the famous recipe for rabbit stew that begins, "Catch the rabbit," most formulas for rational policy choice begin with the admonition, "Identify and rank your values."[2] The problem for any theory of policy evaluation is how this should be done. Contemporary policy theory tends to sidestep the issue. Either the selection of criteria is treated in a highly formal and abstract manner or policy rationality is regarded as a kind of economizing activity and a utilitarian conception of political judgment is implicitly or explicitly endorsed. A third alternative is to rely on a "political" conception of evaluation, in which feasibility or social agreement become overriding norms. In any event, in most contemporary formulations of the problem, the stipulation and ranking of values are regarded as more or less arbitrary, as a "given" in the appraisal of policy. The specification of values is not itself part of the process of rational choice. Rationality is defined in a purely instrumental sense, as "goal-directed behavior" (Riker and Ordeshook, 1973, p. 10). As Dahl and Lindblom write (1953, p. 38), "An action is rational to the extent that it is 'correctly' designed to maximize goal achievement, given the goal in question and the real world as it exists."

What virtually all contemporary policy theories have in common is a positivist or "emotivist" theory of evaluation. Values cannot be justified in terms of objective criteria. Hence, they must be regarded as "preferences" on the part of the policy maker. "Technical" or "rational" policy analysis can only begin once relevant values have been stipulated, either by an authoritative decision maker or through the statement of citizen preferences in a democratic political process. It is impossible to specify what standards ought to be taken into account in rendering a policy evaluation.

This, of course, is not the case. To be regarded as "reasonable," a policy recommendation must be justified as lawful; it must be plausibly argued that it is equitable and that it entails an efficient use of resources. Else it is subject to legitimate criticism.

It does appear that there are certain fundamental considerations that must be accounted for in any policy evaluation, a set of problems that can be identified with the classic concerns of political theory and with a repertoire of basic concepts including authority, the public interest, rights, justice, equality and efficiency. As standards of policy evaluation, these are not simply preferences. They are, in some sense, *obligatory* criteria of political judgment. To justify any policy recommendation, one must argue that it is within the legitimate powers of government, that it is, in some sense, "in the public interest," that it is consistent with lawful rights, that it is fair, and efficient in the use of resources.

The view that "comprehensive" policy rationality is impossible, as argued by Braybrooke and Lindblom (1963), March and Simon (1958) and others, then might not be precisely correct. While there may be an "infinite number of evaluations" for any policy question (as Lindblom argues in criticism of the classic rational model), it may be the case that there are only a limited number of values appropriate to address in rendering a policy evaluation. All policy argument leads back, eventually, to a finite and bounded set of classic principles and problems of political evaluation.

Furthermore, it may be that instrumental rationality is not the only conception of rationality pertinent to policy theory. The sense of rationality as "goal-directed behavior" is perfectly formal; it applies to *any* type of decision and not in any specific sense to *policy* decisions. It is an ideal of formal, logical validity that a given conclusion can be shown to derive from a given set of premises. However, formal validity is not the only tenable meaning of rationality in modern theories of logic. In the spirit of Wittgenstein's *Philosophical Investigations*, modern logicians like Stephen Toulmin (1969, p. 188) have argued that the problem of rational assessment—of telling sound arguments from untrustworthy ones—depends on the characteristics of an arena of discourse and the standards that are pertinent to it; or they have argued with Friedrich Waismann (1951, p. 117) that the known relations of logic can only hold between statements which belong to a homogeneous field of discourse. Thus, it may be possible to say more about *policy* rationality than about rational choice in general, and it may be that certain standards of judgment are necessary to rational policy choice because of the very nature of what we do when we make, and appraise, public decisions.

In the development of contemporary policy theory, what happened was that the ideal of the utility-maximizing individual was simply taken from positive economic theory and applied to the role of the policy maker. Policy rationality then becomes efficiency in the pursuit of any set of utilities. However influential this instrumental conception of rationality may have been in defining the dominant models of contemporary policy analysis, it is by no means the only acceptable use of the term. In modern analytic philosophy, it is also possible to conceive of rationality as performing an action for reasons that an individual correctly or reasonably regards as good reasons (Benn and Mortimore, 1976, p. 2). This conception of rationality as acting for good reasons leads to two related senses in which an action can be called rational. Either we ascribe rationality to individuals who act for reasons which they regard as good, or we call actions rational when we judge that there are reasons to support them, as when we say, "That seemed a rational thing to do." This conception of rationality seems particularly germane to the process of policy discourse and policy argument. And when we consider what would count as a good reason in policy discourse, it would seem that we are inevitably led back to the classic concerns of political evaluation and the classic principles of political thought.

However, merely to invoke the "classic principles" as criteria for policy evaluation is not to have done very much. To talk about "justifying" decisions in the light of such principles seems to lead us down a familiar and none-too-promising path. We begin to ask questions like "What is justice?" and "What is the public interest?" seeking an essentialist definition that would serve as a conclusive test of the propriety or impropriety of public action. It is not my intention to propose an idealist theory of policy evaluation. I want to stay safely within the positivist and pragmatic tradition that has been dominant within this field of political theory, though perhaps to reveal some unexpected implications of what is possible within that tradition. To this end, we must be quite clear about the kind of problem involved in the selection of criteria for policy making and in defining the logical status of the classic principles in any theory of policy evaluation.

The Pluralism of Policy Languages

We can begin from a consideration of a practical problem of policy appraisal. If, as I have argued, standards of evaluation are embedded in specific fields of discourse, if they arise from specific paradigms of inquiry and analysis, then our sense for what counts as a good reason and as a mistake depends on the ideological, disciplinary, or cultural context within which we are operating. This is a familiar problem, both of the sociology of knowledge and of the philosophy of science, that our "plausibility structures" have much to do with social context and social reinforcement. However, the crucial difficulty is not merely the relativity and contingency of standards that such a view entails. The significant issue is how we should proceed when we are aware that public issues can be perceived and appraised through multiple frameworks of evaluation. Given the diversity of the policy sciences in our times, this has become a characteristic dilemma of policy choice and policy rationality.

The proliferation of "policy professions" in the past generation or so has created a great variety of languages and logics of policy evaluation and justification. In such a field as energy policy, for example, the policy maker or citizen must somehow decide what to make of the various arguments and analysis presented by economists, environmentalists, engineers, scientists, lawyers, and so on, each claiming to be authoritative for a specific aspect of the problem, each justified by its own premises of inquiry and rigorous logic of analysis, each containing imperatives for definitive public action.

In the conventional wisdom of policy making, policy makers specify objectives and policy professionals deal only with means to politically designated ends. However, the conventional wisdom may have the matter almost precisely backwards. The actual role of policy professionalism in contemporary government is probably more prescriptive than instrumental. The setting of standards of good practice is a large part of what professionalism means. Most policy professions are such precisely because they provide standards for public policy. In such diverse fields as forestry, public health, nutrition and welfare, the essential function of the expert is often that of setting criteria for the definition of public objectives and the appraisal of public programs.

Policy evaluation takes place within and between such languages of policy analysis. Like scientific disciplines, policy languages constitute a realm of discourse and of argument. What counts as a "problem," and a "good reason," and as a "mistake" in judgment depends on the normative standards embedded in a specific framework of analysis. The process of policy evaluation and argument is different in law, macro-economics, diplomacy, environmental planning and civil engineering. In each of these professions, different rules exist for the identification of the problematic; there are different norms of evaluation and different criteria for what would count as a "solution" to a public problem, for how we would distinguish a "successful" public venture from a policy "failure."

This pluralism of policy languages does not pose any ultimate problems of justification in itself. All arguments trail back eventually to certain normative postulates and assumptions widely shared in liberal political discourse (and arguably, by Marxian and Catholic corporatist thought as well). When we *justify* a policy standard (address the question of why it is appropriately invoked as definitive in making judgments about alternative public projects and purposes) we generally appeal to some higher-order principle with which the criterion of choice is deemed to be consistent (Taylor, 1961, pp. 45–46). Thus, the neoclassical economist, when asked why "market failure" is an appropriate (and perhaps exclusive) test of the propriety of government intervention in the economy, will refer back to the values of freedom and efficiency served by the market mechanism and behind this perhaps to some notion of the moral autonomy of the individual and to a nominalist skepticism toward the possibility of objective standards of public judgment apart from individual preference and wants. Similarly, if one inquired of the committed conservationist why it might not be a plausible energy policy alternative to simply use up all fossil fuels in one generation of grand bacchanalian extravagance and let the future fend for itself, appeal would probably be made, in the final analysis, to some notion of justice between generations (Barry, 1977).

It is not then that the diverse policy professions do not rest on a shared set of justificatory principles. Rather, the problem is that the weight, emphasis and significance given to the various fundamental principles is different in each. Because they endorse different standards of argument (what counts as a good reason) and because they are organized to account for different facets of experience, they entail different orderings of relevant values. Thus, the central normative construct of law is rights, while that of economics is efficiency. While it might be possible to argue considerations of efficiency in delimiting the scope of an established right (a court might plausibly argue potential bankruptcy as a ground for denying counsel to indigent defendants), in legal reasoning, the ordinary procedure for establishing the categories and scope of rights is not that of a calculus of individual utilities. Conversely, while the logic of economic reasoning may rest on certain postulates of rights (such as property rights), the purpose of a calculation of alternative utility functions is not to stipulate a system of rights.

Hence, it makes a great deal of difference whether we choose to adopt the rules of rational discourse of one of these policy professions rather than another in evaluating a policy problem. We may come to very different conclusions if we choose to regard a specific issue as falling in the domain of law rather than economics. As Arthur Okun (1975) suggests, it makes a difference whether we regard a problem like income distribution from the point of view of rights rather than that of efficiency. There is, he suggests, a "big tradeoff" between these two considerations, either of which can be regarded as definitive for policy making.

In such a pluralistic universe of policy discourse and policy rationality, the crucial problem for a theory of policy evaluation becomes that of identifying standards by which we may weigh the claims of various languages of policy analysis. On what grounds should we choose to regard a problem from the point of view of one of the policy professions rather than another? What justifies the choice among the several logics of policy evaluation?

This is to put the "metapolitical" problem in applied form. Consider the following situation. A labor leader is deciding whether to declare an illegal strike. If the decision is made to strike on the grounds that the probable benefits would be greater than the probable costs, we would say that the decision was based on economic reasoning. If the strike is not called because of its illegality, we would say that the decision was based on legal grounds. But what guidance can be given as to whether the leader ought to decide for economic or legal reasons?

Hence, the problem that must be faced in constructing a theory of policy evaluation is also a characteristic practical problem of policy making in our times. How do we judge a judgment? What standards must any system of policy evaluation meet? The problem concerns the justification of the procedures of policy analysis, but it also addresses the concrete question of how we weigh the rival claims and considerations adduced by different "rationalities" of policy appraisal.

The Metapolitics of Policy Evaluation

A few political scientists have begun the process of trying to extend the idea of policy rationality, asking what is logically required in any stipulation of criteria for policy evaluation. For example, Brian Barry and Douglas Rae (1975, pp. 337–401) set forth seven requirements that any system of political evaluation must meet. Their standards derive largely from formal decision theory. They are rules that must be followed if we are to judge rationally among alternatives in the light of standards.

For Barry and Rae, the formal tests of adequacy are these. The standards by which a policy is judged must be *internally consistent*, that is, transitive. It is logically impossible to come to conclusions about preferred policy unless the criteria are clear and hierarchically ranked. Standards must be *interpretable*: we must be able to tell what a standard means in policy discourse, to judge when it has been met or fails to be met. It must be possible to *aggregate criteria*, to rank them, for a variety of standards might be relevant to choice; yet we cannot simply say, for example, that we favor both, say, equity and efficiency, for no alternative may satisfy both criteria equally.

Any theory of policy evaluation, for Barry and Rae, must also account for the problem of forced choice, that not to decide is in fact a policy choice, and there is no a priori reason why the status quo should have a privileged position in policy appraisal. A system of political evaluation must acknowledge *risk and uncertainty* (we cannot say with confidence, that a given choice will actually meet standards) and it must deal with *time* (policies will have both proximate and distant consequences). Finally, choices must be logically justified in terms of some conception of *individual welfare*.[3]

Duncan MacRae (1976) has attempted to develop a "metaethics" for normative policy discourse on the basis of an analogy between the logic of policy evaluation and the rules of scientific inquiry. MacRae suggests that normative discourse can be as rigorous as empirical investigation in politics, that it is not mere assertion, but can be seen as disciplined inquiry to be judged by "higher-order" standards of appropriate procedure. MacRae envisions normative discourse as debate between the proponents of rival evaluative systems. The standards that any system must meet, the grounds of appropriate criticism of any normative judgment, include (1) *generality*, if the proposed system fails to apply to a choice about which both discussants have moral convictions and to which the critic's system does apply; (2) *internal consistency*, in which the proponent's system yields contradictory recommendations where the critic's does not; (3) *inconsistency with shared convictions*, that the proposed system leads to conclusions at odds with presumably shared evaluations.

I offer no critique of the position of either Barry and Rae or MacRae. Both have extended and clarified the domain of rationality in policy evaluation. Yet, I think the logic of their analysis can be carried further. They emphasize procedural norms, formal rules of consistency and logical rules of validity in rational choice and ethical judgment. However, it seems possible to continue this line of logic to assimilate certain substantive principles that distinguish policy judgment from the more general language regions of rational choice or normative discourse. Barry and Rae, to be sure, do take up the place of the classic principles in policy analysis. However, they view such concepts as justice, rights, the public interest, etc., primarily as "simplifying devices," culturally derived constructs that somehow pull together and focus attention on certain facets of our shared political experiences. The logical status of such principles is somehow different from that of the formal norms of rational decison making. My own view is that something more can be said for and about the place of such principles as "metapolitical" standards, as criteria for judging the worth of any system of policy evaluation.

The Place of Principles in Policy Analysis

It is not immediately apparent that any systematic relationship exists among the classic principles of political thought. Words like *right, the public interest, justice, freedom* and *community* can seem to be no more than an array of discrete "good things." We are used to the idea that political argument can fasten arbitrarily on one or a few of these concepts and that they can be arranged in different patterns in ideological thinking, invested with a variety of meanings and given different degrees of emphasis.

To make the point that the criteria which enter into a policy evaluation are not merely preferences, but that certain substantive standards need be accounted for in any rationally defensible policy judgment, one must show that certain principles do form, in some sense, a finite and bounded set and one must establish in what specific way such criteria are mandatory in the activity of policy evaluation. It is also necessary to show that these principles can be stated in such a way as to be free from any partisan or ideological quality. They must reflect no more than the logical characteristics of any form of political judgment.

The essence of my argument is this: a defensible policy judgment must meet certain formal standards of rational choice—it must have regard for such problems as the transitivity of values and forced choice—but it must have other qualities as well. By virtue of the fact that these are policy judgments, certain political values must be taken into account. It is not that these values can be justified in any ultimate sense. I will not argue the Kantian position that there are certain normative propositions that any rational thinker must endorse to remain consistent, nor will I argue, with Rawls, that there are certain principles that self-interested individuals would be led to accept if placed in the "original position" and called upon to formulate basic norms of political life. Rather, the argument is that certain criteria of choice are inherent in the activity of politics itself, that they are part of what we mean by "making a political judgment" or as Wittgenstein might have put it, that they are part of politics as a "form of life."

My case is that a specific set of principles is *obligatory* in political evaluation in a very special sense. It is important to be very clear about the logical status of such principles as criteria of "metapolitics"—standards for judging the adequacy of any system of political judgment. There is a difference between claiming that certain *concepts* are indispensable in political evaluation and that certain *propositions* are. To say that a comprehensive policy analysis must account for the problem of authority is not to say that a binding policy recommendation must be shown to "derive from the will of the people." As Stephen Toulmin says (1972, p. 418),

> it is one thing to argue that a certain concept is something that a rational thinker or agent cannot very well get along without; it is quite another to establish the necessary truth of certain substantive ethical or scientific principles.

As standards at the "second level," as criteria for evaluating a policy evaluation itself, the classic principles have a particular standing. They are not norms of conduct; rather, they identify those aspects of a policy recommendation that require justification. The status of such principles in normative policy theory is not unlike the standing of a hypothesis in scientific inquiry. As a hypothesis *requires* experimentation to test its validity, so "principles," in the sense I shall be using the term, require justification to demonstrate the rational plausibility of a policy recommendation.

Taken in this sense, it is possible to identify three of the classic principles that appear to be rationally requisite to the construction of a defensible policy evaluation. These are authority, justice and efficiency. The relationship of these to other fundamental political ideas can also be specified. Nonetheless, this statement is to be taken as exploratory and provisional. While I think it is possible to demonstrate that these considerations, *at least*, have to be accounted for in the process of policy evaluation, it is possible that a similar case can be made for other principles as well.

Authority. In the most general sense, authority means that an exercise of power is rightful, which is to say, justifiable. This implies that good reasons can be given for the act of policy making, that an entitlement can be established to decide on the public behalf and a concomitant obligation to abide by such decisions. Thus understood, authority is a necessary characteristic of any legitimate policy decision and a requirement of any system of policy evaluation. A decision which cannot be justified in terms of this standard is simply an act of domination or coercion.

Put another way, as a logical characteristic of any system of policy evaluation, authority functions to structure the terms of the public debate. It locates the burden of proof in political argument. The logic of public policy making requires that the burden of proof rest always with the state (Neuman, 1953, p. 904). It is up to government to justify its actions; it is not up to citizens to demonstrate why policy makers should not do precisely as they please. It is hard to imagine how the presumption could be reversed and retain any meaningful sense of political discourse. If we were to accept that public action might just as well be whimsical and arbitrary, no problem of political evaluation really arises.

To justify a policy evaluation, then, reasons have to be given for regarding a problem as properly resolved through public action. In liberal political thought, the problem of authority is systematically related to such principles as individual freedom and consent. In liberal discourse, the problem of justification takes the form of giving good reasons for overriding the presumption in favor of individual autonomy. Any legitimate public action must be shown to derive, in some sense, from consent or individual wants and interests. However, the problem is not at all peculiar to liberalism. "Divine right" was, after all, a formally rationalized justification for the exercise of authority. Sixteenth- and seventeenth-century doctrines of sovereignty were an attempt to "give reasons" for unlimited authority. Marxism is an elaborate critique of the consistency of the liberal notion of authority and provides an alternative system of criteria for regarding public action as appropriate or inappropriate. (In fact, Marx, like Rousseau, can be regarded as doing no more than making the liberal presumption in favor of freedom a more stringent test of the legitimacy of public action.)

Even the so-called "irrationalist" political theories, those that *argue* that rationality is far from a definitive force in human affairs, rest paradoxically on a reasoned justification for a certain pattern of authority. Thus, A. James Gregor writes (1969, p.19):

> Adolf Hitler's *Mein Kampf* can, in no sense, be conceived as *simply* a statement of the author's personal emotional preferences. Suggestions, admonitions and imperatives are *argued*. The arguments may be elliptical—vital premises may be suppressed—or they may be invalid and their factual premises erroneous, but they are not simply assertions of personal preference. Hitler advocates, for example, the fulfillment of one of mankind's highest aspirations; man's continued evolutionary progress . . . We raise objections when Hitler contends that the fulfillment of such an ideal demands the caste superordination of a specific biological race . . . We demand evidence, for example, that would confirm that a given race is the sole repository of man's foremost creative capacities. But such objections raise questions of fact and definition and as such are subject to cognitive appraisal.

In any rational policy evaluation, then, good reasons have to be given for regarding a problem or project as appropriately the subject of public action. In the contemporary languages of the policy professions, this can be and is done in a variety of ways. The neoclassical political economist may argue that "market failure" or bona fide "public goods" are the only grounds for state intervention that legitimately override the presumption in favor of autonomous, individual choice. The utilitarian may appeal to some aggregate social welfare function as an appropriate test that "authorizes" a public action. The social democrat may argue from some need or desire-regarding conception of distributive justice. The legal positivist may simply hold that a policy option is legitimate if it is apt to be upheld by the courts, while the constitutionalist will admit the propriety of considering a policy option if it squares with the formal powers of government. Whatever the particular reasons offered, the essential point is that *some* justification on the grounds of authority has to be provided. Authority is not simply a "preference" of the policy maker that may be introduced as a criterion for the evaluation of public policy or not as one likes. One simply cannot say, in justifying a policy appraisal, "I don't care if it's blatantly illegal and rides roughshod over established rights; it's still the most efficient way of getting the job done."

There is an intimate connection between the principle of authority, thus understood, and such concepts as freedom, rights and justice. These are grounds of argument, criteria that can be introduced to make claims about authority, or to test propositions about authority. Different conceptions of freedom—the distinction between the "freedom from" imperatives of the classic liberal and the more activist sense of "freedom to" (Berlin, 1969, pp. 118–72)—give rise to different images of legitimate authority. It might be argued that freedom is as much an obligatory consideration in any political judgment as is the concept of authority itself. (Certainly, the very notion of political argument implies a notion of the individual capable of judging the worth of rival claims.) Yet, it is such only in relation to the problem of authority, or justice. We make propositions about human freedom in order to arrive at a conception of legitimate authority. We do not make cases about authority so as to arrive at a conception of human freedom.

The concept of "the public interest" also bears a close relationship to the problem of authority. It is easy enough to demonstrate that there is no definition of the public interest to which all reasonable persons would necessarily repair. It is equally easy to show that any rational policy evaluation must give reasons for regarding a policy proposal as, in some sense, in the public interest. One cannot justify a policy recommendation on the grounds that "it would make me and my friends richer." However refreshing the candor of such an argument might be, it does not and cannot stand as a legitimate warrant for a public action. (When self-interest is argued as a legitimate basis for decision it is always in connection with some theory of how the public interest will arise from the competition or aggregation of individual interests.)

The concept of the public interest is itself logically dependent on other fundamental criteria of political evaluation, among them concepts of individual welfare and community. The connection between individual and collective welfare must somehow be accounted for in any comprehensive policy evaluation and it is necessary to specify precisely which "public's" interest is to be taken into account. Any policy appraisal entails a decision about who is properly regarded as "us" and "the others," whose interests are to be promoted and whose thwarted or ignored. It makes a considerable difference if the relevant community in whose "interest" policy is to be made excludes the adjoining class, county, nation, the rest of humanity or the people who will live five centuries hence.

Thus, a rigorous and comprehensive policy analysis must touch a number of bases to establish the propriety of public action. This does not mean that every policy argument must contain a full-fledged case about authority going back to first principles and premises. To think of policy analysis and debate in this way would be tedious indeed. Authority may not be problematic in all exercises in policy evaluation. It may simply be assumed that the available array of alternatives passes the test of legitimacy. There are short cuts and simplifying devices in the ordinary language of any policy debate. What is certain, however, is that if a policy is controversial, it will be so in relation to one of the fundamental dimensions of evaluation. Implicitly or explicitly, a policy recommendation must be regarded as plausible in terms of each of these considerations.

Justice. John Rawls (1971, p. 3) states that "justice is the first virtue of social institutions, as truth is of systems of thought." It may or may not be the case that justice must rank first in any ordering of criteria for policy evaluation. Justice might be taken as the paramount criterion for policy evaluation, as a test, say, of rival conceptions of authority. This is the thrust of Marxian analysis and modern theories of civil disobedience, which suggest that a system of government is not rightful if it can be shown that prevailing standards of authority do not permit the consideration of the more equitable policy alternatives. On the other hand, one can argue, with Jimmy Carter, that "the world is unfair," that government should deal only with those cases of inequity that meet the tests of authority and efficiency (and therefore, that welfare funds need not be made available to pay for abortions). It does not seem possible to specify a *necessary* priority between the principles of authority and justice. However, this does not mean that the ranking of these standards of policy evaluation is simply a matter of the policy maker's preference. Good reasons must be given to justify assigning priority to one or the other of these values. Furthermore, it would seem possible to show that justice is not an optional but a necessary consideration in any system of policy evaluation.

This is the case not only because any public decision will have distributional consequences but also because it is inherent in the logic of policy making that rules must either be stated universally or so as to apply to particular cases and categories. The maxim of justice, "Treat like cases alike and different cases differently," stands then not as an ethical imperative but as a statement of a problem that requires justification: it raises the question of what counts as a good reason for regarding cases as alike or dissimilar. As Benn and Peters (1959, p. 99) put it: "If, for example, we believe in democratic rights for white men, we must show good grounds for denying them to black, and the simple criterion of skin color alone is not an obviously relevant ground of distinction. There may be other and better grounds—but the onus of proof rests on those who would limit the right, not on those who would give it universal scope."

The concept of equality then is probably best regarded not as an independent consideration in policy evaluation, but as a proposition that stands in a logical relationship to the problem of justice (Perelman, 1963, pp. 1–60; Bedau, 1971; Benn and Peters, 1959, pp. 107–34). In liberal argument, equality locates the burden of proof in making cases about justice, as freedom does in relation to the problem of authority. All individuals are to be regarded as in the same position with regard to policy unless good reasons can be given for treating them differently. Grounds for differentiation may include need or desire, merit, compensation, or some public interest criterion (as in the familiar appeal to the need for incentives as a spur to productivity and economic growth, which stands as a proxy for aggregate social utility in most modern economic analysis). To my knowledge, there has never been a pure egalitarian argument that cases are to be treated alike regardless of circumstances. Most contemporary egalitarian arguments rest on the premise that existing inequalities are unjust, and that failing a reasonable justification for differential treatment, cases should be treated alike. Thus it seems appropriate to regard justice and not equality as the necessary consideration in any system of policy evaluation.

The point then is that any policy evaluation must include a justification of the categories of universal or differential treatment to be established (though liberals might argue that equality requires no justification) (Feinberg, 1973, pp. 98–102). Once again, it does not make sense to regard justice simply as a preference of policymakers, a consideration which they are free to incorporate into policy evaluation or not as they wish. One cannot really vindicate a policy recommendation by asserting, "I know this program is unfair, but it is efficient, and we clearly have the authority to enact it."

Efficiency. It is easy enough to show that efficiency is a necessary consideration in any system of policy evaluation. Means must be appropriate to the ends chosen, and it is a legitimate criticism of any policy recommendation to demonstrate that there are better alternatives for achieving stipulated values. What is more important is to demonstrate that efficiency cannot be the exclusive consideration in rendering a policy appraisal.

In many models of policy evaluation, efficiency is regarded as tantamount to rationality. The problem of policy is "solved" when it can be demonstrated that one alternative yields an optimum level of benefits over costs. As we have noted, rationality is often defined in an instrumental sense, as "goal-directed behavior" in policy theory. Yet, some conceptions of policy rationality carry the matter even further. They argue that the efficient solution to a policy problem is also the solution that is necessarily in the public interest. In fact, latent in the logic of much of contemporary politicial economy, whether founded on neoclassical or utilitarian premises, is the notion that to solve for the problem of efficiency is simultaneously to solve for the problems of authority and of justice.

The cost-benefit analysis is a fundamental paradigm of much contemporary policy analysis. In the most general sense, any cost-benefit analysis rests on a utilitarian foundation. The only appropriate (or possible) criterion of policy is individual wants and interests, somehow aggregated to yield a social utility function. Any policy which reduces social costs or increases net social welfare is "beneficial." The standard of policy evaluation may be cast in terms of Pareto optimality: a desirable policy is one which makes someone better off without making anyone worse off (or in terms of the looser formulation, a desirable policy is one where winners could conceivably compensate losers through costless transfers). In either case, a solution to the problem of efficiency also yields a solution to the problem of the public interest.

Thus, it can be argued, as it has been, that cost-benefit analysis can be justified as a mode of policy evaluation, that it accounts for those considerations that are necessarily incorporated in any rational system of policy appraisal. However, this is not a necessary conclusion, and in fact most economists do not understand the force of cost-benefit analysis in this way. Efficiency is better identified as one element, but not the exclusive element in policy discourse. As E.J. Mishan says (1973, p. 13),

> It cannot be too strongly stressed, however, that even the result of an ideally conducted cost-benefit analysis does not, of itself, constitute a prescription for society. Since it simulates the effects of an ideal price-system, the ideal cost-benefit analysis is also subject to its limitations. Any adopted criterion of a cost-benefit analysis, that is, requires *inter alia* that all benefits exceed costs, and therefore can be vindicated by a social judgment that an economic rearrangement that *can* make everyone better off is an economic improvement. The reader's attention is drawn to the fact that such a judgment does not require that everyone is actually made better off, or even that nobody is actually worse off. The likelihood . . . that some people, occasionally most people, will be worse off . . . is tacitly acknowledged. A project that is adjudged feasible by reference to a cost-benefit analysis is, therefore, consistent with an economic arrangement that makes the rich richer and the poor poorer. It is also consistent with manifest inequity, for an enterprise that is an attractive proposition by the lights of a cost-benefit calculation may be one that offers opportunities for greater profits and pleasure by one group, in the pursuit of which substantial damages and suffering may be endured by other groups.
>
> In order, then, for a mooted enterprise to be socially approved, it is not enough that the outcome of an ideal cost-benefit analysis is positive. It must also be shown that the resulting distributional changes are not regressive, and no gross inequities are perpetrated.

Even an ideal cost-benefit analysis, then, is normatively incomplete; it cannot escape criticism on the grounds that are pertinent to any policy appraisal. However, this is not the only difficulty with the kind of utilitarian calculation that cost-benefit analysis represents. Since it is impossible in practice to know and to aggregate individual utilities, any concrete exercise in cost-benefit analysis requires a stipulation of the costs and benefits to be taken into account. The values postulated, and their ranking, have to be defended on *some* basis. Alasdair MacIntyre (1977, p. 226) points out that "the use of a cost-benefit analysis clearly presupposes a prior decision as to what is a cost and what a benefit" and that this decision has to rest on some ground other than utilitarianism itself.

It is not possible to derive a complete policy evaluation from any form of purely economic analysis. Efficiency is properly regarded as one ground of policy evaluation, a necessary one to be sure, but not as the exclusive consideration in policy appraisal. Efficiency is best regarded as an instrumental value, a tool for comparing policy options in terms of other values. In fact, in any cost-benefit analysis, we do not compare all alternatives but only those that have survived scrutiny on other evaluative grounds. In making an economic analysis of different roadbuilding techniques, we do not draw up a neat comparison of the costs and benefits of *corvee* and slave labor in relation to more conventional methods. In terms of our standards of authority and justice, these options are simply out of bounds.

If efficiency is properly regarded in this instrumental sense, then it is a lower-order criterion of political judgment, basically a "tie-breaker" between policy options that have passed minimum tests of acceptability on grounds of authority and justice. If this is in fact the case, then it is possible to specify not only the values that have to be taken into account in any comprehensive policy evaluation but to advance certain propositions about their ranking as well. Though it is difficult to stipulate a logical priority between authority and justice (some would argue that justice is the supreme test of the propriety of any exercise of public authority, others that government should only act with regard to those forms of injustice that fall within its legitimate powers), it is possible to say that efficiency can never be assigned a higher priority than authority or justice in any plausible value ordering. Again, we simply cannot argue, "I realize that this policy is unjust; nonetheless, it is the most efficient way of achieving our objectives."

The propositions I have outlined would seem to raise problems of democratic theory. If individual wants, somehow aggregated into "public wants," are not to be regarded as a definitive test of policy, then neither, it would seem, is "majority will." To be sure, in any democratic polity, majority will, expressed through prescribed constitutional mechanisms, is accepted as the definitive test of authority. A policy is legitimate insofar as it reflects the "will of the people." However, unless we are very dogmatic "absolute majoritarians" we do recognize that to regard majority will as the exclusive standard for the evaluation of policy is both paradoxical and unsatisfactory. Within most versions of democratic theory, it is an appropriate criticism of majority will to argue that what the majority wants is unjust (as, for example, if the majority wills genocide against a minority) or inefficient (if the policy preferred by the majority would lead to national bankruptcy). The puzzles and quandaries that arise in relation to any simplistic conception of democratic theory suggest that the majoritarian principle cannot be the exclusive ground of justification. In fact, or course, within any democratic polity, we do judge the worth of majoritarian policies on other grounds.

Conclusion

The problem for a theory of policy evaluation is not to discover the right policies but to establish the appropriate grounds for decision making. Not all reasons are good reasons for a policy decision. One cannot justify a public decision simply by invoking a schedule of personal preferences. A justifiable policy evaluation must meet certain standards; it must address specific problems that are characteristic of the activity and enterprise of politics itself.

To say that a policy is justifiable is not the same as saying that one will endorse it. Rather, it means that we regard the basis on which it was made to be plausible, or rationally defensible. A plausible policy argument is one worth taking seriously in the public debate. An impartial observer would weigh its claims and a critic would feel obliged to respond with careful counter-argument.

There are in fact only a finite number of kinds of reasons that can and must be given in justification of a policy recommendation, a logically delimited set of grounds that are appropriate to the appraisal of public policy. It is possible to set standards of comprehensiveness in policy evaluation, to identify those questions that must at least be addressed if a policy appraisal is to appear "worthy of consideration" in our eyes.

It is not simply the stipulation of values to be served that requires reasoned justification but their ordering as well. One cannot state a transitive ranking of values simply as a matter of preference. If efficiency is to be regarded as more than an instrumental value, reasons will have to be given for regarding the most efficient solution as also within the range of "just" alternatives, and as in some sense "in the public interest."

It might be argued that this conception of policy rationality does not transcend our ordinary sense for what is at issue when we face dilemmas of public choice or when we criticize prevailing notions of how public issues ought to be perceived or analyzed. I admit that my discussion of the limitations of instrumental rationality is hardly novel and my conception of the critical political principles unexceptional. And that is precisely the point. There is something wrong when our dominant models of policy rationality are so obviously at odds with what we in fact take to be fundamental considerations in the deliberation of policy choices. My object has simply been to make explicit what we do regard as legitimate grounds of criticism of any framework for policy choice, and to suggest that our "ordinary language" is probably not deceptive, that certain standards are inherent in the logic of policy evaluation itself.

It can also be argued that this analysis has not "solved" the problem of policy choice, that it provides no prescriptive tests which the practitioner might apply in making decisions about desirable and undesirable public purposes or options for action. That, of course, was not in the cards. In order to reduce policy analysis to a routine, rather than an object of deliberation, one must state criteria of judgment in the form of rules. As Barry and Rae suggest, it is a requirement of any "first-order" system of evaluation that standards be interpretable, that we be able to gauge clearly when a policy meets the mark or fails to do so. The sense of policy rationality described here does not pertain to decisions of this type. Rather, it comes into play at the second, or "metapolitical" level, when we are trying to decide how to decide, when we must face the decision of which system of standards to apply to a given situation.

We face a genuine dilemma of decision only when we are aware that public purposes can be perceived and appraised in more than one way. As I noted, given the proliferation of policy languages in our time, we increasingly face quandaries of this type. So long as we are operating within a bounded framework of policy evaluation, we face no such perplexity. We can "justify" first-order decision rules according to the higher-order value propositions with which they are deemed to be consistent. It is when we understand that different frameworks of evaluation could be applied to a given situation of policy choice that we face a decision of a different kind. The standards that apply to such a judgment have a different logical character from those that apply to first-order policy choices. We must invoke criteria that test the adequacy of any system of policy evaluation. The requirements of formal decision theory, as described by Barry and Rae, pertain to decisions of this type. So do the rules of normative consistency proposed by Duncan MacRae. My point has been that a certain conception of the classic political principles, understood as necessary considerations rather than as explicit normative propositions, is essential to complete this expanded sense of policy rationality.

The classic principles, then, have a place in policy theory that is very much like that of the norms of inquiry in scientific investigation. Thus, the sense of the concept "validity" in scientific discourse is not unlike that of "justification" in policy evaluation. Validity has no clear, incontestable meaning as a standard of science and different disciplines endorse different rules concerning what counts as a valid scientific argument and what does not. By the same token, different policy languages and professions endorse different notions of what counts as a justifiable policy proposal.

One basic norm of scientific inquiry is that propositions be stated in "operational" form, that one can at least imagine an objective procedure that would identify the presence or absence of a phenomenon. Again, different scientific disciplines endorse different standards regarding the kind of scientific evidence that is appropriate or obligatory, what kinds of reasons can or must be given to establish the plausibility of a scientific hypothesis. In the same way, the maxim of justice that "like cases be treated alike and different cases differently" establishes no necessary test of the justice of a public project. Different policy languages endorse different standards regarding the equity considerations that would establish the plausibility of a public proposal. Yet just as *any* scientific argument must account for the problem of experimental demonstration, so also *any* given policy argument must account for the problem of the propriety of universal or differential treatment of cases.

There is no final justification for the norms of scientific inquiry or for those of policy evalution. There is no way of showing that a policy *must* be equitable any more than it can be shown that a proposition *must* be verifiable. What can be said instead is that just as there is nothing binding about the norms of scientific inquiry unless we are doing science, there is also nothing binding about the norms of political discourse unless we are engaged in policy evaluation.

Inevitably, the policy sciences will endorse some conception of how one ought to proceed when faced with a problem of public choice. The function of policy theory is not merely to explain why we get the kind of public policies that we do, but to provide guidance as to what is involved in thinking through a public problem to a reasonable conclusion. The very notion of policy evaluation implies that we will make judgments about desirable and undesirable public purposes and projects on some grounds.

The models of instrumental rationality that have provided our dominant strategies of decision do not adequately represent what we acknowledge to be at issue when we confront public decisions. Models of decisions which place the stipulation and ordering of the values which will serve as objectives and constraints on choice outside the realm of policy rationality provide a truncated and unsatisfactory foundation for policy theory. They place the policy analyst in the position of an agent to an authoritative policy maker. The mission of policy analysis becomes that of maximizing the evaluative preferences of a particular client. Either that, or one invokes some equally problematic norm of "public responsiveness" which similarly evades the fact that in policy making we do debate the grounds on which public issues ought to be decided. However, it has generally been assumed that no other moves were possible without introducing some absolute criteria of decision, which would violate the fundamental norms of scientific neutrality and rational generality on which any comprehensive theory for the policy sciences would have to rest.

This analysis suggests that it is possible to treat the question of specifying the substantive standards that are properly introduced in any comprehensive policy evaluation as well as the rules that appropriately guide choice for any stipulated set of values along lines that are perfectly compatible with the fundamental norms of modern policy theory. In doing so, it opens up the possibility of an alternative model of policy rationality, one in which policy making is understood as a process of reasoned deliberation, argument and criticism rather than a pragmatic calculus. However, this more comprehensive vision of policy choice does not displace but rather complements the formal requirements of instrumental rationality. Furthermore, it does not imply that institutional and sociological factors are unimportant elements in the calculus of choice. Rather, it is simply explicitly recognized that to follow dictates of situational or strategic necessity is not a sufficient criterion of good political judgment. Finally, by suggesting that normative political argument has its own strenuous rules and standards, one defines a rather precise relationship between the perennial concerns of political philosophy and the paradigms of practical reason which the policy sciences aspire to develop.

NOTES

[1]Recently, the term "policy evaluation" has been appropriated to designate a sub-specialty within the general field of policy analysis, denoting the technical appraisal of the impact of public programs. I want to reserve the concept for a broader, more essential use, to refer to the process of making deliberate judgments on the worth of proposals for public action as well as on the success or failure of projects that have been put into effect.

[2]Charles E. Lindblom's formulation (1968, p. 13) of the idea of policy rationality will do for an example:

1. Faced with a given problem,
2. A rational man first clarifies his goals, values, or objectives, and then ranks or otherwise organizes them in his mind;
3. He then lists all important possible ways of—policies for—achieving his goals.
4. And investigates all the important consequences that would follow from each of his alternative policies,
5. At which point he is in a position to compare consequences of each policy with his goals
6. And so choose the policy with consequences most closely matching his goals.

For similar formulations, see Dror, 1968, pp. 129–49; Downs, 1957, p. 6, and Zeckhauser and Schaefer, 1968, p. 29. Pragmatic and incrementalist theories differ only in that standards are to be identified and ordered after the fact, in the light of the consequences of policy. See Brecht, 1959, p. 192.

³Barry and Rae also take up a rigorous critique of certain specific criteria of decision, including utilitarianism, equality, Pareto optimality, majority, minimax and dominance and they do consider the place of principles in political evaluation, about which more further on.

REFERENCES

Barry, Brian and Douglas W. Rae. 1975. "Political Evaluation." In Fred I. Greenstein and Nelson W. Polsby (eds.), *Handbook of Political Science, Vol. 1*. Reading, Mass.: Addison-Wesley, pp. 337–401.

_____. 1977. "Justice Between Generations." In P. M.S. Hacker and J. Raz (eds.), *Law, Morality and Society: Essays in Honour of H. L. A. Hart*. Oxford: Clarendon Press, pp. 268–84.

Bedau, Hugo, ed. 1971. *Justice and Equality*. Englewood Cliffs, N.J.: Prentice-Hall.

Benn, S.I. and R.S. Peters. 1959. *Social Principles and the Democratic State*. London: George Allen and Unwin.

_____ and G.W. Mortimore, eds. 1976. *Rationality and the Social Sciences*. Boston: Routledge and Kegan Paul.

Berlin, Isaiah. 1969. *Four Essays on Liberty*. Oxford: Oxford University Press.

Braybrooke, David and Charles E. Lindblom. 1963. *A Strategy of Decision*. New York: Free Press.

Brecht, Arnold. 1959. *Political Theory*. Princeton, N.J.: Princeton University Press.

Dahl, Robert A. and Charles E. Lindblom. 1953. *Politics, Economics and Welfare*. New York: Harper and Row.

Downs, Anthony. 1957. *An Economic Theory of Democracy*. New York: Harper and Row.

Dror, Yehezkel. 1968. *Public Policymaking Re-examined*. San Francisco: Chandler.

Feinberg, Joel. 1973. *Social Philosophy*. Englewood Cliffs, N.J.: Prentice-Hall.

Gregor, A. James. 1969. *The Ideology of Fascism*. New York: Free Press.

Lindblom, Charles E. 1968. *The Policy-Making Process*. Englewood Cliffs, N.J.: Prentice-Hall.

MacIntyre, Alasdair. 1977. "Utilitarianism and Cost-Benefit Analysis: An Essay on the Relevance of Moral Philosophy to Bureaucratic Theory." In Kenneth Sayre (ed.), *Values in the Electric Power Industry*. Notre Dame, Ind.: Notre Dame University Press.

MacRae, Duncan. 1976. *The Social Function of Social Science*. New Haven: Yale University Press.

March, James G. and Herbert A. Simon. 1958. *Organization*. New York: John Wiley.

Mishan, E.J. 1973. *Economics for Social Decisions*. New York: Praeger.

Neuman, Franz L. 1953. "The Concept of Political Freedom." *Columbia Law Review* 53:901–14.

Okun, Arthur M. 1975. *Equality and Efficiency: The Big Tradeoff*. Washington, D.C.: Brookings.

Perelman, Chaim. 1963. *The Idea of Justice and the Problem of Argument*. New York: Humanities Press.

Rawls, John. 1971. *A Theory of Justice*. Cambridge, Mass.: Harvard University Press.

Riker, William H. and Peter C. Ordeshook. 1973. *An Introduction to Positive Political Theory*. Englewood Cliffs, N.J.: Prentice-Hall.

Taylor, Paul W. 1961. *Normative Discourse*. Englewood Cliffs, N.J.: Prentice Hall.

Toulmin, Stephen. 1969. *The Uses of Argument*. Cambridge: Cambridge University Press.
_____. 1972. *Human Understanding: Vol. 1*. Princeton, N.J.: Princeton University Press.
Waismann, Friedrich. 1951. "Verifiability." In G.N. Flew (ed.), *Logic and Language: First Series*. Oxford: Oxford University Press.
Zeckhauser, Richard and Elmer Schafer. 1968. "Public Policy and Normative Economic Theory." In Raymond A. Bauer and Kenneth J. Gergen (eds.), *The Study of Policy Formation*. New York: Free Press.

11

Utilitarianism and the Presuppositions of Cost-Benefit Analysis: An Essay on the Relevance of Moral Philosophy to The Theory of Bureaucracy

Alasdair MacIntyre

The practical world of business and government is haunted by unrecognized theoretical ghosts. One of the tasks of moral philosophy is to help us to recognize and, if possible, to exorcise such ghosts. For so long as philosophical theories in fact inform and guide the actions of men who take themselves to be hard-headed, pragmatically oriented, free of theory, and guided by common sense, such theories enjoy an undeserved power. Being unrecognized they go uncriticized. At the same time the illusion is encouraged that philosophy is an irrelevant, abstract subject, part of the decoration of a cultured life, perhaps, but unnecessary in and even distracting from the activities of the practical world. The truth is, however, that all nontrivial activity presupposes some philosophical point of view and that not to recognize this is to make oneself the ready victim of bad or at the very least inadequate philosophy.

Consider, for example, the way in which the business executive or the civil servant characteristically defines and conceptualizes the activities of himself, his colleagues, and his clients. He or she does so in a way which appears to exclude both moral and philosophical considerations from arising within his everyday decision-making tasks. Certainly some large moral con-

From Kenneth Sayre, ed., *Values in the Electric Power Industry*, Notre Dame: University of Notre Dame Press, 1977, pp. 217–237. Copyright 1977 by the Philosophic Institute of the University of Notre Dame. Reprinted by permission.

siderations may have been involved in the executive's choice of a corporation; some might not be prepared to work for an armaments firm or in the making of pornographic movies. And certainly there may have been moral grounds for some of the legal constraints imposed by government—the imposition of safety regulations, for example. But once the executive is at work, the aims of the public or private corporation must be taken as given. Within the boundaries imposed by corporate goals and legal constraints, the executive's own tasks characteristically appear to him as merely technical. He has to calculate the most efficient, the most economical way of mobilizing the existing resources to produce the benefits of power at the lowest costs. The weighing of costs against benefits is not just his business, it is business.

The business executive does not differ in this view of his task from other bureaucrats. Bureaucracies have been conceived, since Weber, as impersonal instruments for the realization of ends which characteristically they themselves do not determine. A bureaucracy is set the task of achieving within the limits set by certain legal and physical constraints the most efficient solution of the problems of realizing such ends with the means available. The impersonality of bureaucracy has two closely related aspects. The first is that those who deal with a bureaucracy over time must be able to have continuous relationships of an intelligible kind with it, no matter which individuals within the bureaucracy retire, die, or are replaced during that relationship. Correspondence is correspondence with the organization rather than with the individuals who dictate the letters. Hence the existence of files or of computerized records is essential to bureaucratic organizations. From this aspect of impersonality a second emerges. Reasons cited as explanations for or justifications of actions in correspondence or in other external or internal transactions must hold as good reasons for the members of the organization independently of whoever actually on a particular occasion enunciates them. Thus established and agreed criteria of sound reasoning are presupposed in the successful functioning of all bureaucratic organizations. This is the point at which their impersonality and their commitment to means-ends rationality can be understood as two aspects of the same phenomenon.

The presupposed agreement on ends allows all disagreement within the organization to take place on questions of means, that is on the merits or rival policies for achieving the agreed ends. If these arguments are to be settleable, then there must also be presupposed agreed methods both for isolating all the relevant elements in each situation and for estimating the costs and the benefits of proceeding by this route rather than that. In other words, the norms of rationality which on a Weberian or a neo-Weberian view of bureaucracies must govern public discourse within bureaucracies and between bureaucracies and their masters, clients, customers, or other external agents are such that the cost-benefit analysis provides the essential normative form of argument.

The effect of this is that questions of alternative policies appear to become settleable in the same way that relatively simply questions of fact are. For the question of whether these particular means will or will not bring about that particular end with less expenditures of this or that resource than some other means is of course a question of fact.

The moral philosopher will at once recognize that the discourse of bureaucracy thus conceived reproduces the argumentative forms of utilitarianism. Not the forms, perhaps, of utilitarianism largely conceived as a morality capable of dealing with every area of life, but one that has accepted J.S. Mill's judgment upon "what a philosophy like Bentham's can do. It can teach the means of organizing and regulating the merely *business* part of the social arrangements." Poetry, music, friendship, family life may as Mill sees it not be captured by the Benthamite calculus; but there is a part of life which may be so captured, which may be rendered calculable.

If it is correct that corporate activity embodies the argumentative forms of utilitarianism, then we ought to be able to identify the key features of utilitarianism, including its central errors and distortions, within corporate activity. The guide that I shall use to identify the argumentative forms of corporate activity will be the textbook versons of cost-benefit analysis. For such textbooks are not only the instruction manuals which form the mind of the corporate executive; but in their successive versions they incorporate more and more paradigmatic examples drawn from actual practice. The question to be put to the textbook will be: do we discover in their pages precisely the lacunae and the incoherences of classical utilitarianism or not? It will be necessary first therefore to characterize these lacunae and incoherences.

Utilitarianism and Its Deficiencies

The doctrines of classical utilitarianism appear at first sight simple and elegant. Every proposed course of action is to be subjected to the test: will it produce a greater balance of pleasure over pain, of happiness over unhappiness, of benefits over harms than any alternative course of action? It is right to perform that action which will be productive of "the greatest happiness of the greatest number," which will have the greatest utility. In calculating the greatest happiness, everybody is to count for one and nobody for more than one. Utilitarianism sometimes has entangled itself, but perhaps need not entangle itself in questions about the meaning of such words as 'right' and 'good'. Bentham at least made no pretence that his doctrine was an analysis of what moral agents had hitherto meant in using such words; he proposed it instead as a rational substitute for the confusions and superstitions of earlier moral theory, and it is as such that I shall examine it.

Two main versions of utilitarianism have been advanced: that which holds that the utilitarian test is a test of actions and that which holds that it is a test of rules. On the former view, generally known as act-utilitarianism, rules simply summarize our findings to date about what classes of action generally tend to produce the greatest happiness of the greatest number; they are rough and ready guides to action, but if it appears on a given occasion that an action which transgresses a rule hitherto employed will produce a greater balance of pleasure or pain than one which conforms to that rule, then the former action ought to be preferred to the latter. On the other rule-utilitarian view, we perform those actions which the best moral rules we have prescribe; and we decide which moral rules are best by applying the "greatest happiness" test. But David Lyons has argued cogently that any case in which an act-utilitarian would have a good reason for breaking a rule would be a case in which a rule-utilitarian would have an equally good reason for emending his rule. Hence in practice they come to the same theory and our discussion can safely ignore their differences.

About any version of utilitarian doctrine five major questions arise. The first concerns the range of alternative courses of action which is to be subjected to the utilitarian test. For clearly at any moment an indefinitely large range of alternative courses of action are open to most agents. In practice I may consider a very limited set of alternatives: shall I use this money to paint my house or to educate my child? But perhaps I ought to weigh every proposed expenditure of energy, time, or money against the benefit that might accrue from devoting it to the solution of world population problems or the invention of labor-saving devices or the discovery of new methods of teaching music to young children or . . . If I try to construct a list of this kind of indefinite length, all decision-making will in fact be paralyzed. I must therefore find some principle of restriction in the construction of my list of alternatives. But this principle cannot itself be utilitarian; for if it were to be justified by the test of beneficial and harmful consequences as against alternative proposed principles of restriction, we should have to find some principle of restriction in order to avoid paralysis by the construction of an indefinitely long list of principles of restriction. And so on.

Utilitarian tests therefore always presuppose the application of some prior non-utilitarian principle which sets limits upon the range of alternatives to be considered. But this is not all that they presuppose. Bentham believed that there was one single, simple concept of pleasure or of hap-

piness. It did not matter what you called it. Indeed Bentham believed that
there were no less than fifty-eight synonyms for pleasure of which 'happiness' is one. Nor is there any good which is not either pleasure itself or a
means to pleasure. Moreover, the difference between pleasures is only
quantitative. Given these beliefs the notion of summing pleasures on the
one hand and pains on the other to calculate which course of action will
produce the greatest happiness of the greatest number is not mysterious.
But Bentham's beliefs are of course false and were recognized as false even
by his immediate utilitarian heirs.

Consider for the moment only genuine pleasures. It is clear that the-
pleasure-of-climbing-a-mountain, the-pleasure-of-listening-to-Bartok and
the-pleasure-of-drinking-Guinness-stout are three very different things.
There is not some one state to the production of which the climbing, the
listening and the drinking are merely alternative means. Nor is there any
scale on which they can be weighed against each other. But if this is true of
pleasures, how much more complex must matters become when we seek to
weigh against each other such goods as those of restoring health to the sick,
of scientific enquiry or of friendship. A politician has to decide whether to
propose spending a given sum of money on a new clinic for aged patients or
on a new infant school; a student has to decide between embarking on a
career as a musician or becoming an engineer. Both wish to promote the
greatest happiness of the greatest number, but they are being called upon to
decide between incommensurables—unless they can provide some prior
scheme of values by means of which goods and evils, pleasures and pains,
benefits and harms are to be ranked in some particular way. Such a method
of rank-ordering will, however, have to be non-utilitarian. For like the principle which specified the range of alternatives to be considered it has to be
adopted before any utilitarian test can be applied.

Thirdly, there is the question of whose assessment of harms and benefits
is to be considered by the agent making his assessment. For it is clear not
only that there are alternative methods of rank-ordering, but also that different types of people will adopt and argue for different methods. The old
do not weigh harms and benefits in the same way as the young; the poor
have a different perspective from the rich; the healthy and the sick often
weigh pain and suffering differently. "Everybody is to count for one and
nobody for more than one," declared Bentham; but others—Sir Karl Popper, for one—have suggested that the relief of pain or suffering always
should take precedence over the promotion of pleasure or happiness. So
that we have at least two contingently incompatible proposals immediately,
for the outcome of Bentham's rule will clearly often conflict with the results
of applying Popper's maxim.

Fourthly, there is the question of what is to count as a consequence of a given action. We might be tempted to suppose this a very straightforward question, but it is not. For the apparently straightforward answer "All the predictable effects of my action are to be counted as consequences of my action" at once raises the question, "What are reasonable standards of prediction?" How much care and effort am I required to exert before I make my decision? Once again certain maxims must be adopted prior to the utilitarian test. But this is not the only difficulty which arises over the notion of a consequence. In the Anglo-Saxon legal tradition chains of cause-and-effect arising from an action are often thought to be modified when they pass through another responsible agent in such a way that the later effects are no longer held to be consequences of my action. I am a teacher grading a student's examination. I give him a well-deserved C-. The student who has hoped for an A goes home and in his anger beats his wife. Suppose that I could somehow or other have reasonably predicted this outcome; ought I to have counted the wife-beating as a consequence of my action in grading the paper? Ought I to have weighed this consequence against others before deciding on what grade to give the paper? Classical utilitarianism appears to be committed to the answer "Yes"; the Anglo-Saxon legal tradition by and large to the answer "No." About what are they disagreeing? Obviously it is about the range of effects of an action for which the agent can be held responsible. Thus it turns out that some particular theory of responsibility must be adopted before we can have a criterion for deciding what effects are to count as consequences.

Fifthly, a decision must be made about the time-scale which is to be used in assessing consequences. Clearly if we adopt a longer time-scale we have to reckon with a much less predictable future than if we adopt a shorter one. Our assessment of long-term risks and of long-term probabilities is generally more liable to error than our assessment of short-term risks and probabilities. Moreover, it is not clear how we ought to weigh short-term harms and benefits against long-term contingencies; are our responsibilities the same to future generations as they are to the present one or to our own children? How far ought the present to be sacrificed to the future? Here again we have a range of questions to which non-utilitarian answers have to be given or at least presupposed before any utilitarian test can be applied.

Utilitarianism thus requires a background of beliefs and of evaluative commitments, a fact that has usually gone unnoticed by utilitarians themselves. They are able to apply the test of utility only because they have already implicitly decided that the world ought to be viewed in one way rather than another, that experience ought to be structured and evaluated in one way rather than another. The world which they inhabit is one of discrete variables, of a reasonably high degree of predictability; it is one whose questions of value have become questions of fact and in which the aim and the vindication of theory is its success in increasing our manipulative powers. The utilitarian vision of the world and the bureaucratic vision of the world match each other closely.

Yet this is not just a matter of resemblance; the bureaucratic world contains a number of devices for ensuring that thought, perception and action are organized in a utilitarian way. The most important of such devices in contemporary bureaucracy is probably the cost-benefit analysis.

Cost-Benefit Analysis and Bureaucratic Decision-Making

The cost-benefit analysis is an instrument of practical reason and it is one of the central features of practical reason that it operates under time constraints in a way that theoretical reason does not. Nothing counts as a solution of a practical problem which does not meet any required deadline; it is no good achieving a perfect solution for defeating Wellington at Waterloo on June 19, if the battle had to be fought on June 18. Hence problems cannot be left unsolved to await future solutions. But problems of a cost-benefit kind—of a utilitarian kind in general—can only be solved when all the elements of the problems are treated as belonging to the realm of the calculable and the predictable. Hence the executive is always under pressure to treat the social world as predictable and calculable and to ignore any arbitrariness involved in so doing. This pressure may operate in either of two opposite ways. It may appear in a tendency to restrict our operations to what is genuinely predictable and calculable; one manifestation of this will be a tendency to prefer short-term to long-term planning, since clearly the near future is generally more predictable than the more distant future. But the same pressure may equally appear in an opposite tendency to try and present all that we encounter as calculable and predictable, a tendency to overcome apparent difficulties in calculation by adopting *ad hoc* devices of various kinds. These conflicting pressures may appear in the way in which decisions are taken or evaluative commitments are made in any of the five areas which define the background to utilitarianism and which in a precisely paralleled way define the background to cost-benefit analyses.

There is first of all the restriction of alternatives so that the benefits and the costs of doing this rather than that are weighed against one another, but neither alternative is assessed against an indeterminately large range of other alternatives. Yet ever so often in corporate or governmental or private life the range of alternatives for which cost-benefit analyses are sought changes; and thus change always signals a change in underlying evaluative commitments. Up to a certain point in the history of a marriage, divorce remains an unthinkable alternative; up to a certain point in the history of a foreign policy, embarking on an aggressive war remains an unthinkable alternative; up to a certain point in the history of a war, truce or withdrawal remains unthinkable. Corporate parallels are not difficult to think of. The history of publishing or of automobile manufacture abound with them. The one-volume novel or the cheap intellectually substantial paperback were once unthinkable; so was the car which could be advertised primarily for safety factors.

Corporate executives may respond to this by saying that what restricts the range of alternatives which they consider is simply profitability. They can attend only to those alternatives which in the shorter or longer run will yield their stockholders a competitive return in the market. What this reply fails to notice is that what is profitable is partly determined by the range of evaluative commitments shared in the community. Sir Allen had to *make* the intellectual paperback profitable for the very first time and for that a firm conviction about intellectual values was required. What attitude both automobile manufacturers and the public take to death on the roads *changes* what is profitable. Consumer markets are *made*, not just given. Underlying the restricted range of alternatives considered by corporate executives we may therefore find both covert evaluative commitments, but also unspelled-out assumptions about human wants and needs.

It is not at all mysterious why these commitments and assumptions should go unnoticed. For in the vast majority of cases the devices which presupposed the commitments and assumptions and which delimited the range of thinkable alternatives were not made by the executive him- or herself, but were simply imposed upon him as a defining part of the environment in which he is to carry out his task. This is especially so in the case of public utility companies, such as the telephone company or power companies, where the company is legally chartered for certain specific public ends. What is fascinating is that such companies are dominated not by the legal charter itself, but by an orthodox, taken for granted, interpretation of that charter which each generation of executives in herits from its predecessors and transmits to its successors. It is interpretations of this kind, unrecognized as interpretations, which limit the thinkable alternatives in many government bureaucracies as well as in public utility companies.

Secondly the use of cost-benefit analyses clearly presupposes a prior decision as to what is a cost and what a benefit; but more than that it presupposes some method of ordering costs and benefits so that what would be otherwise incommensurable becomes commensurable. How are we to weigh the benefits of slightly cheaper power against the loss forever of just one beautiful landscape? How are we to weigh the benefits of increased employment and lessened poverty in Detroit against a marginal increase in deaths from automobile accidents? Once somebody has to consider both factors within a cost-benefit analysis framework these questions have to be answered. Considerable ingenuity has in fact been exercised in answering them.

Consider for example how we may carry through a calculation where one of the costs we may have to take into account is the shortening of human life. One recent example occurred in the argument over whether the Anglo-French supersonic aircraft *Concorde* should be allowed to land at United States airports. It is quite clear that the greater the use of *Concorde* the greater—as a result of the effects on those layers of the atmosphere which filter the sun's rays—the number of cases of skin cancer. How are we to include such deaths in our calculations?

Writers on cost-benefit analysis techniques have devised four alternative methods for computing the cost of a person's life. One is that of discounting to the present the person's expected future earnings; a second is that of computing the losses to others from the person's death so as to calculate their present discounted value; a third is that of examining the value placed on an individual life by presently established social policies and practices, e.g. the benefits in increased motor traffic which society at the present moment is prepared to exchange for a higher fatal accident rate; and a fourth is to ask what value a person placed on his or her own life, by looking at the risks which that person is or was prepared to take and the insurance premiums which he or she was prepared to pay. Clearly those four criteria will yield very different answers on occasion; the range of possible different answers to one and the same question that you can extract from the same techniques of cost-benefit analysis makes it clear that all the mathematical sophistication and rigor that may go into the modes of computation may be undermined by the arbitrariness—relative to the mathematics—of the choice to adopt one principle for quantifying rather than another. Thus there once more appears behind the ordered world of discrete, calculable, variable elements in which the cost-benefit analysis is at home a range of relatively arbitrary decisions presupposed—and sometimes actually made by the analyst himself.

Thirdly, once more as with utilitarianism in general, the application of cost-benefit analysis presupposes a decision as to *whose* values and preferences are to be taken into account in assessing costs and benefits. Indeed the choice of a method for weighing costs against benefits, the adoption of the type of principle discussed immediately above, will often involve equally a decision as to which voices are to be heard. Consider once again the different methods employed to estimate the cost of a human death. One of these considers the individual's own earnings; one the losses to others;

one certain socially established norms; and one the individual's own risk-taking. The first is an attempt to give the individual the value which he sets on himself; the second gives him the value he has to others; the third the value he has in the eyes of "society"; the fourth perhaps the value that he has in the eyes of the taxation system. To adopt one of these methods rather than another is precisely to decide *who* is to decide what counts as a cost and what counts as a benefit.

Consider the range of possible decision-makers with whom a corporate executive might be concerned: his superiors, the consumers of his product, the stockholders, the labor force, the other members of his profession (if he is, say, a lawyer or an actuary); the community in which the corporation is sited, government, and the public at large. What makes the question "Who decides?" so crucial is another feature of cost-benefit analyses. Very often, perhaps characteristically, neither future costs nor future benefits can be restricted to identifiable individuals. After the event we can say who died in the road deaths created by an increase in automobile traffic, or which children were deformed by the side-effects of a new drug or who in fact got skin-cancer as a result of increased and more powerful jet aeroplane use. But beforehand all that is at best predictable is what proportion of a given population will be harmed (or will benefit). It is a chance of harm or benefit which is assigned now to each member of the population. Therefore the question is: who should decide how the chances are distributed over a population?

There are some alien cultures where a family's ancestors are given an important voice in decision-making; so it is in traditional Vietnamese culture, for example. There are cultures where the old have a very special voice. In our own culture our explicit beliefs label the former as a superstition and our dominant practices show that we implicitly label the latter a superstition too. This is directly relevant to, for example, the policies of public utility companies. Light and heat are peculiarly important to old people; ought therefore the old to receive special consideration from public utility corporation executives in determining what is to count as a cost and what as a benefit? Implicitly or explicitly a decision will have been taken on this point whenever a cost-benefit analysis is offered in a relevant context.

Fourthly, the parallel with utilitarianism is maintained in the way in which the questions of what is to count as a consequence of some particular action or course of action arises for cost-benefit analyses. Any answer to this question, as I suggested earlier, presupposes a prior answer to the question: for what range of effects of his actions is an agent to be considered liable or responsible? What answer to this latter question is in fact presupposed by corporate practice? A necessary starting point is to recognize that in advanced societies today, and most notably in the United States, individuals often see their moral lives as parcelled out between the different roles which one and the same individual plays. Parts of his moral self are allocated to each sphere of activity and within each sphere responsibilities—and therefore consequences—are understood in very different ways. So the individual *qua* father or husband has one role and one way of envisaging responsibilities and consequences; but *qua* consumer, *qua* citizen or *qua* corporate executive he may see matters quite differently. The effects of the division of the self are characteristically to exempt the individual in any one role from considering those responsibilities which he is prepared to acknowledge only too readily in other roles. The individual learns to confine different aspects of his evaluative commitments to different spheres. Consider in particular how this may define the situation of the executive in a public utility company. For what is to some degree present in the situation of many corporate managers in America is present in his situation in a highly explicit form. Public utility companies—and the Bell Telephone Company is in some ways the best example—from the outset accepted public governmental regulation as the price to be paid for the privilege of monopoly. The case for monopoly is quite simply that competition involves extremely expensive reduplication of equipment and—especially in the case of rival telephone companies, each of whom serves only a portion of the subscribers—grave inconvenience for consumers. But if monopoly is permitted, then the consumer must find elsewhere the protection which otherwise would—in theory, at least—be provided by competition. Hence the activities of public utility companies are to be regulated and restricted by government designated agencies. The company's is the sphere of activity; the government's is the sphere of restriction. The executive himself inhabits both spheres: *qua* corporate executive he represents the company; *qua* citizen and consumer the government represents him. Parts of his self are allocated to each area.

Other types of corporate executive have often come to embrace government regulation in a similar way; but the executive in the public utility company was forced to seek it out for himself. His acknowledgement of restriction, in that sphere at least, must not appear even to himself reluctant. He operates thereafter under a quasi-legal mandate which prescribes this definition of spheres. I say quasi-legal, because in the case of both power companies and the telephone company, the various statutes which govern the operation of the company do not exhaust the mandate as the executives understand it. For that mandate is one to supply individual and corporate consumers with a good—electrical power. Hence it is not after all only the statutory restrictions on their activities which define a moral dimension in their activities; there is also a goal conceived of as a goal of public service. (Chester Barnard who wrote what is still the single most influential—even if now usually unread—book on management theory laid it down that service is the true goal of corporate activity; it is, I think, no coincidence that he spent his entire working life with the telephone company.)

Morally then the executive faces in at least two directions: towards the morality of restriction where it is the duty of others and not himself—or if you like, his duty *qua* citizen and not *qua* executive—to discipline his activities and also towards the morality of service which defines a goal external to, but justifying his day to day activity. What do I mean when I call this goal external?

The power company executive is able at this point to avail himself of a picture of his activities which has nothing particular to do with his serving a public utility company, but is one common to many executives in many industries. This picture is one of a moral contract, prior to and providing warrant for, all legal contracts, between an autonomous supplier and an autonomous client. Their autonomy entails that each is the sole authority as to his own needs and wants. The acts of production by the supplier are undertaken for the sake of the client's consumption. Everyone is both in one aspect supplier and in another client. A simple model of economic value informs their exchanges (something very like a labor theory of value is presupposed). The moral contract has replaced the crude rule of *caveat emptor*. Autonomy also entails that the supplier has no responsibility for the use that the client makes of the goods which he supplies. Moreover since the contract is between individuals no transactions transcend one generation. The supplier is morally bound to give the client what *he* wants; for the nature of the client's wants and the consequences of the act of supply he is not answerable. To make him so would be to injure the autonomy necessary for such a contract.

Only one kind of moral distinction needs to be made by the supplier: that which divides off genuine goods from dubious commodities. Many suppliers will not worry over this distinction except insofar as it is enforced by law; but many do. Goodrich and Goodyear clearly take pride in as well as make profit from making first-rate tires; many businessmen would not wish to involve themselves in selling second-hand napalm or pornographic movies. But once a man is assured of the goodness of what he supplies he has a sanction for what he does that leaves him free not to think about this aspect of his activity any more. He in his dealings with consumers, in his investment policies, in his dealings with his labor force can press ahead exactly as he would do with any other product (except for technological consideration). The wants of the consumer for the good supplied are to be taken as given; whatever is asked for in the form of market demand will, so far as possible, be supplied. It is only as creators of demand that consumers appear in this picture.

It follows that the consequences of any course of action terminate for such an executive when the consumer has been successfully supplied. The further consequences of supplying demand—the trivialization of the culture by the major television networks, for example—are beyond the scope of any consideration by those who supply the electric power for such enterprises. Once again the cost-benefit analysis is not an evaluatively neutral instrument of choice.

The fifth and last parallel with utilitarianism concerns the time-scale on which costs and benefits are to be assessed. When we make a decision—implicitly or explicitly, recognizing it or failing to recognize it—about the time-span within which we are going to reckon up costs and benefits, at least three different kinds of consideration will affect our decision. The first of these concerns the fact that both types and rates of change for different cost and benefit factors may vary so that by choosing one time-length rather than another the relation of costs to benefits will appear quite differently. If I am deciding how to transport commodities from one place to another—by building a road, building a railway, maintaining a canal or whatever—changes in the price of land, the prices of raw materials, the size of the labor force, the demand for utilization of surplus carrying capacity, the technologies involved, the alternative uses to which each type of resource might be put will all change in such a way that, even if I am a perfect predictor, the choice of dates within which costs and benefits are to be assessed may give strikingly different results. Of course in a private profit-seeking corporation the current rates of return expected on investment will place constraints on such a choice of dates; and in public corporations the need to vindicate policies within terms ultimately specified by electoral laws will set not dissimilar constraints. Nonetheless even within such limits a certain arbitrariness is likely to appear.

Secondly, it is not just that the different factors in a situation will be subject to different types and different rates of change; they will also differ in the degree to which they are predictable. Three key types of unpredictability are likely to be generated in the relevant types of situation. One springs from the sheer complexity of so many of the relevant types of situation and their vulnerability to contingencies of an in practice unpredictable kind: earthquakes, viruses, panics. A second springs from the systematic unpredictability of all innovation that involves radical conceptual invention. We could not before the event have predicted Einstein's definition of "simultaneity" or Kant's doctrine of the transcendental ego or Turing's proof of the effective computability theorem just because to have predicted these we would have had to specify their character and to have specified their character would be to have anticipated Einstein or Kant or Turing and so prevented their being the discoverers that they were.

It may be said that the author of a cost-benefit analysis simply cannot be expected to deal with unpredictability at all. If this were indeed so it would be equivalent to saying that he must exclude from his view a central feature of social reality—as in fact seems to happen with many studies of organization and management as well as with many conventional texts on the methodology of the social sciences. But of course this consciously or unconciously willed blindness is not necessary. Reasoning of a cost-benefit analysis kind may include—often does include—some provision for unforeseen contingencies. But once again how much and what types of unpredictability are allowed for will rest upon judgments independent of and prior to the cost-benefit analysis itself. Among these judgments will once again be those as to the length of time within which costs and benefits are to be reckoned; and once again there is, relative to the cost-benefit analysis, an element that seems purely arbitrary.

It seems less arbitrary, but perhaps no less difficult to handle, if we turn to the third factor impinging upon judgments about time-scales. This concerns the view taken by individuals of the existence, identity, interests and responsibilities through time of the organization for which they are working. Let me make an initial point about the interests of individuals. We know that individuals vary in the degree to which their identification of their own interests ranges beyond their individual selves and their present state in time. A man may see his interests as being those of his family or of his trade association or of his church; he may envisage his interests as being those of a man with a future of a certain kind rather than a present of a certain kind. So a man may for considerations of interest vote for a measure which benefits the aged, although he himself is young, because it is in his family's interest that the aged be supported. Or he may vote for a tax measure which benefits forty-five year old married men with high incomes, although he himself is a low paid, unmarried twenty-five year old, because he votes on the basis of the interests of his predicted future self rather than his present self. As with individuals acting for themselves *qua* individuals, so also for individuals acting in their organizational roles. What time span is assumed to be appropriate for determining costs and benefits will depend on how the organization's interests are envisaged through time and on how the interests of related institutions—the state, the local community, the profession or whatever—are envisaged through time. This becomes very clear if we look at the limiting case, that of organizations constructed and maintained only for some temporary purpose, such as a relief mission whose task is to feed and provide schooling for three thousand children for a period of four months.

The reason why the time-scale within which costs and benefits are to be assessed is in such cases much less arbitrary and debatable is *not* merely that the time within which the project is to be completed is specified; for even with projects whose duration is specified costs and benefits may range in time far beyond the actual duration of the project. What limits the time-scale in a non-arbitrary way is rather the clear restraints placed on goals, tasks and resources in this kind of temporary organization and the consequent ease in identifying both the interests and the responsibilities of the organization. This limitation is, as it were, part of the legal or quasi-legal charter of the organization. But with permanent or at least long-term organizations the criteria for imputing responsibility for and defining interests in a variety of consequences are not assigned in this clear way; and the adoption of different time-scales for the assessment of costs and benefits may presuppose the adoption of different views of how organizational responsibility is to be imputed and how organizational interests are to be defined.

Consider the example of a university. What counts as a cost or a benefit to a university may—and, it is to be hoped, characteristically will—depend upon a distinction between the essential and long-term purposes which a university serves and the short-term *ad hoc* projects with which universities necessarily become involved. A university which undertakes remedial teaching of adolescents from deprived groups in a situation of social and educational crisis or which organizes some of its research in terms of the immediate practical needs of its community may and often does pay costs in terms of the damage done to its contract with those long dead and those yet to be born in the distant future to whom it is committed to transmit in living form to the unborn the cultural tradition of the dead. A public utility company or a country club is committed to no such contract; and this means that the appropriate time-scale for assessing costs and benefits will be a different one from that appropriate to a university. But *any* time-scale may presuppose some view of its identity.

Note that I have written 'may' and not 'will'. For those who inhabit organizations are often unclear and confused as to what precisely they are doing, and the implicit presuppositions of their actions may be similarly unclear. Sometimes what appears arbitrary in choice of time-scale just *is* arbitrary; but not always.

Any cost-benefit analysis therefore has to be understood against *some* background of assumptions about identity and time; and because it is impossible to speak of the identity of organizations except in terms of some evaluative commitment, these assumptions will be in part evaluative. Consider the concept of the university embodied in my remarks in the last paragraph. The concept in terms of which I wrote may have been the dominant one in the Western world, but it is far from being without rivals. What concept of the university you adopt will involve one out of a set of rival views of the place of knowledge and education in human life. There is no way to employ the concept of a university without adopting some such value-laden conception. And what is true in the case of universities is equally true, if less often noticed, in the case of such organizations as public utility companies and indeed in the case of private and public corporations in general.

Less often noticed? In fact of course not usually noticed at all. The moral structure underlying the corporate executive's thinking is one of which he remains almost entirely unaware. He does not recognize himself as a classical utilitarian; and he cannot therefore recognize that the presuppositions of classical utilitarianism which he shares—which the utilitarians themselves did not recognize—must go doubly unrecognized by himself and his colleagues. His vision of himself remains that of a man engaged in the exercise of a purely technical competence to whom moral concerns are at best marginal, engaging him rather *qua* citizen or *qua* consumer than *qua* executive. Does this false consciousness of the executive, whether in the private corporation or in government, itself have a function? It is plausible to suppose that it does. To consider what that function is imagine what would occur if all these considerations became manifest rather than latent.

The executive would then be presented with a set of moral problems, or moral conflicts, on which he would have to make overt decisions, over which he would have to take sides in the course of his work. What sort of issues are these? The claims of the environment *versus* the claims of cheaper power, the claims of need (for example, of the old) against the claims of demand, the claims of future generations against those of the urgent present, the claims of rival institutions—government, church, school—in certain respects, the claims of rival judgments of intelligence, integrity and courage. Now it is a crucial feature of our moral culture that we have no established way of deciding between radically different moral views. Moral arguments are in our culture generally unsettleable. This is not just a matter of one party to a dispute generally being unable to find any natural method to convince other contending parties. It is also the case that we seem unable to settle these matters within ourselves without a certain arbitrary taking of sides.

It follows that to allow moral issues to become overt and explicit is to create at least the risk of and more probably the fact of open and rationally unmanageable conflict both between executives and within each executive. The avoidance of such conflict necessitates two kinds of device. Where the recognition of moral considerations is unavoidable they must be apportioned out between the different areas of the self and its social life, so that what is done and thought in one area will not impinge upon, let alone conflict with what is done and thought in another. Boundaries must be drawn between areas of social action whose effectiveness will depend upon them not being recognized for what they are.

Where however it is unavoidable that moral issues arise *within* one and the same area, then they must be disguised from the agent so that he can deal with them, so far as is humanly possible, as merely technical issues. Their moral and evaluative character must be relegated to a realm of latent presuppositions. But it is obvious at once that both these devices are central to the structures of life of the corporate executive, as I described them earlier. The morality of contract with the autonomous consumer and the morality of governmental regulation operate in carefully defined areas so that questions of their coherence or conflict with each other or with other moral considerations are prevented from arising. The moral considerations underlying cost-benefit analysis are simply suppressed.

REFERENCES

Barnard, Chester I. 1938. *The Functions of the Executive*. Cambridge: Harvard University Press.
Leavis, F.R., ed. 1950. *Mill on Bentham and Coleridge, Chatto and Windus*. London.
Lyons, David. 1964. *Forms and Limits of Utilitarianism*. Oxford: Clarendon Press.
Mishan, E.J. 1971. *Cost-Benefit Analysis*. New York: Praeger.
Popper, Sir Karl. 1966: *The Open Society and its Enemies*. 5th Ed., Vol. 1. London: Routledge & Kegan Paul.

12

Cost-Benefit Analysis and Environmental, Safety, and Health Regulation: Ethical and Philosophical Considerations

Steven Kelman

At the broadest level, cost-benefit analysis may be regarded simply as systematic thinking about decision making. Who can oppose, indignant proponents of cost-benefit analysis frequently ask critics, efforts to think systematically about the various consequences of alternative decisions? The alternative, it would appear, is unexamined or idiosyncratic decision making.

Equating cost-benefit analysis with an attempt to ponder systematically the consequences of decisions deprives the concept of many implications for actual decisions faced by regulatory officials. I will assume therefore, that those who argue that "more cost-benefit analysis is needed" in decisions involving environmental, safety, and health regulation hold views such as the following:

- An act should not be undertaken unless its benefits outweigh its costs. (More formally, economists would argue that the right decision is one in which the excess of benefits over costs is maximized. Thus, a decision with benefits of $100\times$ and costs of $99\times$ would be wrong if there were an alternative decision with benefits of $100\times$ and costs of $95\times$.)
- To determine whether benefits outweigh costs, all benefits and costs should be expressed in a common metric, so that they can be compared

From Steven Kelman, *Cost-Benefit Analysis and Environmental Regulations: Politics, Ethics, and Methods* (The Conservation Foundation, 1982). Reprinted by permission.

with one another, since some benefits and costs are not traded on markets and hence have no established dollar values.

- Efforts to increase both the degree to which decision makers account for costs and benefits and the accuracy of calculating costs and benefits are important enough to warrant the use of persuasion and politics (as well as the expenditure of money) to give these efforts greater public priority than other types of decision analysis.

I wish to examine each of these three views from a perspective of philosophical discourse, and more particularly from the perspective of formal ethical theory; that is, the study of what actions are morally right (or wrong) to undertake. About the first of the presumptions—the view that an act is right if its benefits outweigh its costs and wrong if its benefits do not—there is an enormous amount of discussion in ethical theory; indeed, it is one of the central issues in ethical theory. There is considerably less literature on the other viewpoints; in fact, the ethics of monetizing nonmonetary benefits and costs are on the frontiers of discussions within ethical theory. The conclusions of my analysis will be:

- In areas of environmental, safety, and health regulation, there may be many instances when a certain decision might be right even though the benefits of that decision do not outweigh the costs.
- There are a number of reasons to oppose efforts to put dollar values on nonmarketed benefits and costs, beyond the technical difficulties of doing so.
- Given the relative frequency of occasions in the areas of environmental, safety, and health regulation when it is not desirable to use a "benefits outweigh costs" test as a decision rule, and given the reasons to oppose the monetizing of nonmarketed benefits or of costs—a prerequisite for cost-benefit analysis—it is not justifiable to devote major resources to generate data to be used in cost-benefit calculations or to undertake an effort to "spread the gospel" of cost-benefit analysis further.

Should Benefits Outweigh Costs?

How do we decide whether a given action is morally right or wrong and, assuming the desire to act morally, why it should be undertaken or refrained from? Like the Moliere character who spoke prose without knowing it, economists advocating the use of cost-benefit analysis for public decisions are philosophers without knowing it: the answer given by cost-benefit analysis, that actions should be undertaken so as to maximize net benefits, represents one of the classic answers given by moral philosophers. This is the doctrine of utilitarianism, associated with philosophers such as Bentham, Mill, and Sidgwick. Utilitarians argue that the right action under a given set of circumstances is the one that maximizes net satisfaction. To determine whether an action is right or wrong, all the positive consequences of the action in terms of human satisfaction should be totaled, and the act that maximizes attainment of satisfaction considered the right act.[1] The fact that the economists' answer is also the answer of one school of philosophers should not be surprising. Originally, economics was a branch of moral philosophy—Bentham and Sidgwick are famous not only among philosophers but are regarded by economists as their intellectual forebears. Only later on did economics separate from moral philosophy.

Before proceeding, the subtlety of the utilitarian position should be noted. For example, the positive and negative consequences of an act for the sum total of satisfaction in the world may go beyond the act's immediate consequences. A facile version of utilitarianism would give moral sanction to a lie, for instance, if the satisfaction an individual attained by telling the lie were greater than the suffering imposed on the victim of the lie.

Few utilitarians would agree, however. They would add to the list of negative consequences the effect of the one lie on the tendency of the person who lied to tell other lies, especially when those lies would produce less satisfaction for the liar than the dissatisfaction produced in others. They also would add the negative effects of the lie on general social respect for truth telling, a respect with many positive consequences. In addition, a negative consequence of a lie that some maintain must be added to the utilitarian calculation is the feeling of dissatisfaction produced in the individual (and perhaps in others) because, by telling a lie, one has "done the wrong thing." Correspondingly, in this view, among the positive consequences to be weighed into a utilitarian calculation of telling the truth is the satisfaction of "doing the right thing." This view rests on an error, however, because it assumes what it is the purpose of the calculation to determine—that telling the truth in the instance in question is indeed the right thing to do. For a utilitarian, there is nothing wrong about lying independent of its negative consequences (broadly regarded) for human satisfaction.

This last error is revealing, however, because it begins to suggest a critique of utilitarianism. Utilitarianism is an important and powerful moral doctrine. Few philosophers, including opponents of utilitarianism, would disagree that, for many actions, a utilitarian balancing of costs and benefits is an appropriate guide to moral choice. But it is probably fair to say that utilitarianism is a minority position among contemporary moral philosophers. It is indeed amazing that economists can proceed in unanimous endorsement of cost-benefit analysis as if unaware that in the discipline from which the conceptual framework for cost-benefit analysis arose, namely moral philosophy, this framework is, to put it mildly, highly controversial.

On the one hand, the notion that something is wrong unless its benefits outweigh its costs initially seems to be just common sense. On the other hand, the logical error discussed before indicates that our notion of certain things being right or wrong—such as telling a lie—predates our calculation of costs and benefits. Let us explore these contradictory intuitions with several examples.

Imagine the case of an old man in Nazi Germany who is hostile to the Nazi regime. He is wondering whether he should speak out against Hitler. If he speaks out, he will lose his pension. His action will do nothing to increase the chances that the Nazi regime will be overthrown since he is regarded as somewhat eccentric and nobody has ever consulted his views on political questions. Recall that any satisfaction from doing "the right thing" cannot be added to the benefits of speaking out because the purpose of the exercise is to determine whether speaking out is the right thing. The utilitarian calculation would determine that the benefits of speaking out, as the example is presented, would be nil. The cost would be the loss of the old man's pension. The costs of the action, therefore, would outweigh the benefits. By the utilitarian cost-benefit calculation, it would be morally wrong for the man to speak out.[2]

In another example two very close friends are on an Arctic expedition. One man becomes very sick in the snow and bitter cold, and he sinks quickly before anything can be done to help him. As he is dying, he asks his friend one thing, "Please, make me a solemn promise that 10 years from today you will come back to this spot and place a lighted candle here to remember me." The friend solemnly promises but does not tell a soul. Now, 10 years later, the friend must decide whether to fulfill his promise and return to the spot. It would be inconvenient for him to travel all the way back. Since he told nobody, his failure to go would not affect the general social faith in promise keeping. And the incident was unique enough so that it is safe to assume that failure to go would not encourage the man to break other promises. Again, the costs of the act outweigh the benefits. A utilitarian would believe that it would be morally wrong to travel to the Arctic to light the candle.

A third example: a wave of thefts has hit a city. The police are having trouble finding any of the actual perpetrators. But they believe, correctly, that punishment of someone for theft will have some deterrent effect and will decrease the number of crimes. Unable to arrest any real perpetrator, the police chief and the prosecutor arrest a person whom they know to be innocent and, in cahoots with each other, fabricate a convincing case against him. The police chief and the prosecutor are about to retire, so the act will not affect their future actions. The fabrication is perfectly executed, and nobody finds out about it. In determining whether the act of framing the innocent man is morally correct, is the only question the one of whether the man's suffering from conviction and imprisonment will be greater than the suffering avoided among potential crime victims? A utilitarian would need to believe that it is morally right to punish the innocent man as long as it can be demonstrated that the suffering prevented outweighs his suffering.[3]

And a final example: imagine two worlds, each with the same sum total of happiness in them. In the first world, this particular total of happiness came about from a series of acts that included a number of lies and injustices. The sum total of happiness in this hypothetical world would consist of the immediate gross sum of happiness the acts created, minus any long-term unhappiness occasioned by lies and injustices. In the second world, the identical sum total of happiness was produced by a different series of acts, none of which involved lies or injustices. Are there any reasons to prefer the one world to the other? A utilitarian would believe that the choice between the two worlds is a matter of indifference.[4]

To those who believe that it would not be morally wrong for the old man to speak out in Nazi Germany or the man to venture to the Arctic to light a candle for his deceased friend, that it would not be morally right to convict the innocent man, or that the choice between the two worlds is not a matter of indifference, utilitarianism is insufficient as a moral view. Some acts whose costs are greater than their benefits may be morally right while some acts whose benefits are greater than their costs may be morally wrong.

This does not mean that the question of whether benefits are greater than costs is morally irrelevant. Few would claim such. Indeed, for a broad range of individual and social decisions, whether or not an act's benefits outweigh its costs is a sufficient question to ask. But not for all such decisions. There are situations in which certain duties—duties not to lie, break promises, or kill, for example—make an act wrong, even if the act would result in an excess of benefits over costs.[5] Another reason that an act might be wrong even though its benefits outweigh its costs is if that act violates someone's rights. We would not permit rape even if it could be demonstrated that the rapist derived enormous happiness from his act, while the victim only experienced a minor displeasure. We do not conduct cost-benefit analyses of freedom of speech or trial by jury. As the Steelworkers Union noted in a comment on the economic analysis of the Occupational Safety and Health Administration's (OSHA's) proposed regulation to reduce worker exposure to carcinogenic coke-oven emissions, the Emancipation Proclamation was not subjected to an inflationary impact statement. Similarly, the Bill of Rights is not subject to the Regulatory Analysis Review Group. The notion of human rights involves the idea that people may make certain claims to be allowed to act in certain ways, or to be treated in certain ways, even if the sum of benefits achieved thereby does not outweigh the sum of costs.[6] It is this view that lies behind statements like "workers have a right to a safe and healthy workplace," and behind the expectation that OSHA decisions will reflect that judgment.

In the most convincing versions of nonutilitarian (or deontological) ethics, various duties or rights are not absolute, but each has a *prima facie* moral validity such that, if duties or rights do not conflict, the morally right act is the act that reflects a duty or respects a right. If duties or rights do conflict, a moral judgment, based on deliberative reflection, must be made. One of the duties that deontological philosophers enumerate is the duty of beneficence (the duty to maximize happiness), which in effect incorporates all of utilitarianism by reference. Thus, a nonutilitarian, faced with conflicts between the results of cost-benefit analysis and the results of nonutility-based considerations, will need to undertake deliberative reflections. But additional elements in such deliberations, which cannot be reduced to whether benefits outweigh costs, exist. Indeed, depending on the moral importance we attach to the right or duty involved, questions of benefits and costs may, within wide ranges, become irrelevant to the outcome of the moral judgment.

In addition to questions of duties and rights, there is a final sort of question in which the issue of whether benefits outweigh costs should not determine moral judgment. I noted earlier that, for the common run of questions facing individuals and societies, it is possible to determine actions by calculating whether the benefits of the contemplated act outweigh the costs. Thus, one way for people to show the great importance or value attached to an issue is to say that decisions involving the issue should not be determined by cost-benefit calculations. This applies, I think, to the view many enviromentalists have of decisions involving our natural environment. When decisions are being made about pollution levels that will harm certain vulnerable people—such as asthmatics or the elderly—while not harming others, issues of the rights of those people not to be sacrificed on the altar of somewhat higher living standards for the rest of us may be involved. Some environmentalists, in addition, speak of the "rights of nature" involved in environmental decisions. But more broadly than this, I believe many environmentalists object to the use of cost-benefit analysis for environmental decisions because the very act of using cost-benefit analysis for decisions about cleaning the air or water removes these questions from the realm of specially valued things where such calculations are not applicable.

Using a Common Metric

In order for cost-benefit calculations to be performed, all costs and benefits must be expressed in a common metric, typically dollars. This creates an undisputed technical problem when placing a value on things not normally bought and sold on markets and to which no dollar price is attached. The most dramatic example of such things is human life itself, but many other benefits, such as peace and quiet, fresh-smelling air, swimmable rivers, or spectacular vistas, achieved or preserved by environmental policy also are not traded on markets.

Economists who use cost-benefit analysis have regarded the quest after dollar values for nonmarket things as a difficult challenge—and one joined with relish. Economists have tried to develop methods for imputing people's "willingness to pay" for nonmarket things. Essentially, the method involves searching for bundled goods that are traded on markets and whose price varies by whether or not they include a feature that is, by itself, not marketed. Thus, fresh air is not marketed but houses in different parts of Los Angeles that are similar except for the degree of smog are. Peace and quiet are not marketed but similar houses inside and outside airport flight paths are. The risk of death is not marketed but similar jobs that have different levels of risk are. Economists have made often ingenious efforts to impute dollar prices to nonmarketed things by calculating, for example, the premiums that homes in clean air areas attract over similar homes in dirty areas or of the premium of risky jobs over similar non-risky jobs. To the extent these efforts succeed, the ability to place nonmarket things into a common metric for the purpose of cost-benefit analysis succeeds.

Efforts to place nonmarket things into a common metric can be criticized on a number of technical grounds. First, the attempt to control and account for all the dimensions by which the bundled good can vary except for the nonmarketed thing may be difficult. More importantly, in a world where people vary in their preferences and the constraints to which they are subject, the dollar value imputed to nonmarket things that most people would wish to avoid will be lower than in a uniform world. This is because people with unusually weak aversion to these commodities or with unusually strong constraints on choice would be willing to take the bundled good in question at less of a discount than the average person. Thus, to use the property value discount of homes near airports as a measure of people's willingness to pay for quiet means to accept as a proxy for the rest of the population the behavior of those least sensitive to location, or of those susceptible to an agent's assurances that "it's not so bad." Similarly, to use the wage premiums accorded hazardous work as a measure of the value of life is to accept as proxies for the rest of us the choices of people who do not have many choices or who are exceptionally risk seeking.

A second problem is that the attempts of economists to measure people's "willingness to pay" for nonmarketed things do not differentiate between the price people will need to be paid to give up something to which they have a preexistent right and the price they would be willing to pay to gain something to which they enjoy no right. Thus, the analysis assumes no difference between how much a homeowner would need to be paid in order to give up an unobstructed mountain view that he or she already enjoys and how much the homeowner would be willing to pay to get an obstruction moved once it is already in place. Evidence suggests that most people would insist on being paid far more to assent to a worsening of their situation than they would be willing to pay to improve their situation. Such factors as habituation with the familiar and psychological attachments to that which people believe they enjoy a right account for the difference. This would create a circularity problem, for any attempt to use cost-benefit analysis would first have to determine whether to assign, for instance, the homeowner the right to an unobstructed mountain view. For the "willingness to pay" will be different depending on whether the right is initially assigned or not assigned. The value judgment about whether or not to assign the right must thus be made first.[7] (Actually, an analyst could assume assignment of the right to the person and determine how much he or she would need to be paid to give it up. This could set an upper bound on the benefit; if the costs were still greater, then by any test the costs of the measure outweigh the benefits.)

A third problem with placing nonmarket goods in a common metric is that the efforts economists make to impute willingness to pay all involve bundled goods exchanged in private transactions. People using figures garnered from such analysis to provide guidance for public decisions assume there is no difference between how people value certain things in private, individual transactions and how they would wish a social valuation of those same things to be made in public, collective decisions.

In assuming this, economists insidiously slip an important and controversial value judgment into their analysis—the view that there should be no difference between private, individual values and behavior, and the values and behavior displayed in public, social life. The view that public decisions should seek to mimic private, individual behavior grows naturally out of the highly individualistic microeconomic tradition. But it remains controversial nonetheless. An alternative view—one that enjoys wide resonance among many citizens—would be that public, social decisions provide an opportunity to give certain things a higher valuation than we choose, for one reason or another, to give these things in our private, individual activities.

Opponents of stricter regulation of health risks often argue that our daily risk-taking behavior indicates that we do not value life infinitely, and therefore our public decisions should not reflect the high value of life that proponents of strict regulation propose. However, an alternative view is equally plausible. Precisely because we fail in everyday personal decisions, for whatever reasons, to give life the value we believe it should have, we wish our social decisions to display the reverence for life that we espouse but do not always show. By this view, people do not have fixed, unambiguous "preferences" which they express through private activities and which, therefore, should be expressed in public decisions. Rather, people may have what they themselves regard as "higher" and "lower" preferences. The latter may dominate in private decisions, but people may want the higher values to dominate in public decisions. For example, people may sometimes display racial prejudice but support anti-discrimination laws. They may buy a certain product after seeing a seductive ad but be skeptical enough of advertising to want the government to keep a close eye on it. In such cases, the use of private behavior to impute values for public decisions violates a view of citizen behavior that is deeply engrained in our democratic tradition. It is a view that denudes politics of any independent role in society, reducing it to a mechanistic recalculation based on private behavior.

Finally, putting a price on a nonmarket commodity and hence incorporating it into the market system may be opposed out of a fear that doing so will reduce the thing's perceived value. To place a price on the benefit of clean air, for example, may reduce the value of clean air. The act of cost-benefit analysis, thus, may affect the values of otherwise nonpriced benefits and costs.

Examples of the perceived cheapening of a thing's value by the very act of buying and selling it abound both in everyday life and language. The horror and disgust that accompany the idea of buying and selling human beings are based on the sense that this practice would dramatically diminish human worth. Epithets such as "he prostituted himself" and "he's a whore" applied as linguistic analogies to people who have sold something reflect the view that certain things should not be sold because doing so diminishes their value. One reason that pricing decreases something's perceived value is that nonmarket exchange often is associated with certain positively valued feelings that market exchange, using prices, is not. These may include feelings such as spontaneity and emotions that come from personal relationships.[8] If a good becomes disassociated from positively valued feelings because of market exchange, the good will lose its perceived value to the extent that those feelings are valued.

This loss can be seen clearly in instances when a thing may be transferred both by market and by nonmarket mechanisms. The willingness to pay for an apple in a store is less than the perceived value of the same apple presented as a gift by a friend or a stranger. The willingness to pay for sex bought from a prostitute is less than the perceived value of the sex consummating love. (Imagine the reaction if a practitioner of cost-benefit analysis computed the benefits of sex in our society based on the price of prostitute services.)

If a nonmarket sector is valued because of its connection with certain valued feelings, then any nonmarketed good is valued as a representative and part repository of values represented by the nonmarket sector. This status removed, the thing loses its repository character and, hence, part of its perceived value. This seems to be the case for the values placed on things in nature, such as pristine streams or undisturbed forests.

The second way that placing a market price decreases a thing's perceived value is by removing the possibility of proclaiming that the thing is "not for sale." The very statement that something is "not for sale" affirms, enhances, and protects a thing's value in a number of ways. Proclaiming a thing "not for sale" is a way of showing that the thing is valued for its own sake. By contrast, when a thing is sold for money, the thing sold is valued only instrumentally and not for its own sake. Furthermore, many goods sold are exchangeable for other goods of an unrelated nature. To state that something cannot be transferred in that way places it in an exceptional category.

If we do value something very highly, one way of stamping the thing with a cachet affirming its high value is to announce that it is "not for sale." Such an announcement does more, however, than just reflect—and affirm—a preexisting high valuation. It signals a thing's distinctive value to others and helps us exhort them to value the thing more highly than they otherwise might. And it also expresses our resolution to safeguard that distinctive value. To state that something is "not for sale" is thus also a source of value for that thing since, if a thing's value is easy to affirm, to exhort others to recognize, or to proclaim a desire to safeguard, it will be worth more than an otherwise similar thing without such abilities.

If something is declared "not for sale," a once-and-for-all judgment has been made of its special value. When something is priced, its perceived value is constantly being assessed, and a standing invitation exists to reconsider that original price. If people were constantly faced with questions such as "how much would you sell your vote for if you could?" the perceived value of the freedom to speak or the right to vote would soon become devastated, since, in moments of weakness, people might decide that these values are not worth so much after all. Something similar did in fact occur when the slogan "better red than dead" was launched by some pacifists during the Cold War. Critics pointed out that the very posing of this stark choice—in effect, "would you really be willing to give up your life in exchange for not living under communism?"—reduced the value people attached to freedom and thus diminished resistance to attacks on freedom.

Some things valued very highly are said to be "priceless," that "no price is too high" for them, or that they have "infinite value." This is not the case for all things considered "not for sale." Suppose a daughter has some inexpensive candlesticks used many years earlier by her long-dead mother. She might well wish to proclaim that they are not for sale as a way of affirming and protecting their value to her. But she probably would not go so far as to use the word "priceless" or "of infinite worth" to describe them. Such expressions are reserved for a subset of things not for sale, such as life or health.

For an economist to state that something is "priceless" or that "no price is too high" is to say that the economist would be willing to trade off an infinite quantity of all other goods for one unit of priceless good, a situation that empirically appears highly unlikely. Economists thus tend to scoff at talk of "pricelessness." What economists miss when they so scoff is the effect of the word "priceless" on the thing to which the word is applied. The world "priceless" may ring silly to an economist's ear, but to most people it is pregnant with meaning.

The value-affirming and value-protecting functions cannot be bestowed on expressions that merely denote attribution of a determinate, albeit high, valuation. John F. Kennedy in his inaugural address proclaimed that the nation was ready to "pay any price (and) bear any burden . . . to assure the survival and the success of liberty." Had he stated instead (as most economists probably would have preferred) that we were willing to "pay a high price" or "bear a large burden" for liberty, the statement would have rung hollow.[9]

Conclusion

An objection that advocates of cost-benefit analysis might well make to the preceding argument should be considered. I noted earlier that, when various nonutility-based duties or rights conflict with maximization of utility, it is necessary to make a deliberative judgment about what act is finally right. I also argued earlier that the search for commensurability might not always be a desirable one, that the attempt to go beyond expressing benefits in terms of, say, lives saved and costs in terms of dollars is not something devoutly to be wished.

In situations involving things not expressed in a common metric—where a lie is on one side and a certain amount of happiness on the other, or lives on

one side and dollars on the other—advocates of cost-benefit analysis frequently argue that people making judgments "in effect" perform cost-
benefit calculations anyway. If government regulators promulgate a regulation that saves 100 lives at a cost of $1 billion, they are "in effect" valuing a
life at a minimum of $10 million, whether or not they say that they are will-
ing to place a dollar value on a human life. Since, in this view, cost-benefit
analysis "in effect" is inevitable, it might as well be made specific.

This argument misconstrues the real difference in the reasoning processes
involved. In cost-benefit analysis, equivalencies are established in advance
as one of the raw materials for calculation. We determine costs and
benefits, we determine equivalencies (various costs and benefits are put into
a common metric), and then we tote things up—waiting, as it were, with
bated breath for the results of the calculation. The outcome is determined
by the arithmetic; if the outcome is a close call, we do not know how it will
turn out until the calculation is finished. In the kind of deliberative judgment that is performed without a common metric—rights and utility,
dollars and lives—there is no establishing equivalencies or calculations. The
equivalencies that the decision maker, according to this argument, "in effect" uses, are not aids to the decision process. In fact, the decision maker
might not even be aware of what the "in effect" equivalencies are, at least
before they are revealed to him afterwards by someone pointing out what he
or she had "in effect" done. The decision maker would see him or herself as
simply having made a deliberative judgment; the "in effect" equivalency
number did not play a causal role in the decision but at most merely reflects
it.[10] Given this, the argument against making the process explicit is the one
advanced earlier in the discussion of problems with putting specific quantified values on things that are not normally quantified—that the very act of
doing so may reduce the value of such things.

My own judgment, in conclusion, is that modest efforts to assess levels of
benefits and costs are justified, although I do not believe that government
agencies ought give a cachet to efforts to put dollar prices on nonmarket
things. I do not believe that the cry "we need more cost-benefit analysis in
regulation" is, on the whole, justified. If sensitivity about regulatory costs
were sufficiently primitive among regulatory officials to not even provide
acceptable raw material for deliberative judgments (even of a nonstrictly
cost-benefit nature), this conclusion might be different. But this does not, it
seems, reflect the current reality of the regulatory environment. The danger
now would seem to come more from the other side.

NOTES

[1]For accounts of utilitarianism and its critics, see any standard textbook in ethical theory, such as Richard Brandt, *Ethical Theory* (Englewood Cliffs: Prentice Hall, 1959), Ch. 15–17; or William Frankena, *Ethics* (Englewood Cliffs: Prentice Hall, 1973). See also J.J.C. Smart and Bernard Williams, *Utilitarianism: For and Against* (Cambridge: Cambridge University Press, 1973).

[2]This example is adapted from Thomas E. Hill, Jr. "Symbolic Protest and Calculated Silence," *Philosophy and Public Affairs*, 9 (Fall 1979), p. 84.

[3]This example is adapted from Brandt, *op. cit.*, p. 494.

[4]This example is somewhat analogous to one found in G.E. Moore, *Principia Ethica* (Cambridge: Cambridge University Press, 1903), pp. 84–5.

[5]The independent status of such duties as moral concepts—independent, that is, of the question of utility maximization—may be regarded as an unanalyzable ultimate moral concept, similar as an ultimate concept to the concept that maximizing satisfaction is right. In other words, asking "why is lying wrong?" cannot be answered more satisfactorily than the question, "why is making someone unhappy wrong?".

[6]For more on rights, see for instance, Ronald Dorkin, *Taking Rights Seriously* (Cambridge: Harvard University Press, 1977), particularly Ch. 6–7, and A.I. Melden (editor), *Human Rights* (Belmont, California: Wadsworth Publishing, 1970).

[7]For a further discussion, see Mark Kelman, "Consumption Theory, Production Theory, and Ideology in the Coase Theorem," *Southern California Law Review*, 52 (March 1979).

[8]For a further discussion, see Steven Kelman, "Economic Incentives and Environmental Policy: Politics, Philosophy, Ideology" (manuscript, 1980), pp. 85–118.

[9]For a more detailed discussion, see *Ibid.*, pp. 119–29.

[10]In these circumstances, the value of the "in effect" equivalency number would be for use in future decisions, to achieve "consistency." But the decision maker might be uneasy about applying the results of one deliberation automatically to other deliberations, either out of an unwillingness to cast deliberative judgment in stone or out of a belief that different circumstances may not show enough in common.

13

Ethical Dilemmas in Forecasting for Public Policy

Martin Wachs

Introduction

Forecasts are part and parcel of policy making. Governments deploy military forces and construct weapons systems on the basis of forecasts of actions by potential future enemies. Transit systems, power plants, hospitals, and airports are constructed only after forecasts have demonstrated that a "need" exists for their services and that their costs are justified by expected benefits. Testimony before Congress advocating increased expenditures for housing or education is considered incomplete unless forecasts of future need are carefully detailed. Economic forecasts are so influential as to be the subject of national media coverage, and of evaluations of national monetary or employment policy by competing candidates for high office.

The requirement to prepare forecasts is written into law and government regulation. For example, highway networks built in American metropolitan areas have been based upon a "comprehensive, continuing, and cooperative" planning process, institutionalized by the Highway Act of 1964. This act was interpreted as requiring that highway plans be evaluated against a 20-year forecast of travel demand, with the 20-year forecast being updated periodically to ensure that the plans remain valid. The Urban Mass

The author gratefully acknowledges the support of a Rockefeller Foundation Humanities Grant which made this study possible.

From *Public Administration Review*, Vol. 42, No. 6 (November/December 1982), pp. 562–567. Reprinted with permission © 1982 by The American Society for Public Administration, 1120 G Street, N.W., Washington, D.C. All rights reserved.

Transportation Administration requires that state and local governments submit "alternatives analyses" as part of requests for funds under its capital grants program. The analysis must show that the course of action for which funding is sought clearly constitutes a superior use of public funds in comparison with all reasonable alternatives. Guidelines for the program require, among other things, that cost and patronage levels be forecast for each alternative. Similarly, airport authorities produce long-range forecasts of air traffic in their regions to arrive at proposals for new facilities, metropolitan planning organizations base housing programs on forecasts, and national energy policy debates have been motivated by competing forecasts of the demand for and availability of fuels.

Forecasts can be made by politicians, clairvoyants, philosophers, or prophets. In policy making, however, forecasts taken seriously for any practical purpose are likely to be produced by technical experts, and it is technical forecasting to which this study is addressed. In a society influenced by technology and technique, prediction is accomplished by applications of standarized methods to carefully collected files of information. Forecasts in most instances are produced by manipulations of computers which are probably understood by relatively few of the people who act on the basis of the results. Forecasters are usually experts, serving as staff or consultants to those in decision-making positions. Public officials who employ forecasts as the basis for action rarely comprehend all of the mathematical procedures involved in the predictions. They are likely to be unfamiliar with the data series employed and unaware of the technical assumptions hidden under the cloak of expert judgment.

The political salience of many forecasts and the technical complexity of the forecasting process combine to create for the forecaster an important ethical dilemma. Forecasts which support the advocacy of particular courses of action are often demanded by interest groups or public officials. Forecasters must rely upon so many assumptions and judgmental procedures that it is usually possible to adjust forecasts to the extent that they meet such demands. On the other hand, forecasters are likely to view themselves as technical experts rather than politicians, loyal to supposedly objective criteria according to which their work is judged in technical terms rather than political ones. Public policy heightens this dilemma by requiring through laws and regulations forecasts which are supposedly technically objective and politically neutral, while distributing political rewards to those whose forecasts prove their positions most emphatically.

Consider a situation described by Peter Marcuse who changed the name of the community in which it occurred in order to avoid embarrassing those involved:

In Oldport, the mayor retained a planning firm as consultant to develop a comprehensive twenty-year plan for urban renewal, housing, schools, and social service facilities. The planners' preliminary report projected moderate population growth but a dramatic and continuing shift in racial composition, with minority groups reaching a majority in twelve years. A black majority was predicted within five years in the public schools.

The mayor reacted strongly to the preliminary report. If these findings were released, they would become a self-fulfilling prophecy. All hope of preserving an integrated school system and maintaining stable mixed neighborhoods or developing an ethnically heterogeneous city with a strong residential base would disappear.

The planners were asked to review their figures. They agreed to use the lower range of their projections—minority dominance in the public schools after eight years and a majority in the city in sixteen. The mayor was not satisfied. He told the planners either to change the figures or to cut them out of the report. They refused, feeling they had bent their interpretation of fact as far as they could. Without a discussion of these facts, the balance of the report could not be professionally justified.

The mayor lashed out at them privately for professional arrogance, asked a professional on his own staff to rewrite the report without the projections, and ordered the consultants not to release or disclose their findings on race under any circumstances. The professional on the mayor's staff initially demurred from rewriting the report but ultimately complied. The consultants remained silent, completed the formal requirements of their contracts, and left. The mayor never used professional planning consultants again.[1]

Here we have in a nutshell the central ethical dilemma of forecasting. Those who use forecasts, prepare them, or critique them, invariably use the language of technical objectivity. A model used for prediction is assumed to be unbiased, a tool in the hands of a forecaster who is a technical expert rather than a decision maker—a scientist more than a politician. Yet, so many technical assumptions are required to make any forecast that the process can ultimately be quite subjective, while the consequences have great significance. By choosing particular data or mathematical forms, many a forecast can easily be changed to transform increases into decreases, growth into contraction, gain into loss. These transformations can produce rewards or remove threats for those who accomplish them, they can often be made to masquerade as technical details rather than value judgments, and the outcome is frequently unverifiable.

Little attention has been given in the field of public administration to the role which forecasting plays in decision making. Even less attention has been given in the education of policy makers and technical experts to the ethical dimensions of forecasting. Without pretending to prescribe appropriate courses of action for those engaged in forecasting, this paper explores the nature of this dilemma. Its roots are sought in both the technical aspects of forecasting and the political uses to which forecasts are put. This explication of this dilemma should help forecasters recognize the volatile situations in which it appears, and to address it more effectively in the education of policy makers.

The Inherent Dilemma of Circularity

The role of forecasts in policy making is fascinating largely because it always involves an inherent dilemma of circularity. The future is made by people, and is not beyond our control. But to choose wisely from among alternative actions we seek information about conditions which will form the context of those actions. We want to know what the future will be like so that we can act, yet actions will determine what the future will be, and may negate the forecast. Because of this circularity, rarely may the accuracy of a forecast made in the public policy arena be literally verified.

A forecast of dire future events is made for the purpose of bringing about actions to avert that future. Having taken action and thus avoided the gloomy prospect, we can never be sure that the forecast events would have happened in the absence of that action. For example, if responsible medical authorities forecast that a particular disease will reach epidemic proportions unless mass inoculations are undertaken, a prudent government would surely conduct an inoculation program before victims begin to expire. If they did so, an incorrect forecast—with no epidemic in the offing—would yield the same measurable result as a correct one. The accuracy of the forecast could only have been proven had no action been taken and had the epidemic come about. Prudent policy makers would surely avoid the possibility of proving such forecasts correct, largely because of the dangerous potential consequences of inaction. Unless a forecast is considered frivolous, the salience of its consequences may be more influential than the probable accuracy. The international attention recently given to the Club of Rome's forecast of world ecological disaster follows more from its tenebrous visions than from its probable accuracy.[2]

A forecast of growing demand for some service, facility, or commodity and its provision in response to the forecast, give rise to a similar dilemma. The demand which is later observed might have been "correctly" forecast, or it might have been instigated by the forecast and the action which it spurred. In past decades, for example, electric utilities foresaw enormous growth in the demand for electricity, and expanded their generating capacity accordingly. Later, having huge capacity, they advertised electric appliances, lowered the price of electricity to users of large quantities, and invented new uses for electricity. Do the earlier forecasters of great demand now have the right to claim that their forecasts were "accurace"? Only in a superficial sense were they correct. It is the intertwining of forecast and action which is more important than any mathematical measure of consistency between forecast and actual consumption of electricity. Such examples serve to illustrate that there can be no absolute criteria of accuracy in forecasting for public policy, and that the supposed accuracy of any forecast can nearly always arouse suspicion among skeptics. From the inherent dilemma of circularity there follow many questions for those who prepare forecasts for government agencies, and those who employ their forecasts.

Forecasts Require Numerous Assumptions

Many authors have drawn a distinction between forecasts on the one hand, and projections or extrapolations on the other. A projection or extrapolation is merely a calculation of the likely consequences of mathematical relationships between variables. A simple population projection, for example, would extend in time the relationships among birth, death, and migration rates. A forecast is more than a projection, for it involves also committing oneself to the selection of particular values of the variables which are involved. Thus, a forecast of population requires first that certain birth, death, and migration rates be selected as those most likely to prevail, and secondly, projecting the consequences of the specific rates selected. Clearly, the estimation of appropriate future values for these rates is a much more challenging task than calculating their implications. Technical expertise, however, contributes far more to one's ability to do the calculations that it does to one's ability to form the appropriate assumptions about future values of the parameters.

In a complex society, policies set by one organization or institution are inherently dependent upon the actions of many others. The demand for automobiles, for example, depends partly upon decisions made in Detroit, but also upon international politics, current wage rates, residential preferences, investment programs in highways and transit, changes in economic and family roles of men and women, and many other underlying conditions. Health care, housing, energy, and educational programs all present challenges to understanding and forecasting which are equally complex. These intricate interrelationships among the areas of modern society make it difficult to isolate clear cause and effect sequences which would allow forecasting with confidence. This is why Michel Godet has observed: "Forecasting in the classic sense of the word is possible only when man, through his past actions, has overcommitted his future to such a degree that the outcome can only take one or two forms."[3] Unable and unwilling to exert tyrannical control over events, we instead make forecasts which are conditional upon many assumptions about the likely behavior of some factors, so that we can estimate probable variations in others. Even a simple projection involving relationships among five or six variables would yield an unmanageable range of combinations of future conditions unless some of the variables were constrained by assumptions about the limits of their future values.

Without assumptions, forecasting would be impossible. But assumptions can be self-serving, and in the end can dominate the outcome of the forecast. William Ascher studied the accuracy of forecasts made over a period of 50 years in the fields of population, economic, energy, transportation, and technological forecasting. He concluded that "core assumptions" were more important determinants of the accuracy of any forecast than were any other factors:

> The core assumptions underlying a forecast, which represent the forecaster's basic outlook on the context within which the specific forecasted trend develops, are the major determinants of forecast accuracy. Methodologies are basically the vehicles for determining the consequences or implications of core assumptions that have been chosen more or less independently of the specific methodologies. When the core assumptions are valid, the choice of methodology is either secondary or obvious. When the core assumptions fail to capture the reality of the future context, other factors such as methodology generally make little difference; they cannot "save" the forecast.[4]

Reliance on assumptions is heightened by the fact that forecasts are often necessarily based on historical trends in variables, yet archives of data on social systems frequently provide historical information for only one or two points in time. It is difficult to project a trend on the basis of few data points, but this is often done by assuming a particular mathematical form for a curve and "calibrating" the trendline on the basis of only one or two observations. On technical grounds it may be quite risky to project a trend forward some 10, 20, or 50 years if the trendline is based upon information extending backward in time only 10 to 15 years, yet this is frequently done for practical reasons.

Extending a trendline based upon inadequate evidence of a relationship between variables is often a manifestation of a problem in forecasting which Ascher refers to as "assumption drag," and which he considers to be "the source of some of the most drastic errors in forecasting."[5] Assumption drag consists of reliance upon old core assumptions, sometimes after they have been positively disproven. He shows, for example, that population forecasters working in the late 1930s and 1940s continued to assume declining birthrates into the fifties and sixties, although the assumption of declining birthrates had already been authoritatively invalidated. Similarly, feminists point out that, while the majority of married women are today in the work force, many predict future household and labor force characteristics on the assumption that the single-worker household will continue to be the norm.

Assumption drag is due, in large part, to the simple fact that it is often more appropriate to incorporate into a forecast an historical trend than it is to anticipate a future deviation from that trend. The forecaster who projects the continuation of past trends may risk criticism for failing to anticipate systemic changes. Conversely, the analyst who forecasts coming systemic changes always risks criticism for going out on a limb, following hunches, or departing from conventional wisdom or established practice. It is usually difficult to decide whether a recent deviation from a long-term trend is a temporary secular variation or a permanent change in the trendline. It may take many years to recognize a systemic change in a policy variable. Furthermore, most forecasters are specialists who use information produced by other specialists as raw materials for their work. A forecaster of transportation or electricity demand may know far less about demography than a population forecaster, but may rely upon population forecasts as a source of change in transportation or electricity usage. While up-to-date on the latest analyses in his or her own area of expertise, the transportation or electricity forecaster may have access only to published population analyses which are out of date, and may not know of newer theories or conclusions in that area of study.

For these several reasons, analysts often conclude that variables which have been stable will continue to be so during the period for which a forecast is being prepared. Forecasting models may even reflect an assumption of stability by omitting from the model a variable deemed to be stable and hence less influential than others which are more volatile. This can have disastrous consequences if the passage of time proves the assumption incorrect. Consider the elaborate set of models widely used to forecast highway traffic throughout the world. These models, involving hundreds of equations, have been institutionalized through the widespread availability of standardized computer packages. The forecast procedures have been in use for more than 20 years, and were developed at a time when gasoline was inexpensive and in ample supply. Thus, while the models are notable for their level of detail, they do not explicitly represent the price or availability of gasoline as determinants of travel. When the forecasting models were formalized, gasoline was so widely available and inexpensive that statistical associations between these variables and the frequency or duration of trips were difficult to identify. The decision to omit these factors seemed rational on technical grounds. With hindsight, having experienced large changes in the price and availability of fuel and consequent fluctuations in travel, we may certainly question the wisdom of omitting them. The omission illustrates Godet's contention that: "certain forecasting errors are explained by our tendency to look at the 'better lit' aspects of our problems. The light dazzles us and hides from us what lies behind it."[6]

We more often assume stability than discontinuity, so assumption drag introduces into forecasting a systematic tendency toward conservatism. The centrality of core assumptions in forecasting makes this a serious problem, although attempting to overcome the conservative bias often means adopting critical assumptions on the basis of little supporting evidence. This dilemma contributes to the ethical quandary which forecasters face, because the absence of evidence supporting assumptions can easily reduce forecasts to statements of advocacy.

Technical Expertise in Forecasting

Despite the fact that assumptions play a larger role in forecasting than do the methods which elaborate upon them, forecasters are usually drawn from the ranks of social scientists, engineers, and planners whose education and professional identity are based primarily upon technical methodological skills. They are likely to believe and promote the belief that forecasting is impossible without the use of computers, mathematical methods, and complex data sets.

Sophistication in the technique of forecasting is more apparent, however, than real. Computers are used because there is often a great deal of data: many variables, many units of analysis for each, several time periods. These conditions lead to the requirement for training and experience in mathematics, statistics, data manipulation, and computer programming. But together, such skills ensure no special perspective on the future, and there is relatively little theory derivable from the social sciences to help one arrive at reasonable core assumptions.

Most forecasts result from extrapolations and assumptions rather than theoretical models incorporating representations of causality. Curve fitting and statistical tests of association may be employed, but extending a quadratic polynomial 25 years beyond the present is disturbingly similar to sketching a simple line on graph paper if the extrapolation is based on goodness of fit rather than an understanding of the underlying phenomena. Mathematical finesse enables one to connect models in series with the outputs of one forming the inputs to others, but if the models are associative rather than causal, errors may multiply so rapidly that they quickly dominate the forecasts. For these reasons, the technical elegance of some forecasting models is an illusion, obfuscating the central importance of assumptions which require or utilize no special expertise.

It would seem obvious that complex social or environmental phenomena can be forecast best using models which capture their complexity by representing the causal chains which underlie them. Thus, a simple model, predicting crime rate or air pollution on the basis of one or two indicators, is likely to be inadequate because we know that crime and air pollution result from many factors working in concert. In technical terms, simplistic models of complex phenomena are likely to have large "specification errors"—they fail to represent the processes by which outcomes are actually determined. By adding complexity—linking larger numbers of variables in longer causal chains—more sophisticated forecasting models can be developed which would appear to promise better predictions.

But complex models raise other problems. As more and more variables are included in the mathematical representation of a social or technical process, more data are required to use such a model in the preparation of a forecast. Of course, every bit of data used in a model is subject to error, and as more variables are used these "measurement errors" tend to increase more rapidly than the number of variables employed. A tradeoff must be made. Simple models, involving few variables, minimize measurement errors at the expense of large errors of specification. Complex models, involving many variables and equations, may reduce errors of specification, but only at the price of rapidly escalating measurement errors. An "optimum" forecasting model would be designed to the level of complexity which would minimize the sum of errors of the two types, but for most real phenomena analysts have no way of actually estimating the magnitude of each kind of error. Many feel that forecasting models of social, economic, and environmental phenomena have been developed to such a level of complexity that measurement errors are multiplied dramatically.[7]

Complex models are attractive for tactical reasons. They appear to be sophisticated and for this reason lend credibility to the advice given by those who understand them. Their very complexity makes it difficult to criticize or question their validity. In reality, they may be no more valid than very simple forecasting models which require less technical expertise.

There is a dangerous impression that forecasting is nothing more than data processing and extrapolation. Often, prescribed steps are followed to get a result even though the connections among the variables may not be known to be causative. No matter how accurate the data used and whether or not the structure of the model is appropriate, the specificity of the results often makes them more plausible and authoritative than they ought to be.[8]

The Political Uses of Forecasts

Governments with limited resources to allocate, and citizens who rely upon public services and pay their costs, would seem on the surface to assume that forecasts of future need and cost are executed with objectivity. The complexity of pluralistic and technological societies, however, places many burdens upon those who prepare forecasts, which make objectivity difficult to attain. Public resource allocation is competitive in that the decision to fund a project in one jurisdiction may deprive another of a similar opportunity. Political influence, financial gain, jobs, and prestige all flow from "winning" competitions for public projects. Technical experts are often employed by agencies which advocate particular solutions to certain problems: nuclear vs. fossil fuel plants for power; highways vs. rapid transit for urban transportation, and so on. A forecaster might be in the employ of an engineering firm which received a small contract to estimate the need for a bridge. If the bridge is shown to be justified, additional consulting fees for design and engineering may produce hundreds of times the income derived from the preparation of the forecast itself. If the bridge is shown to be unnecessary, no further contracts may be awarded. In such settings, it is obvious that forecasters are under pressure to adjust their predictions for self-serving purposes.

This pressure is intensified by the issues mentioned earlier: (1) a forecast is inherently unverifiable; (2) the outcome of a forecasting exercise is to a great extent determined by its core assumptions; and (3) the activity of forecasting is technically complex, revealing to most users its results but not its mechanisms or assumptions. It is indeed difficult to withstand pressures to produce self-serving forecasts which are cloaked in the guise of technical objectivity. By politely agreeing to speak of forecasts as objective, planners, engineers, or economists who prepare them can maintain their self-respect and professional identity. Simultaneously, advocates of particular positions gain strength for their arguments by virtue of the supposedly "unbiased" technical analyses which they can cite. And politicians who finally make resource allocations calmly accept forecasts which confirm their particular preconceptions with far less critical review than those which do not. All three sets of actors—technical forecasting experts, advocates for a particular point of view, and politicians—gain by pretending that a forecast is an objective scientific statement, and gain more if it is also an effective statement of advocacy in a struggle for resources.

In keeping with the illusion of technical objectivity, when the passage of time has shown the vast majority of demand and cost forecasts for public services to have been inaccurate, critics generally have contended that "imperfect techniques" and "inadequate data" were the sources of the prob-

lems. Rarely has it been argued that forecasts have deliberately been designed to place certain projects in a favorable light and others at a disadvantage. Rarely has it been argued that the structure of governmental decision
making makes such ethically troublesome uses of forecasts inevitable.

Consider, as an example, the well-known case of San Francisco's Bay
Area Rapid Transit System (BART). Capital cost forecasts for the 71-mile
system, which formed the basis for the 1962 bond issue election, amounted
to $994 million in construction costs plus $70 million for rolling stock. The
final capital cost is now actually estimated to have been in excess of $2.4
billion (deflated to 1962 dollars). Design changes contributed to the deviation from the initial estimate, but there is no doubt that the initial estimate
of capital costs was simply too low. The cost estimates may have been
deliberately kept unrealistically low for political reasons. The value of
general obligation bonds that could be sold was limited to $792 million, 15
percent of the assessed valuation of the real property in the proposed
district which for 1960–61 was $5.3 billion. It appears that the estimate of
the construction cost was at least influenced by legal restrictions on the borrowing limit of the district.[9]

The example of BART illustrates an age-old problem in forecasting the
demand for and the cost of public works. If demand for a water supply
system, bridge, or port facility is overestimated and cost is underestimated,
the benefits of the project can easily be made to seem to outweigh the costs.
Once the decision to build the project has been made, and expenditures of
public monies have taken place, the realization that initial cost estimates
were too low will rarely kill the project. Somehow, more money will be
found to finish a project which is already underway. This was well
understood by Robert Moses, as he planned and built the parkways,
bridges, and parks of New York City. His biographer, Robert A. Caro, has
written:

> 'Once you sink that first stake,' he would often say, 'they'll never make you
> pull it up.' . . . If ends justified means, and if the important thing in building
> a project was to get it started, then any means that got it started were justified.
> Furnishing misleading information about it was justified; so was
> underestimating its costs.
>
> Misleading and underestimating, in fact, might be the only way to get a project
> started. Since his projects were unprecedentedly vast, one of the biggest dif-
> ficulties in getting them started was the fear of public officials . . . that the
> state couldn't afford the projects (which) . . . beneficial though they might
> be, would drain off a share of the state's wealth incommensurate with their
> benefits.
>
> But what if you didn't tell the officials how much the projects would cost?
> What if you let the legislators know about only a fraction of what you knew
> would be the project's ultimate expense?

Once they had authorized that small initial expenditure and you had spent it, they would not be able to avoid giving you the rest when you asked for it. How could they? If they refused to give you the rest of the money, what they had given you would be wasted, and that would make them look bad in the eyes of the public. And if they said you had misled them, well, they were not supposed to be misled. If they had been misled, that would mean that they hadn't investigated the projects thoroughly, and had therefore been derelict in their own duty. The possibilities for a polite but effective form of political blackmail were endless.[10]

The situation described is indeed an ethical dilemma because of the ambiguity and competing allegiances inherent in forecasting. The forecaster, in all likelihood, was educated according to a tradition of scientific-technical rationality, having allegiance to a set of methods and techniques rather than to particular outcomes in a policy debate. It is necessary to make assumptions so that the techniques can produce useful forecasts, and reasonable assumptions are not necessarily a betrayal of a commitment to technical objectivity. The agency for which the forecaster works, however, has a commitment to certain programs or solutions and believes that they can be shown to be superior to others on the basis of reasonable criteria.

In addition to commitment to a body of tools and techniques, the forecaster must also have loyalty and responsibility to the agency which he or she serves, either as employee or consultant. The employee wishes to advance and wants to be considered both competent and cooperative by his or her superiors. The consultant wishes to be considered for future contracts. Rewards flow from effective service as an advocate for the interests clearly identified by the organization. Should the forecast be made on the basis of core assumptions which seem most favorable to the furtherance of the organization's goals? Forecasts often require so many assumptions that there is leeway to allow the forecaster to satisfy both organizational goals and technical criteria. Indeed, if he or she has become a "team player" and has internalized the goals of the agency, there may not even appear to be a conflict between the two loyalties. In cases where the forecaster is aware of the conflict, and where reasonable technical judgment may deliver forecasts which the agency would rather not hear about, the forecaster faces the problem of choosing between advocacy and objectivity. The rewards for advocacy are clear, while even the criteria for judging objectivity are ambiguous.

Dahl and Lindblom observed: "someone must control those who run the calculations and machines. Someone must control the controllers, etc. At every point there would be opportunities for attempting to feed into the calculator one's own preferences. Doubtless, pressure groups would organize for just such a purpose."[11] It is critically important that public administrators recognize the limits of technical forecasts. There are few ethical guideposts included in the education of professionals, the canons of professional societies, or the processes of public policy making to suggest how such choices should be made. The choices are personal and sometimes troublesome. Frequently, the options boil down to serving the agency or leaving its employ. Because the agency itself, and the political process in which it is embedded, continue to describe, respond to, and reward advocacy as if it were technically objective and neutral expertise, only the most sensitive of analysts would choose not to serve as advocate. The result is that many forecasts are statements of hope and intention, while analysts, agency boards, and politicians cooperatively maintain the fiction that they are value-free projections of trends. Few forecasters engage in blatant falsification in order to receive a commission or promotion. Many, however, are transformed in subtle steps from analyst to advocate by the situation in which they perform their work.

NOTES

[1] Peter Marcuse, "Professional Ethics and Beyond: Values in Planning," *Journal of the American Institute of Planners*, Vol. 42, No. 3 (July 1976), pp. 264–274.

[2] Donella H. Meadows, Dennis L. Meadows, Jorgen Randers, and William W. Behrens, III, *The Limits to Growth: A Report for the Club of Rome's Project on the Predicament of Mankind*, Second Edition (New York: Universe Books, 1974).

[3] Michel Godet, *The Crisis in Forecasting and the Emergence of the Prospective Approach* (New York and Oxford: Pergamon Press, 1979).

[4] William Ascher, *Forecasting: An Appraisal for Policy-Makers and Planners* (Baltimore and London: Johns Hopkins University Press, 1978), p. 199.

[5] *Ibid.*, p. 202.

[6] Michel Godet, *The Crisis in Forecasting and the Emergence of the Prospective Approach*, p. 15.

[7] William Alonso, "Predicting Best with Imperfect Data," *Journal of the American Institute of Planners*, Vol. 34, No. 3 (July 1968), pp. 248–255.

[8] Solomon Encel, Pauline K. Marstrand, and William Page, *The Art of Anticipation: Values and Methods in Forecasting* (London: Martin Robertson and Company, Ltd., 1975), p. 66.

[9] Martin Wachs and James Ortner, "Capital Grants and Recurrent Subsidies: A Dilemma in American Transportation Policy," *Transportation*, Vol. 8 (1979), pp. 3–19.

[10] Robert A. Caro, *The Power Broker: Robert Moses and the Fall of New York* (New York: Vintage Books, 1975), pp. 218–219.

[11] Robert A. Dahl and Charles E. Lindblom, *Politics, Economics, and Welfare* (New York: Harper, 1953).

14

Normative Criteria for Organizational Discourse: A Methodological Approach

Frank Fischer

In political and social theory generally, the neglect of ethics and normative discourse in modern ogranizational life has been an enduring theme. Max Weber (1947), for example, warned against the denigration of values under the spreading influence of instrumental rationality that has accompanied the bureaucratization of industrial society. In more recent times, Jacques Ellul has documented the extension of an ever-expanding and irreversible rule of technical rationality in the normative domains of social life. Portraying modern civilization as a commitment to the quest for continually improved means to unexamined ends, he advanced the thesis this way:

> From the political, social, and human points of view, this conjunction of state and technique is by far the most important phenomenon of history. It is astonishing . . . that we still apply ourselves to the study or political theories or parties which no longer possess anything but episodic importance, yet we bypass the technical fact which explains the totality of modern political events [Ellul, 1964: 233].

The emergence of technical rationality and its organizational form—bureaucracy—is largely the product of the normative imperatives of the industrial revolution of the 18th and 19th centuries and the accompanying rise of modern science. Under the industrial revolution large-scale organization, characterized by the division of labor and functional specialization, evolved as the efficient instrument for transforming scientifically derived technological achievements into economic progress. In fact, the overwhelming

Frank Fischer, "Ethical Discourse in Public Administration," *Administration & Society*, Vol. 15, No. 1 (May 1983), pp. 5–42. Reprinted by permission of Sage Publications, Inc.

success of the convergence of these phenomena—industrialization, the economies of large-scale bureaucracy, technological progress, and economic growth—has served to establish the fundamental premises that govern the dominant operational ideologies of industrial nations, both under capitalistic and socialistic regimes (Jacoby, 1976).

One of the central by-products of this fusion has been the emergence of the scientifically-trained expert, or "technocrat." As the "ideal type" dominating the contemporary bureaucratic landscape, the function of the expert is to translate technological progress into organizational output (Hummel, 1977). Accomplished through the mastery of the calculus of instrumental rationality, symbolized today by the computer sciences, the essential function of the technocrat is scientific decision-making.

Technocracy obtains its legitimacy from two sources. The first is the material progress that has resulted from a pragmatic adherence to its methodological principles. Modern bureaucratic organization, as the institutional embodiment of technical rationality, has made possible unprecedented economic growth measured in quantitative terms. Secondly, technical rationality is legitimated by the dominant epistemological theory governing twentieth century science, namely, positivism. Technical rationality is essentially the handmaiden of positivism's fact-value dichotomy (Habermas, 1970: 50–122; Weisskopf, 1971).

Under the methodological prescriptions of positivism, only technical decisions about the instrumental relationship of means to ends lend themselves to the rules of rational assessment. Value judgments, as decisions about which ends or goals to choose, are ruled to be beyond the reach of scientific methodology and, therefore, must be relegated to philosophy and metaphysics. Unlike factual questions (such as, What is the case? or What is the most efficient means to pursue that which is to be done?), the answers to value questions must ultimately be based on emotional judgments, matters of personal conviction, taste, or faith (Frohock, 1974).

In a science founded upon these epistemological distinctions, the only admissiable value statements are the following: (1) the logical explication and elaboration of the internal consistency of value judgments, which determine alternative attitudes along with an examination of their conceptual implications for thought and action; (2) the investigation of the factual premises and their empirical consequences; and (3) the determination of optimal means-ends relationships between goals and the methods of achieving them. What science cannot do is establish the truth or falsity of values. Discussion of normative principles and assumptions in this view can only lead to a "bottomless morass" (Meehan, 1967).

There is something of a paradox here in the fact that these basic tenets of the fact-value separation are attributed to the man known for his critique of bureaucratic rationality, Max Weber. By now it is almost a forgotten fact that Weber initially set forth the fact-value dichotomy as a guard against technocratic encroachments (Simey, 1968). Worried about the rising power of bureaucracy emerging with the welfare state under Bismarck, Weber argued that values were too important to be left in the hands of the technocracy. Sharp distinctions between empirical and normative discourse were necessary to establish a limit on technocratic authority.

Although designed to emphasize the supremacy of values over technical facts, the modern interpretation of Weber's value-free social science, conditioned by the pervasive sway of scientific ideology, has ironically led to the denigration of values and normative discourse. Insofar as values are held to be beyond the reach of rational methods defined as scientific methodology—they can only be understood to reflect irrational judgments properly consigned to "the intellectual limbo of personal preference" (Weldon, 1953).

For organizational science, these methodological principles provide the framework for organizational decision-making processes that emphasize empirically oriented technical criticisms of means designed to efficiently achieve goals or ends posited by the industrial imperative and its supporting ideologies. Carried to its logical extreme, technical efficiency emerges as the essence of rational organizational action. For example, Ludwig von Mises, an ardent advocate of positivism, maintained that "the economic principle is the fundamental principle of all rational action, and not just a particular feature of a certain kind of rational action" (von Mises, 1960: 148). Therefore, all rational action is reducible to the technical calculation of economic efficiency. The task of the managerial policy maker is to calculate the costs and benefits of alternative means for achieving goals hammered out by (and justified through) legitimated political processes. For many writers on the subject, the value-laden political dimensions of decision-making are to be denigrated. They are viewed as representing irrational interruptions that impede the methodological requirements of efficient decision-making (Wildavsky, 1966).

To a growing number of theorists, however, this conception of rationality operates as an ideology that places severe limitations on the development of organizational theory and decision-making techniques (Kramer, 1975). While leaving questions about goals and ends to the political processes may foster value neutrality *within* the decision-oriented policy sciences, in substantive terms it operates to serve the socioeconomic values established by the play of political power. In this sense, the value neutrality of decision-making techniques only serves to mask the presence of the underlying metaphysic of contemporary society and, worse yet, denies the epistemological validity of the modes of inquiry required to uncover it. This leaves us in a dilemma that Paul Diesing has summed up rather succinctly: "It seems unfortunate to have rational procedures available for the relatively less important decisions of life and to have none for dealing with the most important decisions" (Diesing, 1962: 1).

Recent Themes

In the late 1960s, the concern about overemphasis on technical rationality at the expense of ethical and political content emerged as a primary theme in the literature of the "new" public administration (Marini, 1971). The critique of public administration put forth by these writers centered around the theoretical failures resulting from the discipline's conceptual separation of politics and administration. Not only has the "politics-administration dichotomy" underemphasized the uniquely value-laden character of public organizational goals, it has also failed to anticipate public management's expanding discretionary powers in the governing processes. As the politics-administration dichotomy is essentially a substantive expression of the methodological fact-value dichotomy, the new public administration critique led inevitably to a more fundamental denunciation of the idea of a value-free social science. In the 1970s, these concerns were reinforced by Watergate, which revitalized interest in ethics in the curricula of public administration and policy analysis (Fleishman and Payne, 1980).

One of the most important statements of the need for attention to ethical concerns in the organizational literature during the past decade has been the writings of David Hart and William Scott. Building upon themes drawn from Ellul and the new public administration writers, Hart and Scott (1973, 1979) stressed the "neglect of metaphysical speculation" as the root cause of what they call the contemporary "administrative crisis." Where the standard managerial prescription is for better administrative technology, they argue that management's underlying technocratic value system is the basic cause of our organizational failures. They outlined their argument in these words:

> We maintain that the values of the administrators are the most basic aspect of this crisis. This assertion is made on the grounds that (1) an administrative elite performs the functions of leadership in advanced societies, and (2) this elite subscribes to a metaphysic that influences its decisions and its behavior in the management of technology in complex organizations, but (3) this administrative metaphysic is unarticulated, and, therefore, is unexamined. Thus, the crisis in administration is the neglect of metaphysical speculation [Hart and Scott, 1973: 416].

For Hart and Scott, the principles of technical rationality that underlie this unarticulated metaphysic must become a subject for deliberation in the organizational literature. Toward this end, administrative theorists must begin to introduce moral discourse into both organizational policy-making and the professional-managerial curriculum. For this purpose, they suggest that administrative theorists use political philosophy as an example. Ethical discourse in political philosophy points to the necessity of focusing on two fundamental aspects of moral discourse: "(1) a vision of the innate moral nature of man, and (2) the value criteria used for judging the morality of behavior" (Hart and Scott, 1973: 416). The task for organizational and administrative theorists is to bring out the assumptions and value criteria derived from the technical image of people in organizations, hidden behind the epistemological screen of scientism, and to submit them to intellectual discourse.

Hart has attempted to take the problem beyond the task of rigorous explication of existing organizational values. Drawing on the work of the new public administration writers stressing the normative criterion of "social equity," Hart advanced John Rawls's principles of justice as an alternative metaphysic for an ethical theory of applied public administration. Leaving aside the question of whether Hart has demonstrated the applicability of Rawls's theory, his essay offers some useful guidelines to the kind of work involved in the search for alternative ethical foundations. But perhaps the main lesson to be gleaned from Hart's exercise is an appreciation of the complexity of the assignment. Hart not only points out, but in fact demonstrates, that further work in this direction requires the skill of the scholar versed in both political philosophy and public administration. As Hart puts it, "this means there is an urgent need for a tradition of public administration philosophers" (Hart, 1974: 10).

In many ways, the validity of Hart's argument is also its downfall. While it is clear that Hart has a grip on the fundamental problem, it is less obvious that his solution speaks to the pragmatic requirements facing public managers and the public administration curriculum. Even if the case for a tradition of public administration philosophers addresses critical problems in organizational and administrative theory, it does not deal directly with normative deliberation as it arises in the public organizational context. While it is essential to understand that organizational discourse operates under the premise of a philosophical metaphysic, it is equally important to recognize that the manager's task is not by definition concerned with the explication of metaphysical assumptions, let alone the philosophical exploration of alternative metaphysics. The problem appears to be less a matter of the irrelevance of philosophical investigation than a dilemma associated with the level of analysis. From this perspective, the problem is better viewed

as concerned with establishing the logical and empirical relationships between concrete policy decision-making and the abstract theoretical model
that supplies fundamental value criteria.

John Rohr harbors similar reservations about Hart and Scott's
philosophical orientation and has attempted to supply a more managerially
oriented practical alternative. Rohr, for example, is unpersuaded that the
"rigor of the philosophical tradition" is the solution to ethics in public administration (Rohr, 1976, 1978). Taken seriously, as he points out, this
would require administrative policy decisions to be considered in a complex
framework of issues raised in linguistics, epistemology, psychology, and
metaphysics. This, to be sure, suggests the impracticality of such an approach for the public management curriculum. Even in philosophy itself
this broader framework has been as much a frustration as a glory. With
regard to curriculum, Rohr (1976: 399) wrote:

> If a public administration curriculum is to maintain its professional focus, cer-
> tain valuable intellectual investigations must be sacrificed . . . [We] can [not]
> prudently demand extensive philosophical investigations from public ad-
> ministration students after they have started their professional studies. To set-
> tle for a smattering of political philosophy as part of a course in ethics would
> not be fair either to the students or to philosophy itself.

Rohr's proposed alternative is more closely rooted in the practical concerns of the discipline. Rather than the study of political philosophy per se,
he has suggested that the study of "regime values" provides a more appropriate foundation for the study of ethics in the public administration
curriculum. Addressed to the fundamental normative obligation of
bureaucrats in a democratic government—namely, to exercise their discretionary power within the value context of the people for whom they
govern—the method of "regime values" is developed around an identification of American values and the search for meaningful statements about
them. As a practical device enabling career-oriented students to think about
public values, Rohr proposed the study of major Supreme Court decisions.
Court cases involving salient values such as freedom, property, and equity
are well suited for ethical reflection in public administration for a number
of reasons. First, Supreme Court decisions are concerned with concrete
cases involving established patterns of institutional values. Justices must be
disciplined by social realities in a manner that political philosophers are not.
As Rohr (1976: 403) put it, "A Justice may soar to the highest levels of
abstraction in discussing such lofty generalities as due process of law, but
eventually he must decide whether the confession was admissible, or the
book obscene, or the statement libelous." The Justice must at the key point

in the deliberative process apply his wisdom to the concrete problem pressing for a solution.

Furthermore, Rohr is correct in his contention that this dimension of the Supreme Court's work can be warmly appreciated by public managers who are frequently asked to exercise similar judgmental functions in the administrative process. Court opinions, in his words, not only "offer reflection on American values, but they show what these values mean in practice as well." As a decision model, such deliberation can be very helpful to administrative decision makers who "might be bored by discourse that is purely theoretical." Supreme Court arguments "provide an excellent illustration of how theory and practice combine to generate public policy" (Rohr, 1976: 404). In this respect, Rohr concurs with Theodore Lowi, who has chastised policy-oriented political theorists for reading "philosophers rather than law."[1]

Also, the relation of practical affairs to fundamental values can be examined through the study of court cases. Frequently Supreme Court cases are not decided on legal issues alone. Exercising its potential discretion, the Court must, in the words of Justice Brennan, occasionally push "beyond the established contours to protect the vulnerable and to further basic human values" (Rohr, 1976: 404). For administrators, especially those concerned with social equity, a careful examination of such decisions can offer insights about the responsible exercise of their own administrative discretion, which may lie beyond the established contours of regime values.

Finally, the dialectical character of concurring and dissenting Court opinions offers the administrative student "the opportunity to follow a public debate in a highly structured and formal context." More specifically, Rohr (1976: 403) puts the advantage this way: "Since constitutional cases usually turn on the interpretation of such vague phrases as 'due process of law,' 'equal protection,' or 'commerce among the states,' these public debates necessarily point to higher questions on the nature of the common good." In cases concerning the constitutionality of an antimiscegenation law or a minimum wage statute, Justices almost always include their views on the nature of the just society in their concurring and dissenting arguments. The dialectical character of the argumentation offers instruction to the administrative policy maker on the meaning of American values by illustrating alternative ways of viewing the same value problem. Such instruction helps to avoid uncritical acceptance of the dominant values.

Both Hart and Rohr have a grip on key aspects of normative discourse in public administration theory and education. But it is not clear that either of their proposals constitutes a successful solution. The purpose of the remainder of this article is to put forth a third approach that integrates the major strengths of these two proposed solutions while avoiding their primary pitfalls.

Toward an Alternative

Hart is correct to stress the rigor of the philosophical tradition. Rigorous thinking about normative questions is the essence of proper ethical training. However, Rohr's reservation about the study of substantive metaphysical theories is well taken. Given the sheer complexity of an argument such as Rawls's, fruitful discussion at this level of analysis presumes elaborate training in philosophical theory and method. Even within the philosophical tradition itself, a widely heralded contribution such as Rawls's never receives unanimous acceptance by political philosophers. The problem involved in reading Rawls is essentially that it is *too* rigorous. It is difficult not to believe that the value of the exercise would be lost on career-oriented public administration students.

In this regard, Rohr's emphasis on the relationship of ethical theory to practical cases is a turn in the right direction. Furthermore, he is correct to point to the logic of legal argumentation as an exercise in this mode of reasoning. His contention, however, that the study of "regime values" reflected in court decisions is the best exercise suited for imparting the art of normative thinking is not entirely convincing. There are a couple of difficulties here.

The most obvious limitation of an approach geared to regime values is that they insufficiently ground the study of ethics. To cite the standard ethical example, few today would argue that bureaucratic ethics in a state such as Nazi Germany should be limited to the study of regime values. While this illustration does not speak to the cultural context of American public administration, it does point to an essential level of ethical education. In fact, this aspect of normative discourse was evident in the literature of the new public administration (Marini, 1971). Questioning the appropriateness of specific regime values, many of these theorists advocated values that lay outside the operating system. Regardless of whether such an appeal is appropriate, an adequate framework for ethical discourse should be able to systematically incorporate this level of discussion when it arises.[2]

Second, the nature and logic of ethical reasoning do not stand out sharply in legal argumentation. More frequently the ethical logic of a legal argument is lodged in the complexity of the substantive issue with which it is concerned. In many cases, it is deliberately buried in the camouflage of an argument designed to persuade and cajole. It is therefore best to assume that the logic of ethical debate is not highly explicit in the language or rhetoric chosen to defend a legal argument. While it is correct to recognize legal argumentation as a special form of ethical discourse, it is equally important to appreciate the separate and distinct purposes for which legal and ethical theory have been designed. Rohr's recognition of the value of studying the dialectical character of the formally structured context of legal discourse is the strength of his argument; but it fails to sufficiently confront the fact that the substantive study of legal cases does not, ipso facto, impart this value. Rohr has laid out an important insight upon which a viable alternative can be constructed, but it remains to be worked out.

What is needed is a rigorous, systematic alternative that paves a middle course between these two approaches. Such an approach would have to be based on rigorous normative methods, but remain anchored to the realities of public administrative discourse. It is the contention here that such an alternative can be developed by shifting the emphasis from the study of the content of specific ethical arguments—whether philosophical or legal—to the underlying metaethical study of how to engage in normative discourse in evaluation. Essentially, the proposal involves turning from a primary focus on substantive issues to an emphasis on methodology. Building upon Rohr's appeal to formal argumentation, this approach directs attention to the nature and logic of the argumentation process. To accomplish this, however, requires the appropriation of rigorous analytical methods employed in philosophical analysis.

While this approach underscores Hart's emphasis on rigorous philosophical thinking, it confronts the problem on a different level of analysis. In place of the study of metaphysical theories, the shift to normative methodology proposed here turns instead to analytical philosophy, especially variants of the ordinary-language approach concerned with the study of the nature and rules of normative discourse in everyday affairs. Much of this work remains abstract, requiring translation for use in more practical contexts; but as the next section attempts to show there is a growing body of precedents for this task.

The following discussion is an effort to show that an approach based on the normative logic of evaluation permits exploration of the questions actually raised about value judgments in the context of ordinary language communication. It establishes logical connections between functional regime values and other levels of ethical reasoning, and it facilitates the exploration of the practical relationship linking facts and values in "real world" deliberation. As such, it is offered as groundwork for the construction of a tool designed for probing specific concrete cases, such as Supreme Court decisions or actual policy deliberations in organizational discourse. The development of such a methodological tool would serve both to guide discussions between the ethical public manager and the participants in the relevant policy environment—both inside and outside the organization—and as a pedagogical aid for the classroom student preparing for the task ahead.

Normative Methodology

The basic threads of the approach presented here have begun to emerge in the literatures of organization theory and policy analysis, although they do not as yet represent a fully developed systematic scheme. Most of them have been, in one way or another, advanced as responses to the fact-value problem and reflect a turn to methodological concerns.

In general, the frustrations generated by failure to find answers to complex problems tend to lead to a retreat to basic methodological questions. As a return to the epistemological drawing board, such inquiry involves a more basic level of concern with how we actually reason about the problems perplexing us (Cohen and Lindblom, 1979).

A similar transition took place in the public administration literature of the middle and late 1970s. The frustrations encountered by the new public administration writers attempting to espouse alternative social values frequently led to a less obstreperous but more rigorous retreat to fundamental methodological issues underlying value problems. During this period, for instance, Mitroff and Pondy (1974) argued that the search for new directions in normative decision-making requires organizational theorists and policy analysts to turn to the contributions of analytical philosophy and the philosophy of science—fields traditionally conceived to be far removed from their own focus of inquiry.

At the same time, partly in response to such concerns, political theorists in the philosophical tradition similarly suggested the relevance of their methods to the practical problems of policy decision-making (Barry, 1979; Anderson, 1979). In work emerging from analytical philosophy and the philosophy of science, we can find developments that speak directly to the task of constructing a methodological alternative to the problems raised by Hart and Rohr. Through a synthesis of related lines of investigation, a new direction can be set out that combines both analytical rigor and formal argumentation based on a jurisprudential model. The purpose here is to outline such an alternative.

The general framework of the approach emerges from an effort to advance a "forensic" model of social science. Writers such as Churchman (1971; also Churchman and Shainblatt, 1969), Brown (1976), and Rivlin (1973) have suggested that normative analysis in organizations can be facilitated by the introduction of a formally organized dialogue (or forensic debate) between normative and empirical perspectives. In such a scheme, policy analysts and administrative decision makers would take on the assignment of preparing briefs for or against policy positions emerging from the organizational decision process. As Rivlin (1973: 25) put it, they would "state what the position is and bring together all the evidence that supports their side of the argument, leaving to the brief writers of the other side the job of picking apart the case that has been presented and detailing the counter evidence."

Such policy argumentation starts with the recognition that the participants do not have solid answers to the questions under discussion, or even a solid method for getting answers. With this understanding, the policy analyst and decision maker attempt to work out a meaningful synthesis of perspectives, both normative and empirical. Some writers, such as Churchman, have suggested that the procedure take the form of a debate. Each party confronts the other with a counterproposal based on alternative sets of facts (or varying perceptions of the same facts). The participants in the exchange organize the established data and fit it into the competing world views that underlie their own respective arguments. The grounds or criteria for accepting or rejecting a normative proposal must be the same grounds for accepting or rejecting a counterproposal; and each must be subjected to corresponding types of data, judged or tested by the same rigorous empirical methods.

In this scheme, the formalized debate itself is the most instructive part of the analytical process. The free exercise of normative judgment, released from the empirical restrictions of the formal policy model, increases the possibility of developing a synthesis of normative perspectives that provide a legitimate basis for politically acceptable decisions and action. Where the scientific approach attempts to adapt qualitative data about norms and values to an empirical model through quantification, this forensic model reverses the process by fitting quantitative data into the framework of a normative world view. What is lost in logical and theoretical elegance is compensated for through relevance and practicality. Rather than attempt to "prove" policy decisions, analysts and decision makers base their judgments on the strongest possible arguments, employing both empirical methods and the discursive logic of normative argumentation.

This approach is an important step toward the development of a dynamic methodology designed to facilitate a dialectical interplay between empirical and normative processes in organizational policy-making. Moreover, as a rigorous practical method, it offers a solid foundation for the development of a middle course between the types of proposals advanced by Hart and Rohr. Like any step forward, however, it only brings the methodologist to the next set of hurdles. The logical question that arises is this: If both analysts and decision makers must employ the same grounds or criteria in their respective arguments, what are these criteria? What are the rules governing the integration of empirical and normative judgments?

Here the technique encounters the fundamental fact-value problem, particularly the question of normative criteria. There is little question about criteria governing empirical discourse, but the question as to whether there are criteria or grounds for mediating normative discourse is methodologically problematic. The introduction of normative debate brings the value dimensions of policy into sharper focus, but this is not to be confused with methodology, per se. Given the long history of arguments in philosophy and the social sciences about value judgments, it is reasonable to surmise that the methodological success of the forensic model ultimately rests on the elaboration of rules that govern the exchanges between empirical and normative perspectives. In such an exchange it is often easy to agree that one argument is more persuasive than another, but it is not always clear how that is known. It is the absence of such rational procedures for dealing with normative judgments that has led to the epistemological demise of normative theory in the contemporary social sciences.

In recognition of the methodological limbo posed by normative argumentation, a number of writers have begun to borrow methods from both analytical philosophy and legal argumentation. One proposal suggested extending the forensic approach's emphasis on brief-writing to include the concept of "rules of evidence" (Cain and Hollister, 1972). As a methodological counterpart to Rohr's emphasis on substantive legal arguments, this idea involves study of the rules and procedures of evidence that govern legal argumentation in the courtroom. From these processes, organizational analysts and decision makers might gain insight into the rules of argumentation which, in turn, can be adapted to the organization's policy deliberation process.

Duncan MacRae, for one, has stressed the value of the legal analogy. He has suggested a number of advantages that would result from supplying organizational policy-making with a methodologically regulated normative discourse that commands the kind of rigor found in law. Regulated communication, according to MacRae (1976: 85), has the advantage of standing "apart from the discourse of ordinary life in several attributes such as precise definitions, stress on written rather than oral communications, and limitation of meaning to what has been specified in advance." In such discourse, a statement or judgment can be given a precise definition and interpretation by a larger audience. A legal essay, for instance, written by trained legal specialists, directs the attention of similarly trained readers to statements and conclusions that can be systematically reexamined by shared rules and methods. Such an approach permits the analyst to concede the limitations of technically oriented models as decision-making tools while, at the same time, salvaging the heuristic and empirical insights that they offer. By combining empirical analysis, forensic policy debate, and the development of rules of evidence, this alternative clearly introduces a more judicious mix of pragmatism and rigor into administrative policy evaluation.

In conjunction with the study of the methods and procedures of legal discourse, Anderson and MacRae urged the exploration of the possibility of borrowing and adapting the rules of normative analysis employed in political philosophy. As Anderson (1978: 22) put it, evaluators fail to recognize that "their concern with cost-benefit analysis is only an episode in a long Western tradition of defining principles appropriate to judge the legitimacy and propriety of political activity." At the same time, political philosophers are able to examine the policy of representation in the 18th century, but they seem incapable of scrutinizing problems of participation in modern-day economic planning. As a suggestive attempt to bridge this gap, MacRae (1976: 92) introduced three logical tools employed in normative political analysis—logical clarity, consistency, and generality. These are essential principles of normative analysis with a place in organizational deliberation. Most organizational dialogue would indeed benefit from a rigorous application of these logical tests. Unfortunately, they remain too abstract to serve as a basis for a methodology. It is not clear from MacRae's work what the operational rules for the analytical layout and interpretation of policy arguments are, especially arguments involving both facts and values.

Several other writers have sought the logical structure of policy arguments by studying actual policy discussions. Within this framework Hambrick has attempted to explicate the propositional components that constitute a logically complete policy argument. With the assistance of such components, it is possible for the analyst to determine the kinds of evidence needed to support, reject, or modify a policy proposal.[3] Hambrick (1974: 469) offered the following ten propositions as a logical structure for policy analysis.

1. Action Proposal: a statement specifying a proposed policy action.
2. Policy Proposition: a statement indicating both the action(s) and goal(s) believed to lead to the policy action.
3. Grounding Propositions: definitional or conceptual statements stipulating a proven or assumed empirical claim that lays a foundation for the policy proposition.
4. Normative Proposition: a statement specifying the positive or negative value derived from the policy goals.
5. External Impact Proposition: a statement describing the policy action's impact on other than the intended goal(s).

6. Causal Proposition: a statement specifying the immediate cause-and-effect relationship that results in the goal.
7. Instrumental Proposition: a statement that turns the independent variable in the causal proposition into a dependent variable in the evaluation.
8. Time-Place Proposition: statement establishing the temporal and spatial configuration of variables providing an empirical base for assessing the need for policy intervention.
9. Constraints Proposition: a statement of factors that potentially alter the instrumental or causal propositions.
10. Comparative Proposition: a statement about the efficiency or effectiveness of the policy action.

This scheme sets out a useful line of investigation but is limited to an emphasis on the empirical, technical questions that underlie organizational deliberation—questions about cause and effect, costs and benefits of alternative means, and unanticipated impacts. While it avoids the methodological abstractions of political philosophy, it fails to deal adequately with the normative dimensions of analysis. Still missing is a statement of the logical structure that relates factual evidence to normative deliberation.

Practical Reason

The question, then, is how to develop a practical framework capable of incorporating the full range of empirical and normative judgments. An important clue can be gleaned from the work of ordinary-language philosophers engaged in the explication of the logic and purposes of practical discourse. The question posed here is quite similar to the one that concerns ordinary-language philosophers such as Toulmin (1950), Baier (1958), Taylor (1961), and Perry (1976). The similarity of concerns, in fact, is significant enough to suggest the study of practical reason as a potential avenue of methodological exploration for organizational theorists and policy analysts (Fischer, 1980).[4]

In recent decades, as Fred Dallmayr (1976: 64) explained, "philosophical trends in a variety of contexts have pointed toward a revival of normative agruments even in the absence of cognitive premises; by means of a careful and critical scrutiny of normative statements, philosophers of different persuasions have progressively uncovered the distinctive and autonomous status of moral and normative discourse vis-à-vis empirical propositions." Stimulated by linguistic philosophy—especially the ordinary-language approach—a number of political theorists have begun to seek knowledge about values through the metaethical analysis of the structure of normative arguments in politics. The primary purpose of metaethics is to explicate the distinctive logic of practical discourse to determine how people make reasoned judgments, i.e., how they choose and systematically employ rules and standards as criteria to arrive at conclusions. The basic aim is to come to a clear understanding of what it means to be rational in the process of dealing with values and norms, particularly in relation to empirical statements (Taylor, 1961). Whereas conceptual linguistic analysis focuses on the definitions and meanings of concepts employed in practical discourse, metaethics examines the nature of the judgments in which normative concepts are used; it inquires about the logic of practical discourse that governs reasoning about values; and it asks whether value judgments can be justified, proven, or shown to be valid.

An outgrowth of the later work of Wittgenstein, the ordinary-language approach to practical deliberation represents a loosely connected set of orientations characterized as much by ambiguity as by unity and agreement (Wellman, 1961). On the most general level, however, these orientations share a common response to positivism and the fact-value dichotomy. Fundamentally, the study of practical reason represents an effort to circumvent the methodological pitfalls of the fact-value separation, without necessarily resolving the underlying epistemological problems that it poses. Instead of emphasizing the failure of attempts to validate fundamental ideals, ordinary-language writers focus on the rational elements that make normative practical discourse possible in everyday life. Accepting the fact that values may in the final analysis rest on irrational components, they reject the positivistic conclusion that all normative discourse must be relegated to an intellectual limbo.

Such writers point to a number of dimensions of practical discourse that militate against such a conclusion. For example, in everyday life, actors are seldom faced with the lofty intellectual task of establishing the validity of fundamental values. Also, they have succeeded (at least to a degree) in explicating the outlines of an "informal logic" that governs practical deliberation. Such theorists argue that positivists, in their overemphasis on the irrationality of fundamental values, overlook the normative inferential methods that mediate the wide range of normative discussion about practical world affairs carried on within a framework of fundamental values. As most of the deliberation about practical affairs is conducted within a general social consensus about ideal values, it is possible from this view to argue that positivistic philosophers (and mainstream social scientists) have thrown the proverbial baby out with the bathwater.

The analysis of practical reason begins with the recognition that normative and scientific discourse are two distinct types of reason, each with its own logic and purpose. Writers such as Stephen Toulmin (1958) have argued that the fundamental distinction between the two rests on purpose or function: The function of scientific judgment is to alter expectations about what *will* happen, while that of normative judgment is to alter attitudes, behavior, and decisions about what *should* happen. Scientific judgments are based on the formal logic of the hypothetical-deductive model of causal demonstration. In contrast, normative judgments follow an informal logic that can be better understood in terms of something akin to a "jurispruden-tial analogy." Drawing attention to the similarities between normative arguments and those used by lawyers in a courtroom, Toulmin demonstrated that a good lawyer does not simply present the facts of the case, but rather marshals them to stress those aspects of the situation that favor his or her client. The lawyer selects language and structures arguments designed to persuade or convince a jury to decide in favor of the client.

Similarly, moral and political judgments are statements in support of decisions that can be forcefully or poorly defended. They are neither factual nor emotive statements, but are rather like records of practical decisions that can be supported much as a lawyer defends a client. They are rationally constructed, but not proven inductively or deductively like a scientific prop-osition. In this respect, one does not refer to J.S. Mill's "proof" of liberty, but rather to his persuasive defense of it (MacDonald, 1956: 53).

For present purposes, the contribution of a normative logic rests on its ability to provide the logical structure of the rational evaluative argument. The task is to present standards for decision-making that can serve as guides to asking deliberative questions about evaluative judgments. Such questions can be used as pointers or direction finders turning attention to facts, values and norms that might not otherwise be seen (Barry, 1979). They should, as Leys (1952: 11) put it, "help . . . administrators . . . and anyone who par-ticipates in the determination of policy by providing a 'rational-analytic' for reviewers, investigators, auditors, surveyors, and consultants, who are asked to pass judgment upon what others have done." Organized as a framework of questions, it can "improve and systematize practical judgment by finding out whether the right questions are being asked" (Leys, 1952: 12; Forester, 1979).

The identification of such questions has clear implications for organiza-tional policy-making. As a normative foundation, it could serve as a metanormative guide for probing the acceptability of administrative policy judgments. Ideally, such a logical structure would integrate the full range of empirical and normative questions that arise in policy deliberations. It would provide each participant in a policy debate with a common framework for laying out his or her arguments. All parties would be subject to the same methodological questions and rules of judgment. Where agree-ment or consensus proves beyond reach, it should be possible to specify the exact points of tension and disagreement and to suggest the kinds of evidence, if any, that might resolve these tensions.

A Logic of Policy Questions

As a preliminary step toward the development of an informal logic of policy questions for organizational deliberation, it is possible here to suggest twelve points or loci around which discussion and debate might take place. Cutting across both the empirical and normative domains of policy inquiry, they are based on Taylor's (1961) study of the logic of evaluation and an examination of specific policy arguments (Fischer, 1980).

Following Toulmin's lead, Taylor has laid out an informal logic of evaluative discourse. A full evaluation, in Taylor's scheme, has to answer to questions that arise in four distinct but interrelated levels of evaluation. Ranging from the most concrete empirical questions up to abstract normative questions concerning the "way of life," each of the four levels has its own specific logic and purpose in evaluative inquiry. Specified as verification, validation, vindication and rational choice, the first two constitute first-order discourse concerned with reasoning within a specific value system; the second two constitute second-order discourse addressed to fundamental questions about the value system itself. Each of the two levels involves an interplay between empirical and normative questions. Although Taylor's explication of these four phases of evaluation largely speaks to the abstract epistemological concerns of philosophers, it also provides a basis for the development of specific evaluative questions applicable to policy decision-making. The translation from epistemology to practical questions adapted to policy evaluation has been the primary focus of the work presented here. As such, it is offered only as a suggestive beginning, designed to promote further exploration in this direction.

Evaluative inquiry can be initiated by a problem's emerging in any of the four levels of discourse, requiring the participants to proceed to higher or lower levels of inquiry, depending upon the specific nature of the problem. For purposes of systematic presentation, however, it is helpful to present them in a formal order ranging from the lowest concrete level up to the highest abstract questions. The phase or level of verification, then, is the starting point.

Verification is the simplest of the levels to describe. It is addressed to the basic empirical questions that have monopolized the attention of social and policy scientists. At this level, the evaluator will seek answers to problems revolving around the four following questions:

— Is the program objective derived from the policy goal(s)?

— Does the program empirically fulfill its stated objectives?

— Does empirical analysis uncover secondary system effects that offset the program objective(s)?

— Does the program fulfill the objective(s) more efficiently than alternative means available?

These are familiar questions in the empirical methodology of policy evaluation. For purposes of brief illustration, consider the case of the Head Start compensatory education program. After determining whether Head Start policy goals have been properly translated into an empirically measurable program, administrators in the Office of Education must question whether the program in fact efficiently achieves its stated objectives. They have to ask whether it accomplishes its objectives better than alternative programs, without offsetting other relevant objectives pertinent to compensatory educational policies as a whole. As in the case of the public debate about the Head Start findings of the Westinghouse Learning Corporation, much of the deliberation at this level would focus on the concerns of empirical methodology, which include the following: Was the control group adequate? Was sufficient attention paid to program variations? Was the sample random (Williams and Evans, 1972)?

Criticisms directed at the technocratic conception of policy evaluation largely derive from its failure to extend inquiry beyond the verification of program objectives. After technical verification, the logic of evaluation leads to questions of validation, concerned with whether the particular goals from which the policy objectives are drawn are the relevant goals in the particular situation. In this phase, the evaluator must turn from the methodological principles of empirical verification to the logical rules of first-order normative discourse. As a process of reasoning that takes place *within* an adopted value system, it reflects Weber's call for the explication and elaboration of the internal consistency of a value judgment, along with its conceptual implications for thought and action. The focus of discussion here centers around the following questions:

— Is the policy goal(s) relevant? Can it be justified or grounded by an appeal to a higher principle or established causal knowledge?

— Are there circumstances in the situation that require that an exception be made to the policy goal?

— Are two or more goals equally relevant to the situation?

— Does the decision maker's value system place higher precedence on one of the conflicting criteria; or does it make contradictory prescriptions in this situation?

The validation of a policy goal shifts the focus from program objectives to the relevance of the more general goals from which the objectives are derived. The general relevance of a policy goal can be justified by pointing to its logical link to a higher level normative principle (e.g., the goal of efficiency derived from the principles of economic development); or it can be justified by an appeal to data about specific causal consequences that have previously resulted from adhering to the goal. In philosophy, this latter appeal is known as "rule-utilitarianism." Beyond this first step, the evaluator must examine the relevance of the goal to the specific circumstances to which it is applied and, if relevant, determine whether it conflicts with other goals relevant to the same situation.

To pursue the Head Start illustration further, assume that policy evaluators in the Office of Education fail to statistically verify an improvement in the reading scores of Head Start children, leading some to argue for the elimination of the program. Against this judgment, minority leaders might raise questions about the validity of reading scores as a criterion in this situation. Are they a valid criterion for judging the overall success of a program based on policies designed to improve the life opportunities of socially deprived ghetto children? What about providing "socially relevant experiences"? Wouldn't this objective have at least equal bearing on the determination of success or failure of Head Start programs? For those holding equality to be the highest human value, socially relevant experiences would most likely take precedence over academic merit measured as reading scores.

At this point, evaluative discourse shifts fundamentally from first- to second-order discourse. The vindication of a political choice between reading scores and socially relevant experiences requires the evaluator to step outside of the value systems from which these preferences are drawn and to examine their implications for the larger social system as a whole. It is here that we begin to confront the kinds of discourse that Hart and Rohr are attempting to introduce into organizational deliberation.

— Do the practical consequences resulting from a commitment to the decision maker's basic value system facilitate the realization of the ideals of the accepted social order?
— Do other value systems, which reflect interests and needs in the social system as a whole, judge the consequences (as benefits and costs) to be distributed equitably?

The questions of vindication are essentially second-order empirical questions concerned with the functional consequences of individual and group values for the social system as a whole. In this respect, they reflect the types

of concerns advanced by naturalistic philosophers of the systems persuasion, such as Bertalanffy (1968) and Laszlo (1972). As such, vindication is
the second-order counterpart of verification in first-order discourse.

Although the empirical complexity of the questions raised in vindication
is frequently a major obstacle, it is nonetheless possible to locate the concerns of this level of evaluation in policy debates. In the issues surrounding
Head Start, probably the most salient example has been the controversy
about the "culture of poverty" (Moynihan, 1968). If social researchers can
empirically demonstrate that ghetto children are socialized into value
systems that lack instrumentality for the American "way of life," it can be
argued that socially relevant experiences must be the primary consideration.
In addition to Head Start policies, the logic of this argument has also
grounded school integration and affirmative action policies.

The outcomes of such empirical tests form the basis for the second question in vindication. Here the issue is whether the system consequences
satisfy the accepted standards of social equity held by the competing interest
groups or social classes that benefit from or pay for the outcomes.
Disparities between these standards and the empirical results trigger
political debate about the social system itself, which ultimately leads to the
philosophical concerns of the fourth level of evaluation—rational choice.

As Hart made clear, the new public administration's emphasis on social
equity inevitably leads to a more fundamental debate about the nature of
the good society. At the level of rational choice, we encounter political
philosophers like Rawls (1971) attempting to construct models of the "rational" way of life by identifying values (such as equality, freedom, or community) to be adopted as the ultimate goals of all subsequent political
undertakings. While public administration by virtue of function is not concerned with this level of evaluation, it is essential that ethical education for
public administrators shows how to systematically link the normative questions in organizational deliberation to the higher levels of evaluation, including political philosophy.

Summarized in Table 1, these questions are designed to serve as a
rational-analytic guide for policy deliberation. Rather than as a normative
calculus, they are presented as a framework of component parts of a policy
judgment that require investigation. Instead of supplying information per
se, they point to unperceived angles and forgotten dimensions that must be
explored, as well as the kinds of empirical and normative data pertinent to
the deliberative processes in general. The task of the evaluator is to tease out
the answers to these questions and formally organize them in such a way
that the strengths and weaknesses, inconsistencies and contradictions, of
policy decisions are revealed.

TABLE 1

A Logic of Policy Questions

Program Objectives:	Is the program objective(s) logically derived from the relevant policy goals?
Empirical Consequences:	Does the program empirically fulfill its stated objective(s)?
Unanticipated Effects:	Does the empirical analysis uncover secondary effects that offset the program objective(s)?
Alternative Means:	Does the program fulfill the objective(s) more efficiently than alternative means available?
Relevance:	Is the policy goal(s) relevant? Can it be justified or grounded by an appeal to a higher principle(s) or established causal knowledge?
Situational Context:	Are there circumstances in the situation which require that an exception be made to the policy goal?
Multiple Goals:	Are two or more goals equally relevant to the situation?
Precedence:	Does the decision-maker's value system place higher precedence on one of the conflicting criteria? Or does it make contradictory prescriptions in this situation?
System Consequences:	Do the practical consequences resulting from a commitment to the decision-maker's basic value system facilitate the realization of the ideals of the accepted social order?
Social Equity:	Do other value systems, which reflect interests and needs in the social system as a whole, judge the consequences (as benefits and costs) to be distributed equitably?
Ideological Conflict:	Do the fundamental ideals that organize the accepted social order provide a basis for an equitable resolution of conflicting judgments?
Alternative Social Order:	If the social order is unable to resolve value system conflicts, do other social orders equitably prescribe for the relevant interests and needs that the conflicts reflect?

While such a logic of evaluation has prescriptive implications for evaluating the outcomes of organizational deliberation, it is essential that it be recognized as an ideal structure. To properly introduce an ideal logic of communication, an evaluator must be prepared to anticipate the inherent conflicts that it will generate in a modern bureaucratic organization, where the patterns of communication are sharply limited by hierarchical authority and the chain of command. Realistically, it is designed to deliberately exploit the tensions between the real and the ideal, between bureaucratic domination and legitimate human discourse. Dialectically, the explication of such tensions can serve as a critical force facilitating organizational change. In this regard, an ideal logic may better serve those who suffer the consequences of organizational policies than the managers responsible for them. Like policy analysis in general, an ideal logic of evaluation must be approached as a tool for bureaucratic reform (Danke, 1977).

Epistemological Issues

In addition to probing arguments, this approach makes it possible to give some shape to the characteristically general discussions that typify social science literature on normative methodology; it also helps open or facilitate methodological discussion in the organizational and policy sciences about larger epistemological questions being raised in the philosophy of the social sciences. With regard to the literature on normative methodology, an important contribution of this scheme must be its ability to relate factual evidence or data to normative policy deliberations. One way to demonstrate this is by relating the scheme to the naturalistic conception of ethical theory, emphasizing the factual dimensions of evaluative discourse.

Naturalists point to six types of factual knowledge that can be brought to bear on value judgments: (1) knowledge of consequences that flow from alternative actions; (2) knowledge of alternative means available; (3) knowledge of established norms and values that bear on the decisions; (4) the particular facts of the situation; (5) general causal conditions and law relevant to the situation; and (6) knowledge about the fundamental needs of humankind (Kurtz, 1965). These six types of facts and their methodological counterparts in policy evaluation (such as means-ends and comparative input-output analysis, situational and political feasibility studies, causal and systems analysis), can be located across the twelve components of the logic of policy questions. Also, for comparison, Hambrick's empirical questions can be fitted to specific points in the framework. Table 2 shows that all of the factual elements in the framework (identified by number) are incorporated in a practical scheme that encompasses the full range of normative inquiry.

Some organizational theorists and policy scientists will argue that questions about ideological conflict and alternative social systems are beyond the scope of the trade (see Meehan, 1973). To a large extent this is true, at least in terms of the prevailing definitions of these sciences. The point here is not to insist that the organizational scientist turn political philosopher but rather to show the logical relationship between organizational policy research and the full range of normative inquiry. Even though public administration scholars are not directly concerned with the construction of alternative social systems, they are consumers of the ideological framework of the society within which they are working. Knowledge about the

TABLE 2

**Policy Questions: The Role of Empirical
and Normative Analysis**

Policy Questions: Practical Reason	Role of Empirical And Normative Analysis	Hambrick's Policy Questions
Program Objectives	Logical Rules of Normative Analysis	
Empirical Consequences	Empirical Knowledge of Consequences (1)	Causal Proposition Instrumental Proposition
Unanticipated Effects	Knowledge of Consequences (1)	External Impact Proposition Constraint Proposition
Alternative Means	Knowledge of Alternative Means (2)	Comparative Proposition
Relevance	Knowledge of Established Norms (3), Causal Conditions and Laws (5)	Normative Proposition Grounding Proposition
Situational Context	Particular Facts of the Situation (4)	Time-Place Proposition
Multiple Goals	Normative Logic	
Precedence	Normative Logic	
System Consequences	Causal Conditions, Laws (5), and Consequences (1)	
Social Equity	Normative Logic, Knowledge of Norms (3), and Consequences (5)	
Ideological Conflict	Normative Logic	
Alternative Social Orders	Knowledge of Fundamental Needs (6), Normative Logic	

Source: From Frank Fischer, Politics, Values, and Public Policy: The Problem of Methodology, p. 212, Westview Press, 1980.

ideological system is indispensable to the policy maker who must translate research findings into the political language of public discussion. An evaluative framework based upon ordinary-language deliberation can facilitiate such communication between the worlds of theory and practice. Clarification of the full range of connections between normative assumptions and empirical relationships would eliminate the ideological shroud that hangs over the technocratic approach to organization and policy analysis (Kramer, 1975; Habermas, 1973).

The second methodological advantage of this approach, which has origins in the deeper epistemological issues raised by the relationship of empirical to normative judgments, deserves at least brief mention, even though the scope of this issue is well beyond the limits and purposes of this discussion. Given the interplay between empirical research (facts) and ideology (values), it is clear that the construction of policy arguments necessarily remains as much an art as a science. Accordingly, organizational theorists must begin to confront the less scientific, more interpretive dimensions of policy evaluation and the methodological problems they imply. As Mitroff and Pondy (1974) pointed out, this requires methodological exploration of the more recent developments in the philosophy of the social sciences.

Careful reading of this literature, in fact, confirms that some of the main "technical" problems plaguing policy decision-making are less matters of research design and data collection than problems with normative epistemological assumptions (Rein, 1976). To the extent that the development and logical analysis of organizational policy proposals are deliberative exercises employing conjecture and speculation, analogy and metaphor, and extrapolation from empirically established causal propositions, policy-making methodology must be attuned to questions concerning the relation of cause to understanding, and of insight and discovery to demonstration and proof.

Particularly important in this regard are the epistemological contributions of phenomenological sociologists and political philosophers emphasizing the socially constructed, interpretive character of organizational realities (Bernstein, 1976). From these works it is clear that theorists and evaluators must confront more directly the fact that organizational policy arguments—unlike scientific arguments based on closed and generalizable models—must be open and contextual (Walsh, 1973). Where scientific judgment can be based on a computational algorithm, the validity of a normative-based policy argument is in the final analysis determined by the communicative power or persuasive force it has for the organizational participants. Such judgments are not true or false in the scientific sense of the term; rather, they portray policies as better or worse, powerful or weak, persuasive or unconvincing for members of the policy audience. The test criteria for the proposal are the breadth of its appeal, its ability to synthesize conflicting arguments, the number of people willing to accept it, and so on.

While it is difficult to state precise rules governing these test criteria, the existing literature provides some important clues as to how or where to begin such studies. Barry and Rae (1975), for example, suggested that those interested in evaluation should place greater emphasis on the study of "political rhetoric"—that is, the way in which arguments are marshaled in politics to reconcile people pursuing different goals and objectives. House (1980) and Anderson (1979) similarly have called for the study of the "metapolitical" languages of evaluation, and Johnson (1975) alluded to instructive parallels that can be drawn between literary criticism and policy evaluation viewed as criticism. Outside of mainstream social science, the study of the rules and principles of criticism are widely endorsed as a serious, systematic endeavor. It may well be here, through further exploration of policy languages and modes of argumentation, that analytical political philosophers can make their most important contributions to the normative processes of organizational deliberation. The analytical insights offered by ordinary-language philosophers make it clear that the logic of practical criticism is not beyond rational inquiry. As a logical structure based on such investigation, the methodological framework suggested here is in large part designed to facilitate the exploration of this dimension of the evaluative process.

Concluding Remarks

The discussion here has attempted to sketch out an approach to organizational policy deliberation based on the informal logic of evaluation. In the process, I have argued that such an alternative approach facilitates the exploration of both the normative and empirical questions actually raised about policy value judgments. It does this in the context of ordinary language, which is the communicative medium of the public administrator, both on the job and in the classroom. By delineating the levels of evaluative discourse, it illuminates the kinds of connections that must be drawn between Hart's emphasis on abstract ethical theory and Rohr's concern for real-world deliberations. It also promotes epistemological exploration of the practical linkages between facts and values.

It is the contention here that if organizational theorists and policy scientists are to take seriously the concerns of ethics and normative discourse, they must begin to introduce these kinds of epistemological issues into their own discussions. This will require much more attention to the study of the levels of practical discourse in organizational settings and to the task of converting such a methodology into a pedagogical tool for ethical education in the public administration curriculum.

The nature of the task clearly underscores the need for a tradition of public administration philosophers, trained in both ethics and public affairs. The prospects for such a possibility depend upon the development of a much closer interaction between political philosophers and public administration theorists than has existed heretofore. In fact, as experience at the Harvard Business School suggests, this may mean that Ph.D.'s in moral philosophy need to add the Master's degree in management to their training. To facilitate this kind of interaction, Harvard's course entitled "Ethical Aspects of Corporate Policy" is taught jointly by professors from both the schools of business and divinity to a class combining students from the two programs. Another sign of more integration is the appearance of journals of applied ethics such as *Philosophy and Public Affairs*, although the concept of an "applied ethics" has received criticism from a number of intellectual quarters.[5]

On the administrative side, organization theorists must devote more attention to the process of argumentation in public organizational debate. Already this discussion has reviewed some encouraging contributions in this direction, particularly the work of Churchman and his associates. Beyond the introduction of formal debate, however, organizational theorists must analyze the implications of argumentation for specific functional relationships in the organizational process. Technical rationality has emerged as an intellectual framework geared to a specific organizational form designed to promote and perpetuate particular configurations of power and authority. Organization theorists must study the functional tensions that the introduction of ideal standards would generate under a bureaucratic distribution of power, as well as to determine the organizational forms implied by the ideal logic of debate. One promising approach in this direction has been set out by managerial psychologists such as Kolb (1974). Kolb and his colleagues have sought to map out the cognitive domains of organizational structures and to assess their implications for normative problem-solving. Much of this work is still in its infancy, but it does provide some encouraging insights into the kind of research that must be placed on the agenda.

In contrast to the sophisticated nature of the challenge, claims about the present discussion must remain modest. The purpose here has been only to point to difficulties that arise in two approaches that tend to typify much of the writing on the problem—particularly the gap between the abstract concerns of ethical theory and the more practical issues that confront public organizational discourse—and to suggest an alternative direction for further exploration. It is hoped that this discussion will encourage others concerned with ethics and evaluative discourse to explore this particular line of investigation. At this stage, however, the most important assignment should not be so much a matter of arguing about which specific approach is best, but rather a concern for nurturing the dialogue about organizational ethics and evaluation.

NOTES

[1]The remarks mentioned here were made by Theodore Lowi during a panel discussion on "Political Theory and Public Policy" at the annual meeting of the American Political Science Association, August 29, 1980.

[2]It can argued that Rohr advocates "regime values" only after one is convinced of the fundamental justice of the regime itself. Surely this is true. The point here is that the methodological relationship between these two levels of evaluation needs to be clarified. That is, what is the nature and relationship of argumentation within a set of regime values to the nature of argumentation about the justice or validity of these values?

[3]Brock et al. (1973) approached the problem from the point of view of argumentation theory in public speaking and the systems perspective. Designed specifically as a tool for research and analysis in forensic debate, they offered a series of question formats for the description and evaluation of policy alternatives organized around a systems framework.

[4]Dunn (1981), House (1980), and Klosterman (1978) are among those who have also recognized the possibility of borrowing and adapting methods for policy evaluation from the study of practical reason.

[5]For criticisms of "applied ethics" see Euben (1981) and Lilla (1981). Euben's critique emerges from a left-liberal perspective, while Lilla's analysis is anchored to a neoconservative point of view.

REFERENCES

Anderson, C. 1979. "The place of principles in policy analysis." Amer. Pol. Sci. Rev. 73 (September): 711–723.

_____. 1978. "The logic of public problems: evaluation in comparative policy research," pp. 19–41 in D. Ashford (ed.) Comparing Public Policies. Beverly Hills, CA: Sage.

Baier, K. 1958. The Moral Point of View. Ithaca, NY: Cornell Univ. Press.

Barry, B. 1979. Political Argument. Atlantic Highlands, NJ: Humanities.

_____ and D. Rae. 1975. "Political evaluation," pp. 337–401 in N. Polsby and F. Greenstein (eds.) The Handbook of Political Science. Reading, MA: Addison-Wesley.

Bernstein, R. 1976. The Restructuring of Social and Political Theory. New York: Harcourt Brace Jovanovich.

Bertalanffy, L. 1968. General Systems Theory. New York: George Braziller.

Brock, B., J. Chesebro, J. Cragen, and J. Klumpp. 1973. Public Policy Decision-Making: Systems Analysis and Comparative Advantages Debate. New York: Harper & Row.

Brown, P. 1976. "Ethics and policy research." Policy Analysis 2 (Spring): 325–340.

Cain, G. and R. Hollister. 1972. "The methodology of evaluating social action programs," pp. 131–139 in P. Rossi and W. Williams (eds.) Evaluating Social Programs. New York: Seminar.

Churchman, C. 1971. The Design of Inquiry Systems. New York: Basic Books.

_____ and A. Schainblatt. 1969. "PPB: how can it be implemented?" Public Administration Rev. 29 (March-April): 178–189.

Cohen, D. and C. Lindblom. 1979. "Solving problems of bureaucracy," pp. 125–138 in C. Weiss and A. Barton (eds.) Making Bureaucracies Work. Beverly Hills, CA: Sage.

Dallmayr, F. 1976. "Beyond dogma and despair: toward a critical theory of politics." Amer. Pol. Sci. Rev. 70 (March): 64–79.

Danke, G. 1977. "Policy analysis as bureaucratic reform." Southern Rev. of Public Administration 1 (Summer): 109–128.

Diesing, P. 1962. Reason in Society. Urbana: Univ. of Illinois Press.

Dunn, W. 1981. Public Policy Analysis: An Introduction. Englewood Cliffs, NJ: Prentice-Hall.

Ellul, J. 1964. The Technological Society. New York: Knopf.

Euben, P.J. 1981. "Philosophy and the professions." Democracy 1 (April): 112–127.

Fischer, F. 1980. Politics, Values, and Public Policy: The Problem of Methodology. Boulder, CO: Westview.

Fleishman, J. and B. Payne. 1980. Ethical Dilemmas and the Education of Policy Makers. Hastings-on-Hudson, NY: Hastings Center.

Forester, J. 1979. Questioning and Shaping Attention as Planning Strategy: Toward a Critical Theory of Planning. Department of City and Regional Planning, Working Paper 7. Ithaca, NY: Cornell University.

Frohock, F. 1974. Normative Political Theory. Englewood Cliffs, NJ: Prentice Hall.

Habermas, J. 1973. Legitimation Crisis. Boston: Beacon.

_____. 1970. Toward a Rational Society. Boston: Beacon.

Hambrick, R. 1974. "A guide for the analysis of policy arguments." Policy Sciences 5 (December): 469–478.

Hart, D. 1974. "Social equity, justice, and the equitable administrator." Public Administration Rev. 34 (January-February): 3–17.

Hart, D. and W. Scott. 1979. Organizational America. Boston: Houghton Mifflin.

_____. 1973. "Administrative crisis: the neglect of metaphysical speculation." Public Administration Rev. 33 (September-October):415–422.

House, E. 1980. Evaluating with Validity. Beverly Hills, CA: Sage.

Hummel, R. 1977. The Bureaucratic Experience. New York: St. Martin's.

Jacoby, H. 1976. The Bureaucratization of the World. Berkeley: Univ. of California Press.

Johnson, R. 1975. "Research objectives for policy analysis," pp. 75–92 in K. Dolbeare (ed.) Public Policy Evaluation. Beverly Hills, CA: Sage.

Klosterman, R. 1978. "Foundations for normative planning." J. of Amer. Institute of Planners 44 (January): 37–46.

Kolb, D. 1974. "On management and the learning process," pp. 27–42 in D. Kolb, I. Rubin, J. McIntyre (eds.) Organizational Psychology: A Book of Readings. Englewood Cliffs, NJ: Prentice-Hall.

Kramer, F. 1975. "Policy analysis as ideology." Public Administration Rev. 36 (September-October): 509–517.

Kurtz, P. 1965. Decision and the Condition of Man. New York: Dell.

Laszlo, E. 1972. The Systems View of the World: The Natural Philosophy of the New Developments in the Sciences. New York: George Braziller.

Leys, W. 1952. Ethics for Policy Decisions. Englewood Cliffs, NJ: Prentice-Hall.

Lilla, M. 1981. "Ethos, ethics, and public service." Public Interest (Spring): 3–17.

MacDonald, M. 1956. "Natural rights," pp. 35–55 in P. Laslett (ed.) Politics, Philosophy and Society. Oxford: Oxford Univ. Press.

MacRae, D. 1976. The Social Function of Social Science. New Haven, CT: Yale Univ. Press.

Marini, F. [ed.] 1971. Toward a New Public Administration. Scranton, PA: Chandler.

Mason, R. and I. Mitroff. 1981. "Policy analysis as argument." Policy Studies J. 9 (Special Issue, No. 2): 579–585.

Meehan, E. 1973. "Science, values, and policies." Amer. Behavioral Scientist 17 (September-October): 53–100.

_____. 1967. Contemporary Political Thought. Homewood, IL: Dorsey.

Mitroff, I. and L. Pondy. 1974. "On the organization of inquiry: a comparison of some radically different approaches to policy analysis." Public Adminstration Rev. 34 (September-October): 471-479.

Moynihan, D. [ed.] 1968. On Understanding Poverty. New York: Basic Books.

Perry, T. 1976. Moral Reasoning and Truth. Oxford: Clarendon.

Rawls, J. 1971. A Theory of Justice. Cambridge, MA: Belknap.

Rein, M. 1976. Social Science and Public Policy. NY: Penguin.

Rivlin, A. 1973. "Forensic social science." Harvard Educ. Rev. 13 (February): 61-75.

Rohr, J. 1978. Ethics for Bureaucrats. New York: Dekker.

_____. 1976. "The study of ethics in the p.a. curriculum." Public Administration Rev. 36 (July-August): 398-406.

Simey, T. 1968. Social Science and Social Purpose. London: Constable.

Taylor, P. 1961. Normative Discourse. Englewood Cliffs, NJ: Prentice-Hall.

Toulmin, S. 1958. The Uses of Argument. Cambridge: Cambridge Univ. Press.

_____. 1950. An Examination of the Place of Reason in Ethics. Cambridge: Cambridge Univ. Press.

von Mises, L. 1960. Epistemological Problems of Economics. Princeton, NJ: Van Nostrand.

Walsh, D. 1973. "Sociology and the social world." pp. 15-35 in P. Filmer et al. (eds.) New Directions in Sociological Theory. Cambridge: MIT Press.

Weber, M. 1947. The Theory of Social and Economic Organization. New York: Free Press.

Weisskopf, W. 1971. Alienation and Economists. New York: Delta.

Weldon, T. 1953. The Vocabulary of Politics. London: Penguin.

Wellman, C. 1961. The Language of Ethics. Cambridge, MA. Harvard Univ. Press.

Wildavsky, A. 1966. "The political economy of efficiency." Public Administration Rev. 26 (November-December): 292-310.

Williams, W. and J. Evans. 1972. "The politics of evaluation: the case of Head Start," pp. 249-269 in P. Rossi and W. Williams (eds.) Evaluating Social Programs. New York: Seminar.

IV

The Emergence of an Environmental Ethic

15

Land Planning in an Ethical Perspective

Jerome L. Kaufman

Economic and ecological forces assuredly will affect how land resources are used in this country in the next generation. The need for land resource conservation would be much less were it not for the success of the economic system, which has produced such a high standard of living for many Americans, but left in its wake a lot more sprawl and a lot less farmland and natural areas for the public at large. As a countervailing force, the ecological approach is being looked at more as a check on the economic system's incessant drive to "progress," having the potential to pull us back to a more harmonious balance between people and nature, a balance set awry by past economic forces.

In contrast, the influence ethics will have as a force in shaping future land resource use appears much more problematical and uncertain. Despite the occasional land and environmental ethic manifestos, ethical reasons are rarely cited in day-to-day formulation of land resource policies or in land resource decision-making. I use the term "ethics" as it commonly applies to those weighty matters of right and wrong, good and evil, and duty and obligation(5).

Consider, for example, the reasons environmentalists and land planners give for preserving prime agricultural land, certainly a policy central to any discussion of why a land planning urgency exists. Rarely is the call for such a policy based on grounds that it is right or obligatory to protect such lands. Instead, the reasons given hew to principles of efficiency, economy, or resource protection: Prime agricultural land is the best land for farming

From the *Journal of Soil and Water Conservation* (November-December 1980), pp. 255–258. Copyright © 1980 by the Soil Conservation Society of America.

because it is generally flat or gently rolling or susceptible to little soil erosion; prime agricultural land is our most energy-efficient land, producing the most food with the least fuel, fertilizer, and labor; preserving prime agricultural land will help control urban sprawl and protect open space and critical resource areas, such as wetlands and marshes; or measures to preserve prime agricultural land will reduce the farmer's tax burden that is rapidly increasing because such lands are assessed at urban speculative value rather than at present use value.

Despite the lack of references to specific ethical principles in ongoing deliberations about land resource issues, it is clear that an ethical perspective could hardly be dismissed as inconsequential to land planning. But that perspective is a difficult one to grasp and articulate. Why? Because ethics is one of those nebulous subjects. Most of us can appreciate ethical principles in the abstract, but when it comes to applying them in specific, concrete situations, more often than not we fail to do so.

What I propose to do here is to shake off some of the cobwebs that shroud the ethical perspective on land resource issues. Specifically, I propose to do three things: Show that ethical considerations, although often camouflaged, are alive and present in the land resources planning and development process; discuss patterns of ethical thinking and ethical dilemmas that underlie that process; and suggest how an ethical perspective might become more prominent and useful in dealing with issues related to future land planning.

I do not intend to argue for an ethical perspective as essential to resolve land resource issues. Rather than to pose as a moralist, my intention is to be descriptive and analytical about ethics.

Two Kinds of Principles

There are two kinds of ethical principles—ends- and means-oriented principles. Both come into play as far as land resource issues are concerned, but in different ways. In a recent article, "A New Land Use Ethic," Graham Ashworth of Salford University in England developed 10 land ethic prescriptions that embody his personal perspective on American land use ethic issues and imperatives(2). Presented in proper ethical form, as a list of obligations, two of them read:

- "You ought to consider land as a resource that may be yours for a time but is also held in trust for the future. Land is not a commodity that any of us can own in the ordinary sense of the word."

● "If you are presently trusted with the management of a piece of land, you ought to use it in a manner that benefits the land and does not damage it. Some land uses are abuses that have irreversible consequences, and you ought to avoid such abuses."

These are examples of ends-oriented ethical principles because they imply directions for land policy to follow—view land as a trust, use it in a way that does not damage it, and avoid abusive land uses with irreversible consequences.

Ashworth goes on to contend that land use controls should be developed in the interest of the community and that "you ought to be ready to give time and talents to fight for the land use control." In this instance, the ethical imperative applies to how one should specifically behave—fight for the land use control. This is an example of a means-oriented ethical principle. It is not unlike the standards found in professional codes of ethic, which stipulate how the profession's members should behave in everyday practice.

The distinction between ends- and means-oriented principles is important. Both are needed. Ends without means tend to be impotent, and means without ends tend to be blind. In the context of Ashworth's land ethic prescriptions, it is not enough to say that society should avoid abusive land uses (and end) without also addressing how public officials and others should conduct themselves (the means) in trying to achieve this and other ends.

On the other hand, overemphasizing behavioral norms—be fair, be truthful, be loyal to your employer, be objective, etc.—without stipulating the ends to be sought provides insufficient direction to guide personal conduct. Aside from specifying more clearly ends- and means-oriented ethical principles that apply to land resources, a balance between them would be helpful to guide the activity of those involved in the land resources planning and development process.

Right and Wrong in Land Planning

Previously, I noted the absence of references to specific ethical principles in ongoing deliberations about land resource issues. This does not mean that principles of economy, efficiency, and resource protection, or others such as equity, growth, or individual freedom, which are often mentioned in justifying land resource policy decisions, are necessarily void of ethical content. Although I am neither an expert in moral philosophy nor in metaethics, I recently have done some reading in these subjects in preparing a course on ethical issues in planning and the public policy professions. So with the excuse of partial knowledge to fall back upon, let me try to make the case that notions of right and wrong, which in part are what ethics deals with, are subsumed, albeit often unconsciously, in the reasoning that underlies a lot of land resource policy and decision-making.

If a moral philosopher happened to listen in on a conversation between land resource planners as they ticked off the reasons for an agricultural land preservation policy, he would probably conclude that the planners believe the consequences of implementing such a program would lead to more good than bad things for the public—more open space, more wetlands preserved, more energy efficiencies, and more fairness to farmers as well as less urban sprawl.

On the other hand, he would probably conclude from the discussion that the planners believe that without such a program the public will end up with less of these "goods" and more of the "bads"—more sprawl, less wetlands, less open space, etc. The high-falutin technical term that best describes the ethical reasoning process used by the planners is teleology. And the moral philosopher would conclude that in this instance the planners are reasoning like teleologists.

A teleologist would say that the basic standard for judging what's ethically right, wrong, or obligatory is the nonmoral value or good that is brought about as a consequence of some action. In this example, more open space, less sprawl, etc., are the nonmoral goods valued by the planners. And since the consequence of acting to preserve prime agricultural land is assumed to produce more of these nonmoral goods than would no action, our land planners (teleologists) therefore reason that such action is right or ethical.

Going further, utilitarians, who are a class of teleologists, might reason that it is right to preserve prime agricultural land because such action would lead to at least as great a balance of good over bad as other available alternatives. This then leads to the familiar utilitarian precept that those actions are right that produce the greatest good for the greatest number. Gifford Pinchot, an esteemed figure in the annals of the conservation movement, clearly spoke as a utilitarian in another context when he announced many years ago that resource conservation should provide the "greatest good for the greatest number for the longest time"(1).

There is yet another form of ethical reasoning that applies to the land resource policy area. It goes by the name of deontology. In contrast to teleologists, deontologists assert that considerations other than an act's consequence of producing nonmoral goods are what makes the act right or obligatory. In effect, deontologists contend that the act itself is what is right or wrong, regardless of its consequences.

Examples of deontological thinking are numerous. The Golden Rule to "do unto others as you would have others do unto you" or Immanual Kant's categorical imperative to "act only on that maxim which you can at the same time will to be a universal law" are well-known examples drawn from religious and moral philosophy. When Aldo Leopold asserted that actions disrupting the biotic community are wrong, he too was speaking as a deontologist(6). For that matter, so is Graham Ashworth, when he says, "You ought to use land in a manner that benefits the land and does not damage it"(2).

While to my knowledge no one has yet asserted that the act of preserving prime agricultural land is ethical in itself, deontological principles form the cornerstone of land and environmental ethic statements. To the extent these principles are drawn upon—indirectly or even subconsciously—in shaping land resource policy, the influence of deontological thinking can be seen.

My feeling, however, is that the teleological approach is more often used than the deontological when an ethical perspective enters into a discourse on land resource issues. I say this because most policy officials characteristically consider the costs and benefits of proposals, even in rudimentary fashion, before recommending or taking any action. And more often than not, this entails some sort of weighting of the nonmoral goods and bads likely to result from the contemplated action. The list of specific "do's and dont's" in land ethic statements, which reflects the deontological approach, might occasionally enlighten a discussion on a land policy issue, but the principles embodied in these statements in themselves are rarely the grounds upon which land resource policy decisions are forged.

The Question of Values

I have attempted to sort out some of the ways an ethical perspective can enter the land resources planning process by highlighting distinctions between ends- and means-oriented ethical principles and between the teleological and deontological modes of ethical thought. But what makes the ethical perspective considerably more difficult to apply to land resource issues than either the economic or ecological perspectives is the multiplicity of values built into that perspective. Unlike the economic or ecological perspectives—each of which basically springs from a unified, coherent set of values—the ethical perspective on land covers a much wider range of values, some of which work at cross purposes. One of the knottiest problems in using an ethical perspective, therefore, stems from the conflicts among competing "goods" built into the perspective. As one well-known ethics scholar contends, "most moral problems arise in situations where there is a conflict of duties, where on ethical principle pulls one way and another pulls the other way''(3).

This dilemma is illustrated well in a recently published book, where the author lays out some conflicting values that often butt up against each other in the real world, compounding the difficulty of making ethical choices affecting environmental issues(4):

- Economic fuel needs (coal, oil, etc.) versus environmental concerns.
- The psychological need to grow (inducing a quest for economic growth, jobs, and material products) versus the need to conserve resources.
- Passive acceptance of nature (based on the Judaic-Christian belief that nature is there to serve man) versus preserving and improving nature (based on an ecological belief).
- The philosophy of individual freedom versus the philosophy of collective restraint and collective decision-making.
- Faith in human abilities (for example, technology has the answer) versus caution about human error (for example, the problem of nuclear safety).
- Human rights and needs versus plant and animal welfare.

The author's categorization of these value conflicts is helpful because it clarifies our understanding of the complex ethical milieu in which environmentalists and to some extent land resource planners must operate. One could add other value conflicts to his list that are particularly applicable to the land resources area, for example, environmental protection versus equity and social justice for the have-nots; the growth ethic (producing more jobs and goods) versus the ecological ethic (favoring a steady state economy and use of more appropriate technology).

The point is that numerous ethical imperatives compete for attention in the real world, which makes it more difficult to sort out right from wrong in a practical sense. Consider the difficulty facing those who would like to achieve the commendable but numerous ethical imperatives embodied in one of Ashworth's land ethic prescriptions(2):

> You ought to ensure that the land use controls developed in your area prevent irreversible damage, avoid waste, protect your natural and cultural heritage, stimulate visual order, regulate and control the unsightly, and safeguard individual liberties (such as mobility and a choice in housing and schooling, so long as those liberties do not impede the liberties of others).

A tall order indeed!

Education a Critical Need

Given the difficulty of coming up with a clear, internally consistent ethical perspective on land resource issues, what then might be done to make that perspective a more potent and useful instrument for shaping future land resource policy? I see education of those who will shape future policy as a critical need. By this I mean educating the environmentalists, planners, developers, farmers, and public officials to think more carefuly, systematically, and analytically about ethics.

Here we can turn for assistance to the work of those currently rethinking how to teach applied ethics or "moral inquiry directed to making actual choices in moral conflicts" that deal with concrete human problems(5). Interest in applied ethics has increased steadily in the past decade. This interest rises out of symptoms of a moral vacuum in our society, a sense of moral drift and of ethical uncertainty. The field turns on exceedingly difficult ethical dilemmas that are also present in the sphere of land resources planning—tensions between freedom and justice, individual autonomy and government regulation, efficiency and equity, and the rights of individuals and the rights of society.

Drawing upon the summary report(5) of the recently completed nine-volume study by The Hastings Center on how applied ethics is taught in various professional schools, I would suggest a four-pronged educational agenda.

First, we must sort out more clearly the ethical issues and numerous ethical dilemmas involved in working in the land resources area, dilemmas arising out of conflicts among competing ethical principles as well as out of the clash between ends- and means-oriented ethical principles.

Second, we must elicit a greater sense of moral obligation and personal responsibility about what is done to the land resource in our system. We especially need to raise the level of moral anxiety of the public at large about what is being done with our land. As a starting point, those who work as custodians of the public's interest in land should seriously discuss and grapple with the ethical principles embodied in land and environmental ethic statements. If the land custodians pay only lip service to these principles, little progress will be made in educating the general public.

Third, we must develop, hone, and then use the skills of ethical analysis to arrive at ethical judgments. Attention to the following is especially needed:

- Carefully examining the multiple concepts of growth, equity, ecology, fairness, justice, individual rights, and others that underlie ethical issues in the land resource area.
- Tracing the implications of these concepts, an effort requiring both reason and imagination.
- Asking if consequences of ethical choice and action are the only pertinent criteria in judging their validity—characteristic of a teleological approach.
- As a corollary, asking if there are some ethical principles so central and critical to resolving land planning issues that the principles must be embraced regardless of the consequences.

And fourth, we must tolerate disagreements and be prepared to accept the inevitable ambiguities in attempting to examine ethical problems. At the same time, no less an attempt should be made to locate and clarify the sources of disagreement to resolve ambiguity as much as possible and to see if ways can be found to overcome differences in ethical views.

What I am proposing is essentially a vigorous, concerted effort at moral education of those in the business of shaping and affecting land resource policy and decisions. This is a formidable task, but in my judgment a necessary one if the ethical perspective is really to become a significant factor in coping with the land planning urgency our society faces.

REFERENCES CITED

1. Applegate, Rick. 1978. *Consider the future systematically*. J. Soil and Water Cons. 33(2): 54–55.
2. Barnes, Chaplin B. 1980. *A new land use ethic*. J. Soil and Water Cons. 35(2): 61–62.
3. Frankena, William K. 1973. *Ethics*. Prentice-Hall, Englewood Cliffs, N.J. 125 pp.
4. Fritsch, Albert J. 1980. *Environmental ethics*. Anchor Press, Garden City, N.Y. 309 pp.
5. Hastings Center Institute of Society, Ethics, and the Life Sciences. 1980. *The teaching of ethics in higher education*. Hastings-on-Hudson, N.Y. 103 pp.
6. Leopold, Aldo. 1966. *A Sand County almanac*. Ballantine Books, New York, N.Y. 295 pp.

16

Is There an Ecological Ethic?

Holmes Rolston III

The Ecological Conscience[1] is the arresting title of a representative environmental anthology. The puzzlement lies neither in the noun nor in the by now familiar modifier, but in their operation on each other. We are comfortable with a Christian or humanist ethic, but the moral noun does not regularly take a scientific adjective: a biological conscience, a geological conscience. In a celebrated survey, *The Subversive Science*,[2] where ecology reaches into our ultimate commitments, Paul Sears entitles an essay "The Steady State: Physical Law and Moral Choice." To see how odd, ethically and scientifically, is the conjunction, replace homeostasis with gravity or entropy.

The sense of anomaly will dissipate, though moral urgency may remain, if an environmental ethic proves to be only an ethic—utilitarian, hedonist, or whatever—*about* the environment, brought to it, informed concerning it, but not in principle ecologically formed or reformed. This would be like medical ethics, which is applied to but not derived from medical science. But we are sometimes promised more, a derivation in which the newest bioscience shapes (not to say, subverts) the ethic, a resurgent naturalistic ethics. "We must learn that nature includes an intrinsic value system," writes Ian McHarg.[3] A *Daedalus* collection is introduced with the same conviction: Environmental science "is the building of the structure of concepts and natural laws that will enable man to understand his place in nature. Such understanding must be one basis of the moral values that guide each human generation in exercising its stewardship over the earth. For this purpose ecology—the science of interactions among living things and their environments—is central."[4] We shall presently inquire into the claim that an eco-

From *Ethics*, Vol. 85, No. 2 (January 1975), pp. 93–109. © 1975. Reprinted by permission of The University of Chicago Press.

logical ultimacy lies in "The Balance of Nature: A Ground for Values." Just what sort of traffic is there here between science and morality?

The boundary between science and ethics is precise if we accept a pair of current (though not unargued) philosophical categories: the distinction between descriptive and prescriptive law. The former, in the indicative, marks the realm of science and history. The latter, including always an imperative, marks the realm of ethics. The route from one to the other, if any, is perhaps the most intransigent issue in moral philosophy, and he who so moves will be accused of the naturalistic fallacy. No set of statements of fact by itself entails any evaluative statement, except as some additional evaluative premise has been introduced. With careful analysis this evaluation will reappear, the ethics will separate out from the science. We shall press this logic on ecological ethics. Environmental science describes what is the case. An ethic prescribes what ought to be. But an environmnetal ethic? If our categories hold, perhaps we have a muddle. Or perhaps a paradox that yields light on the linkage between facts and values.

We find representative spokesmen for ecological morality not of a single mind. But the multiple species can, we suggest, be classified in two genera, following two concepts that are offered as moral sources. (*A*) Prominent in, or underlying, those whom we hear first is the connection of homeostasis with morality. This issues largely in what we term an ethic that is secondarily ecological. (*B*) Beyond this, surpassing though not necessarily gainsaying it, is the discovery of a moral ought inherent in recognition of the holistic character of the ecosystem, issuing in an ethic that is primarily ecological.

But first, consider an analogue. When advised that we ought to obey the laws of health, we analyze the injunction. The laws of health are nonmoral and operate inescapably on us. But, circumscribed by them, we have certain options: to employ them to our health, or to neglect them ("break them") to our hurt. Antecedent to the laws of health, the moral ought reappears in some such form as, "You ought not to harm yourself." Similarly the laws of psychology, economics, history, the social sciences, and indeed all applied sciences describe what is (has been, or may be) the case; but in confrontation with human agency, they prescribe what the agent must do if he is to attain a desired end. They yield a technical ought related to an if-clause at the agent's option. So far they are nonmoral; they become moral only as a moral principle binds the agent to some end. This, in turn, is transmitted through natural law to a proximate moral ought. Let us map this as follows:

Technical Ought	*Natural Law*	*Antecedent If-Option*
You ought not to break the laws of health	for the laws of health describe the conditions of welfare	if you wish not to harm yourself.

Proximate Moral Ought	Natural Law	Antecedent Moral Ought
You ought not to break the laws of health	for the laws of health describe the conditions of welfare	and you ought not to harm yourself.

Allow for the moment that (in the absence of overriding considerations) prudence is a moral virtue. How far can ecological ethics transpose to an analogous format?

A

Perhaps the paramount law in ecological theory is that of homeostasis. In material, our planetary ecosystem is essentially closed, and life proceeds by recycling transformations. In energy, the system is open, with balanced solar input and output, the cycling being in energy subsystems of aggradation and degradation. Homeostasis, it should be noted, is at once an achievement and a tendency. Systems recycle, and there is energy balance; yet the systems are not static, but dynamic, as the forces that yield equilibrium are in flux, seeking equilibrium yet veering from it to bring counterforces into play. This perpetual stir, tending to and deviating from equilibrium, drives the evolutionary process.

1. How does this translate morally? Let us consider first a guarded translation. In "The Steady State: Physical Law and Moral Choice," Paul Sears writes: "Probably men will always differ as to what constitutes the good life. They need not differ as to what is necessary for the long survival of man on earth. Assuming that this is our wish, the conditions are clear enough. As living beings we must come to terms with the environment about us, learning to get along with the liberal budget at our disposal, promoting rather than disrupting those great cycles of nature—of water movement, energy flow, and material transformation that have made life itself possible. As a physical goal, we must seek to attain what I have called a steady state."[5] The title of the article indicates that this is a moral "must." To assess this argument, begin with the following:

Technical Ought	Ecological Law	Antecedent If-Option
You ought to recycle	for the life-supporting ecosystem recycles or perishes	if you wish to preserve human life.

When we replace the if-option by an antecedent moral ought, we convert the technical ought to a proximate moral ought. Thus the "must" in the citation is initially one of physical necessity describing our circumscription by ecological law, and subsequently it is one of moral necessity when this law is conjoined with the life-promoting ought.

Proximate Ought	*Ecological Law*	*Antecedent Moral Ought*
You ought to recycle	for the life-support-ing ecosystem recy-cles or perishes	and you ought to pre-serve human life.

The antecedent ought Sears takes, fairly enough, to be common to many if not all our moral systems. Notice the sense in which we can break ecological law. Spelling the conditions of stability and instability, homeostatic laws operate on us willy-nilly, but within a necessary obedience we have options, some of which represent enlightened obedience. To break an ecological law, means then, to disregard its implications in regard to an antecedent moral ought.

Thus far ecological morality is informed about the environment, conforming to it, but is not yet an ethic in which environmental science affects principles. Antecedent to ecological input, there is a classical ethical principle, "promoting human life," which, when ecologically tutored, better understands life's circulations, whether in homeostasis, or in DDT, or strontium 90. Values do not (have to) lie in the world but may be imposed on it, as man prudentially manages the world.

2. Much attention has focused on a 1968 address, "The Tragedy of the Commons," given by Garrett Hardin to the American Association for the Advancement of Science. Hardin's argument, recently expanded to book length, proposes an ecologically based "fundamental extension in morality."[6] While complex in its ramifications and deserving of detailed analysis, the essential ethic is simple, built on the model of a village commons. Used by the villagers to graze cattle, the commons is close to is carrying capacity. Any villager who does not increase his livestock will be disadvantaged in the market. Following self-interest, each increases his herd; and the commons is destroyed. Extended to the planet, seen as a homeostatic system of finite resources the model's implication of impending tragedy is obvious. (The propriety of the extrapolation is arguable, but not at issue here.) The prescription of an ecological morality is "mutual coercion, mutually agreed on" in which we limit freedom to grow in order to stabilize the ecosystem to the mutual benefit of all.

To distill the ethics here is not difficult. We begin as before, with ecological law that yields options, which translate morally only with the addition of the life-promoting obligation.

Technical Ought	Ecological Law	Antecedent If-Option
We ought to stabilize the ecosystem thru mutually imposed limited growth	for the life-supporting ecosystem stabilizes at a finite carrying capacity or is destroyed	if we wish mutually to preserve human life.
Proximate Moral Ought	*Ecological Law*	*Antecedent Moral Ought*
We ought to stabilize the ecosystem thru mutually imposed self-limited growth	for the life-supporting ecosystem stabilizes at a finite carrying capacity or is destroyed	and we ought mutually to preserve human life.

To clarify the problem of mutual preservation, Hardin uses an essentially Hobbesian scheme. Every man is an ego set over against the community, acting in his own self-interest. But to check his neighbor's aggrandizement, he compromises and enters a social contract where, now acting in enlightened self-interest, he limits his own freedom to grow in return for a limitation of the encroaching freedom of his competitors. The result is surprisingly atomistic and anthropocentric, recalling the post-Darwinian biological model, lacking significant place for the mutal interdependence and symbiotic cooperation so prominent in recent ecology. In any event, it is clear enough that Hardin's environmental ethic is only a classical ethic applied in the matrix of ecological limitations.

Typically, ecological morality generated by population pressure resolves itself into a particular case of this kind, as for instance in the analysis of Paul Ehrlich in *The Population Bomb*. This is an ethic of scarcity, but morality since its inception has been conceived in scarcity.

3. Let us pass to a more venturesome translation of homeostasis into moral prescription, that of Thomas B. Colwell, Jr. "The balance of Nature provides an objective normative model which can be utilized as the ground of human value . . . Nor does the balance of Nature serve as the source of all our values. It is only the *ground* of whatever other values we may develop. But these other values must be consistent with it. The balance of Nature is, in other words, a kind of ultimate value . . . It is a *natural* norm, not a product of human convention or supernatural authority. It says in effect to man: 'This much at least you must do, this much you must be responsible for. You must at least develop and utilize energy systems which recycle their products back into Nature' . . . Human values are founded in objectively determinable ecological relations with Nature. The ends which we propose must be such as to be compatible with the ecosystems of Nature.'"[7]

Morality and homeostasis are clearly blended here, but it is not so clear how we relate or disentangle them. Much is embedded in the meanings of "ground of human value," "ultimate value," the mixed moral and physical "must," and the identification of a moral norm with a natural limit. Let us mark out first a purely technical ought, followed by an antecedent moral ought which may convert to a proximate moral ought.

Technical Ought	*Ecological Law*	*Antecedent If-Option*
You ought to recycle	for the value-supporting ecosystem recycles or perishes	if you wish to preserve the ground of human value.
Proximate Moral Ought	*Ecological Law*	*Antecedent Moral Ought*
You ought to recycle	for the value-supporting ecosystem recycles or perishes	and you ought to preserve the ground of human value.

The simplest reading of Colwell is to hold, despite his exaggerated terms, that the "ground of human value" means only the limiting condition, itself value free, within which values are to be constructed. Homeostasis is not "an ultimate value," only a precondition of the value enterprise, necessary but not sufficient for value. But then it is misleading to say that "human values have a root base in ecological relationships." For homeostasis, like scarce resources, or the cycling seasons, or soil characteristics, or the conservation of matter-energy, is a natural given, the stage on which the value-drama is played.

If, seeking to manage my finances wisely, I ask, "How shall I spend my money?" and you counsel, "You ought to balance your budget," the advice is sound enough, yet only preparatory to serious discussion of economic values. The balanced budget is necessary but not sufficient for value, a ground of value only in an enabling, not a fundamental sense; certainly not what we would ordinarily call an ultimate value. It is true, of course, that the means to any end can, in contexts of desperation and urgency, stand in short focus as ultimate values. Air, food, water, health, if we are deprived of them, become at once our concern. Call them ultimate values if you wish, but the ultimacy is instrumental, not intrinsic. We should think him immature whose principal goal was just to breathe, to eat, to drink, to be healthy—merely this and nothing more. We would judge a society stagnant whose ultimate goal was but to recycle. To say that the balance of nature is a ground for human values is not to draw any ethics from ecology, as may first appear, but only to recognize the necessary medium of ethical activity.

Thus far, ecological ethics reduces rather straightforwardly to the classical ethical query now advised of certain ecological boundaries. The stir is, to put it so, about the boundedness, not the morality. The ultimate science may well herald limits to growth; it challenges certain presumptions but rising standards of living, capitalism, progress, development, and so on; convictions that, though deeply entrenched parameters of human value, are issues of what is, can, or will be the case, not of what ought to be. This realization of limits, dramatically shift ethical application though it may, can hardly be said to reform our ethical roots, for the reason that its scope remains (when optimistic) a maximizing of human values or (when pessimistic) human survival. All goods are human goods, with nature an accessory. There is no endorsement of any natural rightness, only the acceptance of the natural given. It is ecological secondarily, but primarily anthropological.

B

The claim that morality is a derivative of the holistic character of the ecosystem proves more radical, for the ecological perspective penetrates not only the secondary but also the primary qualities of the ethic. It is ecological in substance, not merely in accident; it is ecological per se, not just consequentially.

Return, for instance, to Colwell. He seems to mean more than the minimal interpretation just given him. The mood is that the ecological circumscription of value is not itself amoral or premoral, neatly articulated from morality. Construct values though man may, he operates in an environmental context where he must ground his values in ecosystemic obedience. This "must" is ecologically descriptive: certain laws in fact circumscribe him and embrace his value enterprises. And it is also morally prescriptive: given options within parameters of necessary obedience, he morally ought to promote homeostasis. But here, advancing on the preceding argument, the claim seems to be that following ecological nature is not merely a prudential means to moral and valuational ends independent of nature but is an end in itself; or, more accurately, it is within man's relatedness to his environment that all man's values are grounded and supported. In that construction of values, man doubtless exceeds any environmental prescription, but nevertheless his values remain environmental reciprocals. They complement a homeostatic world. His valuations, like his other perceptions and knowings, are interactionary, drawn from environmental transactions, not merely brought to it. In this environmental encounter, he finds homeostasis a key to all values—the precondition of values, if you will—but one which, for all that, informs and shapes his other values by making them rational, corporate, environmental. But we are passing over to moral endorsement of the ecosystemic character, and to a tenor of argument that others make clearer.

Perhaps the most provocative such affirmation is in a deservedly seminal essay, "The Land Ethic," by Aldo Leopold. He concludes, "A thing is right when it tends to preserve the integrity, stability, and beauty of the biotic community. It is wrong when it tends otherwise."[8] Leopold writes in search of a morality of land use that escapes economic expediency. He too enjoins, proximately, recycling, but it is clear that his claim transcends the immediate context to teach that we morally ought to preserve the excellences of the ecosystem (or, more freely as we shall interpret him, to maximize the integrity, beauty, and stability of the ecosystem). He is seeking, as he says, to advance the ethical frontier from the merely interpersonal to the region of man in transaction with his environment.

Here the environmental perspective enters not simply at the level of the proximate ought which, environmentally informed and preceded by homocentrist moral principles, prescribes protection of the ecosystem. It acts at a higher level, as itself an antecedent ought, from which proximate oughts, such as the one earlier considered, about recycling, may be derived.

Proximate Moral Ought	*Ecological Law*	*Antecedent Moral Ought*
You ought to recycle	for recycling preserves the ecosystem	and you ought to preserve the integrity of the ecosystem.

Note how the antecedent parallels upper-level axioms in other systems (e.g., "You ought to maximize human good," or "You ought not to harm yourself or others," or "Love your neighbor as yourself"). Earlier, homeostatic connectedness did not really alter the moral focus; but here, in a shift of paradigms, the values hitherto reserved for man are reallocated to man in the environment.

Doubtless even Leopold's antecedent ought depends on a yet prior ought that one promote beauty and integrity, wherever he finds it. But this, like the injunction that one ought to promote the good, or that one ought to keep his promises, is so high level as to be, if not definitional or analytic, so general as to be virtually unarguable and therefore without any real theoretical content. Substantive values emerge only as something empirical is specified as the locus of value. In Leopold's case we have a feedback from ecological science which, prior to any effect on proximate moral oughts, informs the antecedent ought. There is a valuational element intrinsically related to the concepts utilized in ecological description. That is, the character of what is right in some basic sense, not just in application, is stated postecologically. Doubtless too, the natural course we choose to preserve is filtered through our concepts of beauty, stability, and integrity, concepts whose origins are not wholly clear and which are perhaps nonnatural. But, perspectival though this invariably is, what counts as beauty and integrity is not just brought to and imposed on the ecosystem but is discovered there. Let us map this as follows:

Proximate Moral Ought	*Ecological Law*	*Antecedent Moral Ought*	*Ecosystemic Evaluation*
You ought to recycle	for recycling preserves the integral ecosystem	and you ought to preserve the integrity of the ecosystem	for the integral ecosystem has value.

Our antecedent ought is not eco-free. Though preceding ecological law in the sense that, given this ought, one can transmit it via certain ecological laws to arrive at proximate oughts, it is itself a result of an ecosystemic appraisal.

This evaluation is not scientific description; hence not ecology per se, but metaecology. No amount of research can verify that the right is the optimum biotic community. Yet ecological description generates this evaluation of nature, endorsing the systemic rightness. The transition from "is" to "good" and thence to "ought" occurs here; we leave science to enter the domain of evaluation, from which an ethic follows. The injunction to recycle is technical, made under circumscription by ecological necessity and made moral only by the presence of an antecedent. The injunction to maximize the ecosystemic excellence is also ecologically derived but is an evaluative transition which is not made under necessity.

Our account initially suggests that ecological description is logically (if not chronologically) prior to the ecosystemic evaluation, the former generating the latter. But the connection of description with evaluation is more complex, for the description and evaluation to some extent arise together, and it is often difficult to say which is prior and which is subordinate. Ecological description finds unity, harmony, interdependence, stability, etc., and these are valuationally endorsed, yet they are found, to some extent, because we search with a disposition to value order, harmony, stability, unity. Still, the ecological description does not merely confirm these values, it informs them; and we find that the character, the empirical content, of order, harmony, stability is drawn from, no less than brought to, nature. In post-Darwinian nature, for instance, we looked for these values in vain, while with ecological description we now find them; yet the earlier data are not denied, only redescribed or set in a larger ecological context, and somewhere enroute our notions of harmony, stability, etc., have shifted too and we see beauty now where we could not see it before. What is ethically puzzling, and exciting, in the marriage and mutual transformation of ecological description and evaluation is that here an "ought" is not so much *derived* from an "is" as discovered simultaneously with it. As we progress from descriptions of fauna and flora, of cycles and pyramids, of stability and dynamism, on to intricacy, planetary opulence and interdependence, to unity and harmony with oppositions in counterpoint and synthesis, arriving at length at beauty and goodness, it is difficult to say where the natural facts leave off and where the natural values appear. For some observers at least, the sharp is/ought dichotomy is gone; the values seem to be there as soon as the facts are fully in, and both alike are properties of the system.

While it is frequently held that the basic criterion of the obligatory is the nonmoral value that is produced or sustained, there is novelty in what is taken as the nonmoral good—the ecosystem. Our ethical heritage largely attaches values and rights to persons, and if nonpersonal realms enter, they enter only as tributary to the personal. What is proposed here is a broadening of value, so that nature will cease to be merely "property" and become a commonwealth. The logic by which goodness is discovered or appreciated is notoriously evasive, and we can only reach it suggestively. "Ethics cannot be put into words," said Wittgenstein, such things *"make themselves manifest."*[9] We have a parallel, retrospectively, in the checkered advance of the ethical frontier recognizing intrinsic goodness, and accompanying rights, outside the self. If we now universalize "person," consider how slowly the circle has been enlarged fully to include aliens, strangers, infants, children, Negroes, Jews, slaves, women, Indians, prisoners, the elderly, the insane, the deformed, and even now we ponder the status of fetuses. Ecological ethics queries whether we ought again to universalize, recognizing the intrinsic value of every ecobiotic component.

Are there, first, existing ethical sentiments that are subecological, that is, which anticipate the ecological conscience, and on which we might build? Second, is the ecological evaluation authentic, or perhaps only a remodeled traditional humanist ethic? Lastly, what are the implications of maximizing the ecosystem, and what concept of nature warrants such evaluation?

1. Presumably the evaluation of a biotic community will rest partly on the worth of its elements, if not independently, then in matrix. We have a long-standing, if (in the West) rather philosophically neglected, tradition that grants some moral ought to the prevention of needless animal suffering: "A righteous man has regard for the life of his beasts" (Proverbs 12.10). Consider what we oddly call "humane" societies or laws against cockfighting, bear baiting, and (in our nation) bullfighting, and (in most states) steer

busting. We prohibit a child's torture of a cat; we prosecute the rancher who carelessly lets horses starve. Even the hunter pursues a wounded deer. That one ought to prevent needless cruelty has no obvious ecological foundation, much less a natural one, but the initial point is that animals are so far endowed with a value that conveys something like rights, or at least obligates us.

More revelatory is the increasingly common claim that one ought not to destroy life, or species, needlessly, regardless of suffering. We prevent the wanton slaughter of eagles, whether they suffer or not. Even the zealous varmint hunter seems to need the rationalization that crows rob the cornfield. He must malign the coyote and wolf to slay them enthusiastically. He cannot kill just for fun. We abhor the oilspills that devastate birdlife. The Sierra Club defends the preservation of grizzlies or whooping cranes on many counts as means to larger ends— as useful components of the ecosystem, for scientific study, or for our children's enjoyment. (We shall return to the integrated character of such argument.) But sufficiently pressed, the defense is that one ought not destroy a life form of beauty. Since ecosystems regularly eliminate species, this may be a nonecological ought. Yet it is not clearly so, for part of a species' evaluation arises as it is seen in environmental matrix. Meanwhile, we admit they should continue to exist, "as a matter of biotic right."[10]

This caliber of argument can be greatly extended. A reason given for the preservation of Cades Cove in the Great Smoky Mountains National Park is the variety of rare salamanders there. Certain butterflies occur rarely in isolated hummocks in the African grasslands. Formerly, unscrupulous collectors would collect a few hundred then burn out the hummock to destroy the species, and thereby drive up the price of their collections. I find myself persuaded that they morally ought not do this. Nor will the reason resolve into the evil of greed, but it remains the needless destruction of even a butterfly species. At scattered occurrences of rare ferns in Tennessee I refused to collect, not simply to leave them for others to enjoy, but morally unwilling to imperil a species. Such species are a fortiori environmentally pressed, yet they remain, and even prosper, in selected environmental niches, and their dispatch by human whim seems of a different order from their elimination by natural selection—something like the difference between murder and death by natural causes.

This respect enlarges to the landscape. We preserve certain features of natural beauty—the Grand Canyon, or Rainbow Bridge, or the Everglades. Though it seems odd to accord them "rights" (for proposals to confer rights on some new entity always sound linguistically odd), we go so far as to say that, judged to be places of beauty or wonder, they ought to be preserved. Is this only as a means to an end, that we and others may enjoy them? The answer is complex. At least some argue that, as with persons, they are somehow violated, even prostituted, if treated merely as means; we enjoy them very largely for what they are in themselves. To select some landscapes is not to judge the omitted ones valueless. They may be sacrificed to higher values, or perhaps selected environments are judged sufficiently representative of more abundant ones. That we do preserve any landscape indicates our discovery of value there, with its accompanying ought. Nor are such environments only the hospitable ones. We are increasingly drawn to the beauty of wilderness, desert, tundra, the arctic, and the sea. Planetary forces ever reshape landscapes, of course, and former environments are now extinct; nevertheless, we find in extant landscapes an order of beauty that we are unwilling to destroy.

2. Do we perhaps have, even in this proposed primary ecological ethic, some eco-free ought? If Leopold's preserving the ecosystem is merely ancillary to human interests, the veiled antecedent ought is still that we ought to maximize human good. Were we so to maximize the ecosystem we should have a corporate anthropological egoism, "human chauvinism," not a planetary altruism. The optimum ecosystem would be but a prudential means to human welfare, and our antecedent ought would no longer be primarily ecological, but as before, simply a familiar one, incidentally ecological in its prudence.

Even when richly appreciative of nature's values, much ecological moralizing does in fact mix the biosystemic welfare with an appeal to human interests. Reminiscent of Leopold, Réné Dubos suggests extending the Decalogue with an eleventh commandment, "Thou shalt strive for environmental quality." The justification may have a "resources" cast. We preserve wilderness and the maximally diverse ecosystem for reasons scientific and aesthetic. Natural museums serve as laboratories. Useless species may later be found useful. Diversity insures stability, especially if we err and our monocultures trigger environmental upset. Wild beauty adds a spiritual quality to life. "Were it only for selfish reasons, therefore, we must maintain variety and harmony in nature . . . Wilderness is not a luxury; it is a necessity for the protection of humanized nature and for the preservation of mental health."[11]

But the "were it only . . . " indicates that such reasons, if sufficient, are not ultimate. Deeper, nonselfish reasons respect "qualities inherent" in fauna, flora, landscape, "so as to foster their development." Haunting Western civilization is "the criminal conceit that nature is to be considered primarily as a source of raw materials and energy for human purposes," "the crude belief that man is the only value to be considered in managing the world and that the rest of nature can be thoughtlessly sacrificed to his welfare and whims." While holding that man is the creature who humanizes nature, the ecological conscience is sensitive to other worth. Indeed, somewhat paradoxically, it is only as man grants an intrinsic integrity to nature that he discovers his truest interests. " An enlightened anthropocentrism acknowledges that, in the long run, the world's good always coincides with man's own most meaningful good. Man can manipulate nature to his best interests only if he first loves her for her own sake."[12]

This coincidence of human and ecosystemic interests, frequent in environmental thought, is ethically confusing but fertile. To reduce ecological concern merely to human interests does not really exhaust the moral temper here, and only as we appreciate this will we see the ethical perspective significantly altered. That alteration centers in the dissolution of any firm boundary between man and the world. Ecology does not know an encapsulated ego over against his environment. Listen, for instance, to Paul Shepard: "Ecological thinking, on the other hand, requires a kind of vision across boundaries. The epidermis of the skin is ecologically like a pond surface or a forest soil, not a shell so much as a delicate interpenetration. It reveals the self ennobled and extended, rather than threatened, as part of the landscape, because the beauty and complexity of nature are continuous with ourselves."[13] Man's vascular system includes arteries, veins, rivers, oceans, and air currents. Cleaning a dump is not different in kind from filling a tooth. The self metabolically, if metaphorically, interpenetrates the ecosystem. The world is my body.

This mood frustrates and ultimately invalidates the effort to understand all ecological ethics as disguised human self-interest, for now, with the self expanded into the system, their interests merge. One may, from a limited perspective, maximize the systemic good to maximize human good, but one can hardly say that the former is only a means to the latter, since they both amount to the same thing differently described. We are acquainted with egoism, *égoïsme à deux, trois, quatres*, with familial and tribal egoism. But here is an *égoïsme à la système*, as the very etymology of "ecology" witnesses: the earth is one's household. In this planetary confraternity, there is a confluence of egoism and altruism. Or should we say that egoism is transformed into ecoism? To advocate the interests of the system as a means of promoting the interests of man (in an appeal to industry and to congressmen) is to operate with a limited understanding. If we wish, for rhetorical or pragmatic reasons, we may begin with maximizing human good. But when ecologically tutored, we see that this can be redescribed as maximizing the ecosystem. Our classical ought has been transformed, stretched, coextensively with an ecosystemic ought.

To illustrate, ponder the observation that biotic-environmental complexity is integrally related to the richness of human life. That the stability and integrity of an ecosystem is a function of its variety and diversity is a fairly well-established point; and it is frequently observed that complex life forms evolve only in complex environments. The long evolution of man, accordingly, has been possible only under the stimulation of many environments— marine, arboreal, savannah, tropical, temperate, even arctic. Even when man lives at a distance from some of these, they remain tributary to his life support. Without oceans, forests, and grasslands, human life would be imperiled. Thus man's complex life is a product of and is underlain by environmental complexity.

This complexity is not simply biological but also mental and cultural. For maximum noetic development, man requires an environmental exuberance. So Shepard eloquently introduces the "universal wisdom" of *The Subversive Science*:

> Internal complexity, as the mind of a primate, is an extension of natural complexity, measured by the variety of plants and animals and the variety of nerve cells—organic extensions of each other. The exuberance of kinds as the setting in which a good mind could evolve (to deal with a complex world) was not only a past condition. Man did not arrive in the world as though disembarking from a train in the city. He continues to arrive . . . This idea of natural complexity as a counterpart to human intricacy is central to an ecology of man. The creation of order, of which man is an example, is realized also in the number of species and habitats, an abundance of landscapes lush and poor. Even deserts and tundras increase the planetary opulence . . . Reduction of this variegation would, by extension then, be an amputation of man. To convert all "wastes"—all deserts, estuaries, tundras, ice-fields, marshes, steppes and moors—into cultivated fields and cities would impoverish rather than enrich life esthetically as well as ecologically.[14]

Mountains have both physical and psychic impact. Remove eagles from the sky and we will suffer a spiritual loss. For every landscape, there is an inscape; mental and environmental horizons reciprocate.

This supports, but only by curiously transforming, the preservation of the ecosystem in human self-interest, for the "self" has been so extended as to be ecosystemically redefined. The human welfare which we find in the enriched ecosystem is no longer recognizable as that of anthropocentrism. Man judges the ecosystem as "good" or "bad" not in short anthropocentric focus, but with enlarged perspective where the integrity of other species enriches him. The moral posture here recalls more familiar (if frequently unsettled) ethical themes: that self-interest and benevolence are not necessarily incompatible, especially where one derives personal fulfillment from the welfare of others; that treating the object of ethical concern as an end in itself is uplifting; that one's own integrity is enhanced by recognition of other integrities.

3. This environmental ethic is subject both to limits and to development, and a fair appraisal ought to recognize both. As a partial ethical source, it does not displace functioning social-personal codes, but brings into the scope of ethical transaction a realm once regarded as intrinsically valueless and governed largely by expediency. The new ethical parameter is not absolute but relative to classical criteria. Such extension will amplify conflicts of value, for human goods must now coexist with environmental goods. In operational detail this will require a new casuistry. Mutually supportive though the human and the ecosystemic interests may be, conflicts between individuals and parties, the rights of the component members of the ecosystem, the gap between the real and the ideal, will provide abundant quandaries.

Further, interpreting charitably, we are not asked to idolize the whole except as it is understood as a cosmos in which the corporate vision surrounds and limits, but does not suppress the individual. The focus does not only enlarge from man to other ecosystemic members, but from individuals of whatever kind to the system. Values are sometimes personalized; here the community holds values. This is not, of course, without precedent, for we now grant values to states, nations, churches, trusts, corporations, and communities. And they hold these values because of their structure in which individuals are beneficiaries. It is similar with the ecosystem, only more so; for when we recall its diffusion of the boundary between the individual and the ecosystem, we cannot say whether value in the system or in the individual is logically prior.

Leopold and Shepard do not mean to deep freeze the present ecosystem. Despite their preservationist vocabulary, their care for the biosystemic welfare allows for "alteration, management, and use."[15] We are not committed to this as the best possible ecosystem; it may well be that the role of man—at once "citizen" and "king"—is to govern what has hitherto been the partial success of the evolutionary process. Though we revere the earth, we may yet "humanize" it, a point made forcefully by Réné Dubos.[16] This permits interference with and rearrangement of nature's spontaneous course. It enjoins domestication, for part of the natural richness is its potential in human life support. We recognize man's creativity, development, openness, and dynamism.

Species regularly enter and exit nature's theater; perhaps natural selection currently tests species for their capacity to coexist with man. Orogenic and erosional forces have produced perpetual environmental flux; man may well transform his environment. But this should complement the beauty, integrity, and stability of the planetary biosystem, not do violence to it. There ought to be some rational showing that the alteration is enriching; that values are sacrificed for greater ones. For this reason the right is not that which maintains the ecosystemic status quo, but that which preserves its beauty, stability, and integrity.

What ought to be does not invariably coincide with what is; nevertheless, here is a mood that, recalling etymology again, we can best describe as man's being "at home" in his world. He accepts, cherishes his good earth. Purely scientific descriptions of an ecosystem may warrant the term "stability," neutrally used; they facilitate the estimate of its beauty and integrity. Added, though, is a response of the ecologist to his discoveries, an evocation of altering consciousness. We see integrity and beauty we missed before, partly through new realization of fact—interdependence, environmental fitness, hydrologic cycles, population rhythms, and feedback loops—and partly through transformed concepts of what counts as beauty and integrity, for world and concept mutually transform each other.

Though the full range of that shifting concept of nature and the ecological description which underlies it are beyond our scope, we can suggest their central axis. After Darwin (through misunderstanding him, perhaps), the world of design collapsed, and nature, for all its law, seemed random, accidental, chaotic, blind, crude, an "odious scene of violence."[17] Environmental science has been resurveying the post-Darwinian natural jungle and has increasingly set its conflicts within a dynamic web of life. Nature's savagery is much less wanton and clumsy than formerly supposed, and we are invited to see the ecosystem not merely in awe, but in "love, respect, and admiration."[18] Ecological thinking "moves us to silent wonder and glad affirmation."[19] Oppositions remain in ecological models, but in counterpoint. The system resists the very life it supports; indeed it is by resistance not less than environmental conductivity that life is stimulated. The integrity of species and individual is a function of a field where fullness lies in interlocking predation and symbiosis, construction and destruction, aggradation and degradation. The planet that Darrow characterized, in the post-Darwinian heyday, as a miserable little "wart"[20] in the universe, eminently unsuited to life, especially human life, is now a sheltered oasis in space. Its harmony is often strange, and it is not surprising that in our immaturity we mistook it, yet it is an intricate and delicate harmony nevertheless.

Man, an insider, is not spared environmental pressures, yet, in the full ecosystemic context, his integrity is supported by and rises from transaction with his world and therefore requires a corresponding dignity in his world partner. Of late, the world has ceased to threaten, save as we violate it. How starkly this gainsays the alienation that characterizes modern literature, seeing nature as basically rudderless, antipathetical, in need of monitoring and repair. More typically modern man, for all his technical prowess, has found himself distanced from nature, increasingly competent and decreasingly confident, at once distinguished and aggrandized, yet afloat on and adrift in an indifferent, if not a hostile universe. His world is at best a huge filling station; at worst a prison, or "nothingness." Not so for ecological man; confronting his world with deference to a community of value in which he shares, he is at home again. The new mood is epitomized, somewhat surprisingly, in reaction to space exploration, prompted by vivid photography of earth and by astronaut's nostalgia, generating both a new love for Spaceship Earth and a resolution to focus on reconciliation with it.

We shall surely not vindicate the natural sequence in every detail as being productive of ecosystemic health, and therefore we cannot simplify our ethic to an unreflective acceptance of what naturally is the case. We do not live in Eden, yet the trend is there, as ecological advance increasingly finds in the natural given stability, beauty, and integrity, and we are henceforth as willing to open our concepts to reformation by the world as to prejudge the natural order. The question of evolution as it governs our concept of nature is technically a separate one. We must judge the worth of the extant ecosystem independently of its origins. To do otherwise would be to slip into the genetic fallacy. A person has rights for what he is, regardless of his ancestry; and it may well be that an ignoble evolutionary process has issued in a present ecosystem in which we rightly rejoice. No one familiar with paleontology is likely to claim that the evolutionary sequence moves unfailingly and without loss toward an optimally beautiful and stable ecosystem. Yet many ecological mechanisms are also evolutionary, and the ecological reappraisal suggests as a next stage an evolutionary redescription, in which we think again whether evolutionary history, for all its groping, struggle, mutation, natural selection, randomness, and statistical movement, does not yield direction enough to ponder that nature has been enriching the ecosystem. The fossil record is all of ruins. We survey it first with a certain horror; but then out of the ruins emerges this integral ecosystem. He who can be persuaded of this latter truth will have an even more powerful ecological ethic, for the injunction to maximize the ecosystemic excellences will be an invitation to get in gear with the way the universe is operating. Linking his right to nature's processes, he will have, at length, an authentic naturalistic ethic.

The perils of transposing from a new science to a world view, patent in the history of scientific thought, are surpassed only by the perils of omitting to do so. Granted that we yet lack a clear account of the logic by which we get our values, it seems undeniable that we shape them in significant measure in accord with our notion of the kind of universe that we live in. Science has in centuries before us upset those values by reappraising the character of the universe. One has but to name Copernicus and Newton, in addition to our observation that we have lately lived in the shadow of Darwin. The ecological revolution may be of a similar order; it is undeniably at work reilluminating the world.

Darwin, though, often proves more fertile than his interpreters. When, in *The Descent of Man*, he traces the natural history of man's noblest attribute, the moral sense, he observes that "the standard of his morality rises higher and higher." Initially each attended his self-interest. The growth of conscience has been a continual expansion of the objects of his "social instincts and sympathies," first to family and tribe; then he "regarded more and more, not only the welfare, but the happiness of all his fellow-men;" then "his sympathies became more tender and widely diffused, extending to men of all races, to the imbecile, maimed, and other useless members of society, and finally to the lower animals . . ."[21] After the fauna, can we add the flora, the landscape, the seascape, the ecosystem? There would be something magnificent about an evolution of conscience that circumscribed the whole. If so, Leopold lies in the horizon of Darwin's vision. Much of the search for an ecological morality will, perhaps in necessary pragmatism, remain secondary, "conservative," where the ground is better charted, and where we mix ethics, science, and human interests under our logical control. But we judge the ethical frontier to be beyond, a primary revaluing where, in ethical creativity, conscience must evolve. The topography is largely uncharted; to cross it will require the daring, and caution, of a community of scientists and ethicists who can together map both the ecosystem and the ethical grammar appropriate for it.

Perhaps the cash value is the same whether our ethic is ecological in secondary or primary senses; yet in the latter I find appeal enough that it has my vote to be so if it can. To the one, man may be driven while he still fears the world that surrounds him. To the other, he can only be drawn in love.

NOTES

[1] Robert Disch, ed., *The Ecological Conscience: Values for Survival* (Englewood Cliffs, N.J.: Prentice-Hall, Inc., 1970).

[2] Paul Shepard and Daniel McKinley, eds., *The Subversive Science* (Boston: Houghton Mifflin Co., 1969).

[3] Ian L. McHarg, "Values, Process, and Form," in Disch, p. 21.

[4] Roger Revelle and Hans H. Landsberg, eds., *America's Changing Environment* (Boston: Beacon Press, 1970), p. xxii.

[5] Shepard and McKinley, p. 401.

[6] Garrett Hardin, "The Tragedy of the Commons," *Science* 162 (1968): 1243–48.

[7] Thomas B. Colwell, Jr., "The Balance of Nature: A Ground for Human Values," *Main Currents in Modern Thought* 26 (1969): 50.

[8] Aldo Leopold, "The Land Ethic," in *A Sand County Almanac* (New York: Oxford University Press, 1949), pp. 201–26.

[9]Ludwig Wittgenstein, *Tractatus Logico-Philosophicus*, trans. D. F. Pears and B. F. Mc-Guiness (London: Routledge & Kegan Paul, 1969), 6:421, 522.

[10]Leopold, p. 211.

[11]Réné Dubos, *A God Within* (New York: Charles Scribner's Sons, 1972), pp. 166–67.

[12]Ibid., pp. 40–41, 45.

[13]Shepard, p. 2.

[14]Ibid., pp. 4–5.

[15]Leopold, p. 204.

[16]Dubos, chap. 8.

[17]John Stuart Mill, "Nature," in *Collected Works* (Toronto: University of Toronto Press, 1969), 10:398. The phrase characterizes Mill's estimate of nature.

[18]Leopold, p. 223.

[19]Shepard, p. 10.

[20]Clarence Darrow, *The Story of My Life* (New York: Charles Scribner's Sons, 1932), p. 417.

[21]Charles Darwin, *The Descent of Man*, new ed. (New York: D. Appleton & Co., 1895), pp. 124–25.

17

Are We Ready for an
Ecological Morality?

Ernest Partridge*

A land ethic changes the role of homo sapiens *from conqueror of the land-community to plain member and citizen of it. It implies respect for his fellow-members, and also respect for the community as such.*

Aldo Leopold[1]

Introduction

A call for moral reassessment and reform invariably leads one to ask: "Could we bring it off?" Putting the matter another way, even if we affirm the moral worth of a proposed policy or course of action and acknowledge that we have the physical capacity and the knowledge to bring it about, we are immediately faced with the question: "Have we the psychological resources to do what is required of us?" Can we change long-established attitudes, habits, and patterns of behavior? This question of the psychological capacity for change, which arises alongside such public issues as racial and economic justice, foreign aid, educational reform, etc., may even be crucial to the very moral significance of these issues, for if human beings are essen-

*An earlier version of this paper was presented at the Hutchins Center for the Study of Democratic Institutions, 27 May 1981. The author is grateful to Karen Warren, who commented on the paper at the University of Georgia conference, for helpful suggestions and criticisms.

From *Environmental Ethics*, Vol. 4 (Summer 1982), pp. 175–190. Reprinted by permission of *Environmental Ethics* and the author. Copyright 1982.

tially incapable of carrying out their alleged duties, then, by the rule of "ought implies can," they might be blameless.

In this essay I deal with the question of the relevance of psychology to morality—of capacity to duty. In particular, I focus my attention on the question of the human psychological *capacity* to accept and implement Aldo Leopold's "land ethic" (which I also designate with the term *ecological morality*)—an environmental ethic that has been popular and influential in the "environmental movement" of the past decade. (Note that in this essay, the term *environmental ethics* is generic and thus neutral as to normative *content*. On the other hand, the term *ecological morality* refers to a *type* of environmental ethic—namely, the view that mankind should be regarded, and should act, not as a *master*, but as a *member* of the life community).

Ecological Morality—The Land Ethic

In his splendid essay, "The Land Ethic"—an essay that has profoundly touched and guided a generation of environmental students, scholars, and activists—Aldo Leopold describes a historical "extension" of ethical concern, focusing first upon the family and village, then the community, nation, and international community, and finally (though largely by anticipation) upon nature itself. Leopold observes that during the Homeric era, slaves were regarded as mere chattel and thus outside the realm of moral solicitude. Accordingly, as Homer records, Odysseus could, on whim, put all his slave girls to death, for "the girls were property [and] the disposal of property was then, as now, a matter of expedience, not of right or wrong.[2] Since then we have expanded our ethical criteria and extended their field of application. Leopold thus describes this "extension":

> The first ethics dealt with relation between individuals . . . later accretions dealt with the relation between the individual and society. The Golden Rule tries to integrate the individual to society; democracy to integrate social organization to the individual.

But here, he writes, we have come to a stop, for

> There is as yet no ethic dealing with man's relation to land and to the animals and plants which grow upon it. Land, like Odysseus' slave girls, is still property. The land-relation is still strictly economic, entailing privileges but not obligations.

The pause, however, is momentary for, Leopold continues, "the extension of ethics to this third element in human environment is, if I read the evidence correctly, an evolutionary possibility and an ecological necessity."[3] And what is the content of this "next step" in the ethical extension? Briefly this:

> We abuse land because we regard it as a commodity belonging to us. When we see land as a community to which we belong, we may begin to use it with love and respect. There is no other way for land to survive the impact of mechanized man, nor for us to reap from it the esthetic harvest it is capable, under science, of contributing to culture. That land is a community is the basic concept of ecology, but that land is to be loved and respected is an extension of ethics.[4]

And finally, in that most quotable formula: "A thing is right when it tends to preserve the integrity, stability, and beauty of the biotic community. It is wrong when it tends otherwise."[5]

Anthropologists and historians will find much to criticize in this account. Let us briefly review their complaints, if only to get past them and on to more substantive issues. First, the anthropologist will point out that in many primitive cultures, far greater moral concern may be given to animals (especially to members of one's totem species), or even to trees, rocks, and mountains, than are given to persons in other tribes, or, for that matter, even to persons of other clans within one's own tribe. (Such a pattern of moral solicitude may be more the rule than the exception). Thus, we find not an "extension of ethics," but a "leapfrogging" of ethics, over and beyond persons to natural beings and objects. Worse still for Leopold's view, a primitive culture's moral concern for nature often appears to "draw back" to a human-centered perspective as that culture evolves toward a civilized condition.

The historian might point out that there is abundant record of "ethical shrinkage" in the span of civilized history. Consider, for instance, the supplanting of the politically oriented ethics of Plato and Aristotle with the privatistic ethics of the Stoics and the Epicureans.[6] Later, the cosmopolitan concerns and involvements of the Roman citizen contrasted radically, in the Dark Ages, to involvement within the confines of the baron's feudal manor or at most (once again) the city-state. Finally, within the lifetimes of many of us, we have witnessed an erosion of the internationalism which immediately followed World War II to a resurgence of nationalism and, within nations, of regionalism and tribalism (as for instance in Nigeria, Uganda, Pakistan, and Canada).

The evidence of anthropology and history against Leopold's account of "ethical extension" is, I believe, conclusive—and quite beside the point of Leopold's essay. To appreciate this irrelevance we need only ask: suppose that Leopold, or an ecological moralist of similar views, were to agree to all these fact-claims of the cultural anthropologist and historian. Would he then abandon his position? He probably would not. More to the point, would he have *reason* to abandon his "land ethic"? Again, no—not, at least, if the ecological moralist had a clear idea of the logical status of his claim, for the larger significance of Leopold's land ethic is not as a description of cultural evolution or of historical trends. Instead, it is an *ethic*—a normative claim of the moral superiority of this perspective of man's place in, involvement with, and responsibility toward, nature. Far from being *derived* from the facts of culture and history, the land ethic is a moral position from which the ecological moralist *evaluates* cultural and historical trends. Accordingly, if we wish to evaluate the land ethic, we should not ask if this "extension of ethics" is reflected in the facts of ethnology and history (albeit Leopold comes perilously close to embracing this error). Rather, our questions should be *logical, normative*, and *metaethical*. The logical and conceptual issues are these: what is the content and the claim of ecological morality? Is this claim clear, consistent, and coherent?[7] The normative issue is simply this: is the land ethic a *good* ethic—that is, is it desirable that an individual or a society adopt and act upon it? Finally, the metaethical questions: what reasons might be offered to *justify* this point of view? Could an objective and rational person be persuaded to accept the land ethic? If so, then how? These are the sorts of questions that a moral philosopher would ask the ecological moralist and which that moralist must, if he is to avoid obscurity and dogmatism, be prepared to answer.[8]

Naive Wisdom and the Moral Sense

For some time I have been intrigued by the thought that some clarification and even justification of an ecological morality might be obtained through an application of recent studies in moral psychology, and particularly of moral development, to environmental ethics. In this regard, I am especially interested in the works of the philosopher John Rawls and the psychologist Lawrence Kohlberg. Those familiar with the writings of Rawls and Kohlberg may find this to be a rather surprising suggestion in view of the fact that neither have much, if anything, to say about environmental ethics. Indeed, their disengagement from this topic is at times quite explicit.[9] While I concede all this, I still believe that Rawls and Kohlberg offer some suggestions, and even some implicit points of comfort and support, to the ecological moralist. But if we are to find these, then clearly we have to do some digging and draw some bold implications. I am not at all convinced that attempts to apply developmental and moral psychology to the land ethic will be fruitful enterprise, but I believe that the idea is intriguing and promising enough to attempt some probes in this direction.

My first approach to moral psychology is through the work of John Rawls, from whom I borrow not a theory, but a suggestion. Rawls conceives of moral philosophy, in part and in its preliminary stages, as "the attempt to describe our moral capacity."[10] Like Kohlberg, and like the linguist, Noam Chomsky, Rawls is very much impressed with the capacity of the human mind to organize, structure, and coordinate experience, and to do so preconsciously. Thus, like a great many contemporary moral philosophers, he takes moral intuitions quite seriously—not as finished, refined, and self-sufficient guides to action, but as important *ingredients* of a moral philosophy, deserving careful review and analysis. While naive and uncritical intuitionism can unquestionably lead to atrocious moral hunches, even so one should not discount the value of the moral experiences that are reflected in our intuitions. This experience and these intuitions may be of considerable value even if they have not been subjected to the careful reflection, criticism, and refinement that characterizes a sophisticated moral philosophy.

On reflection, this approach appears to be very suggestive. In many cases, the moral sense can reveal to us deeper and subtler knowledge than we know that we have. Consider, as Rawls does, an analogy from linguistics.[11] Young children, and uneducated persons in general, can speak their native languages with correct grammar and do so without a remote notion of the rules that they are thereby following. Moreover, native speakers acquire a "sense" of grammatical "correctness" without taking courses in grammar that explicate the rules they unconsciously utilize. In a word, one can "know *how*" to speak grammatically without "knowing *what*" the rules are that he is following. Similarly, through the experience of functioning in a moderately just and well-ordered society and in a context of mutual trust and civility, one can acquire a sense of moral propriety, simply through the practical, day-by-day activity of satisfying one's needs and acquiring security, under conditions of moderate scarcity, cooperation and competition.[12] Just as one acquires a grammatical sense by speaking his language in particular circumstances, and not necessarily by reflecting upon the language *as such*, one can acquire a moral sense by facing, as all of us do in our daily lives, a sequence of morally significant circumstances: i.e., by balancing rights with duties, playing roles, perceiving oneself as an equal member of society with an equal allotment of rights and duties, and competing for scarce goods in a context of cooperative norms which optimize the life prospects, the productivity, and the security of each member of the community.

All this activity can be done, and done well, without deliberately engaging in abstract philosophical contemplation and the consequent explication of moral concepts and rules. This capacity accounts for what I call "naive wisdom," which is exemplified by "village sages" and "cracker-barrel philosophers." Such individuals, found in all ages and cultures, are those superannuated persons who, through a lifetime of alert, sensitive, intelligent involvement in the social life of their communities, acquire a sense of moral propriety, and who are honored and valued for this sense by members of their community—even though such individuals are, strictly speaking, formally unlearned, and even unprepared to supply a coherent, comprehensive, and abstract theory of moral philosophy as a foundation and justification of their moral maxims and advice.

"The village sage" illustrates the fact that "we may know more than we know that we know." He illustrates the point, made earlier, that the mind subconsciously organizes, assimilates, and structures the data of experience, clarifies concepts with ever increasing degrees of comprehensiveness, clarity, and cognitive adequacy, and, interestingly, that the mind may do all this without the aid and assistance of conscious, abstract, analytical thought.[13] As a self-confessed, practicing philosopher, I must hasten to add my conviction that the final cognitive product may be far superior if this native wisdom is supplemented, refined, extended, and clarified with the aid of careful, deliberate, explicit, and trained thought processes—namely, by philosophizing. Like Rawls, I believe that the moral sense is not the optimum product of human moral thought, but rather that it is an important ingredient of moral philosophy, and that the optimum product is achieved through a "reflective equilibrium" between our moral sense (Rawls calls it "considered moral judgment") and our critically evaluated, carefully articulated and structured, general moral principles.

Of course, we must always bear in mind that the moral sense is subject to what the computer scientists call "the GIGO rule"—"garbage in, garbage out." We are all too aware of cases in which "conventional morality" has embraced morally atrocious principles and practices. Essential, though not sufficient, to the development of a sound moral sense is an active involvement in a just and well-ordered community. This is the "input" that may lead to an acute moral sense. By extension, if we wish to judge the soundness of a conventional environmental ethic, we would be well-advised to examine the "input"—the society's understanding and utilization of its biotic environment, and that society's perception of its function in its biotic community.

To summarize: the moral sense arises out of a motivation to optimize security and satisfaction in the context of a community. (To oversimplify a complicated distinction: Rawls would emphasize the minimization of risk, while many utilitarians would emphasize the maximization of net satisfaction). Through this experience we learn that in order to "get" we must "give"—that is, in order to maximize our gains, we must regard ourselves as members of a community of like selves, and we must act accordingly. We must in short, assume, and act from, a "moral point of view." From that perspective, we find that the sacrifice of each for the welfare of all leads, ideally and eventually, to the maximization of prospects for each. Thus, we arrive at "the paradox of morality": namely, that in the well-ordered society, it is in one's best interest not to seek directly after one's best interest. The prospects of each are maximized by serving the prospects of all. This, in general, is the *rationale*, the "point," of the activity of social morality. (It would not be inappropriate to call it "the *game* of morality"). This rationale is, I believe, a fundamental coordinating principle, perhaps *the* fundamental principle, in "naive moral wisdom," regardless of whether or not the "sage" in question is aware of this abstract rule.[14] But while we have described here the "point" and function of the moral sense, we have not described the process of cognitive development that leads to mature moral judgment. For that insight, we turn next to the work of Lawrence Kohlberg.

Kohlberg's Theory of Cognitive Moral Development

In a continuing study of over twenty years' duration, Lawrence Kohlberg claims to have identified six distinct stages of moral development. The first two "pre-conventional" stages are characterized by responses to reward and punishment ("stage one") and by "instrumental" calculations of optimum means of satisfying personal (and occasionally others') needs and desires ("stage two"). The next two stages are "conventional," and are marked (in "stage three") by a conscious concern for the approval of significant others (e.g., family and friends) and (in "stage four") by an orientation toward and an obedience to the established order. The final two stages are "post-conventional" (also called "autonomous" and "principled"). With "stage five," a "social contract orientation" becomes dominant, and "right action tends to be defined in terms of general individual human rights, and standards which have been critically examined and agreed upon by the whole society." In "stage six," the highest stage of moral development (achieved by relatively few), "right is defined by the decision of conscience in accord with self-chosen *ethical principles* appealing to logical comprehensiveness, universality, and consistency."[15] Each stage, says Kohlberg, presents a more coherent, comprehensive, universal, rational—in a word, a more "cognitively adequate"—moral perspective. Moral development, then, displays intellectual, rational, affective, and normative growth. In short, the "facts" of psychological development parallel and embody *norms* of "desirable" moral growth.

It is obvious, at a glance, that we are dealing here with the development of *social* morality. Moreover, we are dealing with a theory that is both comprehensive and highly attractive to a cultivated moral sense, and, at the same time, very controversial and the target of severe criticism by both psychologists and philosophers. The theory is attractive to the sophisticated reader (who presumably has achieved a "post-conventional stage" of moral development) in that such a reader finds himself devoutly hoping that the theory is true and that it offers a rational mode of moral education and growth. But it just *seems* too good to be true. Alas, a review of the critical literature, and thoughtful examination of Kohlberg's ideas and methods, may indicate that the theory is just that—"too good to be true." Some philosophers find Kohlberg's account of morality to be oversimplistic and his methodology and data open to subjective and ambiguous interpretation. Most philosophers who have commented on his work readily agree that Kohlberg has "committed the naturalistic fallacy"—that is, that he has drawn *ought*-conclusions from *is*-premises, or *values* from *facts*. However, no philosophers, to my knowledge, will concede that Kohlberg has, in his own words, managed to "commit the naturalistic fallacy and get away with it."[16] Many psychologists find that independent replications of Kohlberg's experiments often produce contrary, or at best mixed, results. Kohlberg himself has recently found it necessary to make significant revisions in his theory of moral development.[17]

Fortunately, for our purposes, we can set much of this aside. We are not immediately interested in either the content or the form of judgments of social morality. Instead, we are concerned with the psychological "mechanisms" that allegedly move children and adults to "advance" to a "higher stage" of moral and cognitive adequacy. If we seek lessons here for the development of ecological conscience and, at the same time, attend too closely to Kohlberg's ideas regarding the refinement and advancement of concepts such as *rights* and of theories of justice, we may lose more than we gain. Ecological morality may well follow rules and stages of development that are unique to it.[18] (There are, after all, fundamental differences between social and ecological morality; the foremost being that *social* morality deals with communities of *persons*, while ecological morality deals with a person's interrelationships with the *natural* community.) Accordingly, we might be best advised to deal with the theoretical core of Kohlberg's thought—those general psychological theories of cognitive change, development, and growth that Kohlberg has ingeniously adopted from the work of the late Swiss psychologist, Jean Piaget. Because it is more general and drawn from a variety of psychological theories and studies, this "core" may be less controversial than the "peripheral" application of social morality. At the very least, the core of Kohlberg's thought, unlike the periphery, is clearly applicable to environmental ethics.

The essential core concepts and principles of Kohlberg's (and Piaget's) thought that might be applicable to the development of ecological conscience and morality are as follows:

(a) First, the human mind seeks order and structure. (This, I understand, is a central principle of cognitive psychology). Cognitive structure is sought both consciously and subconsciously, and once a pattern of cognitive structure is adopted, it tends to be maintained unless and until it is found to be clearly inadequate and inferior to a newly acquired structure. (See item [c], below).

(b) Cognitive structures can only order and reorder, assimilate, and reassimilate concepts that are available and intelligible to the individual at his particular developmental stage. Alien and incomprehensible concepts cannot be components of a cognitive structure.

(c) Cognitive structures are abandoned when they are found to be inadequate for the task of dealing with unique experiences and circumstances (i.e., "inadequate" in that they lack clarity, consistency, coherence, and comprehensiveness)—and when more adequate structures appear to be available and at hand which can be constituted of familiar and available experiences and concepts. It is at this point that the opportunity for cognitive growth arises.

(d) Cognitive growth follows from "dissonance" to "resolution." "Dissonance" may be described as a felt or perceived incapacity of the current cognitive structure to explain, comprehend, and resolve problems that are before the individual; or, it may be a failure, in the face of such problems, to harmonize apparently divergent and inconsistent components of the structure. "Resolution" occurs when the mind "grasps" a superior (or "a more cognitively adequate") mode of organizing cognitive elements—i.e., a new, "higher," state of cognitive structure—which serves to solve the previously recalcitrant problems. Thus, dissonance is essential to resolution and thus to cognitive growth.

(e) The "stages" of cognitive development are ordered *sequentially*, and *completely*; that is to say, cognitive growth takes place in stages that are encountered in invariable *order*, with no "skipping of stages. (But not all individuals achieve the "highest" stage of cognitive development.) This is due to the *logical* ordering of these stages—i.e., earlier stages are logically prerequisite to later stages. Because this final claim might appear unduly dogmatic, some elaboration is in order. Consider, for example, the development of the concept of "equal rights" and "just law." In the first case, to have a sense that others have equal rights to one's own (a concept that emerges in Kohlberg's third stage), one must first have a sense of one's *own* rights (a notion that arises in stage two). In the latter case, to seek, in "postconventional morality" (stages five and six) the grounds of *evaluation* of convention and law, one must first have a concept of "convention" and "legal authority" (which are the grounds of the "conventional" morality of stages three and four). In short, Kohlberg's stages of moral cognition are sequential and complete for the simple reason that each stage logically *incorporates* its predecessors. This explains, of course, why stages cannot be "skipped."

Kohlberg's theory of moral development has some significant implications for teaching method. First of all, the importance of role playing to moral education becomes paramount. Moral thinking and moral judgment beyond the pre-conventional stages requires personal abstraction—i.e., the capacity to view oneself as one of many participants in social interaction and, furthermore, the capacity to think in terms of the good of all rather than the good of oneself merely. Moral philosophers speak of this as "taking the moral point of view."

To encourage and develop this perspective of "the moral spectator," Kohlberg prescribes a teaching method which employs a varied menu of parables and hypothetical problems involving difficult moral decisions. These problems not only test and expand the capacity to view problems from the point of view of others (i.e., to play roles), but they also test and strain one's current stage of moral cognition—put it in a state of cognitive dissonance. If moral teaching is well executed, the method creates a condition of "creative dissonance." Finding that familiar cognitive structures are failing to resolve the problems before him, the student grasps at, and occasionally finds and assimilates, new and more adequate cognitive structures. At that point he is, perhaps, prepared to "ascend" to a higher, more adequate stage of moral cognition.

Kohlberg's teaching methodology is Socratic rather than discursive. The student cannot be "given" a new stage of moral cognition; instead, he must discover it for himself. Higher stages of moral cognition develop "from within'' and are created out of preexisting concepts and experiences. The teacher is not a "conveyer"; he is a "facilitator." The student grows only when he "sees" the greater cognitive adequacy of a newer and "higher" structure. But he must do the "seeing" for himself. If the teacher attempts too much, too soon, the student is not able to reassemble and restructure his thought and thus "make the jump" to a higher stage. Indeed, when faced with the anxiety of apparent moral chaos, he might even regress to an earlier, more "comfortable," stage.[19] It is apparent that Kohlberg has great confidence in the efficacy of "preconscious cognition"—that is, of "naive wisdom." Thus, he relies upon the capacity of the student to evaluate, classify, process, structure, and restructure experience and concepts, even when the student is not explicitly aware that these cognitive processes are taking place.

Kohlberg offers a profoundly optimistic view of moral development. Thus, one of the first critical responses must be: "If all this is true about human moral development, then why is the world in such moral disorder?" Clearly there is something missing in Kohlberg's theory, for while it may, at best, account for moral growth and development, it offers little explanation of moral fixation, moral failure, and moral regression.[20]

Given Kohlberg's cheerful account of moral development, how are we to explain moral atavism? One explanation might be that the individual may find himself amidst circumstances that do not encourage role playing.[21] Another possibility is that excessive dissonance, rather than encouraging greater cognitive scope, may lead to anxiety, rejection, and regression to an earlier stage. Thus, finding oneself in a stage of acute moral anxiety, one may seek, not a more "adequate" cognitive structure among unfamiliar and untried models of thought, but rather one may regress to the comfort of familiar, earlier, modes of thought—regardless of their cognitive inadequacy. (This account, of course, parallels Freud's explanation of regressive behavior. It may also serve to explain reactionary political movements.) Finally, a "higher stage" individual may find himself immersed in a social milieu that exemplifies a lower stage of moral cognition. (Some practical folks might characterize this as "the real world of dog-eat-dog competition.) "Cognitive adequacy" might thus lose out to pressures to "conform" to prevailing moral perceptions and precepts. This last condition might, in fact, explain some of the apparent regression from "post-conventional" to "conventional" stages that some of Kohlberg's subjects have recently displayed. These individuals, now into their thirties, have completed their formal education and have moved into the so-called "real world."

Moral Psychology and Ecological Morality

We are prepared, at last, to consider how these considerations of moral psychology might apply to ecological morality. We may do so by posing these questions: first, is there a "naive wisdom" in the ecological morality expounded by Aldo Leopold in his "Land Ethic" and also advocated by poets, artists, naturalists, adventurers, and environmental activists? What facts, experiences, and insights function preconsciously and prediscursively to bring forth a sense of solicitude, care, and responsibility toward nature? Second, does "The Land Ethic" describe a "higher stage" or morality— "higher" in Kohlberg's sense, in that it provides a greater "cognitive adequacy" for resolving the problems that we face both generally, as natural creatures in a natural environment, and specifically, in the face of the pressing emergencies of our particular time and condition in history? In this brief space I cannot offer a detailed answer to these questions. I might suggest, however, a sketch of a response to them.

Consider first a few items of fact, conjecture, and belief that are widespread, or if not widespread, nonetheless well-founded or strongly supported by scientific evidence—cognitive factors that might well encourage, through preconscious assimilation and explicit reflection, a strong sense of ecological conscience. First, consider some hard facts, largely drawn from the sciences of biology and ecology. It is a fact that man is a natural creature, both in his origin and in his sustenance. During virtually all of his biotic history, *Homo sapiens* has lived in and evolved out of natural environments. And to a degree that we cannot even imagine, he may still require natural environments. It is also a fact that our species is sustained by an integrated and interdependent life community.[22] When Leopold writes of mankind as part of a *community*, he is writing not of a mere ideal; he is describing a hard *fact*. Leopold also appears to be on objectively and factually solid grounds when he writes, "in human history, we have learned (I hope) that the conqueror role is eventually self-defeating." And why is this so? Because "it is implicit in such a role that the conqueror knows, *ex cathedra*, just what makes the community clock tick, and just what and who is valuable, and what and who is worthless in community life. It always turns out that he knows neither, and this is why his conquests eventually defeat themselves." The scientist, Leopold observes, "knows that the biotic mechanism is so complex that its workings may never be fully understood."[23] Leopold is correct, in the first place, because, practically speaking, we cannot understand all there is to know about that which we purport to "conquer"— namely, *nature*. But this omniscience is not only practically impossible, it is also *logically* impossible, for we are, in fact, *members* of the very system of which some of us would pretend to be *masters*. But we cannot *know* that system, for the simple but interesting reason that, as a *part* of that system, our very attempts to *know* the system *alters* the system. An attempt to "get ahead of" *that* process is as futile as an attempt to catch one's shadow or a rainbow.

If all this is so, then the "Abrahamic," "land-as-commodity" ethic will not work under the evolved conditions of modern civilization. Such an exploitative ethic will not work simply because it cannot accomplish what it pretends to accomplish, namely, a maximization of security and enjoyment for mankind, the intended beneficiary of this exploitation. Such a policy clearly fails even the test of utilitarian morality, not to mention other traditional theories of morality.

A moment ago, I made note of the biological fact that our species has, "for all of its biotic history, . . . lived in and evolved out of natural environments." We have scarcely touched upon the enormous implications of that stark fact. One implication of possibly profound significance is that we might have a genetically coded "need" for natural environments. As the botanist, Hugh Iltis, writes:

> . . . Every basic adaptation of the human body, be it the ear, the eye, the brain, yes, even our psyche, demands for proper functioning access to an environment similar, at least, to the one in which these structures evolved through natural selection over the past 100 millions years . . .

> . . . like the need for love, the need for nature, the need for its diversity and beauty, has a genetic basis. We cannot reject nature from our lives because we cannot change our genes.[24]

If Iltis and other biologists are correct, then, in a deep sense (pervading both conscious and preconscious awareness and response) we feel "at home" in natural surroundings. Conversely, a destruction of natural environments and systems, even the mere contemplation of such destruction, might thus strike a deeply dissonant "note" in our biotic-neural-psychological sensitivities. Surely these psychological consequences of our genetic "need" for natural stimuli and environments must play a part in the development and exercise of "naive wisdom" and favorably dispose those "in tune" with their natural surroundings and origins to an ethic of environmental restraint and responsibility.[25]

As both moral philosophers and moral psychologists suggest quite forcefully, healthy human beings need to direct their concern toward and invest their loyalties in enduring projects and ideals. Surely the most pervasive and enduring object of loyalty is the natural environment itself, which preceded mankind, nurtured it as a species, and which sustains it now. To contemplate even the possibility of the destruction of nature and of our species by our own hand and through our own greed and folly—to merely contemplate such calamity—must devastate our collective morale.

To summarize: there appears to be good and compelling reason and evidence for the general public to accept and acknowledge these fundamental facts: that our species has its origin and sustenance in natural environments; that we have evolved a genetic need to encounter and to live "in tune with" natural surroundings; and that we have a basic psychological need for concerns and loyalties that transcend our immediate selves and the immediate places and moments of our lives. All these facts, consciously known and acknowledged, or preconsciously apprehended, might incline even a nonreflective mind to assent to a "land ethic."[26]

We move next to our second summary question: "Does an ecological morality offer greater cognitive adequacy and a resolution of cognitive dissonance?" Well, what "dissonance" do we face, with a man-centered and a "now-centered" orientation? Is the prospect of the destruction of nature, just noted, pleasant to contemplate? Can we contemplate the vastness of time and biotic variety and complexity, and casually consent to the destruction thereof in our brief lifetimes? Can we, without moral anguish, hold the future of civilization in our careless hands—and crush It? When we acknowledge the presence of DDT in mothers' milk, strontium 90 and mercury in our seafood, acid rain falling on our lakes, forests, and farmlands, a daily net increase of a quarter of a million persons on the face of the Earth, the weekly extinction of dozens and perhaps hundreds of species—must we not conclude that we have not qualified ourselves to fulfill the role of "Abrahamic conquerors" and managers of nature? Might we not entertain the possibility that we *cannot* fulfill this role, and that, as a consequence, sizable portions of natural regions and ecosystems should be left to exist in magnificent independence and autonomy? In short, is it not all-too-apparent that the anthropocentric viewpoint has simply not done the cognitive and practical work that we have hoped and expected that it might do?—that it leaves us with too many puzzles and paradoxes? Do we not need, and need desperately, to find and grasp a new orientation? Do we not urgently need to acknowledge that "the moral paradox" obtains also in the natural community—that there is "a paradox of ecological morality" which tells us that mankind's ultimate best interests will be obtained by not directly seeking mankind's best interest, but rather by acknowledging and regarding ourselves to be what we are in fact—"plain citizens" and members of the community of life that created us and which sustains us? If all this is true, and we are aware of these truths, then it is fundamentally inconsistent, which is to say "cognitively dissonant," for us to regard ourselves as community members *in fact* (as the life sciences demonstrate), and yet to pretend to be masters and the ultimate justification of that community *in the moral sense.* It is time to resolve that dissonance into a new stage of moral awareness—into an ecological morality. But the time to do so may be brief, for conditions of our very making, which are now being brought so forcefully to our anguished attention, may soon overwhelm us and leave us with no capacity to respond intelligently and effectively. A resolution to act forcefully and appropriately to the biotic emergency before us may best be grounded in an acknowledgement of the *fact* of our interdependence with the life community, and in responding morally with a revised and reconstructed ethical theory.

According to Kohlberg's scheme, it appears that a historically pivotal moral prophet and teacher, such as a Socrates, a Jesus, a Gandhi, a King, preaches new moral ideas with lasting effect, when they are ideas "whose time has come." The moral prophet has lasting impact and effect when he finds his community in a state of creative cognitive dissonance, and offers a higher stage of resolution which might be enthusiastically and effectively accepted. Our closing question is this: is Aldo Leopold such a prophet? Is the land ethic an idea whose time has come? If so, then the answer to the title of this essay may be affirmative. Perhaps we *are* ready for an ecological Morality.

Rawls and Kohlberg might suggest to us that we *may* have a *capacity* for an ecological morality, but such a capacity, though *necessary* for a moral transformation, is not *sufficient*. We may resolve our dissonance by ascending to this new stage, but we cannot be certain that we will. Mankind's readiness for an ecological morality may be determined within the course of our lives, according to the content and conduct of our lives. Quite possibly the fate of our civilization, our posterity, our species, even of the biotic community itself, rests portentously upon the answer to that question: "Are we ready for an ecological morality?"

NOTES

[1] Aldo Leopold, "The Land Ethic," *A Sand County Almanac*, (New York: Ballantine Books, 1970), p. 240.

[2] Ibid., p. 237.

[3] Ibid., p. 238.

[4] Ibid., pp. xviii–xix.

[5] Ibid., p. 262. Moral philosophers will find much to quibble with here, but as a slogan, this statement is not without merit. Of course, an uncompromising determination to preserve ecological diversity and stability can exact enormous human costs, but as a statement of *prima facie* value, this may not be far off the mark.

[6] Several historians of philosophy attribute this "shrinkage" to the shift of political power from the autonomous Greek city-states to the distant political center of Imperial Rome. See, for instance, W. T. Jones, *A History of Western Philosophy* (New York: Harcourt Brace & World, 1969), vol. 1, pp. 315–17.

[7]These "logical and conceptual issues" are, strictly speaking, *metaethical*. However, the clarity of this presentation is better served by this order: conceptual clarification (metaethics), prescription (normative ethics) and justification (metaethics, again).

[8]Some critics have found the very term *ecological morality* to be suspicious in the sense that, strictly speaking, ecological morality might not qualify as a *moral* philosophy at all. And why not? "Because," notes Karen Warren, "presumably biotic communities consist of at least some nonpersons concerning whom we may have certain responsibilities, but with whom we do not share a moral point of view, and with whom we may not share any relevant moral status." (The quotation is from the excellent commentary by Warren that followed the presentation of this paper at the University of Georgia conference, 19 October 1981). We have here an apparent difference in opinion as to the criteria of *moral relationship*. According to my conception, a moral relationship is defined (a) by the capacities of the *agent* (namely, by the capacities that define him/her as a *person*), (b) by the axiological status of the *patient* (namely, that its value is, to some degree, *intrinsic*, or at least extrinsic to someone other than the agent), and (c) by the quality of the agent's motives, acts, or policies (namely, that these "relationships" with the patient reflect well upon the quality of the agent's character). Missing from my criteria list is the requirement that the patient be *personal* and thus, "share our moral status." The ecological moralist, of course, affirms that there are intrinsic values in nature (b). But ecological morality is more than an expression of aesthetic taste or an attribution of technical excellence (e.g., " 'Guernica' is a great painting" or "a Ferrari is a fine automobile"). It is also more than a set of prudential claims (e.g., "you should exercise more if you want to be healthy"). Statements of aesthetic or technical judgment fail to meet criterion (c), while prudential statements fail to meet criterion (b). The ecological moralist's assertions of environmental responsibility meet all these criteria and thus qualify as moral claims.

[9]Lawrence Kohlberg, "From Is to Ought: How to Commit the Naturalistic Fallacy and Get Away with It in the Study of Moral Development," in T. Mischel, ed., *Cognitive Development and Epistemology*, (New York: Academic Press, 1971), pp. 190–93. See also, John Rawls, *A Theory of Justice* (Cambridge: Harvard University Press, 1971), p. 512.

[10]In all fairness to Rawls, the omitted center portion of that passage should be cited here to indicate Rawls's tentativeness and reservations: "Now one may think of moral philosophy at first (and I stress the provisional nature of this view) as the attempt to describe our moral capacity; or, in the present case, one may regard a theory of justice as describing our sense of justice" (Rawls, *Theory of Justice*, p. 46).

[11]In this regard, Rawls explicitly cites the work of the linguist Noam Chomsky (Rawls, *Theory of Justice*, p. 47).

[12]See Rawls's discussion of "the circumstances of justice," *Theory of Justice*, pp. 126–30.

[13]Interestingly, Aldo Leopold, who, a generation ago, anticipated so much of our generation's moral philosophy, anticipated the significance of "naive wisdom" to moral insight in general, and to ecological ethics in particular. He wrote: "An ethic may be regarded as a mode of guidance for meeting ecological situations so new or intricate, or involving such deferred reactions, that the path of social expediency is not discernable to the average individual. Animal instincts are modes of guidance for the individual in meeting such situations. Ethics are possibly a kind of community instinct in-the-making" *(Sand County Almanac*, p. 239.)

[14]I am, of course, summarizing in this paragraph the findings of writings in philosophy and psychology. Just as a start, consider Garrett Hardin's "Tragedy of the Commons," *Science* 162 (1968): 1243–48, Ullmann-Margalit's *The Emergence of Norms* (Oxford: Clarendon Press, 1977), Rawls's *A Theory of Justice*. See also the writings of Michael Scriven, Stephen Toulmin, Marcus Singer, and Kai Nielsen. And again, for more indications of Aldo Leopold's astonishing anticipation of the "Good Reasons Approach" to moral philosophy, see pages 238–41 of "The Land Ethic," *Sand County Almanac*.

[15]Lawrence Kohlberg, "The Claim of Moral Adequacy of a Highest Stage of Moral Judgment," *Journal of Philosophy* 70 (1973): 632.

[16]Note the title (cited earlier) of one of Kohlberg's important papers: "From Is to Ought: How to Commit the Naturalistic Fallacy and Get Away with It . . ." Important criticisms of Kohlberg's theory have been published by the following philosophers: R. S. Peters and W. P. Alston (following Kohlberg's "From Is to Ought"), and also by R. G. Hensen and K. Baier. I am particularly disturbed by the problem of the ambiguity of Kohlberg's data, and the consequent opportunity for *ad hoc* interpretation and justification of the theory. (In this respect, Kohlberg's theory may share a weakness with that of Freud.)

[17]Critiques of Kohlberg by several psychologists are reviewed in Howard Muson's "Moral Thinking: Can It Be Taught?" *Psychology Today* 12, no. 9 (February 1979): 48-68, 92.

[18]Quite possibly the student of ecological morality might learn more from the cognitive development of nonmoral values, such as *aesthetic* values. After all, an important ingredient of an ecological morality is an appreciation of the experience of natural landscapes and environments. In this regard, see "The Environment and the Aesthetic Quality of Life," *Journal of Aesthetic Education* 4, no. 4 (October 1970): 5-140; also, Michael J. Parsons, "A Suggestion Concerning the Development of Aesthetic Experience in Children." *Journal of Aesthetics and Art Criticism* 34 (1976): 305-14.

[19]This is a conjecture on my part. In his earlier work, Kohlberg denied that "regression" could take place. Recently he has apparently had second thoughts about this. See Muson, "Moral Thinking."

[20]Again, Kohlberg has recently acknowledged that some of his longitudinal study subjects may have "regressed" to earlier stages. See Muson, "Moral Thinking," p. 54.

[21]Herein may be found an unanticipated and troublesome consequence of the evolving preference of children for TV viewing and their involvement in supervised "Little-League" team play in place of the informal, unsupervised playground activity that was the norm of previous generations. Implicit moral lessons may be "forced" upon a group of youngsters that meet, on their own, to play softball or touch football without coaches or referees. For instance, they learn that competition must take place in a context of tacit cooperation and role playing.

[22]Usually this interdependence is described *macro*-ecologically—in terms of our "external" involvements with other species. For a startling account of *micro*-ecology ("internal involvements"), see Lewis Thomas' superb book, *Lives of a Cell* (New York: Viking Press, 1974).

[23]Leopol, *Sand County Almanac*, pp. 240-41.

[24]Hugh Iltis, "To the Taxonomist and the Ecologist, Whose Fight Is the Preservation of Nature," *BioScience* 17 (1967): 887.

[25]I have examined and defended this idea at some length in my paper, "Why Care about the Future," in Partridge, ed., *Responsibilities to Future Generations* (Buffalo, N.Y.: Prometheus Books, 1981), pp. 203-20.

[26]An anonymous editorial writer in the New Yorker observes: "[How presumptuous] for a single generation, such as our own, to imagine that its wants and its political causes might conceivably justify our jeopardizing not just our inheritance, political and otherwise, but our inheritors as well—our sons and grandsons and the myriad unborn generations whose hopes and achievement we cannot know. It takes truly colossal arrogance. Is it possible that our generation thinks its own transient conflicts more weighty than the infinity of the human future?" *New Yorker*, 13 May 1972, reprinted in Partridge, ed., *Responsibilities to Future Generations*, pp. 21-22.

Appendix
1

Code of Ethics and Professional Conduct

American Institute of Certified Planners
(Adopted September 10, 1981)

This code is a guide to the ethical conduct required of members of the American Institute of Certified Planners. The Code also aims at informing the public of the principles to which professional planners are committed. Systematic discussion of the application of these principles, among planners and with the public, is itself essential behavior to bring the Code into daily use.

The code's standards of behavior provide a basis for adjudicating any charge that a member has acted unethically. However, the Code also provides more than the minimum threshold of enforceable acceptability. It sets aspirational standards that require conscious striving to attain.

The principles of the Code derive both from the general values of society and from the planning profession's special responsibility to serve the public interest. As the basic values of society are often in competition with each other, so also do the principles of this Code sometimes compete. For example, the need to provide full public information may compete with the need to respect confidences. Plans and programs often result from a balancing among divergent interests. An ethical judgment often also requires a conscientious balancing, based on the facts and context of a particular situation and on the precepts of the entire Code. Formal procedures for filing of complaints, investigation and resolution of alleged violations and the issuance of advisory rulings are part of the Code.

The Planner's Responsibility to the Public

A. A planner's primary obligation is to serve the public interest. While the definition of the public interest is formulated through continuous debate, a planner owes allegiance to a conscientiously attained concept of the public interest, which requires these special obligations:

1) A planner must have special concern for the long range consequences of present actions.

2) A planner must pay special attention to the interrelatedness of decisions.

3) A planner must strive to provide full, clear and accurate information on planning issues to citizens and governmental decision-makers.

4) A planner must strive to give citizens the opportunity to have a meaningful impact on the development of plans and programs. Participation should be broad enough to include people who lack formal organization or influence.

5) A planner must strive to expand choice and opportunity for all persons, recognizing a special responsibility to plan for the needs of disadvantaged groups and persons, and must urge the alteration of policies, institutions and decisions which oppose such needs.

6) A planner must strive to protect the integrity of the natural environment.

7) A planner must strive for excellence of environmental design and endeavor to conserve the heritage of the built environment.

The Planner's Responsibility to Clients and Employers

B. A planner owes diligent, creative, independent and competent performance of work in pursuit of the client's or employer's interest. Such performance should be consistent with the planner's faithful service to the public interest.

1) A planner must exercise independent professional judgment on behalf of clients and employers.

2) A planner must accept the decisions of a client or employer concerning the objectives and nature of the professional services to be performed unless the course of action to be pursued involves conduct which is illegal or inconsistent with the planner's primary obligation to the public interest.

3) A planner must not, without the consent of the client or employer, and only after full disclosure, accept or continue to perform work if there is an actual, apparent, or reasonably foreseeable conflict between the interests of the client or employer and the personal or financial interest of the planner or of another past or present client or employer of the planner.

4) A planner must not solicit prospective clients or employment through use of false or misleading claims, harassment or duress.

5) A planner must not sell or offer to sell services by stating or implying an ability to influence decisions by improper means.

6) A planner must not use the power of any office to seek or obtain a special advantage that is not in the public interest nor any special advantage that is not a matter of public knowledge.

7) A planner must not accept or continue to perform work beyond the planner's professional competence or accept work which cannot be performed with the promptness required by the prospective client or employer, or which is required by the circumstances of the assignment.

8) A planner must not reveal information gained in a professional relationship which the client or employer has requested be held inviolate. Exceptions to this requirement of non-disclosure may be made only when (a) required by process of law, or (b) required to prevent a clear violation of law, or (c) required to prevent a substantial injury to the public. Disclosure pursuant to (b) and (c) must not be made until after the planner has verified the facts and issues involved and, when practicable, has exhausted efforts to obtain reconsideration of the matter and has sought separate opinions on the issue from other qualified professionals employed by the client or employer.

The Planner's Responsibility to the Profession and to Colleagues

C. A planner should contribute to the development of the profession by improving knowledge and techniques, making work relevant to solutions of community problems, and increasing public understanding of planning activities. A planner should treat fairly the professional views of qualified colleagues and members of other professions.

1) A planner must protect and enhance the integrity of the profession and must be responsible in criticism of the profession.

2) A planner must accurately represent the qualifications, views and findings of colleagues.

3) A planner, who has responsibility for reviewing the work of other professionals, must fulfill this responsibility in a fair, considerate, professional and equitable manner.

4) A planner must share the results of experience and research which contribute to the body of planning knowledge.

5) A planner must examine the applicability of planning theories, methods and standards to the facts and analysis of each particular situation and must not accept the applicability of a customary solution without first establishing its appropriateness to the situation.

6) A planner must contribute time and information to the professional development of students, interns, beginning professionals and other colleagues.

7) A planner must strive to increase the opportunities for women and members of recognized minorities to become professional planners.

The Planner's Self-Responsibility

D. A planner should strive for high standards of professional integrity, proficiency and knowledge.

1) A planner must not commit a deliberately wrongful act which reflects adversely on the planner's professional fitness.

2) A planner must respect the rights of others and, in particular, must not improperly discriminate against persons.

3) A planner must strive to continue professional education.

4) A planner must accurately represent professional qualifications, education and affiliations.

5) A planner must systematically and critically analyze ethical issues in the practice of planning.

6) A planner must strive to contribute time and effort to groups lacking in adequate planning resources and to voluntary professional activities.

Procedures Under the Code of Ethics and Professional Conduct

1. Informal Advice and Formal Advisory Rulings: Any person may seek informal advice on ethics from the Executive Secretary of the AICP or from the Chair of a Chapter Professional Development Committee. Such advice shall not be binding upon the AICP.

Any person may file a written request with the Executive Secretary of the AICP for a formal advisory ruling on the propriety of any professional planner conduct. The request should contain sufficient facts, real or hypothetical, to permit a definitive opinion. If appropriate, the Executive Secretary shall then prepare and furnish a written formal advisory ruling to the inquiring party. This ruling may be published if endorsed by the AICP Ethics Committee. Published rulings, however, shall not include any actual names and places without the written consent of all persons to be named. A ruling may be relied upon by the person who requested it whether or not published. Published rulings shall be binding on all members of the AICP.

2. Charges Alleging Misconduct by an AICP Member: Any person may file in writing with the Executive Secretary of the AICP a charge of misconduct against an AICP member. The charge shall state the facts upon which it is based. The Executive Secretary shall furnish a copy of the charge to the respondent member.

The Executive Secretary shall determine whether the charge warrants an investigation. In the event a field investigation is deemed appropriate, the Executive Secretary will seek the assistance of the Chair of the Professional Development Committee of the appropriate APA Chapter.

The Executive Secretary with or without an investigation may dismiss the charge or issue a complaint against the respondent. In either event, notice shall be sent to the charging party and to the respondent advising of the determination and of the charging party's right to appeal the dismissal of the charge.

The Executive Secretary's decision to dismiss a charge may be appealed by the charging party within thirty days of receipt of written notification. The Executive Secretary shall promptly forward copies of the appeal to the members of the AICP Ethics Committee. The Ethics Committee may remand the charge to the Executive Secretary for further investigation and/or reconsideration, or the Committee may reverse the Executive Secretary's decision if it is contrary to the provisions of the Code or to prior Committee opinions.

If the Executive Secretary issues a complaint against a member, the latter shall have thirty days from receipt of the complaint to respond. In the absence of extraordinary circumstances which, in the opinion of the Ethics Committee, warrant a special exception, the failure of a respondent to deny any fact alleged in the complaint within the thirty day period will be deemed an admission of such fact.

If the response to the complaint reveals any disputed material fact, the respondent shall be granted a hearing before the Ethics Committee of the AICP or before any member or members of the Ethics Committee designated by the Committee's Chair to conduct the hearing. The hearing shall proceed without application of formal rules of evidence; however, the substantive rights of the respondent shall at all times be protected.

If a hearing is held, those conducting it shall promptly issue findings of fact which shall be transmitted to the full Committee, the respondent and the charging party. If no material fact was in dispute and no hearing held, the Ethics Committee need not issue findings of fact.

On the basis of the findings of fact and admissions, the Ethics Committee shall determine whether the Code has been violated and issue an opinion. A copy of the opinion shall be transmitted to the respondent, the charging party and the Commission. The Ethics Committee may concurrently submit a recommendation to the Commission that the respondent be expelled, suspended, publicly censured, or privately reprimanded. The respondent shall be sent a copy of the recommendation and shall be given no less than thirty days' notice to respond, in person and/or in writing before it is voted on by the Commission, which vote shall be within one year of the issuance of the complaint. Disciplinary action against a member and the official publication of an expulsion, suspension or public censure shall require the affirmative vote of six members (two-thirds) of the Commission.

The Executive Secretary shall publish all written opinions endorsed by the Commission or by the Ethics Committee, but shall omit actual names and places unless authorized by an affirmative vote of six members (two-thirds) of the Commission or in writing by the respondent.

Code of Professional Responsibility and Rules of Procedure

(This code is under study, with comprehensive revision in view, by a committee chaired by Lynn Vandegrift, AICP Commissioner).

Applicability to Members

Members of AICP shall be subject to the Code of Professional Responsibility. The code is divided into four parts: Canons, Rules of Discipline, Rules of Procedure for Disciplinary Cases and Opinion as to Conformity with Canons. The standards of professional conduct are expressed in general terms in the Canons, while the Rules of Discipline establish the minimum level of professional conduct. Any member whose professional conduct violates the Rules of Discipline shall be subject to expulsion, suspension or censure in accordance with the Rules of Procedure for Disciplinary Cases established.

Canons

The Canons are statements of axiomatic norms expressing in general terms the standards of professional conduct expected of planners.

(a) A planner primarily serves the public interest and shall accept or continue employment only when the planner can insure accommodation of the client's or employer's interest with the public interest.

(b) A planner shall seek to expand choice and opportunity for all persons, recognizing a special responsibility to plan for the needs of disadvantaged groups and persons, and shall urge the alteration of policies, institutions and decisions which militate against such objectives.

(c) A planner shall exercise independent professional judgment on behalf of clients or employers and shall serve them in a competent manner.

(d) A planner shall preserve the secrets and confidences of a client or employer.

(e) A planner shall assist in maintaining the integrity and competence of the planning profession.

(f) A planner shall avoid even the appearance of improper professional conduct.

Rules of Discipline

The following Rules of Discipline express the minimum level of conduct below which no member may fall without being subject to disciplinary action. The severity of action taken against a member found blameworthy of violating a Rule of Discipline shall be determined by the character of the offense and the circumstances surrounding it.

(a) A planner shall not engage in conduct involving dishonesty, fraud, deceit or misrepresentation.

(b) A planner shall not give compensation in any form to a person or organization to recommend or secure employment or as a reward for having made a recommendation resulting in employment.

(c) Except with the consent of the client or employer after full disclosure, or except as required by law, court or administrative order or subpoena, a planner shall not reveal, use to personal advantage or to the advantage of a third person, information gained in the professional relationship or employment that the client or employer has requested be held inviolative or the disclosure of which would likely be detrimental to the client or employer.

(d) Except with the consent of the client after full disclosure, a planner shall not accept or continue employment if the exercise of the planner's professional judgment on behalf of the client or employer will be, or reasonably may be, adversely affected by the planner's own financial, business, property or personal interest, or the planner's relationship, with another client or employer.

(e) Except with the consent of the planner's client or employer, after full disclosure, a planner shall not accept compensation for planning services rendered the client or employer from one other than that client or employer.

(f) A planner shall not permit a person who recommends, employs, or pays him or her to render planning services for another to direct or regulate his or her professional judgment in rendering such services.

(g) A planner shall not accept employment to perform planning services which the planner is not competent to perform.

(h) A planner shall not neglect planning services which the planner has agreed to perform; nor shall the planner render services without research and preparation adequate in the circumstances.

(i) A planner shall not give, lend or promise anything of value to a public official in order to influence or attempt to influence the official's judgment or actions.

(j) A planner who holds public office or employment shall not use the public position to obtain or attempt to obtain a special advantage in legislative or administrative matters for a client, an employer, or the planner personally under circumstances where the planner knows or it is obvious that such action is not in the public interest.

(k) A planner who holds public office or employment shall not accept anything of value or the promise of anything valuable, including prospective employment, from any person when the planner knows, or it is obvious, that the offer is for the purpose of influencing the planner's action as a public official or employee.

(l) A planner shall not state or imply that he or she is able to influence improperly any public official, legislative or administrative body.

(m) A planner shall not participate in violations of the Rules of Reference to AICP membership.

(n) A planner shall not directly or indirectly discriminate against any person because of said person's race, color, creed, sex or national origin in any aspect of job recruitment, hiring, conditions or employment, training, advancement or termination of employment.

Rules of Procedure in Disciplinary Cases

(a) Any person may file a charge of misconduct against an AICP member by transmitting to the Executive Secretary a statement of the charge, including the facts upon which it is based, the precise Rules of Discipline allegedly violated and all relevant dates. The Executive Secretary shall transmit copies of the charge and the name of the party who filed the charge to the accused member and to the AICP Executive Committee.

(b) If the Executive Secretary determines that the charge may be meritorious the Executive Secretary shall diligently conduct an investigation which shall include an invitation to the accused member to respond to the charge and an opportunity for the person who filed the charge to reply to any new facts raised by the accused member in his response. The investigation shall not be restricted to the precise facts stated in the charge, but may include other related conduct as possible violations of the Rules of Discipline.

(c) The Executive Secretary shall transmit to the Executive Committee a summary report of the investigation and a recommendation as to whether the charge should be dismissed or a complaint issued.

(d) The Executive Committee shall review the Executive Secretary's summary report and recommendations and direct either dismissal of the charge, or the issuance of a complaint.

(e) Upon the direction of the Executive Committee, the Executive Secretary shall prepare a complaint and transmit copies thereof to the accused member ("the respondent") and the party who filed the charge against the member. Service upon the accused member shall be made by certified mail.

(f) Within thirty days from receipt of the complaint the respondent shall file an answer to the complaint. The answer shall follow the paragraphs of the complaint and each fact alleged shall be admitted or denied. If the fact is denied, the answer may contain an affirmative statement of the respondent's version thereof. If the respondent fails to timely answer the complaint, the facts asserted to the complaint shall be deemed admitted, absent a showing by the respondent that the failure to timely answer was caused by extenuating circumstances warranting an extension of time for the respondent's answer.

(g) If the answer denies any facts alleged in the complaint the Executive Committee shall have authority to designate one or more of its members to examine witnesses and take testimony. The ordinary rules of evidence shall not apply to such examination of witnesses and taking of testimony; however, the substantive rights of the respondent shall at all time be preserved. Upon request of either the Executive Committee or the respondent, the testimony shall be transcribed and a copy furnished the respondent at his or her expense.

(h) Following a hearing the Executive Committee member(s) who conducted the hearing shall issue findings of fact and transmit a copy thereof to the respondent.

(i) On the basis of findings of fact at the close of the hearing and/or on the basis of the facts admitted by the answer or failure to timely answer the complaint the Executive Committee shall issue and publish its opinion whether the facts complained of and proved or admitted violated the Rules of Discipline. The name of a member determined to be blameworthy shall be omitted from the opinion.

(j) If the Executive Committee decides to recommend that the respondent be expelled, suspended or censured, the Committee shall transmit its recommendations in writing to the Commission of AICP for its approval or disapproval. A copy of the recommendation shall be transmitted to the respondent.

(k) The imposition of disciplinary action against a member and the official publication by AICP of such action shall require the affirmative vote of a majority of the Commission.

(l) The Executive Secretary shall notify the respondent of any disciplinary action taken by the Commission.

Opinions as to Conformity with Canons

(a) Any person may file with the Executive Secretary a request for an opinion on the propriety of professional conduct engaged in, or proposed to be engaged in, by a planner, provided that the conduct described appears to be the subject of a Canon and is not within the purview of a Rule of Discipline.

(b) The request shall state sufficient facts so that a definitive opinion may be rendered.

(c) If the Executive Secretary determines that the request is in conformity with (a) and (b) above, the Executive Secretary shall transmit the request to the members of the Institute Executive Committee.

(d) If the request identifies a specific planner whose conduct, or proposed conduct, is being questioned, the Executive Secretary shall notify the planner, unless the planner originated the request, transmit a copy of the request to the affected planner, and invite the planner to submit his/her own statement of facts for an opinion by the Executive Committee.

(e) The Executive Committee shall adopt all opinions by a majority vote. Dissenting Executive Committee members and Executive Committee members who voted with the majority or abstained may submit their own opinions, individually, or jointly with other Committee members.

(f) The names of actual persons and places shall not be mentioned or suggested in any opinion pursuant to (e) above, except upon request by the Executive Committee and the Commission of AICP and by an affirmative vote of a majority of the Commission.

(g) Each opinion shall be published by the Executive Secretary in an official publication of AICP or of APA. A copy of the opinion also shall be sent by the Executive Secretary to the requesting party and, if applicable, to a planner described in (d) above.

(h) The Executive Committee will not issue opinions on questions of law, or pertaining to conduct which is the subject of pending litigation.

(i) All facts contained in the request for an opinion, and in any opinion rendered, shall be deemed as hypothetical. The Executive Committee will not make findings as to disputed facts; nor will the Committee represent any facts in its opinions to be actual.

Rules of Reference to AICP Membership

Written. All written references to AICP membership shall be made in such a manner as to clearly indicate the name of the individual member referred to. The name or initials of AICP shall not be used in such a way as to imply that a firm or agency holds AICP membership. Nor shall the name or initials of AICP be used in general lists which indicate that one or more unspecified employees, partners, officers, staff members or contractors hold memberships in named organizations (for example, the phrase "professional affiliations of the staff" followed by a listing of professional or semiprofessional societies).

Written Forms. When making reference to individual membership in AICP on letterheads, publications, etc., the following forms shall be used: (a) Member, American Institute of Certified Planners, or (b) the initials "AICP" following the member's name.

Violations. All members of AICP shall be responsible for making these Rules of Reference known to their associates, employers, employees, or other persons responsible for the preparation of written materials which may include reference AICP membership. AICP members who are responsible for violations of the Rules of Reference shall be dealt with under the Code of Professional Responsibility. The Executive Secretary of AICP shall take steps to assure that non-members do not represent themselves to be AICP members. (The initials "APA" are not to be used with a member's name or in any manner that implies a professional qualification.)

Appendix
2

The Social Responsibility of the Planner

American Institute of Planners, 1973

This booklet contains the Guidelines for the Social Responsibility of the Planner adopted by the Board of Governors of the American Institute of Planners in 1972. These Guidelines were developed and reviewed by the membership of AIP in recognition that the planning profession is closely involved in public policies and decisions which affect the interests of minorities and other disadvantaged groups.

This booklet is published to help create better understanding among professional planners, public officials and the public at large as to the effects which public decisions have on all segments of the population served by planning.

The American Institute of Planners for several years has had a stated objective to foster social equality through the practice of planning. The AIP Code of Professional Responsibility contains a Canon which states that "*A planner shall seek to expand choice and opportunity for all persons, recognizing a special responsibility to plan for the needs of disadvantaged groups and persons, and shall urge the alteration of policies, institutions and decisions which militate against such objectives.*" These Guidelines on the Social Responsibility of the Planner help explain that Canon. This booklet contains General Guidelines and three specific short sections with Guidelines for planners in local areas, regional jurisdictions and state and federal programs.

The American Institute of Planners is the national professional society of urban and regional planners in the United States. Its members work primarily for local and state governments and other public agencies.

General Guidelines

1

The professional planner should recognize that a sound planning process requires familiarity with political and social realities, including the continuing need for, and real value in, working directly with those affected by the planning process. Of special importance is the need to identify the human consequences of alternative public actions, including identification of positive social and cultural values to be preserved, as well as short-term and long-term social costs and benefits of alternative courses of action.

2

The professional planner owes faithful, creative, and efficient performance of work in pursuit of his client's interest, but also owes allegiance to a conscientiously attained concept of the public interest and a primary commitment to maximize opportunity and expand the extent of choice available to those restricted by social, economic, personal or other constraints. When a professional planner considers that planning policies, instruments, organizations or institutions are not in the interests of those intended to be served by the planning process, he must strive diligently to ensure that they are altered to reflect such interests.

3

The professional planner involved in controversial social issues related to planning activities should determine and recommend the soundest course of action based on his professional judgment, regardless of the controversy attendant upon such recommendation.

4

The professional planner should explain clearly to local, state, and national political leaders the seriousness of existing, emerging and anticipated social problems relating to community planning and development, so that solutions will be given proper priority in allocation of resources and other public actions. Similarly, the urgency of social needs and undesirable or inequi-

table human consequences resulting from public actions should be transmitted to those with power to influence those actions.

5

The professional planner should use all available forms of communication
to make effective presentations on planning issues, planning alternatives
and their likely social effects, so that they are more readily understandable
by the public, particularly those directly affected.

6

The professional planner should seek to expand flexibility of governmental
procedures and institutions to ensure greater constructive citizen participation and involvement in the planning process and to foster leadership in all
groups, especially those neglected in public decisionmaking, because of
gaps in organization, leadership, or articulation of values and needs. The
planner should be intimately concerned with the judgments, values and
needs of specific groups and sub-groups.

7

The professional planner should recognize the wide human and intellectual
diversity within a planning area, and devise appropriate institutions to accommodate and respect that diversity, without unwarranted compromise
resulting in mediocrity.

8

The professional planner should carefully examine planning standards and
theory to determine their realism and their applicability to particular situations. This may call for new research or the systematic monitoring of progress or performance.

9

The professional planner should recommend the services of other professionals, whenever their specialized skills are needed in the constructive identification or measurement of social implications.

10

The professional planner should review achievements in collateral fields of social planning, and reconcile such efforts with his own. The role of the advocate planner must be related to the many forms of planning activity, and the advocate's functions acknowledged and supported.

11

The professional planner should seek opportunities to increase minority representation in the planning profession. This could be achieved by increasing minority representation in the Planning Department through adoption of a general minorities hiring policy, promoting planning education among minority groups by providing scholarship support, summer internship programs, and directly involving minorities in professional and paraprofessional duties in areas of predominant minority-group population.

12

The professional planner should seek every available opportunity to assist citizens in understanding the planning process. This should not be limited to citizen advisory committees or other institutional forms of citizen participation in a project, but should be extended to voluntary participation by the planner himself in citizen organizations in which he may have an interest. This will thereby provide useful technical insights, intimate working relationships with other members, assistance in understanding technical steps in the planning process and comprehension of planning nomenclature. However, the professional planner must avoid conflicts of interests in such undertakings, especially the premature or unauthorized revelation of confidential information.

Guidelines for Planners in Local Areas

1. The process of preparing and updating the comprehensive plan and elements thereof deserves critical attention. This process has been considered by critics to have institutionalized economic and social bias, or to have ignored social injustice by focusing on policies which ignore economic and social consequences of physical planning proposals.

2. Participation in plan-making by professionals fully aware of the problems of minorities and the poor, and who can represent the viewpoints of such groups, would aid in ensuring that the comprehensive plan reflects their aspirations. If the requisite combination of skills, understanding and independence is not available in staff personnel, they must be sought elsewhere.

3. Problems affecting areas of minority and low income concentration with which planning should deal include: The quality, supply, availability and location of low and moderate-income housing; transportation accessibility to employment opportunities, shopping areas, medical services, recreation areas, daycare centers, and educational facilities; location and adequacy of community and neighborhood facilities and services reasonably accessible to minorities, the poor, the young, the elderly, and the handicapped; the lower priority often given to environmental or physical development needs when compared to such immediate concerns as jobs, education and housing; location near ghetto areas of employers who utilize labor-intensive operations which can draw on workers who are residents of the area; and opportunities for minority-group members to establish their own businesses.

4. Where leadership in under-represented areas is lacking or obscure, token representation, acknowledgement of self-appointed spokesmen or cooptation of groups in the planning process should be avoided in favor of an effort to develop adequate representation and real spokesmen.

5. The planning process should involve means by which residents of low income and minority neighborhoods with inadequate experience due to prior unfamiliarity, may identify effects of proposed plans on their neighborhood.

6. A key point in the plan-making process is determination of program content. Program components should assure adequate attention to social problems and needs of the community, as well as identification of positive cultural and social values to be preserved. In communities where there is a built-in reluctance to deal directly with controversial social questions, the planner must develop a strategy to ensure their inclusion in the work program.

7. Technical analysis may subordinate social sensitivity unless there is a conscious evaluation of standards and approach. Technical studies must be conducted broadly enough to determine social impacts.

8. Functional or element plans (e.g. for housing, transportation, health, natural resources, personal and public safety, education, etc.) should reflect underlying social concerns. Appropriate coordination among functional planning and programming efforts should assure that activity in one function does not cancel out the social effectiveness of actions in others. This concern for the social impact of planning is as important for natural and man-made physical environment planning as it is for planning dealing with social and economic environments.

Guidelines for Professional Planners in Regional Jurisdictions (County, Metropolitan and Regional)

1. At the regional scale, there is a significant opportunity to reduce inequities established and perpetuated at the local level. Planners in regional jurisdictions should be aware of the unequal effects of local taxation and service costs, residential and economic discrimination, and poor accessibility to employment, and should seek to reduce such inequities, including critical review of local plans.

2. Regional and metropolitan planners should foster communication among local planners who should meet regularly with counterparts in surrounding communities to improve mutual understanding of related or parallel problems.

3. Regional or metropolitan planners should provide information services for local planners, with more limited resources, in evaluating social impacts of planning actions.

Guidelines for Professional Planners in State and Federal Programs

1. Distance from the neighborhood, where social issues are most apparent, demands from the state and federal planner caution in applying general planning standards or theories to a range of diverse situations. At these higher levels, where many decisions affecting the allocation of resources to local jurisdictions are made, social awareness is imperative.

2. State and federal planning should allow flexibility and choice within planning and a recognition that life styles and values vary significantly.

3. Planners working at state and federal levels should be especially careful that in drafting legislation and administrative guidelines, they reflect a con-

cern for the individual's opportunity to develop his abilities and to move socially and economically within American society.

4. Program administration can often provide the most important opportunities to assure freedom of choice and foster economic and social mobility. For instance, often state and federal programs are over-subscribed and choices must be made among the applicants; the planner should make every effort to give priority to proposals and projects which are socially significant.

5. State and federal planners must pursue changes in national priorities and resource allocation that contribute to alleviation of poverty and inequity, and should convey such concerns to those with the power and resources to change them. They should initiate needed legislative change relating to issues which have human consequences.

6. New forms of research and program monitoring should be pursued vigorously to maintain responsiveness and social awareness of ongoing state and federal programs.

Appendix
3

American Society for
Public Administration:

Statement of Principles, 1981

The American Society for Public Administration exists to advance the science, processes, and art of public administration. The Society affirms its responsibility to develop the spirit of professionalism within its membership, and to increase public awareness of moral standards in public service by its example. To this end we, the members of the Society, commit ourselves to the following principles:

1. Service to the public is beyond service to oneself.

2. The people are sovereign and those in public service are ultimately responsible to them.

3. Laws govern all actions of the public service. Where laws or regulations are ambiguous, leave discretion, or require change, we will seek to serve the best interests of the public.

4. Efficient and effective management is basic to public administration. Subversion through misuse of influence, fraud, waste, or abuse is intolerable. Employees who responsibly call attention to wrongdoing will be encouraged.

5. The merit system, equal opportunity, and affirmative action principles will be supported, implemented, and promoted.

6. Safeguarding the public trust is paramount. Conflicts of interest, bribes, gifts, or favors which subordinate public to private gains are unacceptable.

7. Service to the public creates demands for special sensitivity to the qualities of justice, courage, honesty, equity, competence and compassion. We esteem these qualities, and we will actively promote them.

8. Conscience performs a critical role in choosing among courses of action. It takes into account the moral ambiguities of life, and the necessity to examine value priorities: good ends never justify immoral means.

9. Public administrators are not engaged merely in preventing wrong, but in pursuing right through timely and energetic execution of their responsibilities.

Adopted by National Council
December 6, 1981

Appendix
4

A Code of Ethics for Government Service

PL 96–303 Signed by the President on July 3, 1980

    I. Put loyalty to the highest moral principles and the country above loyalty to persons, party or government department.

    II. Uphold the Constitution, laws, and regulations of the United States and of all governments therein and never be a party to their evasion.

    III. Give a full day's labor for a full day's pay; giving earnest effort and best thought to the performance of duties.

    IV. Seek to find and employ more efficient and economical ways of getting tasks accomplished.

    V. Never discriminate unfairly by the dispensing of special favors or privileges to anyone, whether for remuneration or not; and never accept, for himself or herself or for family members, favors or benefits under circumstances which might be construed by reasonable persons as influencing the performance of governmental duties.

    VI. Make no private promises of any kind binding upon the duties of the office, since a Government employee has no private work which can be binding on public duty.

    VII. Never engage in any business with the government either directly or indirectly, which is inconsistent with the conscientious performance of governmental duties.

    VIII. Never use any information gained confidentially in the performance of governmental duties as a means of making private profit.

    IX. Expose corruption wherever discovered.

    X. Uphold these principles, ever conscious that public office is a public trust.

Bibliography

Ethics of Professions

American Institute of Certified Planners. *Ethical Awareness in Planning*. AICP Publication Series No. 4. Washington: American Institute of Certified Planners, October 1983.

Baum, Howell S. "Politics and Ambivalence in Planners' Practice." *Journal of Planning Education and Research*, Vol. 3, No. 1, Summer 1983, pp. 13–22.

Bensman, Joseph. *Dollars and Sense: Ideology, Ethics, and the Meaning of Work in Profit and Nonprofit Organizations*. New York: MacMillan, 1967.

Bowman, James S. "Ethics in the Federal Service: A Post-Watergate View." *Midwest Review of Public Administration*, Vol. 11, March 1977, pp. 3–20.

Bowman, James S., editor. "Special Symposium Issue: Ethics in Government." *Public Personnel Management Review*, Vol. 10, No. 1, 1981.

Brewer, Garry D. *Politicians, Bureaucrats, and the Consultant: A Critique of Urban Problem Solving*. New York: Basic Books, 1973.

Brewer, Garry D. "What Ever Happened to Professionalism?" *Interfaces*, Vol. 8, No. 4, August 1978.

Chalk, Rosemary, Mark S. Frankel, and Sallie B. Chafer. *AAAS Professional Ethics Project: Professional Ethics Activities in the Scientific and Engineering Societies*. Washington: American Association for the Advancement of Science, 1980.

Chandler, Ralph Clark. "The Problem of Moral Reasoning in American Public Administration." *Public Administration Review*, 43, January/February 1983, pp. 32–39.

Euben, J. Peter. "Philosophy and the Professions." *Democracy*, Vol. 1, No. 2, April, 1981, pp. 112–127.

Frankel, Mark S. "Professional Ethics and Self Regulation." *4S: Journal of the Society for the Social Study of Science*, Vol. 4, No. 2, Spring 1979, pp. 13–14.

Galloway, T.D. and J.T. Edwards. "Critically Examining the Assumptions of Espoused Theory: The Case of City Planning and Management."

Journal of the American Planning Association, Vol. 48, No. 2, Spring 1982, pp. 184–195.

Graham, George A. "Ethical Guidelines for Public Administrators: Observations on Rules of the Game." *Public Administration Review*, Vol. 34, January/February 1974.

Hallett, Stanley James. *Ethical Issues in Urban Planning and Development*. Ph.D. Dissertation, Political Science, Boston University Graduate School, 1963.

Hallett, Stanley J. "Planning, Politics, and Ethics," in William R. Ewald, Jr., ed. *Environment for Man: The Next Fifty Years*. Indiana University Press, 1967.

Hirschman, Albert O. *Exit, Voice, and Loyalty*. Cambridge: Harvard University Press, 1970.

Howe, Elizabeth. "Public Professions and the Private Model of Professionalism." *Social Work*, Vol. 25, No. 3, May 1980, pp. 179–191.

Howe, Elizabeth. "Role Choices of Urban Planners." *Journal of the American Planning Association*, Vol. 46, No. 4, October 1980, pp. 398–409.

Howe, Elizabeth and Jerome Kaufman. "The Values of Contemporary American Planners." *Journal of the American Planning Association*, Vol. 47, No. 3, July 1981, pp. 266–278.

Howe, Elizabeth and Jerome Kaufman. "Ethics and Professional Practice in Planning and Related Policy Professions." *Policy Studies Journal*, Vol. 9, No. 4, 1980–81, pp. 585–595.

Kaufman, Jerome L. "Ethics and Planning: Some Insights from the Outside." *Journal of the American Planning Association*, Vol. 47, No. 2, April 1981, pp. 196–199.

Kernaghan, Kenneth. "Codes of Ethics and Public Administration: Progress, Problems, and Prospects." *Public Administration*, Vol. 58, Summer 1980, pp. 207–223.

Klosterman, Richard E. "A Public Interest Criterion." *Journal of the American Planning Association*, Vol. 46, No. 3, July 1980, pp. 323–333.

Levy, Charles S. "On the Development of a Code of Ethics." *Social Work*, Vol. 19, No. 2, March 1974, pp. 207–216.

Lilla, Mark T. "Ethos, Ethics, and Public Service." *The Public Interest*, No. 63, Spring 1981, pp. 3–17.

Livingston, Lawrence, Jr. "Confessions of a Planner." *Planning* 46, March 1980, pp. 30–33.

Mayo, J.M. "Sources of Job Dissatisfaction: Ideals Versus Realities in Planning." *Journal of the American Planning Association*, Vol. 48, No. 4, Autumn 1982, pp. 481–495.

Mosher, Frederick C. *Democracy and the Public Service.* New York: Oxford University Press, Second Edition, 1982.

Patriarche, John M. "Ethical Questions Which Public Administrators Face." *Public Management,* Vol. 57, June 1975, pp. 17–19.

Reamer, Frederick G. *Ethical Dilemmas in Social Service.* New York: Columbia University Press, 1982.

Sherwood, Frank P. "Professional Ethics." *Public Management,* Vol. 57, June 1975, pp. 13–14.

Slayton, Philip and Michael J. Trebilcock, eds. *The Professions and Public Policy.* Toronto: University of Toronto Press, 1978.

Wakefield, Susan. "Ethics and the Public Service: A Case for Individual Responsibility." *Public Administration Review,* Vol. 36, No. 6, November-December 1976, pp. 661–666.

Ethical Dimensions of Public Policy and Policymaking

Aram, John D. *Dilemmas of Administrative Behavior.* Englewood Cliffs, NJ: Prentice-Hall, 1976.

Arkes, Hadley. *The Philosopher in the City: The Moral Dimensions of Urban Politics.* Princeton, NJ: Princeton University Press, 1971.

Appleby, Paul H. *Morality and Administration in Democratic Government.* Baton Rouge: Louisiana State University Press, 1952.

Bailey, Stephen K. "Ethics and the Public Service," in Roscoe C. Martin, ed., *Public Administration and Democracy.* Syracuse: Syracuse University Press, 1965, pp. 283–298.

Baum, Robert. *Ethical Arguments for Analysis.* New York: Holt, Rinehart and Winston, 1975.

Behn, Robert. "Policy Analysis and Policy Politics." *Journal of Policy Analysis,* Spring 1981.

Berger, Peter L. *Pyramids of Sacrifice: Political Ethics and Social Change.* Doubleday, 1976.

Bernstein, Marver H. "Ethics in Government: The Problems in Perspective." *National Civic Review,* Vol. 61, No. 7, July 1972, pp. 341–347.

Beyle, Thad, and George Lathrop, eds. *Planning and Politics.* New York: Odyssey Press, 1974.

Bok, Sissela. *Lying: Moral Choice in Public and Private Life.* New York: Pantheon Books, 1978.

Boulding, Kenneth E. "The Ethics of Rational Decisionmaking." *Management Science,* Vol. 12, No. 6, February 1966, pp. B-161-B-169.

Bowie, Norman E., ed. *Ethical Issues in Government.* Philosophical Monographs, Third Annual Series. Philadelphia: Temple University Press, 1981.

Brown, Peter G. "Ethics and Policy Research." *Policy Analysis*, Vol. 2, 1976, pp. 325–340.

Brown, Peter. "Ethics and Policy: A Preliminary Agenda." *Policy Studies Journal*, Vol. 7, No. 1, Autumn 1978, pp. 132–137.

Caiden, Gerald. "Ethics in the Public Service: Codification Misses the Real Target." *Public Personnel Management*, Vol. 10, No. 1, 1981, pp. 140–152.

Caplan, Arthur L. and Daniel Callahan. *Ethics in Hard Times*. New York: Plenum Press, 1981.

Carritt, Edgar F. *Ethical and Political Thinking*. Greenwood, 1973. Reprint of 1947 edition.

Dagger, R.K. "What is Political Obligation?" *American Political Science Review*, Vol. 71, March 1977, pp. 86–94.

Dallmayr, Fred. "Toward a Critical Reconstruction of Ethics and Politics." *Journal of Politics*, Vol. 36, No. 4, November 1974, pp. 926–57.

Diamond, Martin. "Ethics and Politics: The American Way," in Robert Horowitz, ed., *The Moral Foundations of American Democracy*. Charlottesville: University of Virginia Press, 1977.

Douglas, Paul H. *Ethics in Government*. Greenwood, 1972, Reprint of 1952 Edition.

Dunn, William N., ed. *Values, Ethics, and the Practice of Policy Analysis*. Lexington, MA: Lexington Books, 1983.

Edwards, J.T., and T.D. Galloway. "Freedom and Inequality: Dimensions of Political Ideology Among City Planners and City Managers." *Urban Affairs Quarterly*, Vol. 17, 1981, pp. 173–193.

Fainstein, Susan and Norman Fainstein. "City Planning and Political Values." *Urban Affairs Quarterly*, Vol. 6, No. 3, March 1971, pp. 341–362.

Fischer, Frank. *Politics, Values, and Public Policy: The Problem of Methodology*. Boulder: Westview Press, 1980.

Fleishman, Joel L. et al., eds. *Public Duties: The Moral Obligations of Government Officials*. Cambridge: Harvard University Press, 1981.

Forster, John. "Planning in the Face of Power." *Journal of the American Planning Association*, Vol. 48, No. 1, Winter 1982, pp. 67–80.

Gawthrop, Louis C. "Administrative Responsibility: Public Policy and the Wilsonian Legacy." *Policy Studies Journal*, Vol. 5, No. 1, Autumn 1976, pp. 108–113.

Golembiewski, Robert. *Men, Management, and Morality: Toward an Organizational Ethic*. New York: McGraw-Hill, 1965.

Haughey, John G., ed. *Personal Values in Public Policy: Conversations on Government Decision-Making*. New York: Paulist Press, 1979.

Hoover, Robert C. "A View of Ethics and Planning." *Journal of the American Institute of Planners*, Vol. 27, No. 4, November 1961, pp. 293–304.

Johnson, Wallace. *Responsible Individualism: Perspectives on a Political Philosophy for Our Time*. New York: Devin-Adair Co., 1967.

Jones, Donald G., ed. *Private and Public Ethics: Tensions Between Conscience and Institutional Responsibility*. New York: E. Mellen Press, 1978.

Jonsen, Albert R. and Lewis H. Butler. "Public Ethics and Policy Making." *The Hastings Center Report 5*, August 1975, p. 29.

Kaplan, Abraham. *American Ethics and Public Policy*. New York: Oxford University Press, 1963.

Ladd, John. "Policy Studies and Ethics." *Policy Studies Journal*, Vol. 2, No. 1, Autumn 1973, pp. 38–43.

Lee, James E. "Planning and Professionalism." *Journal of the American Institute of Planners*, Vol. 26, No. 1, February 1960, pp. 25–30.

Leys, Wayne A.R. *Ethics and Social Policy*. New York: Prentice-Hall, 1941.

Leys, Wayne A.R. *Ethics and Policy Decisions: The Art of Asking Deliberative Questions*. New York: Prentice-Hall, 1952.

MacRae, Duncan, Jr. "Scientific Communication, Ethical Argument and Public Policy." *American Political Science Review*, Vol. 65, No. 1, March 1971, pp. 38–50.

Moen, E. "Voodoo Forecasting: Technical, Political, and Ethical Issues Regarding the Projection of Local Population Growth." *Population Research and Policy Review*, Vol. 3, No. 1, January 1984, pp. 1–25.

Orlans, H. "Neutrality and Advocacy in Policy Research." *Policy Sciences*, 6, 1975, pp. 107–119.

Pennock, J. Roland and John W. Chapman, eds. *Compromise in Ethics, Law, and Politics* (Nomos XXI: Yearbook of the American Society for Political and Legal Philosophy). New York: New York University Press, 1979.

Price, David E. "Public Policy and Ethics." *Hastings Center Report*, Vol. 7, No. 6, December 1977, pp. 4–6.

Quade, E.S. *Analysis for Public Decisions*. New York: American Elsivier, 1975.

Rohr, John A. *Ethics for Bureaucrats: An Essay on Law and Values*. New York: Marcel Dekker, Inc., 1978.

Rosenbaum, Walter A. *The Burning of the Farm Population Estimates*. Inter-University Case Program #83. Indianapolis: Bobbs-Merrill, 1965.

Sayre, Kenneth, ed. *Values in the Electric Power Industry*. Notre Dame, IN: University of Notre Dame Press, 1977.

Schneider, Herbert W. *Three Dimensions of Public Morality*. 1973 reprint of 1956 Edition, Kennikat.

Schon, Donald. *The Reflective Practitioner*. New York: Basic Books, 1983.

Simmons, Alan John. *Moral Principles and Political Obligations*. Princeton, NJ: Princeton University Press, 1979.

Sundquist, James. "Reflections on Watergate: Lessons for Public Administration." *Public Administration Review*, Vol. 34, Sept./Oct. 1974.

Swartzman, Daniel et al., eds. *Cost-Benefit Analysis and Environmental Regulations: Politics, Ethics, and Methods*. Washington: The Conservation Foundation, 1982.

Tribe, Laurence H. "Policy Science: Analysis or Ideology?" *Philosophy and Public Affairs*, Vol. 2, No. 1, Fall 1972, pp. 66–110.

Walzer, Michael. "Political Action: The Problem of Dirty Hands." *Philosophy and Public Affairs*, Vol. 2, No. 2, Winter 1975, pp. 160–180.

Weisband, Edward and Thomas M. Frank. *Resignation in Protest*. New York: Grossman, 1975.

Yadlosky, Elizabeth, and Richard Ehlke. "Provisions in the United States Code Prohibiting Conflicts of Interest by Members of Congress and by the U.S. Government Officials and Employees." Congressional Reference Service, Library of Congress, 73-29A, January 1973.

Corruption

Caiden, Gerald and Naomi J. Caiden. "Administrative Corruption." *Public Administration Review*, Vol. 37, No. 3, May–June 1977, pp. 301–309.

Gardiner, John A. and David J. Olson, ed. *Theft of the City: Readings on Corruption in Urban America*. Bloomington: Indiana University Press, 1974.

McCahill, Ed. "Stealing: A Primer on Zoning Corruption." *Planning*, 39, December 1973, pp. 6–8.

Peters, J. and S. Welch. "Political Corruption in America: A Search for Definitions and a Theory." *American Political Science Review*, Vol. 72, 1978, pp. 974–984.

Rose-Ackerman, S. *Corruption: A Study in Political Economy*. New York: Academic Press, 1978.

Environmental Ethics

Ashby, Eric. "The Search for an Environmental Ethic," in *Tanner Lectures on Human Values, 1980*. Salt Lake City: University of Utah Press, 1980.

Barbour, Ian G., ed. *Western Man and Environmental Ethics: Attitudes Toward Nature and Technology*. Reading, Mass.: Addison-Wesley Publishing Co., 1973.

Blackstone, William T., ed. *Philosophy and Environmental Crisis*. Athens: University of Georgia Press, 1974.

DeGeorge, Richard T. "The Environment, Rights, and Future Generations," in K. E. Goodpastor, and K. M. Sayre, eds. *Ethics and Problems of the 21st Century*. Notre Dame: University of Notre Dame Press, 1979.

Frankena, W.K. "Ethics and the Environment," in Goodpastor and Sayre, *Ethics and Problems of the 21st Century*, Notre Dame: University of Notre Dame Press, 1979, pp. 2–20.

Leopold, Aldo. *A Sand County Almanac and Sketches from Here and There*. New York: Oxford University Press, 1949.

Partridge, Ernest, ed. *Responsibilities to Future Generations: Environmental Ethics*. Buffalo: Prometheus Books, 1981.

Regan, Tom. "On the Nature and Possibility of an Environmental Ethic." *Environmental Ethics*, Vol. 3, No. 1, 1981, pp. 19–34.

Sikora, R. I. and Brian Barry, eds. *Obligations to Future Generations*. Philadelphia: Temple University Press, 1978.

Stone, Christopher. *Should Trees Have Standing?: Toward Legal Rights for Natural Objects*. Los Altos, CA: Kaufman, 1974.

Ethical Dimensions of Social Science and Social Research

Beauchamp, Tom L., Ruth R. Faden, R. Jay Wallace, Jr., and Leroy Walters, eds. *Ethical Issues in Social Science Research*. Baltimore: The Johns Hopkins University Press, 1982.

Bermant, Gordon, Herbert Kelman, and Donald Warwick. *The Ethics of Social Intervention*. Halsted Press, 1978.

Callahan, Daniel and Bruce Jennings, ed. *Ethics, The Social Sciences, and Policy Analysis*. Plenum Press, 1983.

Rainwater, L. and D.J. Pittman. "Ethical Problems in Studying a Politically Sensitive and Deviant Community." *Social Problems*, Vol. 14, No. 4, 1967, pp. 357–366.

Rein, Martin. *Social Science and Public Policy*. New York: Penguin Books, 1976.

Reynolds, Paul Davidson. *Ethical Dilemma and Social Science Research*. San Francisco: Jossey-Bass, 1979.

Rivlin, Alice. "Forensic Social Science." *Harvard Educational Review*, Vol. 43, No. 1, February 1973, pp. 61–75.

Rivlin, Alice M. and P. Michael Timpane. *Ethical and Legal Issues of Social Experimentation*. Washington: The Brookings Institution, 1975.

Sjoberg, Gideon, ed. *Ethics, Politics, and Social Research*. Cambridge: Schenkman Publishing Company, 1967.

Sjoberg, Gideon. "Politics, Ethics, and Evaluation Research," in M. Guttentag and E.L. Streuning, eds. *Handbook of Evaluation Research*, Vol. II, Beverly Hills: Sage Publications, 1975.

Thompson, D. "The Ethics of Social Experimentation." *Public Policy*, Vol. 29, No. 3, Summer 1981, pp. 369–398.

Tribe, Lawrence. "Policy Science: Analysis or Ideology." *Philosophy and Public Affairs*, Vol. 2, No. 1, 1972, pp. 66–110.

Weber, Max. "Objectivity in Social Science and Social Policy," in Gresham Riley, ed. *Values, Objectivity and the Social Sciences*. Reading, MA: Addison-Wesley Company, 1974.

Education and Training Related to Ethics in Planning and Public Policy

Bok, Derek C. "Can Ethics Be Taught?" *Change*, Vol. 8, No. 8, September 1976, pp. 26–30.

Callahan, Daniel and Sissela Bok., eds. *Ethics Teaching in Higher Education*. New York: Plenum, 1980.

Carroll, James D. "Education for the Public Trust: Learning to Live with the Absurd." *The Bureaucrat*, Vol. 4, April 1974, pp. 24–33.

Fleishman, Joel L. and Bruce L. Payne. *Ethical Dilemmas and the Education of Policymakers*. Hastings, NY: The Hastings Center, 1980.

Kaufman, Jerome L. "Teaching Planning Ethics." *Journal of Planning Education and Research*. Vol. 1, No. 1, Summer 1981, pp. 29–34.

Mertins, Herman, Jr. and Patrick J. Hennigan, eds. *Applying Professional Standards and Ethics in the Eighties: A Workbook and Study Guide for Public Administrators*. Second Edition. Washington: American Society for Public Administration, 1982.

Whistle-Blowing

Anderson, Robert M., et al. *Divided Loyalties: Whistle-Blowing at BART*. West Lafayette, Indiana: Purdue University Series in Science, Technology, and Human Values, 1980.

Bok, Sissela. "Blowing the Whistle," in Joel L. Fleishman, Lance Liebman, and Mark H. Moore, eds. *Public Duties: The Moral Obligations of*

Government Officials. Cambridge: Harvard University Press, 1981, pp. 204–220.

Bowman, James S. "Whistleblowing in the Public Service: An Overview of the Issues." *Review of Public Personnel Administration*, Vol. 1, Fall 1980, pp. 15–28.

Bowman, James S. et al. *Professional Ethics: Whistle-Blowing in Organizations: An Annotated Bibliography and Resource Guide.* NY: Garland Publishing, Inc. 1983.

Burnett, Arthur L. "Management's Positive Interest in Accountability Through Whistleblowing." *The Bureaucrat*, Vol. 9, Summer 1980, pp. 5–10.

Chalk, Rosemary and Frank Von Hippel. "Due Process for Dissenting Whistle-Blowers." *Technology Review*, Vol. 81, June/July 1979, pp. 49–55.

Coven, Mark. "The First Amendment Rights of Policy Making Public Employees," *Harvard Civil Rights—Civil Liberties Law Review*, Vol. 12, Summer 1977, pp. 559–584.

Elliston, Frederick A. *Conflicting Loyalties in the Workplace.* Notre Dame: University of Notre Dame Press, 1983.

Finkler, Earl. "Dissent and Independent Initiative in Planning Offices." *Planning Advisory Service*, No. 269, Chicago, Illinois: American Society of Planning Officials, 1971.

Hirschman, Albert. *Exit, Voice, and Loyalty.* Cambridge: Harvard University Press, 1970.

Lindauer, Mitchell J. "Government Employee Disclosures of Agency Wrongdoing: Protecting the Right to Blow the Whistle." *University of Chicago Law Review*, Vol. 42, Spring 1975, pp. 530–561.

Nader, Ralph, Peter J. Petkas, and Kate Blackwell, eds. *Whistle Blowing: The Report of the Conference on Professional Responsibility.* New York: Grossman, 1972.

Parmerlee, Marcia A. et al. "Correlates of Whistle-Blowers' Perception of Organizational Retaliation." *Administrative Science Quarterly*, Vol. 27, March 1982, pp. 17–34.

Parris, Judith H. "Whistle Blowers in the Executive Branch." Washington, D.C.: Congressional Research Service, Issue Brief, No. 1B78006, 1979.

Perrucci, Robert et al. "Whistle-Blowing: Professionals' Resistance to Organizational Authority." *Social Problems*, Vol. 28, December 1980, pp. 149–164.

Peters, Charles and Taylor Branch, eds. *Blowing the Whistle: Dissent in the Public Interest.* New York: Praeger, 1972.

Raven-Hansen, Peter. "Do's and Don'ts for Whistleblowers: Planning for Trouble." *Technology Review*, Vol. 82, May 1980, pp. 34–44.

U.S. Congress, House Committee on Post Office and Civil Service. Subcommittee on the Civil Service. *Civil Service Reform Oversight, 1980—Whistle Blower Hearings.* 96th Congress, 2nd Session, 1980.

U.S. Congress, Senate Committee on Governmental Affairs. *The Whistleblowers: A Report on Federal Employees Who Disclose Acts of Governmental Waste, Abuse, and Corruption.* 95th Congress, 2nd Session, 1978.

Weinstein, Deena. *Bureaucratic Opposition: Challenging Abuses at the Work Place.* New York: Pergamon Press, 1979.

Index